D1571142

THE PRACTICAL GUIDE TO FINANCE AND ACCOUNTING

THE PRACTICAL GUIDE TO FINANCE AND ACCOUNTING

SUSAN M. DRAKE
RENÉE G. DINGLER, CPA

PRENTICE HALL

Library of Congress Cataloging-in-Publication Data

Drake, Susan M.
The practical guide to finance and accounting / Susan M. Drake, Renée G. Dingler.
p. cm.
Includes bibliographical references and index.
ISBN 0-13-027006-7 — ISBN 0-7352-0180-3 (pbk.)
1. Finance. 2. Accounting. I. Dingler, Renée. II. Title.

HG173 .D73 2001
657—dc21 00-052848

Printed in the United States of America

10 9 8 7 6 5 4 3 2 1

ISBN 0-13-027006-7

PRENTICE HALL
Paramus, NJ 07652

http://www.phdirect.com

DEDICATION

To the millions of nonfinancial people who have struggled to understand these concepts, and to the financial people who have dealt with them.

May this book help them appreciate each other.

ACKNOWLEDGMENTS

From Susan M. Drake:

Because this is a long book, we have lots of people to thank. Many friends have contributed their knowledge and skills. More importantly, they have given their personal support and been willing to listen to a lot of whining as I immersed myself in the mysterious world of finance and accounting.

This project would never have happened without Luis Gonzalez, who is a truly evolved human being and can really zing out a one-liner. Thank you, Luis, for your belief and patience.

Thanks to Renée, my co-author, for helping me live up to my commitment to write this book. I had no idea how little I knew; you did, but for some crazy reason you agreed to help me anyway. You are a genius and a really good sport. I love you.

I can never thank my husband, Scott, enough for his constant support. He quietly accepts it when I take on projects that will monopolize my time and thoughts.

Renée and I both especially thank Timothy Powell for his amazing intellect and skill and for his willingness to jump on an airplane at the drop of a hat. Tim, your undying friendship is an incredible blessing. Thank you for your ability to live spontaneously and to rise to any challenge.

Lynn Lesher is always my treasured friend and guru. She taught me that there are creative ways to say technical stuff. Thank you for your input and help.

Many more thanks to those who gave their support in so many ways, seen and unseen. Thank you to Colleen Wells, my darling daughter, and to Rob Dingler.

Susan Gross is a continuous inspiration and anchor. (Susan, you were right.)

And, finally, thanks to the Marx Brothers, who can make anything fun.

From Renée G. Dingler:

Behind every public act or kind deed is a host of friends, teachers, and mentors, who sow their seeds of wisdom, love, patience, and encouragement into the person who gets all the public recognition. In my case, here are just a few of the ones who have made a significant impact on my life, bringing me to the point that I could write this book. So, my friends, I honor you now. This work is the fruit of your seeds sown into my life. Thank you.

To my friend and co-author, Susan Drake, who is the creative genius behind this book: Thank you for asking me to share this with you. We've always known that God put us together for a reason; we just didn't know it was to write a finance and accounting book! (Who would've ever thought it?)

To my personal and business mentors, Dr. Marie Dubke, John Boushy, Wilda Wright, and Jerry Lee: Thank you for your wisdom and guidance. Thank you for taking a chance on me and believing in me.

To my parents, Ray and Brenda Gentry: Thank you for teaching me that I could do anything and be anything that I wanted to be, and for showing me that life is too short not to follow my dreams!

To my husband, Rob: Thank you for making me finish my degrees and helping me pursue a business career. Thank you for your love, encouragement, and support (and for not caring that the house got *really* messy right before the deadline for this book).

To my Lord and friend, Jesus Christ, who opened the doors and then pushed me through in order to make my dream of writing a book a reality: Thank you for giving me wisdom and faith. Thank you for loving me and walking with me every step of the way.

CONTENTS

PREFACE .... *xxi*

Introduction

ACCOUNTING AND FINANCE: A SYSTEMATIC APPROACH TO MANAGEMENT

A WAY OF KEEPING SCORE *1*

A BAROMETER OF OUTCOMES *1*

WHAT IS ACCOUNTING? *2*

WHAT IS FINANCE? *2*

FOUR UNDERLYING PRINCIPLES OF ACCOUNTING AND FINANCE *3*

WHO USES ACCOUNTING AND FINANCE INFORMATION? *4*

Chapter 1

WHAT IS ACCOUNTING?

ACCOUNTING RECORDS INFORMATION *7*

PUBLIC AND PRIVATE ACCOUNTING *8*

CAREER PATHS FOR ACCOUNTING PROFESSIONALS *9*

SPECIALIZED FIELDS IN ACCOUNTING *10*

CERTIFICATIONS *13*

Chapter 2

THE RULES OF ACCOUNTING

WHO GOVERNS ACCOUNTING? 15

HOW ACCOUNTING RULES ORIGINATED.................... 16

CREATING CONSISTENCY 16

THE ACCOUNTING PRINCIPLES BOARD (APB) 17

WEAKNESSES OF THE SYSTEM 17

THE BIRTH OF FASB 18

Chapter 3

ACCOUNTING TOOLS

TOOLS OF ACCOUNTING 24

ACCOUNTING FORMATS.................................. 24

THE BASIC ACCOUNTING MODEL 26

DEBITS AND CREDITS.................................. 27

DOUBLE-ENTRY BOOKKEEPING 30

ACCOUNTS 30

RECORDING ACCOUNTING TRANSACTIONS 33

T-ACCOUNTS.. 35

BASIC FINANCIAL STATEMENTS: THE KEY TO
UNDERSTANDING A COMPANY'S POSITION 36

THE ANNUAL REPORT 41

SOME KEY TERMS....................................... 42

Chapter 4

ASSETS

TANGIBLE AND INTANGIBLE ASSETS....................... 45

Liquid Assets 45
Current Assets 46
Cash and Cash Equivalents 46
Short-Term Investments 53
Accounts Receivable 54

Chapter 5

INVENTORIES

Classifications of Inventory 62
What to Include in Inventory 62
Capitalizing Costs 63
Putting Inventory Costs on the P&L 64
How to Determine Inventory 67
Accounting for Inventory 69
Inventory Methods 70
Lower of Cost or Market (LCM) 73
Net Realizable Value 75

Chapter 6

LONG-TERM ASSETS

Property, Plant, and Equipment (PPE) 77
Depreciable and Nondepreciable Assets 78
Gifts and Bartering 81
Other Related Expenditures 82
Depreciation 83

Chapter 7

INTANGIBLE ASSETS

GOODWILL 93
LEGAL RIGHTS OR PRIVILEGES 94
LEASEHOLDS 97
PREPAID EXPENSES 97
ORGANIZATION COSTS 98
DEFERRED CHARGES 98
SPECIAL EXPENSES 99
AMORTIZATION 99
ASSETS YOU WON'T FIND ON THE BALANCE SHEET 99

Chapter 8

LIABILITIES

CURRENT LIABILITIES 103
LONG-TERM LIABILITIES 110

Chapter 9

EQUITY

WHAT IS CAPITAL STOCK? 137
COMMON STOCK 138
PREFERRED STOCK 140
TREASURY STOCK 142
PAID-IN CAPITAL 143
RETAINED EARNINGS 143
SOME KEY TERMS 144

Chapter 10

STATEMENT OF INCOME

Revenues 148
Expenses 150
Cost of Goods Sold 150
Cost of Goods Manufactured 151
Gross Profit 156
General and Administrative Expenses 156
Net Income Before Interest and Tax 158
Other Income and Other Expenses 158
Income Taxes 158
Extraordinary Items 159
Net Income 160
Earnings Per Share 161
Other Information About the P&L 163
Comprehensive Income 164

Chapter 11

FINANCIAL REPORTING

Management Reporting 165
Market Reporting 166
The Securities and Exchange Commission (SEC) 166
The Annual Report 168
Investor Relations 171
Stockholders Meetings 171
Ongoing Communication 172

Chapter 12

FINANCE

WHAT IS FINANCE? 175

WHY IS FINANCE IMPORTANT? 175

HOW FINANCE RELATES TO ACCOUNTING 177

CAREER PATHS FOR FINANCE PROFESSIONALS 177

CERTIFICATIONS 179

Chapter 13

FINANCE TOOLS

PLANNING ENCOMPASSES MANY FACTORS 181

FORECASTING 182

BUDGETING 183

LONG-RANGE PLANNING 184

FINANCIAL MODELS 185

STATISTICAL ANALYSIS 186

COST OF CAPITAL 186

FINANCIAL RATIOS 186

TIME VALUE OF MONEY 187

Chapter 14

FINANCIAL STATEMENT RATIOS

WHAT IS A RATIO? 189

CATEGORIES OF FREQUENTLY USED RATIOS 192

CONSIDERING ALL FACTORS 200

Chapter 15

TIME VALUE OF MONEY

Inflation 204
Interest Rates 206
Compounding 208
Risk 209
TVM Formulas 212

Chapter 16

CAPITAL AND PROJECT BUDGETING

A Scientific Approach 227
Three Essential Considerations 227
Capital Budgeting Techniques 230
To Lease or Not to Lease, That Is the Question! 252

Chapter 17

RESPONSIBILITIES OF NONFINANCIAL MANAGERS

P&L Review 257
Steps to Easy Budgeting 259
Forecasting 262
Managing Costs 265
Managing Payroll and Related Expenses 271
Accruals and Prepaid Expenses 271

Chapter 18

PAYROLL CONCERNS

FEDERAL WAGES AND HOURS LAW (FAIR LABOR STANDARDS ACT) 273

THE DIFFERENCE BETWEEN WAGES AND SALARIES 274

EMPLOYER PAYROLL REQUIREMENTS 274

UNION REQUIREMENTS 276

PAYROLL TAXES AND DEDUCTIONS 276

SOCIAL SECURITY BENEFITS 280

OTHER EMPLOYEE COMPENSATION 282

Chapter 19

EMPLOYEE COMPENSATION AND BENEFITS

SOCIAL SECURITY 288

EMPLOYER-RELATED COMPENSATION AND BENEFITS 289

EMPLOYEE RETIREMENT INCOME SECURITY ACT (ERISA) . . . 290

HEALTH BENEFITS 290

RETIREMENT PLANS 290

EMPLOYEE STOCK OWNERSHIP PLANS (ESOPS) 293

STOCK PURCHASES PLANS 294

ROLLOVERS 294

PERQUISITES (PERKS) 295

REPORTING 295

RETIREMENT PLANS FOR THE SELF-EMPLOYED 296

Chapter 20

BUSINESS OWNERSHIP AND ORGANIZATION

Types of Business Organization 299
Other Information 309

Chapter 21

TYPES OF INVESTMENT

Types of Payback 313
Investment Strategies..................................... 316
Factors in Selecting an Investment 317
Portfolios 318
Stocks 318
Commodities 320
Bonds... 320
Options (or Derivatives) 324
Money Markets 326
Investment Funds 326
Index Shares or Exchange-Traded Funds 329

Chapter 22

STOCK EXCHANGES AND RATING AGENCIES

Stock Markets.. 331
How Stock Exchanges Work.............................. 331
Market Security 331

Trading Times. 332
Stock Exchange Membership 332
Stock Listings 334
Rating Agencies 335
Industry Designations 335
Following the Markets 336

Chapter 23

TRADING

People Who Trade Securities 337
Online or E-Trading 338
Day Trading 339
Institutional Buyers 339
Investment Clubs 340
Buying and Selling Stock 340
Ways to Pay for Securities 343

Chapter 24

MARKET MEASUREMENTS

Bulls and Bears 345
Stock Indexes 345
Market Ratios 347
When Is a Stock Overpriced? 348
Risk Measurements 349
Market Investment Assumptions 350
Fund Managers and the Efficient Market 351
Evaluating Stock. 351

Chapter 25

INTERNATIONAL FINANCE

INTERNATIONAL FINANCE TERMINOLOGY 354
INTERNATIONAL MONETARY FUND 354
WORLD BANK 356
FOREIGN EXCHANGE 358
INTERNATIONAL TRADE 363
REPORTING INTERNATIONAL OPERATIONS IN U. S. FINANCIAL STATEMENTS 368
OTHER INTERNATIONAL INFORMATION 368

Chapter 26

FEDERAL RESERVE SYSTEM

PURPOSE 373
ORGANIZATION AND GOVERNING BODY 374

GLOSSARY 379
APPENDIX (CHARTS) 407
BIBLIOGRAPHY 437
INDEX 443

PREFACE

If you're in business, it helps to know whether you're making money, losing money, or just breaking even. To do that, you need to at least understand the basics of finance and accounting, because they're the nuts and bolts of running a business.

The professionals who practice finance and accounting (which we'll refer to as F&A) must know every detail of the rules and regulations that govern financial matters. But if you're not a professional in one of those fields, you still need to understand the principles of these disciplines to use the information they convey to run your business. Whether you're a corporate manager, a small business owner, an investor in the stock market, or someone who deals with accounting and finance people in your daily work, understanding F&A will help you make sound business decisions.

Unfortunately, writing a book about those subjects is like writing a book about brain surgery; you can't tell people just a little and then send them out into the world to do an operation. Those who want only a general understanding of F&A discover that there is no shortcut to either subject. A little knowledge is a dangerous thing. The good news is that these matters don't have (quite) the potentially serious side effects as brain surgery.

Like many professions, F&A is built on concepts and language that defy decoding by the average person. What's more, books written by F&A professionals do little to alleviate confusion, because they're cloaked in the same jargon. We don't blame the pros. It's really not their fault. They've been steeped in it since they cracked open their first Accounting 101 book. We only realized the difficulty when Susan—the creative one—began digging into the why's and wherefores that Renee—the analytical one—was giving her. To our surprise, simple words like *account* or symbols like parentheses (a negative sign to mathematicians but a credit sign to accountants) had completely different meanings in nonfinancial and financial settings. The uninformed, attempting to become educated about the subject, can become just further confounded.

Because our team combines the strengths of a right-brain creative type and a left-brain analytical person, in this book we are able to accomplish several things. We

- Look at processes from both perspectives, which helps us explain them in accurate yet understandable ways.
- Challenge prevailing F&A beliefs about how things must be done.
- Find creative solutions to seemingly impossible tasks (such as explaining things like subordinated debentures)!

This book is designed as a practical guide, not in the usual sense of textbook practicality, but as a translation; it offers information to be used by laypersons to better understand the highly technical concepts that underlie accounting and finance. While we wrote it as a comprehensive, accurate reference, we did not write it as a legal document or as a textbook for those who would practice the art—or science—of financial matters.

Although individuals may need to understand F&A as it relates to their personal lives, this book is written primarily from the perspective of business. The concepts are universal, but the application we describe is based on its uses in corporations. We hope that this book will provide a foundation that will allow corporate managers to confidently move through the ranks of an organization, to talk at ease with experts, and to know when to seek advice from professionals. Ideally, it will enhance their decision-making ability. The same holds true for small business owners, who can use this book to learn what their accountants are talking about, and to understand how to talk intelligently with them.

Finally, despite some popular beliefs, neither accounting nor finance are black-and-white subjects. Both are open to opinion to a greater or lesser degree. This book represents our opinions.

Introduction

ACCOUNTING AND FINANCE: A SYSTEMATIC APPROACH TO MANAGEMENT

A WAY OF KEEPING SCORE

The words *accounting* and *finance* may call up images of calculators and spreadsheets, but they encompass much more than mathematical processes. Two distinct disciplines, they work hand-in-glove to measure an organization's progress and help shape its future. By reporting and interpreting all of the financial dealings that increase or decrease wealth or value, they create a picture of a company's current and potential well-being. In a sense, accounting and finance is a way of keeping score.

A BAROMETER OF OUTCOMES

An old joke says that accounting and finance is the tail that wags the dog. Why? Because a potential action that makes good, sound business sense from every other point of view can be vetoed with one word from the accounting or finance people. It seems like a lot of power to give one group, yet there's a good reason: These professionals have the information necessary to determine whether any undertaking will be in the company's best interest financially. Sound financial strategy, above all, is what shareholders are interested in, which means the accounting and finance people can call the shots.

WHAT IS ACCOUNTING?

Accounting is a way of organizing information to tell a story. By collecting, recording, and reporting information about a company's financial position, an accountant creates a body of data that can be used to make decisions.

There are generally two reasons to perform accounting:

- So people inside or outside a company will know how the company is doing financially.
- To provide information that will help a manager run a business.

Accounting is a sort of financial diary of everything that happens to a company in the course of a day, a quarter, a year.

When all is said and done, accounting is a way for people to communicate.

WHAT IS FINANCE?

If accounting is concerned with compiling information in a readable, consistent format, finance is all about interpreting the information, predicting outcomes, and planning to achieve favorable results. And as exacting as accounting is purported to be, finance is equally inexact, relying as it does on predictions and estimates. Oddly, together these two disciplines form an indispensable team. Accounting paints a picture of the existing landscape; finance paints a picture of the future.

Continuously faced with decisions about how to operate, management needs input—something to help them choose between alternative paths. That's where finance comes in. It is the science of analyzing a company's financial history and determining how the company can increase its value to shareholders. The main difference between accounting and finance is that

- Accounting states facts based on history.
- Finance interprets facts and then makes judgments and recommendations about future strategy.

The accountant asks, "What have we done? Where have we been?" The financial analyst asks, "Where should we go? What should we do now?" And while a great deal of the information associated with accounting and finance is factual, in both disciplines interpretation and subjectivity are important parts of painting the picture.

Armed with the facts and assumptions provided by accounting and finance professionals, management is able to draw conclusions about the impact of decisions on performance, and to map a plan for the future.

FOUR UNDERLYING PRINCIPLES OF ACCOUNTING AND FINANCE

Just as three-year-olds ask, "Why?" a seemingly inordinate number of times a day, we have asked ourselves, "Why?" with regard to the rigid rules and regulations that guide finance and accounting. We realize that it is a record-keeping system, a way of outlining a company's performance, a systematic way to figure out the taxes we owe. But beyond that, why do we need the rigid systems we use?

There are four reasons why we've developed systems for accounting and finance:

1. ***Disclosure.*** Anyone who is going to make a decision must have all the information that's pertinent to the subject. For example, if you invested in a company thinking that it was making money but later discovered that the company had been insolvent all along, you would be justifiably upset. It wouldn't be wise for you to make an investment decision without having as many facts as are available. (You'll never have all the facts.) One of the premises of accounting and finance is that the systems we use require full disclosure of information that's related to the operation of the company.
2. ***Consistency.*** There are different right ways to get to answers, and there are also different right answers. By having systems, accounting and finance can ensure that the information delivered in a financial report allows apples-to-apples comparisons. For

instance, suppose that one year a company reported its revenues for 11 months but the next year reported revenues for 12 months. It would be very difficult to determine how well the company was performing. Now imagine that every company used a different reporting calendar. That would be certain chaos. You couldn't compare competitors' results or decide what investment was better. Thus, accounting and finance specifies ways of keeping information consistent, so everyone is reading from similar pages.

3. ***Timing.*** In financial terms, timing can dramatically influence outcomes. The length of a lease, the timing of debt payments, and the dates represented by a financial report can all be important information. Accounting and finance specifies the timing of all transactions so that people can accurately assess situations.
4. ***Facts and predictions.*** In the scope of accounting and finance there are two types of information: factual data that has been recorded as it happened, and predictions, or forecasts, based on factual data and extrapolated to suggest what might happen in the future. Those who make decisions about how to run a company or otherwise evaluate its worth must know not only the facts but also what is forecast for the future. Accounting and finance creates a means by which to learn those things.

The rationale for accounting and finance, therefore, is to provide information that helps people make informed decisions. The methods we use to get there ensure that we know what we need to about the circumstances of a company's operation, that the company is consistent in the way it reports things, that we know when events take place, and that we have experts' opinions about the facts of the current situation as well as what can be logically predicted.

WHO USES ACCOUNTING AND FINANCE INFORMATION?

Financial reports are used by a number of people who are in a position to make a decision about how a company operates and what its potential might be. Here is the list of the key people who might use financial reports:

1. ***Internal financial analysts.*** Analysts inside a company evaluate whether the company's current strategy is paying off and what other strategies might be advantageous.

2. ***Internal management.*** Division and department managers use financial information as a guide to planning activities, timing, and other factors associated with their budgets. The manager's ultimate job is to create wealth for shareholders.

3. ***Employees.*** Those who work for or are considering working for a company are interested in its stability and ability to provide opportunities.

4. ***Creditors and lenders.*** Anyone who is considering providing products, services, or credit to a firm will want to know how well the company can pay its bills.

5. ***Customers.*** A company's reputation for performance affects customers' decisions to buy.

6. ***Shareholders and prospective shareholders.*** The people who own stock in a company use its financial information to make decisions about issues such as whether to buy or sell stock, or how to vote on company issues at the annual shareholders meeting. Shareholders elect members of the board of directors, and they may base their decision to re-elect members on how well the company has performed.

7. ***Financial brokers and fund managers.*** In determining whether to recommend a stock to their clients as a good investment, financial managers evaluate the company's performance over a period of time and try to predict its future results.

8. ***External financial analysts.*** Professional analysts outside a company make a career of providing unbiased assessments of companies' performance, often specializing in a particular industry, such as lodging or banking. A corporation considering acquiring or merging with another company might hire an analyst to evaluate whether that would be a wise move.

9. ***Institutional investors.*** When investors are considering putting money into a company, they look at its financial performance to

make sure it will be a wise investment. Certain indicators give them a clue as to whether their money will grow at a rate that compares favorably with other investments they might choose.

10. ***Government organizations.*** Regulatory agencies require information about whether a company is performing in acceptable ways, following required policies and laws, and operating fairly.

These groups have greater or lesser interest in a company's performance and may look at financial reports in detail or may simply look at an overview.

As a manager or business owner you'll have specific reasons for understanding basic financial concepts such as monthly statements, budgets, and forecasts, which we cover in detail later. In addition, we look at financial terms and concepts from an outsider's point of view, so you'll also understand what others are looking at in your company's financial statements. Finally, we take a global view in examining the Federal Reserve and how it affects our economy and international issues.

Before we look at the large topics, let's talk about the foundation: Where does accounting come from, and what is the basis for financial statements?

Chapter 1

WHAT IS ACCOUNTING?

As early as 3300 B.C., the Egyptians etched tax accounting records in hieroglyphics on clay tablets, creating what is now considered to be the first known example of writing. Over the centuries, record keeping evolved from clay to papyrus to paper, and was used for a variety of purposes: to validate merchant sales, as a means to create a written contract, or to monitor government storage of "in kind" tax payments.

Today, thanks to the ingenuity of the 14th-century Italians, we have double-entry bookkeeping, the revolutionary system on which our modern methods are based. We've moved from clay to computer and from a primitive system of record keeping to an excruciatingly detailed methodology that is directed by tomes of rules and enforced by government regulations. We call this *accounting.*

ACCOUNTING RECORDS INFORMATION

Accounting is a system of recording information about financial transactions. By providing a consistent method of shorthand, it ensures that no matter who is keeping the records or who is looking at the records, the information will be interpreted in a similar way.

TWO TYPES OF ACCOUNTING

Accountants perform two types of accounting:

1. ***Managerial*** (for internal decision making). To give people inside a company information that will help them make decisions about their areas of responsibility.

2. ***Financial*** (for external decision making). To give people outside a company information about the company's past and current health as well as its potential for the future.

PUBLIC AND PRIVATE ACCOUNTING

Accountants may practice in one of several venues:

1. Public
2. Private
3. Government

A certified public accountant (CPA) is a person who has the credentials to perform accounting services for others, whether they're inside or outside a company.

PUBLIC ACCOUNTING

A *certified public accounting* firm (also known as public accounting) is an independent organization that looks at a company's financial statements objectively and gives an opinion about whether they are presented according to Generally Accepted Accounting Principles (GAAP). A CPA firm probably also offers tax work including research and tax return preparation and assistance in case of a tax audit, and also may engage in management consulting. The main reason to hire a public accounting firm is to gain an independent opinion and expert advice. For example, there are industry specialists, transaction specialists, and other accounting professionals who can recommend the best systems for a company's particular position.

PRIVATE ACCOUNTING

Private accounting is done by a person working inside a company who accumulates and reports financial information, and works with the company's managers to develop budgets and plans.

DIFFERENCES BETWEEN PUBLIC AND PRIVATE ACCOUNTING

While the work of public and private accountants may seem the same, the point of view is vastly different in public and private accounting.

Government Accounting

Government accountants may work in federal, state, or local agencies, and often do work related to budget management, government spending, and taxes.

CAREER PATHS FOR ACCOUNTING PROFESSIONALS

There are numerous accounting and finance specialties and positions both inside and outside corporations. They require various degrees of education, certification, and experience.

In public accounting, the accountants are somewhat like salespeople, those who drive revenues. The accountant's image may be one of a miser counting pennies. On the contrary, the public accountant understands that it's necessary to spend money in the interest of making a client happy and thus bringing in more business.

Conversely, in private accounting, the accountants are the behind-the-scenes people who are considered cost centers; that is, they don't generate any income, they just cost the company money. Because of that perspective, private accountants tend to watch the pennies in order to serve as a role model for the rest of the corporation.

Accounting Positions

Those who practice accounting techniques may work in positions with varying levels of responsibility. There are a considerable number of specialties, including such areas as sales and use tax, income tax, payroll tax, fixed assets, construction, domestic and international, accounts payable, and accounts receivable. The list goes on.

Accounting Clerk. In a large corporation, a clerk usually deals with one specific aspect of accounting, such as payroll or accounts payable. A clerk may have a financial degree and is usually supervised by an accountant.

Bookkeeper or Full-Charge Bookkeeper. Bookkeepers generally work for small companies and typically have full responsibility for keeping a complete set of books, meaning assets, liabilities, owners' equity, profit and loss statement, and so on. They post (or record) entries and do the day-to-day work associated with keeping records.

Some have two-year or four-year degrees. Bookkeepers usually refer difficult issues to an outside CPA.

Accounting Staff. These persons have four-year degrees and may be CPAs. In a large company, the accounting staff works with one group of accounts such as payroll or fixed assets. In small companies, they may handle a group of accounts, such as the balance sheet or income statement accounts.

Accounting Supervisor or Manager. Supervisors perform hands-on review of staff work and manage the performance of a group. They usually have charge of a section of an accounting function, such as balance sheet, consolidation, or plant.

Controller (Comptroller). The controller has a four-year degree and usually a CPA or a certified management accountant (CMA). In large companies, he may have had public accounting experience. In all companies, the controller is responsible for all of the financial statements. The controller is an officer of the company and usually reports to the chief financial officer.

Chief Financial Officer (CFO). The CFO is a company officer who has control of all accounting and finance activities. In smaller companies the controller doubles for this position.

SPECIALIZED FIELDS IN ACCOUNTING

There are three major areas of specialty in public accounting:

1. Auditing
2. Tax
3. Management consulting

AUDITING

The term *audit* sends chills through most people, who equate an audit with either the Internal Revenue Service or an auditor coming into a company to find fraud or outright negligence. Not necessarily so.

Auditors are more concerned with events that have broad implications or a major impact than on individual situations or events. While they may work inside or outside a corporation, auditors answer to the board of directors, not to management. An auditor will make sure the company

1. Has internal financial controls (checks and balances).
2. Adheres to the financial policies and procedures set out by the company.
3. Follows the rules of regulatory agencies.
4. Presents financial statements fairly, in accordance with accounting rules. (In Chapter 2 we will discuss Generally Accepted Accounting Principles, known as GAAP, the procedures that guide all accountants.)

Internal Auditor. Auditors have accounting degrees and experience, and may have a background in management information systems (MIS). Their concern is that there are adequate processes for protecting the company's assets, and that people follow established procedures. For example, they might look at an information technology division to make sure there is appropriate security to protect assets such as computers, as well as the information that goes through the computers.

External Auditor. Working for a public accounting firm, an auditor comes into a business to analyze its financial statements, seeing that they follow accepted accounting and auditing guidelines. External auditors work with the internal auditors, using their work as a base. They will also perform as much special investigation as needed to raise their comfort level to the point they can sign the opinion. External auditors also report to the board of directors.

Management is supposed to cooperate in every way necessary to provide auditors with the information they need. The auditors must do everything they can to build relationships with the CFO, controller, financial managers, and others associated with their work because they must develop a trust level that facilitates their job. Because the board is the ultimate decision-making body, auditors always answer to the board, not to the managers.

Auditors do three basic things:

- ***Compilation.*** Accountants gather all financial information and present it in the proper format. They do not change any numbers, but merely arrange things in accord with accounting practices. The result of the compilation is a set of reports (formal financial statements) that together create a picture of a company's health.
- ***Review.*** They look at accounting records and make sure all entries are put where they need to be, changing things that may be recorded incorrectly. This service is usually requested by a private company in preparation for seeking financing or for other banking purposes.
- ***Audit.*** This is a detailed study of "material items" that could impact your financial statements. Typically, the accountant (in this case an auditor) looks at every account, but only focuses on accounts that could have a major financial impact on your business. The image of an accountant going over every number with a fine-tooth comb is an overstatement. It would be impossible and impractical for an auditor to study records in this much detail.

When the auditor is finished examining the books, she *issues an opinion,* which means writing a formal letter verifying that financial statements are fairly presented, and specifying the guidelines she used to determine the fairness.

TAX

Tax specialists know how to keep books, but they concentrate their efforts in tax research and tax preparation, ensuring that a company meets IRS and state requirements. Companies also hire tax planning specialists who take maximum advantage of the law to create the most favorable tax situation possible.

Tax specialists hold four-year degrees plus a CPA and may also have a masters degree in taxation or a J.D. degree in tax law. They may also hold power of attorney for signing tax returns and can assist in case of tax audits.

Management Consulting

Management consulting covers a wide range of services, involving the application and use of accounting throughout a business. It is focused on how to run the business more efficiently or effectively, rather than on reporting financials to the investors or the government. There are three classifications of businesses:

1. Service
2. Merchandising
3. Manufacturing

Each of these types of businesses may have its special needs. In manufacturing, for example, cost accounting is a very important issue. Cost accounting is concerned with how much it costs to produce goods. Cost accountants actually compute how much it costs to produce each unit of a product. In other words, they figure out the cost to make one toaster or one stapler.

CERTIFICATIONS

Accountants can earn two certifications:

1. Certified public accountant
2. Certified management accountant

In both certification classifications, members must meet requirements involving education, experience, and ethics and must pass an examination. Following their licensing they must update their skills by completing a minimum number of hours each year of continuing professional education (CPE) hours. They must also stay current with ever-changing rules and guidelines related to their field.

Certified Public Accountant (CPA). To become certified, accountants must complete an accounting degree. (Some states require a five-year degree.) They must also pass the Uniform CPA Examination administered by the American Institute of Certified Public Accountants (AICPA). A CPA is licensed by the state board of accountancy.

Certified Management Accountant (CMA). A CMA is a professional designation for management accountants. Requirements for certification include a baccalaureate degree, a CPA certificate, and a satisfactory score on the Graduate Management Admissions Test (GMAT) or Graduate Record Examination (GRE). To become a CMA, an accountant must pass a CMA examination administered by the Institute of Management Accountants (IMA).

Chapter 2

THE RULES OF ACCOUNTING

Accountants are reputed to be zealous in their attention to detail. That's because accountants are bound by clearly defined rules designed to ensure consistency among accounting practices and reports. They must be meticulous in their methods and must adhere to standards set by their peers, accounting academicians, and regulatory agencies.

WHO GOVERNS ACCOUNTING?

There are four organizations in the United States that affect how accounting is practiced:

1. AICPA, the American Institute of Certified Public Accountants, a national professional association for all public accountants in the United States. The AICPA is the most dominant influence in the accounting profession.
2. FASB (pronounced *faz-bee*), the Financial Accounting Standards Board, an independent nongovernmental board that outlines accounting practices.
3. SEC, the Securities and Exchange Commission, a government agency that administers policies governing the sale of securities. While the SEC is the official governing authority for financial reporting, it generally works closely with the accounting profession, allowing AICPA to regulate the behavior of accounting professionals.

4. AAA, the American Accounting Association, a group of accounting educators who research principles and publish reports and opinions. While the AAA has had input into the development of accounting principles, its presence has not been felt to the extent of the AICPA's.

HOW ACCOUNTING RULES ORIGINATED

Accounting has its roots in ancient practice, but the modern form of accounting we use today was very recently established after a long and painful evolutionary process.

In the late 1800s and early 1900s, the U.S. financial picture was a roller coaster. Two events spotlighted significant problem areas:

- In 1913, the U.S. Congress passed a constitutional amendment instituting the federal income tax. This amendment required not only that individuals pay personal tax, but also that corporations pay tax on their net income. What the income tax law brought to light was that different corporations were keeping records and reporting their results in different ways. This meant there was a lot of doubt about how much tax they owed. Also, the vastly different reporting methods meant that companies' information was subject to interpretation and impossible to compare.
- While the problem of inconsistent income reporting had existed for quite a while, it became more obvious because of information unearthed following the stock market crash of 1929 and the subsequent Great Depression.

CREATING CONSISTENCY

The American Institute of Certified Public Accountants began in 1887 as the American Association of Public Accountants (AAPA). AICPA had struggled for some time to formulate solutions to the accounting issues.

In 1938 AICPA created the Committee on Accounting Principles, which developed principles that would bring some consistency to reporting standards. Despite the committee's efforts, there were still several problems:

- The committee worked part-time and acted slowly.
- Industries needed special techniques to suit their unique needs, but the committee didn't seek input from industry experts. Thus, the committee's theoretical principles didn't always work in practice.
- The principles were merely recommendations, not binding requirements.

THE ACCOUNTING PRINCIPLES BOARD (APB)

By the mid-1950s, the committee had become relatively inactive. In 1959, AICPA set up the Accounting Principles Board (APB) to

- Define a theoretical foundation of accounting.
- Issue pronouncements on current issues.

Like its predecessor, the APB tried simply to persuade people to abide by its recommendations. Again, the concept of voluntary participation failed. Finally, in 1964, the governing council of AICPA agreed to follow Generally Accepted Accounting Principles in the CPA's rule of ethics.

WEAKNESSES OF THE SYSTEM

Making the system mandatory, however, didn't make all its problems disappear. Even accountants thought the rules were flawed, and, although they had to follow them, they didn't like them. These complaints about the system continued into the 1960s and 70s:

- There was lack of participation by organizations other than AICPA, and many felt that operating in a vacuum, without feedback from other agencies or involved parties, limited the effectiveness of the principles.

- In the view of many CPAs, the "APB Opinions" were not thoroughly researched and sought no middle ground on industry issues.
- APB never set up objectives and principles underlying financial statements.
- It was slow!

THE BIRTH OF FASB

Inevitably, these problems led to a major AICPA study that recommended that an independent organization develop accounting standards. In 1973, the Financial Accounting Standards Board, known popularly as FASB, was organized.

Today, the framework that guides accountants includes:

- FASB Concept Statements, which are assumptions and broad principles that define the environment in which accounting is done.
- Generally Accepted Accounting Principles (GAAP, pronounced *gap*), a set of statements issued by FASB that tell accountants how to record transactions. These numbered statements are called Financial Accounting Standards (FAS). FASB rules are published in sets of books that are bigger than the tax code! They change regularly (although slowly). This is the framework for all accounting practices in the United States. Accountants who don't follow GAAP may have to undergo an investigation and may ultimately have their certification taken away.
- Code of Professional Ethics. All CPAs are expected to uphold the code of ethics which guides their actions and relationships. If a CPA violates the code, the AICPA may impose sanctions or expel the CPA from the profession.

FASB Framework

While FASB has developed a framework that delineates its principles, statements, and assumptions, making distinctions among those may be more confusing than helpful. For the sake of simplicity, we outline the elements of the framework that prescribe how accountants work. Once again, the elements are designed to make sure that financial statements are consistent and timely, and have full disclosure, of facts and pertinent predictions. Here are the key FASB elements.

Knowledge of the Audience. This statement assumes that accountants are preparing their information for people who

- Lack the authority to get the financial information they need.
- Have a reasonable understanding of business and economic activities.
- Are willing to study the information they're given.
- Could be investors or creditors, or the people who represent investors or creditors.

In other words, FASB assumes that the people who use financial statements will have a certain level of knowledge. Thus, accountants don't have to create statements that can be understood by just anyone.

Relevance. The accountant must report all information that *bears upon the matter at hand,* leaving out information that has little effect on the company's financial outcomes. For example, if the company acquires a competitor, sells a division, incurs debt, and so on, it is reported because it has a significant effect on the business. The principle of relevance ensures disclosure of all facts, but prevents the reporting of needless information that won't affect the situation one way or another. (While interested parties may need to know that the company has acquired another company, they don't need to know that Joe was promoted to supervisor.)

Reliability. Information must be relatively free from error and must represent what it says it represents. If a company releases a financial statement indicating it has $100,000 in cash, you expect it to have

$100,000 in cash at the reporting date. If it only had $10,000, the information would be unreliable.

Comparability. The information should be computed in a way that's consistent with the way it's been done before and with the way other companies in the industry do it. For instance, if you're reporting financial results for this fiscal year, you should be able to compare the results with identical information for preceding fiscal years. You should also be able to compare the information inside your company from one time period to another and compare it with information from across the industry.

Materiality. Materiality means that the information makes a substantial difference, and FASB has a formula for determining at what level things become material. The amounts may vary, but usually, if items don't represent at least 5% of net income or assets, it is considered unnecessary to follow GAAP. For example, if a company shows $5 billion in net income, a $25,000 loss would probably not be material.

Constraint. The idea of weighing the benefit of reporting something correctly with the cost of reporting it to the penny is called a *constraint.* For instance, when a company conducts a fixed asset inventory, it doesn't count trash baskets because it would be very inefficient. What you would gain from requiring people to report their trash baskets wouldn't be worth what it would cost to track the information.

Separate Entity (or Economic Entity). This rule stipulates that an organization has a life of its own, that is, it is legally a separate entity apart from the owners. Under this rule, company money and other assets are kept separate and not "co-mingled" (mixed) with those of the owners.

Going Concern. The term *going concern* means that the business is expected to continue in the future. If a business is not a going concern, a CPA is required to disclose it. For example, if the company is planning to sell out or close its doors in six months, the CPA would note that in the financial statements.

Unit of Measure. Simple as it may seem, the accountant must measure and report economic transactions in a monetary unit such as a dollar.

Time Period Assumption. Because there is lag time in debt payments, receivables, and other income and outgo, it's virtually impossible to know to the penny how a company is doing until it literally closes its doors. Therefore, reports must record a company's position only for a specific period of time. Many companies use a 12-month year, some use a 52- to 53-week year. The important point is that the periods be defined and consistent.

Cost Principle. GAAP says you will use *cash equivalent basis* to indicate the initial cost you paid for an item on your financial statement. This means you report what you paid (also known as *historical cost*), not what it would cost to replace the item or what it's currently worth.

Revenue Principle. When should you report revenue? The simple answer would be, when you receive the money. But the simple answer isn't necessarily the correct one. Suppose you're in the construction business. You undertake building an office complex that will take two years to complete. The contract may call for your client to pay you in three installments: at job start, halfway through, and when the building is completed. Should you report the income now, since there is a contract for the money, or should you report it three years from now when the building is complete? The revenue principle tells you to report income when you *earn* it.

The revenue principle also makes the assumption that a transaction has occurred. In other words, you're not only merely planning to build a building; you've actually signed a contract to do so.

Matching Principle. The matching principle states that you must have the same timing for certain income and outgo. You record how much you spent to make money at the same time you record how much money you made. That means you record your expenses related to earning revenues at the same time you record the revenues you earn.

Change in Accounting Principle. GAAP may seem very strict, but it's not. There is some flexibility in how it's applied. This principle states that if you change the way you apply GAAP, you must disclose the change in the financial statements to let people know about the change.

Here's how it works: You may choose a way of recording an item or transaction, and later decide to record it a different way that you believe will be more representative of the facts. GAAP allows you to change your mind about how you will report things, as long as you tell people about it. On your financial statements you label this as a "Change in Accounting Principle." This doesn't mean you were doing anything wrong in the beginning, it simply means you may have gained some information that leads you to choose a different method.

Full Disclosure Principle. All the financial statement disclosures that you are required to make (by SEC and other regulators) must be made in the appropriate format. This allows investors to quickly grasp events or transactions that impact financial statements. For example, if a company shows $100,000 in accounts receivable, there would be a footnote to the balance sheet telling how much of accounts receivable is current and how much is old. Clearly, there would be a big difference if $10,000 was current, but $90,000 was more than 180 days old. An investor would invariably question whether that debt was collectible.

Conservatism. Accounting and finance is not black and white, so there may be more than one way to report something. This principle says, given a choice of two paths, an accountant will report the least favorable effect on total income or total assets. In other words, it shows less profit (or revenue) and more loss (or expense).

Industry Peculiarities. While accounting is designed to make everything consistent, there must be some deviations because of the peculiarities of certain industries. For example, banking is a regulated industry with very specific federal regulations about how it reports its transactions. The federal regulations are different than what GAAP prescribes. One example of this is in the way you show bad loan reserves (or bad debt). Needless to say, the accountants must follow the government's way. Other differences exist in other industries, and an accountant must recognize these.

ACCOUNTING EVOLVES

This framework is the foundation for all of accounting, but it is not a static framework by any means. Accounting is an evolving discipline, with changes very carefully considered before they are adopted.

Chapter 3

ACCOUNTING TOOLS

Just as plumbers use wrenches and dentists wield drills, accountants employ a variety of tools to help them do their jobs. In particular, they use a language to communicate concisely. This accounting shorthand can be confusing to amateurs for several reasons.

1. Some highly technical accounting terms have been casually interpreted, and we use them in our daily lives quite differently than the way accountants use them.
2. Some of the tools and language of accounting are outmoded or even extinct, yet accountants have continued to use the original language.
3. Some things in accounting have multiple names, so you must know all the names for each thing to keep them straight.

Thus, to understand accounting (and not be overwhelmed by it), we must overcome our preconceptions about what things mean. Never assume that anything means what you thought.

As we outline the various concepts and practices of accounting, remember that no element can be understood in isolation. To introduce the foundation of the disciplines, however, we'll briefly describe some key elements, knowing that it will be impossible to understand them completely out of context. This chapter just lets you get your feet wet. Later we'll offer more detailed explanations where they are pertinent in the text.

TOOLS OF ACCOUNTING

Like any profession, accounting uses a variety of tools. The basic tools of accounting are

- Journals and ledgers in which transactions are recorded.
- Journal entries, a system of noting incoming and outgoing funds.
- A system called *debits* and *credits,* another way of describing how accountants record transactions.
- Accounts, separate areas within journals and ledgers where different types of funds are shown.
- The basic accounting model, a formula that accounts for everything a company owns, everything it owes, and who owns it.
- T-accounts, a simple way of charting transactions.
- Contra accounts, which are the reverse of the way things are normally recorded.
- Financial statements, which are standardized formats for reporting information.

ACCOUNTING FORMATS

Since some accounting language is anachronistic, a history lesson can be helpful. Let's talk a little bit about how things were done in the old days.

Before we became computerized, accountants plied their trade by hand, making handwritten entries in lined notebooks. Now that we have computers, it seems unnecessary to understand the manual techniques. But since old habits die hard, certain terminology is still in use, even though it doesn't apply to our current methods. The easiest way to understand the language is to understand how the manual system worked.

Originally, accountants used two types of columned books to record information about accounts:

- A general journal
- A general ledger

These two forms contain essentially the same information but are organized in different ways. The general journal lists transactions in chronological order, and the general ledger lists them according to what account they're being applied to, such as the cash account, the receivables account, or the fixed asset account.

THE GENERAL JOURNAL AND JOURNAL ENTRIES

A *general journal* in an accounting sense is a diary of all the financial events or transactions (debits and credits) that happen in a month and are recorded in order by date. In a regular diary you would describe the events in words; in an accounting journal you describe them with numbers.

Each event you record is called a *journal entry,* and each journal entry has debits and credits. By looking at the journal you can determine if the debits equal the credits, just as they always should.

When do you make a journal entry? Anytime you buy something, pay for something, earn money for something, or owe something.

Journal entries are triggered by two types of transactions:

- Internal events. This would be when you depreciate equipment or pay workers' salaries.
- External events. A vendor sends you a bill that you need to pay, or a customer buys a product from you.

THE GENERAL LEDGER

The general ledger has the same information as the general journal but sorts it in a different way. While the *general journal* tracks transactions by date, the *general ledger* puts the transactions in the accounts that are affected by the journal entries (still in date order). The act of moving general journal information into your general ledger is called *posting,* and it's separate from making an entry in the general journal.

In accounting today, with the use of computers, the general journal is still available but is not really used. Thus, posting is a thing of the past.

THE BASIC ACCOUNTING MODEL

The starting point for all accounting is the *basic accounting model* (or *equation*). The equation is

Assets = Liabilities + Equity

This is the foundation of everything accountants do.

The model (equation or formula) describes what you own (assets) and who owns you (liability to debtors and equity to shareholders or owners). In the formula, you're describing the two ways you can pay for your assets:

- Through *liabilities* or debt, which means you borrow money to finance something you need, such as equipment, personnel costs, plant expansion, or other expenses.
- Through *equity* or investment, which means owners have put money into the company.

There are two important things to remember about the model:

- It answers the question, How were your assets paid for?
- It follows simple algebra. Whatever you do to one side of the equation, you must also do to the other.

Accounting is the process of recording every financial event that affects your assets, liabilities, or equity. By looking at the general ledger you can see if your assets equal your liabilities plus owners' equity.

Keep in mind that all of accounting is merely an attempt to show where a company's money goes. Understanding this simple concept will set the stage for your understanding of accounting.

HOW DOES THE PROFIT AND LOSS STATEMENT (P&L) FIT INTO THE BASIC ACCOUNTING MODEL?

The P&L is a component of equity. On the balance sheet it is called *retained earnings*.

SUBSIDIARY (OR SUB) LEDGER

A subsidiary ledger shows the detail of one specific account in the general ledger. For example, in the general ledger you would see one number for fixed assets. The subledger would show the detail of all the assets that make up the total balance of the fixed assets account.

DEBITS AND CREDITS

Like many technical terms, debits and credits have been misrepresented in common use. Many of us have grown up believing two myths:

- Myth 1. Debits mean subtractions, and they are bad.
- Myth 2. Credits mean additions, and they are good.

Overcoming the Myths of Debits and Credits

To grasp accounting you must overcome these myths because they are absolutely wrong.

- Truth 1. Debit means recording something on the *left* side of an account.
- Truth 2. Credit means recording something on the *right* side of an account.

And, finally, debits and credits are neither bad nor good; they just are.

The old-fashioned general ledger and general journal were lined, and the last two columns on the far right of the page were for debits and for credits. The debit column was always on the left, and the credit column was always on the right.

Confusion Squared

To completely understand the debits and credits issue, it helps to have an *AHA!* about how we've misused them. Let's explore where the myths come from.

Part of our confusion stems from our banking system and its use of the technical accounting terms *debit* and *credit* in day-to-day transactions.

When you deposit money in the bank, the bank records the amount. From your point of view, your money is an asset to you. But from the bank's point of view, it's a liability because, at some point, the bank will have to pay you that money. So they record it as a credit. (See our previous discussion of the basic accounting model.) But really, the statement shows withdrawals from your account as debits, so it may seem that debit means subtract. You see, you're looking at someone else's books, and their entries will be the exact opposite of yours.

At the first of the month, the bank will send you a statement showing your money as a "credit." All that means is that the bank recorded it on the right side of the basic accounting model. However, because you see it as a deposit (asset), you may interpret *credit* to mean adding to your account. Since you don't keep accounting books for your personal records, this would be a perfectly logical assumption. Logical, but incorrect. That belief leads to the conclusion that credit is in your favor and debit is not.

The irony is that in a computerized accounting system, all credits are shown as a minus, and all debits are shown as positives. This twist should serve to confuse us even more with regard to the meaning of debits and credits!

CONFUSION CUBED

Our bank accounts aren't the only source of confusing debit and credit information. After all, we use "credit cards" and "debit cards," and we buy "on credit," using those words lightly without truly understanding what they mean. What were originally terms limited to an accountant's use are now in common parlance and serve to reinforce our faulty beliefs about their definitions.

Taken a step further, modern methods of displaying accounting information don't really use left and right columns. Even our checkbooks have changed the format for recording deposits and withdrawals. So, as you can see, the terms *debit* and *credit* no longer fit the way we do business; however, when we study the subject of accounting, we continue to hear those terms.

NORMAL DEBIT BALANCE, NORMAL CREDIT BALANCE

Accountants refer to a *normal balance,* which sounds as if it means the balance is normal versus abnormal. It really means *the balance under normal circumstances.* Thus, when they say *a normal debit balance,* this means that under normal circumstances, there will be a balance in the debit column. Conversely, a normal credit balance means there will usually be a balance on the credit side.

Assets	=	**Liabilities + Owners' equity**
Left		Right
Debit		Credit
Normal debit balance		Normal credit balance
Debits increase asset accounts.		Credits increase liabilities and owners' equity.
Credits decrease asset accounts.		Debits decrease liabilities and owners' equity.

That's how it works under normal circumstances. When would circumstances not be normal? If you write checks for more money than is in your cash account, in accounting terms that would mean that you would have a balance in your credit column. Since cash is an asset, it should have a "normal debit balance" (a positive number in the debit column). The credit balance (which reflects your negative cash situation) is not normal.

Laypeople would say you were *overdrawn,* but accountants don't consider an account overdrawn until the checks have cleared the bank.

Contra Accounts

Contra accounts are accounts that have a normal balance that is contrary (opposite) to what you might think. For example, an asset account has a normal debit balance. A contra asset account would have the opposite—a normal credit balance. As confusing as debit and credit balances can be, why would accountants purposely use an account that is contrary?

Sometimes accountants need to "write down" (or reduce) an account but want to keep a record of the original balance. To do that, they create a separate account to record the reduction. The regular account stays the same, and the contra account records the reduction. When you add the two together, you show what the net balance should be.

For example, property, plant, and equipment are recorded at cost in an account called fixed assets. Each accounting period, accountants record the depreciation (reduction in value) of the fixed assets in a contra asset account. If you were to add these two accounts together, you would know the net value of the fixed assets. The contra account is called *accumulated depreciation.*

Contra accounts are used to record accumulated depreciation, accumulated amortization, and allowance for doubtful accounts.

DOUBLE-ENTRY BOOKKEEPING

There are two ways of checking to see whether you have errors in your bookkeeping:

- By checking your debits and credits to make sure they are equal.
- By checking to see that assets = owners' liability and equity.

Because there are two methods of checking, we call it the *double-entry bookkeeping system.*

Having a double- (or dual-) entry system literally allows you to double-check yourself. In the basic accounting model—as algebra—the left side of the equation must always equal the right side. Thus, debits must always equal credits, and the assets must always equal the liabilities.

Accountants will check to see that the equation is equal, because if it isn't, then your accounts are out of balance. They must then look for the discrepancy.

Double-entry bookkeeping was developed to ensure error-free recording of manual entries. Computers now do that work for us, and accounting programs typically won't even allow you to do things that would cause the sides of the equation to be unequal.

ACCOUNTS

The term *account* is used to describe where the transaction is recorded. It is a place where all transactions that affect a particular item, such as cash, are accumulated. For example, there is a cash account, accounts receivable, inventory account, fixed asset account, and so on.

General Ledger Accounts

There are two types of general ledger accounts:

- *Temporary* (revenue and expense or P&L accounts). They are called temporary because these accounts don't accumulate a balance over the years. Instead, at the end of the year, the accountant makes a journal entry to move the total balances to the retained earnings account on the balance sheet. (Retained earnings shows the cumulative total of all prior-year and current-year net income. It is a component of equity.) Therefore, at the beginning of each year all your temporary accounts begin with a zero balance. During the year they accumulate transactions. And, again, when you close your books at the end of the year, all these accounts go back to zero.
- *Permanent* (or balance sheet). These accounts are called permanent because they accumulate all the transactions of a business from start to finish. You don't close them out at the end of each year. In fact, the only time all of the permanent accounts would go to zero is if the company closed its doors or if there were a serious accounting mistake!

Types of Accounts on a Balance Sheet

There are three types of accounts on a balance sheet:

- Assets.
- Liabilities.
- Shareholders' equity.

ASSETS

Assets are things a company owns that are used to produce income. For example, cash is used to purchase employees' time, which is used to manufacture or sell products and services. Fixed assets (property, plant, and equipment) are the physical items used to produce that income.

There are two major classifications of assets:

- Current assets (those that can be converted to cash within a year).
- Long-term assets (those that can be converted to cash in over one year).

Current assets include

- Cash or cash equivalents.
- Short-term equity.
- Accounts receivable.
- Prepaid expenses.
- Inventory.

Long-term assets include

- Long-term accounts receivable.
- Property, plant, and equipment.
- Intangibles (goodwill, patents, royalties, etc., as discussed in Chapter 7).

LIABILITIES

Liabilities are the amounts the business owes to other businesses or individuals. They are the portion of assets purchased using some type of financing arrangement. For example, trade accounts payable (typically paid within 60 days) is a short-term financing arrangement to buy inventory, which a business then uses to build products for sale. (You don't often think of invoices being a financing arrangement with vendors, but they are. That's why some vendors make you pay up front until they check your company's credit record.)

There are two classifications of liabilities:

- Current (those that must be paid within a year).
- Long-term (those that can be paid in over one year).

Current Liabilities

- Accounts payable.
- Short-term other payables (salaries and wages, income tax, etc.).
- Accrued liabilities (items or services that you have purchased before the end of the accounting period but for which you haven't received a bill).

Long-Term Liabilities

- Long-term debt (such as equipment financing or leases).
- Bonds (or debentures).

SHAREHOLDERS' EQUITY

Shareholders' equity is the amount of money the shareholders are entitled to. The types of shareholders equity are

- Common stock.
- Preferred stock.
- Paid-in capital (also known as *contributed capital in excess of par).*
- Retained earnings (a record of the cumulative total of net income, or P&L) the company has earned since it opened its door.

RECORDING ACCOUNTING TRANSACTIONS

ACCOUNTING PERIODS

Remember that accounting statements are reports of specific financial activity that always specify what period of time is covered. The period of time is known as an *accounting period.* An accounting period may be a year, a quarter, or a month.

The GAAP *matching principle* states that you must always match up revenues and expenses incurred for the period. In other words, revenues must be matched to the expenses incurred to generate that specific revenue. This can sometimes be difficult because of timing differences. A timing difference occurs when you create a product in July (incurring the production expenses), but you may not sell the product until September, when you send out an invoice. You may not receive payment for that invoice until October or November. To keep things straight, accountants use two types of accounting systems that are based on when you record and report transactions: cash basis accounting and accrual basis accounting.

CASH BASIS ACCOUNTING

In the cash basis system, transactions are officially recorded when the cash comes in or goes out. This is a very straightforward system, though somewhat inaccurate because of the timing differences described above. It is mainly used by small businesses that don't have to report to any outside companies, investors, or agencies.

ACCRUAL BASIS ACCOUNTING

Accrual basis accounting is the type of accounting required by GAAP. It is based on the matching principle and results in handling revenues and expenses like this:

- Revenue is recorded in the period when it's earned, whether or not payment has been received. It's recorded to accounts receivable, which represents future payments to be received.
- Expenses are recorded when they're incurred rather than when they're paid. They are recorded to accounts payable, which represents the bills you have to pay by their due dates.

WHY USE ACCRUAL BASIS ACCOUNTING?

The whole purpose of accounting is to show

1. Where a company stands, financially, at any given point in time (balance sheet).
2. Whether a company is making money on the products and services it sells.

This is difficult to do if you use cash basis accounting, because the financial statements will show that you have a certain sum of money in the bank, but they will never show how much of that cash is already committed for paying invoices. Remember, in cash basis accounting, you record expenses when paid, not when incurred. So, the financial statements may misrepresent the company's financial status.

Many small business owners get into cash flow problems because they see that they have cash in the bank, but forget that the money must be used to pay current commitments.

It's also difficult with cash basis accounting to see if the revenue a product or service has generated is adequate to cover the expenses incurred to generate that revenue. If your revenue doesn't exceed the related expense, you are losing money! But you may never know it with cash basis accounting.

ACCRUALS

You may hear people say, "We need to do an accrual." This means recording an expense when it's incurred, even though you haven't received documentation of it or paid it. An accrual is a way of recording an expense in the period in which it occurs. Accruals are very important at the end of the year, because you want to make sure all your transactions are accounted for in the right year.

There are three types of accruals:

- For revenues generated but not yet invoiced.
- For expenses for which you'll never receive an invoice, such as payroll, vacation time, and sick time.
- For expenses you haven't received an invoice for yet.

Companies that use cash basis accounting don't do accruals at all.

MAKING JOURNAL ENTRIES TO ACCOUNTS

Accountants make entries to accounts for two reasons:

- To keep track of all transactions.
- To come up with a total of all activities.

T-ACCOUNTS

To simplify the process of understanding debits and credits, accounting students use T-accounts, so called because they look like the letter T. The T-account shows the debits on the left side of the vertical leg of the T, and shows the credits on the right side. While the T-account is a simplified method of charting transactions, experienced accountants also use them to map complex activities.

BASIC FINANCIAL STATEMENTS: THE KEY TO UNDERSTANDING A COMPANY'S POSITION

Once accountants have compiled all the important information about a company's transactions, they put them into summaries (or reports) that are quick and easy for people to read. These summaries, called financial statements, are the foundation of understanding a company's health and well-being. In a sense, a financial statement sums up the thrill of victory and the agony of defeat.

THE FOUR KEY STATEMENTS

There are many financial statements that report information, but there are four key financial statements that accountants and analysts use to judge a company's overall progress or lack thereof. The four are commonly referred to as the

1. Statement of financial position (balance sheet).
2. Statement of income (income statement or profit and loss, also known as P&L).
3. Statement of cash flows (cash flow statement).
4. Change in stockholders' equity.

The first names listed are the formal document names that appear in annual reports and other formal statements. The names in parentheses are the informal names, which we will use throughout this book

THE BALANCE SHEET

The *balance sheet* is a snapshot of a company's health at *one certain point in time.* It lists everything a company owns, everything it owes, and the difference between the two.

There are three main sections on the balance sheet:

- ***Assets.*** This section lists everything a company owns that has a probable future benefit.
- ***Liabilities.*** This section lists everything a company is obligated to pay through cash, products, or services.

- ***Owners' or shareholders'/stockholders' equity.*** This is how much of the company the owners own—in other words, the sum of what's left after you subtract the liabilities from the assets.

CHART 3.1—EXAMPLE OF BALANCE SHEET

XYZ Company Inc.
Statement of Financial Position
as of December 31, 20xx

Assets		
Cash		$ 10,000
Accounts receivable		12,000
Inventory		65,000
Fixed assets	$105,000	
Less: Accumulated depreciation	25,000	80,000
Patents		35,000
Total assets		$202,000
Liabilities		
Accounts payable	$ 30,000	
Notes payable	65,000	
Total liabilities		$ 95,000
Owners' Equity		
Common stock	$ 50,000	
Retained earnings	57,000	
Total owner's equity		$107,000
Total liabilities & owner's equity		$202,000

This statement is called a *balance* sheet because it is the equivalent of the basic accounting model, assets = liabilities + owners' equity. The two sides of the equation must match (balance). This is the main financial report, and the remaining reports all fit into or further explain this one.

THE INCOME STATEMENT (PROFIT AND LOSS OR P&L)

If the balance sheet is a snapshot, the *income statement* is a video that depicts a company's earning history over the accounting period. While the balance sheet shows how things stand on one particular calendar date, the income statement expresses what's happened over a defined period of time, such as one month or one year. The income statement lists everything you've earned and everything you've spent. The difference between how much you've earned and how much you've spent is called either *net income* or *net loss.* This statement is also called a *profit and loss statement* or, more commonly, *P&L* for short.

CHART 3.2— EXAMPLE OF INCOME STATEMENT (PROFIT AND LOSS OR P&L)

XYZ Company Inc.
Statement of Income Position
as of December 31, 20xx

Revenues		
Merchandise sales	$100,000	
Less: Sales returns	5,000	
Net sales		$95,000
Cost of Goods Sold		
Inventory	$ 20,000	
Labor	35,000	
Equipment depreciation	10,000	
Total cost of goods sold		65,000
Gross margin		$30,000
Operating Expenses		
Advertising	$ 1,500	
Office supplies	500	
Salaries	10,000	
Rent	2,000	
Utilities	800	
Total operating expenses		14,800
Net income		$15,200

So how does the P&L fit into the balance sheet? It is actually part of an account called retained earnings, which is a component of owners' equity. It may be easy to visualize this way:

Balance sheet

DR	=	CR + CR
Assets	=	Liabilities + Owners' equity (i.e., Stock + Paid-in capital + Retained earnings)

The P&L includes accruals for a variety of items so it isn't clear how and where the company is spending actual cash. For that purpose, we use the cash flow statement.

CASH FLOW STATEMENT

The *cash flow statement* describes where a company's money came from and where it is going. Basically, it demonstrates how well the company is managing its money. It may also be known as the *statement of cash receipts and disbursements.*

An analyst could look at the cash flow statement to determine things such as how well a company was able to pay its bills, or how much cash was available to pay debts and dividends or to reinvest in the company.

How Does the Cash Flow Statement Fit into the Balance Sheet? Typical financial statements show this year's balance sheet next to last year's balance sheet. This helps managers and investors compare the changes that occurred in each account. Since cash is such an important asset, investors want to know what is the difference between last year's cash balance and this year's. This is what the cash flow statement does.

The main section of the cash flow statement shows where cash came from and where it went. When all this is added and subtracted, it equals the difference between last year's cash balance and this year's (or the change in the cash account). So the next line on the statement shows the beginning year's cash balance (which is the same as last year's ending balance). Add the two together and voilà! You have the cash balance shown on the balance sheet. See Chart 3.3 for an example of a cash flow statement.

CHANGES IN OWNERS' EQUITY

The changes in owners' equity describes what happened to the portion of the company owned by stockholders. It includes what the price of the stock was and how it changed, how many shares were outstanding, and dividends paid, as well as how much money was kept and reinvested in the company.

How Do the Changes in Owners' Equity Fit in the Balance Sheet? In a way similar to the cash flow statement, this fits into the balance sheet by explaining the difference between last year and this year. See Chart 3.4 for an example.

CHART 3.3—EXAMPLE OF CASH FLOW STATEMENT

XYZ Company Inc.
Statement of Cash Flows
as of December 31, 20xx

Net Cash Flow from Operating Activities:		
Net income	$15,200	
Noncash expenses:		
Depreciation	10,000	
Increase in accounts receivable	(7,000)	
Increase in inventory	4,000	
Decrease in accounts payable	(5,000)	
Net cash flow from operating activities		$17,200
Cash Flows from Investing Activities:		
Purchase of equipment		(15,000)
Cash Flows from Financing Activities:		
Increase in long-term debt		2,000
Net increase in cash		4,200
Beginning cash balance, December 1, 20xx		5,800
Ending cash balance, December 31, 20xx		$10,000

CHART 3.4—EXAMPLE OF CHANGES IN OWNERS' EQUITY

XYZ Company Inc.
Statement of Changes in Owners' Equity
As of December 31, 20xx

Owners' Equity, December 31 (prior year)	$ 91,800
Additions:	
Current year net income	15,200
Owners' Equity, December 31, 20xx	$107,000

FINANCIAL STATEMENT SHORTHAND

Financial statements are primarily numbers, with a few words of description for each line. There are also some symbols that express certain mathematical actions or that describe what a line means. For example,

- A double line under a number means this is a grand total.

- A single line under a number indicates an equal sign or says this is a new subtotal.
- Parentheses mean the number is being subtracted.

To make the reports easier to read, numbers are shortened too, being reported in thousands or millions, so that the number 300,000 would be shown as 300. A heading on the chart will indicate this, saying something such as "in 000's," or "in thousands."

THE ANNUAL REPORT

The annual report is just what its name says: It is a year-end description in words and financial statements of the preceding year's activities. It also compares this year's financial status with last year's. Generally speaking, only public companies publish annual reports, and they are sent to shareholders in conjunction with the reports that are required to be issued by the government.

An annual report usually includes these things:

- A letter to shareholders, which gives an overview of the company's progress and outlook.
- Management's discussion and analysis (MDA), which is management's narrative and detailed explanation of operations and financial results.
- Financial statements, which include the balance sheet, income statement, cash flow statement, changes in financial position, and other financial information that is pertinent to the company or the industry.
- Summaries of the key events involving the companies products, brands, or divisions, with an outlook for the coming year or years.
- The auditor's report—in any financial statement there should be an auditor's report or opinion. This statement confirms that an outside auditing firm has reviewed the information included in the report and has verified that it has been fairly stated. The auditor's report does not imply that the information is 100% correct or true, but only that the preparation of the information follows GAAP.

USING STATEMENTS TO FORM A PICTURE

Financial statements provide only quantitative information. Individually, they're just pieces of the puzzle. Accountants and financial analysts must look at all the pieces as a whole, adding insight and interpretation to gain a qualitative perspective. To see the company clearly, you must use the statements together.

SOME KEY TERMS

Now that we've described some of the key concepts, here are some commonly used shorthand terms in accounting:

- *DR* means debit.
- *CR* means credit.

The words *debit* and *credit* are also used as verbs, as in *to debit* an account, meaning to make an entry on the left side of the journal.

- *AP* means accounts payable.
- *AR* means accounts receivable.
- *GL* means general ledger.
- *JE* means journal entry.
- *Line item* refers to an individual account on any financial statement.
- *Transfer journal voucher* is a journal entry made between companies that are owned by the same holding company.
- *Expense it* reflects a noun being used as a verb. Accountants "expense" an item, meaning they record it as an expense on the profit and loss statement.
- *Capitalize* means you're not going to expense the transaction yet. You will put it on the balance sheet as an asset and expense it in portions over time.
- *Write down* means to decrease an account balance.
- *Write up* means to increase an account balance. (This is seldom done.)

- *In the black* means that the company has a positive balance. In other words, it has more assets than liabilities.
- *In the red* means that the company has a negative balance (more liabilities than assets). The reason this term arose is that accountants used to write negative numbers in red ink to differentiate them.
- *Reconcile an account* means to compare the debits and credits to make sure they match.

Chapter 4

ASSETS

The term *assets* (or resources) describes all the things of *value* that a company possesses. The only things considered of value are those that can be used or exchanged to make products or to provide services in return for revenues. These products or services can, in turn, create income for the company. For example, machinery used in the production process is considered valuable; however, scrap materials (which are manufacturing by-products) aren't valuable. They aren't considered assets.

TANGIBLE AND INTANGIBLE ASSETS

Some assets are *tangible,* things you can see and touch, such as property or money. Others (such as reputation or patents) are *intangible* in that they aren't able to be perceived by the senses. Even though they may not be visible, certain intangible assets may still be very valuable. For example, although you can't see a company's reputation, it may be just as important as the company's product. If a company has a reputation for excellent service, that reputation will contribute to its making money.

LIQUID ASSETS

In financial statements, assets are typically described according to how *liquid* they are—how quickly they can be turned into cash. The first assets listed on the balance sheet are the most liquid, the last are the least liquid.

CURRENT ASSETS

Current assets appear in the first section of a balance sheet because it contains a list of the assets most easily converted into usable form. Current assets, listed on the balance sheet in order from high liquidity to low liquidity, include

1. ***Cash.***
2. ***Cash equivalents,*** which are as good as cash. These include certificates of deposit (CDs), letters of credit, and other things that can be readily converted into cash.
3. ***Marketable securities,*** that is, stocks and bonds. (Stock of major companies is easier to sell than bonds and is, therefore, more liquid.)
4. ***Accounts receivable.*** This is the amount of money you're waiting for customers to pay your company. It may be more or less liquid, depending upon how easily you can collect it, but the assumption is that it is very liquid because you can always sell it.
5. ***Inventory.*** Inventory may include actual products waiting to be sold, or it may mean the ingredients for creating the product. Once again, inventory may be more liquid if it's ready to be sold, or not so liquid if it has to be manufactured before going to market.

CASH AND CASH EQUIVALENTS

The most liquid asset is actual cash or items that are virtually the same as cash. These are described as *cash or cash equivalents.* Examples are

- Currency
- Coin
- Checks
- Bank drafts
- Money orders
- Checking accounts
- Savings accounts

Types of Cash Accounts

Companies have different types of cash accounts on the balance sheet.

- ***Petty cash.*** This is a small amount of cash, perhaps 100 to $300, that a company (or department) keeps on hand to buy miscellaneous items such as birthday cakes, postage, or pizza for employees who are working overtime. The person responsible for petty cash keeps a log of the expenses that are paid from this fund. When the money in the petty cash drawer is low, she gets accounting to write a check to petty cash, reimbursing it for the amount already spent, and making an entry in the general journal for the receipts (or expenses).

Petty cash on balance sheet	$100.00
Receipts for items paid with petty cash:	
Postage due	$ 2.50
Birthday cake	35.00
Overtime pizza	50.00
Total paid out of petty cash	$ 87.50
Remaining cash in petty cash	$ 13.50

  To bring the petty cash balance back up to $100.00, the company will cash a check for $87.50 and record the postage due, birthday cake, and overtime pizza as expenses on the P&L. (Note: The petty cash balance of $100.00 on the balance sheet remains the same.)

- ***Cash on hand.*** This refers to any currency or coins in your possession that you haven't deposited into the company's bank account. In most cases, you will not see this entry on a financial statement because cash is usually not kept on hand for long. The deposit would have been made by the time a financial statement is issued. Cash on hand usually applies to a retail store with cash registers, and in that case it is recorded like petty cash.

- ***Cash in bank.*** This would be cash that is actually in the bank. The bank will send you monthly bank statements, which you can review and compare with your own records. A bank statement lists other information such as interest income and bank fees charged to your account during the month.

The total of all these accounts is shown as *Cash* on the balance sheet.

RECONCILIATION

The purpose of doing a reconciliation is to verify that the balance is accurate. To do that, you must compare the numbers with something outside the actual account.

Reconciling an account is a two-step process:

1. Looking at an account on the general ledger and verifying the information with another outside source such as a bank statement, credit card statement, or long-term debt statement. Sometimes you verify it against a subledger such as fixed assets, accounts receivable, or accounts payable, which has more detail than the general ledger.
2. Producing a report that shows what the differences are between the general ledger and the outside source, and explaining what needs to be done to align the two.

TIMING DIFFERENCE

In some cases, you don't have to do anything to align the accounts because the differences will clear up automatically during the next accounting period—for example, if you show a difference between a bank statement and a checking account because of three outstanding checks. You wrote the checks close to the date the bank statement was issued. The checks will probably clear the bank in the next month and will show up on that statement. In this case, you don't have to take any action at all. This type of situation is called a *timing difference.*

BANK RECONCILIATIONS

We've probably all used a checkbook, and we know the challenge of trying to balance our checking account and making the balance agree with how much the bank states we have. This process is called a *bank reconciliation.*

Technically, the reconciliation process begins with comparing your general ledger balance with your bank statement. When the balances don't agree, there are a few areas where differences frequently originate:

- Interest payments that may be recorded on the bank statement but not in your general ledger.

- Service charges from the bank that you have not recorded.
- Checks written but not cleared or listed on the current bank statement (called outstanding checks) that do appear in your general ledger.
- Deposits you've received but not yet recorded on your bank statement.
- Addition or subtraction errors the company or the bank has made. (Don't always assume you're wrong. Banks make mistakes too!)

The bank reconciliation itself is the formal report showing the bank statement balance and all the reconciling items, totaling to your cash balances.

How Companies Manage and Control Cash

Cash is a convenient asset, but it must be managed to the company's advantage. There are four important things to consider when dealing with cash:

- Monitoring and managing cash to make sure it's working to the company's benefit, so that the money is not just sitting idle in an account. This might include switching funds from a lower- to a higher-interest–paying account or investing funds in the money market overnight.
- Controlling the use of cash to protect against theft and carelessness.
- Accounting for all cash transactions accurately.
- Making sure there is enough money to pay the company's bills.

Cash is the most easily mishandled asset a company has. Once cash is in someone else's pocket, it's very hard to prove it should be in yours instead.

CASH MANAGEMENT

Most companies have short-term accounts in which they invest cash for short periods, sometimes just overnight. This allows them to earn interest, rather than letting the money sit unused in a checking account. When a company is dealing with huge sums of money, gaining interest even for a very limited time can be quite advantageous.

Some companies that have a headquarters and several outlying operating units also use a *sweep* account to pool the company's money in one location. They set a minimum amount to be kept in each location's cash account. As the cash accumulates in each location's account, the main bank regularly sweeps all the cash accounts and leaves only the minimum as an operating unit fund, depositing the excess money in an account that will earn interest.

FLOAT: ALLIES AND FOES

There are appropriate and inappropriate ways to manage cash to the company's benefit. One that is open to debate is called *float*. Here's how it works: A person writes a check to pay bills, knowing the company won't receive the funds to pay the bills until a day or two later. Since the check usually won't reach a vendor for a day or two, the company will have time to deposit its payments before the check clears the bank. This is called *using float*.

While some people question the ethics of floating, it can actually be a method of good cash management if you don't get caught short by late customer payments. The issue may soon be irrelevant, however, because electronic transfers from one account to another make the transaction instantaneous. Float may soon be a thing of the past.

SAFEGUARDING CASH

Whenever more than one person handles money, there's always the possibility of error, fraud, and even theft. That's why most companies have several means to oversee financial aspects of their operation. Here are five ways to guard cash (known as internal controls):

1. Segregation (or separation) of duties. Cash is especially easy to steal, so anytime there's cash involved, there should be more than one person watching it. These duties should be handled by more than one person:

   a. Taking in and paying out cash.

b. Handling cash (e.g., at a cash register) and recording cash transactions.

c. Writing and signing checks to vendors.

d. Signing checks for payment and preparing bank receipts.

e. Authorizing payments and signing checks.

f. Having access to cancelled checks and writing and signing checks.

2. Close supervision of those who handle cash.
3. Surprise audits and verification of funds.
4. Required daily reports of cash receipts payments and balances.
5. Required vacations. (Anyone who is involved in fraud will not want to take time off!)

OTHER CASH CONTROLS

There are a number of other controls that help to ensure the security of cash.

1. Approve all disbursements and pay by check or petty cash. Keep a permanent record of each disbursement. Note: Most companies use checks to pay liabilities because it provides a better record of transactions than paying with cash.
2. Number checks serially, and limit access to people who have the authority to write the checks.
3. Require two signatures on a check.
4. Require approved documents to support checks. These include vendor invoices, expense requests, and travel invoices.
5. Mark *paid* on accounts payable, and show the check number and payment date. (This helps to avoid paying an invoice twice.)
6. Prepare a bank reconciliation each month.
7. When voiding a check, mark *VOID* over the signature or tear off the signature and keep it to prevent someone unauthorized from using it.

STEALING: TYPES OF FRAUD

Call it fraud or call it embezzlement; either way, it amounts to stealing from a company. Some fraud is considered a crime and is frequently prosecuted. Other fraud is seen as a cost of doing business so it's fully expected in the day-do-day operations of any company.

Fraud can involve property or money, and there are a variety of ways to accomplish it. Here are a few of the most common methods.

- ***Kiting.*** A person receives a check, cashes it in the company's name, pockets the money, and then uses other customers' checks to cover the amount in accounts receivable. The trick is to keep a customer from getting a second notice for the invoice. Kiting is a crime of time; the secret to being successful is always putting the next check in before the first one clears. The vicious circle for the person committing the crime is that he must always be there to cover the next check, or the customer—and the business owner—will find out. (This is difficult to do in a large corporation.)
- ***Fictitious expenses.*** An employee makes a check request for a made-up expense. Busy bosses don't always pay much attention to what they're approving, and an employee can easily slip a relatively small expense in without raising suspicions. In an even worse case, the employee could be in league with a vendor. The vendor sends the company an invoice, and the two split the profit. (As a caution, watch out for firms owned by your employees' relatives!)
- ***Travel expenses.*** Anyone who travels regularly can *pad* an expense report, adding a few dollars here and there. Companies don't require receipts for items under a certain amount, so it's quite easy to claim tips, cab fares, or other small cash expenses without being questioned.
- ***Long-distance fraud.*** Long-distance phone fraud may be the most widely perpetrated white-collar crime. A call to mom here, a chat with an old friend there. It's not commonly caught, and it's even less frequently mentioned, unless the amount is exorbitant.
- ***Personal item fraud.*** When an employee has the company pay for personal items that are not used in business, that's fraud. For example, buying a computer to use at home with the kids is a form of fraud.

- ***Office supply fraud.*** Some people feel it's justifiable to take small items such as pens or paper for their personal use. Regardless of the size of the crime, it's still fraud. Added up, the office supply fraud that takes place at all the companies would undoubtedly amount to a staggering figure.
- ***Time fraud.*** It's not a concept accountants normally deal with, but perhaps it could or should be. That's when *employers* steal *employees'* time by expecting them to work overtime regularly for no additional pay.

SHORT-TERM INVESTMENTS

Short-term investments are stocks, bonds, or commercial paper that the company intends to sell within one year of the financial statement date. *Short-term* refers to the time when the investment will be sold, not the length of time it's been held. Thus, even though they're called short-term because management is going to sell them within the next year, these could be investments the company has held for a long time. Usually the only thing that distinguishes a short-term investment from a long-term investment is when management intends to sell it.

Some examples of short-term investments are

1. Common and preferred stock of *other* companies
2. Bonds
3. Commercial paper
   - Certificates of deposit (CDs)
   - Money market certificates
   - Treasury bills
4. Savings accounts

RECORDING SHORT-TERM INVESTMENTS

You record a short-term investment at the time of purchase and at the cost you paid. The cost may include commissions, transfer taxes, or other costs related to the acquisition.

If you don't pay cash for it, but instead trade stock or something of value, you record it at the full market value.

ACCOUNTS RECEIVABLE

Accounts receivables (AR) are your claims for all the money, goods, services, or noncash assets owed to you by other companies.

A receivable can be

- Informal, such as a revolving credit account you would use to sell a computer on the installment plan, or just having an account with a customer such as a printer.
- Formal, such as a loan agreement.

An accounts receivable is classified under *current assets* if it will be collected within a 12-month period. It is classified as a *long-term asset,* or *long-term trade receivable,* if it will be collected in a period longer than 12 months. Suppose, for example, that you are contracted to construct a building, and you will receive your payment in increments according to the completion of the work. The building may take 18 months to construct. The money you will receive at the completion of the job would be considered a long-term trade receivable.

INVOICE TERMS

Invoice terms spell out how a bill is supposed to be paid. Typical terms would include an acceptable time period such as 15 or 30 days from the date the invoice was issued. Some invoices ask for payment at the time the invoice is received.

When a company offers a discount for quick pay, it's usually indicated in shorthand. For example, 2/10, net 30 means you can take a 2% discount if you pay within 10 days.

Another common invoice term designates a percentage of the invoice amount that will be charged if payment is late, such as 1-1/2% per day past the due date.

Here are some examples of invoice terms:

- ***Net due upon receipt.*** Payment is expected now.
- ***Net 30.*** This is the most common payment. Payment is due within 30 days past the invoice date.
- ***2/10, net 30.*** You may take a 2% discount if you pay within 10 days; payment is required within 30 days.
- ***1/10, net 30.*** You may take a 1% discount if you pay within 10 days; payment is required within 30 days.

MANAGING COLLECTIONS

When do you require customers to pay, and when do they actually follow through? That can be important information to help you manage your cash flow. You need to know what to expect so that you can plan to pay your own debts or arrange financing.

An aging report is a tool that helps you manage your money by examining how much of your money is in each category of payment: not past due, or past due by particular amounts of time.

PAST DUE ACCOUNTS

The accounts receivable aging report shows categories in terms of the number of days past the invoice date that a bill hasn't been paid. Thus, past due (1–30 days) means 1 to 30 days past the invoice due date. Categories include

- Not past due (under 30 days).
- Past due (1–30 days).
- Past due (31–60 days).
- Past due (over 60 days).

Amounts are usually listed by customer, so you can see who is paying on time and who is not. Here is what an aging report might look like:

Customer	Receivable Balance	Not Past Due	1–30 Days	31–60 Days	Over 60 Days
Mr. Brown	15,000	7,000	8,000		
Ms. Doe	20,000	3,000	12,000	5,000	
ABC Cleaners	38,000	38,000			
XYZ Printer	25,000	18,000			7,000
PQR Quality	22,000	11,000	11,000		
	120,000	77,000	31,000	5,000	7,000

INTERPRETING THE AGING REPORT

The aging report tells you the amounts of your outstanding invoices, and where they are in the payment cycle. Take it a step further and analyze the report. You can see that of the $120,000 AR balance, $77,000 isn't past due; you're simply awaiting payment. However, look at the $7,000 that is over 60 days past due from XYZ printer. The printer has one other substantial invoice outstanding ($18,000), and this alerts you to what could be a potential problem.

There are several reasons the $7,000 might be overdue.

- The check or your invoice could have been lost in the mail. (Did you call them the last time you did an aging report to find out why the payment was late?)
- The amount may be under dispute.
- The printer may not have received all the merchandise ordered, and is withholding payment for the undelivered amount.
- They may be waiting for repairs or replacement of damaged goods.
- They may have financial problems and are not able to pay.

Under any circumstances, you would want to know the reason, and could take action in several cases to speed resolution.

You should analyze the 31–60 days past due column in the same way.

The last thing you would look at in this report is the column of the 1–30 days overdue amount. Here you would probably seek additional information such as

- In each case, is the payment one day overdue, or is it 30 days?
- Does the customer have a history of late payment?
- Is it a new customer? Do you have sufficient credit information to believe this customer will pay? Might it have limited cash flow and be waiting to pay you until it gets paid?

After this analysis, you may choose to call the customer and ask for payment. Depending upon which category the overdue amount is in, you might decide to work out new terms. If you find that the situation is going nowhere, you might choose to call a collection agency to handle the problem for you, or you could write it off as bad debt. But if you believe you will be paid, you won't want to write this off as bad debt.

RECORDING ACCOUNTS RECEIVABLE

Typically, you will record the exact amount of money you're owed, but you may not always collect that amount. For example, small companies often offer a discount to clients who pay quickly, because this helps them to maintain a good cash flow. The discount is only supposed to apply if the bill is paid according to the specified time limit. (Unfortunately, many large companies may not play by the rules. They may take the discount, even when they don't pay within the required time.)

You should record the amount of money you *expect to collect*, rather than the amount of the invoice. If your company has a policy regarding discounts, and one of your regular customers routinely pays right away at the reduced amount, you should record the amount the customer normally pays.

OTHER FEES

Some companies assess additional fees for certain situations.

- *Finance fees.* These are required if payment is past due, and standard fees are usually shown at the bottom of each invoice so the customer is aware in advance of what will happen if payment is late. Usually these fees are computed monthly, but some are computed daily.

- *Returned check charges.* These fees are more common in retail businesses because they sell to individuals rather than to businesses, and individuals are more likely than companies to write checks with insufficient funds. When a check is returned by the bank for insufficient funds, a company may tack on a fee to cover the bank charges and additional processing costs as well as for its loss of use of the money during the time.

DISCOUNTED ACCOUNTS RECEIVABLE

Accounts receivable is the money you're waiting for customers to pay for goods or services you've delivered. You can't always be certain when customers will pay. If your customers are difficult to collect from, you may decide to sell your accounts receivable to a firm that will pay you a percentage of what's owed to you and take the rest as its fee for collecting it. These are called *discounted accounts receivable.*

The amount of the fee you pay will depend on how well your customers have paid historically: the better their payment record, the lower the fee.

INTERNAL CONTROLS

The internal controls for managing receivables are similar to those for cash. Primarily, the person recording the sales shouldn't be recording accounts receivables collections, because it's very easy to write up AR with fictitious sales. (Auditors look carefully at this because companies can use it to manipulate their current ratio and their P&L, making them both look better than they actually are.)

BAD DEBTS

Most companies have some amount of bad debt (accounts receivable that they can't collect). There may be many reasons for this:

- A company that owes you money may be unable to pay because of financial difficulties.
- A company may go out of business without enough money to pay its debts.
- The company may be disputing the amount it owes you because of damaged goods or other issues.

THE AUDITOR'S PERSPECTIVE

Risk and collectibility drive how much you have to reserve for bad debt (a reserve is an estimated amount that you set aside to cover bad debts). If you have a customer who pays slowly and inconsistently, an auditor will require you to record the accounts receivable under bad debt, even though you know it will eventually pay.

Bad debt expense is detrimental because you won't get paid!

For a small company, having too much bad debt can also be detrimental to getting financing for projects or other reasons. Lenders frown upon bad debt that amounts to more than 10% of receivables, reasoning that the company is not selective enough about to whom it sells.

WRITING OFF BAD DEBT

When you can't collect all of your accounts receivables, you record a *bad debt expense.* This is called *writing it off.*

There are two ways to write off bad debt:

1. Specific identification.
2. Allowance for bad credit.

Specific Identification. When you know for certain that money cannot be collected, you reduce your accounts receivables by that specific amount. For example, if a small company owes you $1,000, and the company goes bankrupt, you *write off* the specific $1,000.

Allowance for Bad Credit. It's not always possible to write off the specific amount because you can't be certain how much you will receive. For that reason, most large companies use a method called *allowance for bad credit.* This is a procedure in which you take an average of your bad debt expense for the past three to five years and create an allowance or a reserve for that amount.

Suppose ABC company knows that it will have some amount of bad debt, but doesn't know who won't pay. The company decides to set up an allowance account. It takes an average of the past five years of bad debt, which we will say is 10%. On the balance sheet, it sets up an allowance for bad debt, also known as *doubtful accounts.*

Here's how it works. At the end of the first year, you set up an account for your average bad debt. Say it's $10,000. Then, at the end of the second year, your accounts receivable has become $120,000, and your bad debt expense is still running about 10%. You must increase your allowance to $12,000 (10% of your $120,000 accounts payable) from the original $10,000, which is a $2,000 increase.

Your only goal is to keep about 10% in the reserve account. You're reserving it just in case, to cover what you think your bad debt write-off will be. If your bad debt begins to go down, you can always adjust your account.

One thing to keep in mind is that you're only truly writing it off (removing it from accounts receivable) when an invoice is actually not paid. In the meantime, you're adjusting your allowance account just in case.

In the preceding example, for the first year you set up the account you would take a bigger hit on your P&L, writing off the full $10,000. In the second year, however, you would only write off the difference between the original $10,000 allowance and the increase to $12,000. Therefore, in the second year you're only writing off $2,000.

INDUSTRY DIFFERENCES FOR BAD DEBT

We described industry peculiarities earlier, and this is an instance where that applies. When you read a bank's financial statement, you won't find an entry for bad debt expense. Instead, banks list *loan loss reserves.* It is a more complex calculation, but means the same thing as bad debts. It's the amount of money that customers owe on loans that will not be repaid.

Anyone considering investing in a bank looks at loan loss reserves, because it reveals the institution's lending practices. If the bank has set aside a high percentage for loan loss reserves, it means that it is not selective in deciding to whom to loan money. That's considered an unwise business practice.

Chapter 5

INVENTORIES

Inventory is the dollar value of the goods you have on hand for resale to customers. There are three reasons you need to stay abreast of how much inventory you have:

1. You need to manage your stock in any of several ways: making sure that older items are sold first, that there is plenty of stock on hand, that materials are used up in an acceptable time period, that you are not purchasing an overabundance of items and having to store them, and so on.
2. You want to control what you own and to make sure that there isn't theft or loss going on.
3. You must account for inventory on your financial reports and tax documents.

To accurately assess your inventory, you must know two things:

1. A measurement of the items you have in number, weight, length, or other pertinent unit of measure.
2. The dollar value per item for each item you possess. Basically, the inventory value equals the number of items (or other measurement) multiplied by the dollar value per item.

CLASSIFICATIONS OF INVENTORY

There are three classifications of inventories:

- ***Raw material.*** This is material that must be processed before it can be sold to customers. Raw materials might be crude oil, corn that's not yet cornflakes, steel that will be molded, or fabric to make clothing.
- ***Work-in-progress or work-in-process (WIP).*** This includes partially completed products. If you are a clothing manufacturer, and you have cut the fabric and sewed two seams in a garment, but the garment is not finished, it is considered inventory.
- ***Finished goods.*** Finished goods inventory is product that is ready to be sold.

For manufacturing, distribution, and retail businesses, inventory may be the most expensive asset they own. For example, a car dealership has the majority of its money in inventory (new and used cars), and a jewelry store might have most of its money tied up in expensive jewelry.

WHAT TO INCLUDE IN INVENTORY

The only goods you include in inventory are those you hold legal title to. That might seem logical, but there are times when that could be in question.

For example, some stores take goods on consignment, meaning that they don't own the goods and will be paid only if the items sell. Consignment goods are not included in inventory on financial statements. (However, they may be included in a physical count.)

The Uniform Commercial Code (UCC) provides rules about when the title to goods passes from one person to another. The title to goods may change at any time agreeable to the buyer and seller. It's up to them to determine what terms they want to use.

There are two common methods of determining ownership:

1. ***F.O.B. (free on board) shipping point.*** This means that the title to goods passes when the seller delivers the goods to the shipper.
2. ***F.O.B. destination.*** The title doesn't pass until the goods arrive at the customer's site.

When the Goods Are in Transit

When an accountant examines inventory at the end of an accounting period, some goods may be in transit. Those that are F.O.B. shipping point must be added to inventory. Since there may be no way to track the goods at a specific time, the accountant will look at invoices for several days before and after the accounting period to make sure everything has been included.

Here's an example: On December 31 your company sends 100 diamonds F.O.B. shipping point because you want to record the sale for this year. The diamonds should not be recorded in your inventory. Technically, however, if you ship them F.O.B. destination, you can't record the sale yet because the diamonds are still in your inventory. While the concept of tracking these goods is fine, it is rarely practiced, so there are always goods in limbo. Auditors look for this.

CAPITALIZING COSTS

Putting something on the balance sheet is called *capitalizing cost.* Including something in inventory is an example of *capitalizing the cost.* That means taking something that would normally appear on the P&L as expense and putting it on the balance sheet. (In other words, it makes your expenses lower and your assets higher.) You can benefit from that; however, you can't capitalize costs simply to manipulate your P&L or your assets. For example, say you're going to the bank for a loan. Your assets look a little low, and your net income isn't very favorable. Thus, you decide to capitalize an expense to make everything look better. As long as the expenses are directly related to inventory and you're capitalizing the same expenses consistently, that's all right.

WHAT COSTS CAN YOU CAPITALIZE?

- Direct materials. This includes product costs (actual costs of material, shipping, taxes, freight, insurance of the shipment, handling, warehousing, and processing).
- Direct labor (labor for processing the raw materials).
- Overhead costs directly related to inventory such as depreciation on equipment used, or the rent on the building in which you do the processing.

PUTTING INVENTORY COST ON THE P&L

One term you may hear often in cost accounting is *COGS (cost of goods sold)*, which appears on the P&L. The term *COGS* refers to how much it costs you to produce the items you sell.

COGS is computed and recorded in different ways by different type of companies:

- ***Service companies.*** They don't have COGS because they don't produce any goods.
- ***Merchandising companies.*** Merchandisers usually buy products in volume and them resell them at a profit. Before the product is sold, it's known as inventory and is considered an investment. After it's sold, it's called COGS and is considered an expense on the P&L. For a merchandiser, the formula for computing COGS is

	Beginning merchandise inventory
+	Net purchases
	Cost of goods available for sale
–	Ending merchandise inventory
	COGS

- ***Manufacturing companies.*** A manufacturing company takes materials in various stages of completion and changes them to form a finished product to be sold. Computing COGS is more complicated for a manufacturing company than for a merchandiser, because it includes not just the price of the materials but also the manufacturer's operating costs (such as labor, plant management, utilities, equipment, and building depreciation).

Before the time of the sale, at any given time a merchandiser may have a combination of materials including:

1. Raw materials.
2. Work in process.
3. Finished goods (goods ready for sale).

After it's sold, the inventory is combined with other expenses to add up to COGS. The formula for computing COGS for a manufacturing company is

Beginning finished goods inventory
+ Direct material costs
+ Direct labor costs
+ Manufacturing overhead
Cost of goods available for sale
− Ending finished goods inventory
COGS

The formula is only used for finished goods, not for raw materials or for work in progress. Thus, you can see how difficult it is to calculate because of the many components and the many stages the work is in. As a result, accountants use something called *standard cost* to value finished goods. They analyze everything is takes to make a product (such as how long it takes to make one piece, the labor involved, and equipment usage) and define a standard cost per item. That's the amount charged to COGS. After the fact, they adjust for any variances.

Valuing inventory incorrectly directly affects the P&L, as shown in the following chart:

Overstated inventory (your inventory asset is overvalued or too high)
↓
Understated cost of good sold (your expenses are too low)
↓
Overstated net income (net income is too high)
↓
Overstated owners' equity or stockholders' equity

Everyone is happy . . . for a while . . . but next year, just the opposite will happen:

Overstated inventory is corrected to actual
↓
Overstated cost of goods sold (your expenses are too high)
↓
Understated net income (net income is too low)
↓
Owners' equity is corrected.

In other words, the mistake comes to light and now your net income looks unfavorable.

Companies also may try to manipulate inventory to reduce taxes by increasing COGS, but the same problem occurs.

Understated inventory (your inventory value is too low)
↓
Overstated cost of goods sold (your expenses are too high)
↓
Understated net income (and LOWER taxes)
↓
Understated stockholders' equity

Once again, everyone is happy short-term because of lower taxes; however, next year is a different story.

Understated inventory is adjusted to actual
↓
Understatement of COGS (your expenses are too low)
↓
Overstatement of net income (and HIGHER taxes)
↓
Owners' equity is corrected.

Unless you continue to manipulate the inventory every year, the situation will become obvious.

HOW TO DETERMINE INVENTORY

The way you determine your inventory is simple: Count it. That may be an easy process, or it may be quite difficult.

For measurement you can use

- Number of items, such as cars in a dealership.
- Weight, such as tons of corn or bolts and nails.
- Specific measurement of length, for items such as cloth or wire.
- Estimated amounts, such as the geometric calculations used to estimate inventory such as grain in bins. (Usually an expert does the estimating.)

Taking physical inventories is not part of an accountant's responsibilities; inventories are performed by operations. Taking inventory disrupts business and can be extremely time consuming. In fact, some facilities close for inventory.

Inventory tags with a detachable stub facilitate the process and contribute to accuracy. The person taking inventory affixes the tag and removes the stub. On the tag she describes or identifies the product number or inventory number, where the item is located, and the number counted, as well as the initials of the person counting.

In a public company, auditors will check the inventory report and will go back and pull counts to make sure of accuracy.

AN INVENTORY CONTROL

One notable item missing from an inventory tag is the number of the items you think you have in the system. Why? It's an internal control procedure. Unfortunately, not everyone is completely honest. If a person doing the counting discovered there were more items on the shelf than were in your record he could simply adjust them to match by marking the inventory number down without counting. Or, he could make them match by taking the excess items home!

When an inventory is complete, accountants compute the inventory on-hand.

SCHEDULING PHYSICAL INVENTORY

How often must you do inventory? All companies should do inventory at least once a year. Public companies may choose to do it more often to make sure that quarterly results match inventory. High-value inventory, such as jewelry or autos, may need to be counted as often as monthly or weekly.

Regulations also drive frequency. In controlled industries such as pharmaceuticals, agriculture, and banking, inventory is required by law.

TYPES OF PHYSICAL INVENTORY SYSTEMS

There are two types of physical inventory systems: perpetual and periodic.

Perpetual Inventory System. Most companies use a system that tracks inventory daily, and they conduct a physical count regularly to verify that the computer system is accurate.

Before the 1900s, perpetual inventory was done by hand, and it was only used by businesses that had low quantities but high dollar-value inventory such as cars.

With the widespread use of personal computers came inexpensive inventory programs such as the point-of-sale (POS) systems used in retail businesses. POS systems track purchase orders and customer order information, individual inventory items, and cost of sales. Inventory items are increased when the business receives the goods and automatically decrease at the point of sale (cash register). Bar code scanners in grocery stores are point-of-sale systems.

For retail stores, some POS systems are fancy enough to track the day and hour the sales are highest so you can schedule employees according to high-demand periods. Some POS systems even allow customers to check themselves out, put in cash or coupons, and receive change. The only reason to go to the cashier is when you're paying by check or debit card or credit card.

Perpetual inventory systems have become such a part of our lives, it's hard to imagine that only recently have they been available. Grocery stores began scanning just a few years ago, and some small stores are still punching in prices by hand.

Even with the new computerized formats, a perpetual inventory system can get off track in a variety of ways: through key-punching errors, theft, or waste or as a result of damaged goods being discarded or returned.

Periodic Inventory System. Small retailers do not maintain their inventory on a day-to-day basis. They adjust it only when they take a physical inventory. Today, however, software for keeping perpetual inventory has become so inexpensive that it seldom makes sense even for a small business owner to use a periodic inventory system. The only times it might be feasible are:

- If a company keeps manual books for its inventory and does not have access to a computer system, or
- If the inventory parts are so small that it doesn't make sense to track each individual part.

When you use a periodic inventory system, you perform a physical count, compute its value, and compare it with the value shown on your general ledger. You either add or subtract for the difference.

To see how this would look on your general ledger or your P&L, take this example. You have a physical inventory count of 1,000 diamonds valued at $100,000. On the balance sheet the diamond inventory is valued at $85,000. The difference between the physical inventory and the balance sheet is $15,000 so you need to increase the account by that amount.

NORMAL INVENTORY DIVERGENCE

It's not unusual for a company's inventory to be off; typical amounts vary by industry. If your inventory is consistently off or if there's a sudden dramatic shift in the pattern, look for problems.

ACCOUNTING FOR INVENTORY

Physical Inventory Measurement

Why is it important to value your inventory properly?

1. Because incorrect inventory amounts affect both assets and net income (and ultimately owners' equity).
2. Because any current year misstatement will be carried over into the next year. This year's ending inventory is next year's beginning inventory, which flows into cost of goods sold.

3. Because any misstatement will reverse itself the next year, which means that you look really good this year and really bad the next (or vice versa).

MEASUREMENTS

Costs and pricing for inventory items and products vary during the year. You may buy steel at $100 per pound at the beginning of the year, $120 per pound in August, and $135 per pound in December. Similarly, you may sell your product for $150 in January, $145 in July, and $180 in December. How can you accurately record the value of items in inventory?

There are two inherent problems in inventory valuation:

- Inventory costs increase a lot over a short time. Everywhere else on the balance sheet you use a historical cost, but which one is the right one to use if costs are volatile?
- Most companies buy a lot of the same thing at different costs. How do you know which ones cost a certain price? It is too time consuming to keep up with each piece of inventory.

Both of these situations come down to the same point: What cost do you use to value inventory? Fortunately, FASB allows accountants to choose among several methods of accounting for inventory, each of which is appropriate for different situations. But, as in most accounting issues, consistency in methods is part of the requirement in accounting. A company cannot decide to use one method this year and another next; manipulation is against accounting principles.

Companies choose their inventory methods according to what makes sense for their business.

INVENTORY METHODS

There are four common inventory methods:

- Specific identification.
- First-in, first-out (FIFO).

- Last-in, first-out (LIFO).
- Weighted average or average cost.

Specific Identification

Specific identification requires you to value each item you sell specifically according to what you paid for it. This method works only for low-volume, slow-moving inventory items such as automobiles. Those items can be tracked by serial number and matched with the price paid, whereas for smaller items such individual tracking is impractical.

First-In, First-Out (FIFO)

FIFO involves selling the oldest item in your inventory first. Using FIFO results in your showing more profit and higher inventory values, because you're selling an item at yesterday's cost but today's price.

Last-In, First-Out (LIFO)

LIFO involves selling the newest inventory item first and valuing it at today's price. This results in less profit and undervalued inventory because the older costs remain in inventory. Another way of saying it is that your cost of goods sold is higher, so your profit is less.

From an investor's viewpoint, if you're using LIFO, your assets are undervalued. And in accounting you can never write up your inventory to market value, because you can't take a gain on inventory you haven't sold.

The IRS allows you to use LIFO for tax purposes only if you also use it for book purposes. LIFO results in lower income taxes than FIFO.

Weighted Average or Average Cost

Just as it sounds, weighted average takes an average of all the different prices you pay for an inventory item. In many accountants' opinions, there is less opportunity to manipulate the profit and loss statement using this method.

An Example of the FIFO, LIFO, and Weighted Average Methods

Suppose you are a retailer who sells television sets. You've purchased them from a major manufacturer according to this schedule:

January	100 units @ $ 95
May	75 units @ $105
August	200 units @ $110
November	50 units @ $115

During the week of Thanksgiving you sell 375 television sets for $250 each. What is your cost of goods sold?

FIFO

100 @ $95=	$ 9,500		
75 @ 105	=		$ 7,875
200 @ 110	=		$22,000
COGS	=		$39,375

The items remaining in inventory are 50 @ $115 = $5,750

You sold 375 @ $250 each	=	$93,750
Less COGS	=	$39,375
Gross profit	=	$54,375

LIFO

50 @ $115=	$ 5,750		
200 @ $110	=		$22,000
75 @ $105	=		$ 7,875
50 @ $95	=		$ 4,750
COGS	=		$40,375

The items remaining in inventory are 50 @ $95 = $4,750

You sold 375 @ $250	=	$93,750
Less COGS	=	$40,375
Gross profit	=	$53,375

Weighted Average

You must first compute the average cost of inventory items:

100 units	@ $95	=	$ 9,500	
75	@ $105	=	$ 7,875	
200	@ $110	=	$22,000	
50	@ $115	=	$ 5,750	
425 units		=	$45,125	the total inventory value
$45,125 / 425		=	$106.18	average cost per unit
COGS		=	375 @ $106.18 = $39,817.50	

The items remaining in inventory are 50 @ $106.18 = $5,309

Sold 375 @ $250	=	$93,750.00
COGS	=	$39,817.50
Gross profit	=	$53,932.50

	Remaining Inventory	COGS	Gross Profit
FIFO	$5,750	$39,375	$54,375
LIFO	4,750	40,375	53,375
Weighted Avg.	5,309	39,817.50	53,932.50

Note: Weighted average least distorts the balance sheet and the P&L.

LOWER OF COST OR MARKET (LCM)

All of the inventory valuation methods are subject to a rule called *lower of cost or market (LCM).* LCM means that if your inventory depreciates (instead of appreciating as it usually does), you must write your inventory down to the depreciated cost.

How do you define the market value? It is how much it would cost today to replace the item either by purchasing a duplicate or by reproducing it.

There are upper and lower limits for market price:

- Upper limit *(ceiling):* Market value cannot exceed the net realizable value (NRV), which is the amount you could sell it for.
- Lower limit *(floor):* Market value cannot be less than the NRV minus an average profit margin.

If you're looking at the LCM, the replacement cost is used only if it falls between the ceiling and the floor.

- If it's higher than the ceiling, you use the ceiling.
- If it's lower than the floor, you use the floor.

Remember, you only use the LCM if your inventory is depreciating.

RECORDING LCM ON THE BOOKS

When you do a journal entry for LCM, you don't take the write-off directly to your inventory account because there's always the possibility that inventory that's decreasing in value today could increase tomorrow. Thus, you use a contra asset account called *allowance to reduce inventory cost to market.* The expense account is called *loss on reduction in inventory cost.*

For example, say you have $100,000 worth of diamonds. The world's largest diamond dealer releases a huge amount of new diamonds on the market, which depreciates all of your inventory by 30%. The journal entry to record this reduction in cost looks like this:

		DR	CR
P&L	Loss on reduction of inventory cost	$30,000	
Balance sheet	Allowance to reduce inventory cost to market		$ 30,000

The balance sheet presentation is

Inventory at cost	$100,000
Less: allowance to reduce inventory cost to market	30,000
Net inventory	$ 70,000

If inventory appreciates, you can reverse this entry; however, you can't ever increase the inventory above its original cost of $100,000.

NET REALIZABLE VALUE

Most of the time, inventory value is based on its historical cost plus what it cost you to produce it. There are times, however, when that calculation isn't appropriate. For example, suppose your inventory is damaged, or that something has happened in the market that makes your goods much less valuable. (This happened to the makers of black-and-white TV sets when Japanese companies began manufacturing them and selling them at a severely reduced price.)

Your merchandise isn't worth what you originally paid for it, so you won't be able to charge the full price. Therefore, you estimate how much you believe you can receive for the goods, creating an allowance for the change. In other words, you write down the inventory value to the *net realizable value.*

Chapter 6

LONG-TERM ASSETS

Assets are anything that brings income to a company. Since in accounting *long-term* means over a year, *long-term assets* are anything that brings in income value after one year or more. Current assets pay the bills, whereas long-term assets theoretically bring in future revenues.

Often, long-term assets are considered depreciable. The word *depreciable,* which we'll discuss later in this chapter, is just an accounting term. It means to record a portion of an asset's cost on the P&L, or to expense it, over a period of time. The time period is usually the asset's expected useful life.

PROPERTY, PLANT, AND EQUIPMENT (PPE)

Long-term assets that fall under the heading *property, plant, and equipment* have many other names:

- Fixed assets.
- Plant assets.
- Physical assets.
- Tangible assets.

Some of those are old terms, some are new.

Two Requirements of PPE

To qualify as PPE, your assets must meet two requirements:

- You're not buying them to sell but to help you run your business.
- They have rather long lives (that is, more than a year), and you expense them over the term of their productive life.

DEPRECIABLE AND NONDEPRECIABLE ASSETS

Depreciation is a way of taking a portion of an asset's cost to the P&L in different accounting periods, indicating that its value is used up over time. Here are the nondepreciable and depreciable long-term assets in the order they appear on a balance sheet.

LAND

Some PPE is not subject to depreciation. For example, land typically appreciates in value, so it is never depreciated. (If the land actually depreciated in value, you would take the loss when you sold it.)

The cost of land that goes on the books includes

- Acquisition price.
- Commissions.
- Legal fees.
- Cost of surveys.
- Cost of removing unwanted buildings, less proceeds from salvage.
- Unpaid taxes assumed by the purchaser.
- Cost of permanent improvements such as grading, landscaping, and sewers.

WHAT HAPPENS WHEN YOU BUY THE LAND AND BUILDING TOGETHER?

Strange as it may seem, you must separate the purchase prices of the land and of the building, because land is not depreciable, but the building is. The best way to do that is to use the land and the building's *proportionate appraised values.* Appraisals, of course, must be done by experts hired specifically for that purpose.

For example, assume you bought a property for $750,000. The appraised value of the land is $600,000. The appraised value of the building is $350,000. Thus, the total appraised value of the property is $950,000. The land, then, represents 63% (600,000 ÷ 950,000) of the appraised value, and the building represents 37% (350,000 ÷ 950,000).

If you record the land on the books at $472,500 ($750,000 × 0.63), the building is recorded at $277,500 ($750,000 × 0.37).

DEPRECIABLE PPE

The types of PPE that are depreciable include

- Buildings.
- Machinery.
- Equipment.
- Furniture.
- Fixtures.
- Self-constructed assets (such as machinery you couldn't buy).
- Land improvements.

BUILDINGS

Buildings are obtained in one of two ways:

1. Purchase.
2. Construction.

When you purchase a building, the depreciable costs include

- Purchase price.
- Renovation costs to prepare for use, such as building permits, repair, or remodeling.
- Legal costs.
- Real estate commissions.
- Unpaid taxes assumed by the purchaser.

When you construct a building, you can include many more costs, such as

- Architect and engineering fees (including plans, blueprints, specifications, and estimates).
- Building permits.
- Excavation fees.
- Materials.
- Labor.
- Interest on any loans related to the construction.
- Overhead including
  - Salaries of those supervising construction.
  - Employee benefits associated with the salaries.
  - Insurance.
  - Property or payroll taxes.

Only a building's permanent fixtures are included in the building's price. Removable assets, such as a refrigerator in a break room, are treated as separate depreciable assets. (By contrast, an unremovable asset would be a toilet.)

MACHINERY, EQUIPMENT, FURNISHINGS, AND FIXTURES

When you purchase machinery, equipment, furnishings, and fixtures, you may include the following items in the depreciable cost:

- Acquisition price (the net invoice price, less discounts). For example, if you bought a fax machine for $500, and the terms were 1/10, net 30, you would enjoy a discount of 1% if you paid within 10 days. Therefore, you would record the cost as $500 less the 1% discount for quick payment.
- Freight (plus insurance on freight).
- Handling costs.

- Cost of installation:
  - Preparing the site.
  - Assembly and installation of equipment.
- Trial runs.
- Cost of reconditioning if the equipment is used.

You may not include the cost of removing and disposing of old assets that you're replacing. These costs are expensed.

SELF-CONSTRUCTED ASSETS

Self-constructed assets are those built by your company to generate revenue, such as building expansions or specialized equipment. The cost of self-constructed assets includes

- Materials.
- Labor directly associated with construction of the asset.
- Indirect costs such as
  - Interest on loans.
  - Related utilities.
  - Supplies.

LAND IMPROVEMENTS

Although land is not depreciable, certain things you do to land are. Improvements that have limited lives (such as driveways, parking lots, lighting, or fences) are defined as *attachments,* and they are depreciable.

GIFTS AND BARTERING

Sometimes assets come to you in ways other than direct purchase. Someone might give you a gift, or you might trade assets with someone.

VALUING A GIFT OR BARTERED ASSET

Since you have not paid a specific price for a gift or bartered item, how would you determine what amount to record?

If you were ever fortunate enough to be given an asset as a gift, you would record the asset at fair market value (what you'd pay for it on the open market).

If you bartered for an asset (that is, exchanged it for something such as shares of stock or other nonmonetary items), there are three ways to value the assets you received:

1. ***Fair market value.*** Fair market value is what a willing buyer would pay.
2. ***Appraised value.*** If it's difficult to determine the fair market value, you would use appraised value, meaning an expert's opinion about what the item's value would be if it were sold. Appraisals are more commonly used for art, antiques, rare books, and the like.
3. ***The value of the asset you're giving up.*** For example, if you traded a used automation machine for 100 shares of General Electric stock, it would be a simple matter to value the shares. And, obviously, it would be much easier than trying to determine the fair market value of the machine.

OTHER RELATED EXPENDITURES

In the course of the life of an asset, there may be costs associated with keeping it in top condition or improving it to maintain its usefulness. There are two types of expenditures of this nature:

- Repairs and maintenance.
- Major improvements.

REPAIRS AND MAINTENANCE

The definition of repairs and maintenance is expenses required to maintain the current operation or sustain the usefulness of the asset. This may include all manner of things from cleaning to minor repairs, preventive maintenance, inspections, and service contracts. These costs are expensed as they are incurred.

Examples of repairs and maintenance are painting, installing new carpet, and fixing an air conditioning system.

Major Improvements

Major improvements, also called capital expenditures, are improvements you make that extend the useful life of the improved PPE beyond one year. They are considered capital items, or items that are capitalized. Examples of major improvements are a plant expansion, a renovation without adding space, and adding onto a building.

DEPRECIATION

Buy a new car now. Several years later, when you sell it, it's worth less than when it was new. The value of the car has depreciated. In accounting, *depreciation* is the process of expensing a portion of the value to the P&L during the accounting time periods over which an asset is used. The value of the item is thus written off, bit by bit.

There are several methods of computing depreciation. Some are based on the concept that you use up an asset equally over its useful life. Others assume that you use up more on the front end.

Though it sounds unlikely, the IRS follows GAAP regulations about depreciation, rather than the other way around. Years ago, the IRS tried to establish depreciation schedules by Standard Industry Codes (SIC) but gave up because it was too massive an undertaking. Today, the IRS publishes depreciation standards that must be followed for tax computation, but these are based on GAAP. (See the Modified Accelerated Cost Recovery System [MACRS] table in appendix for IRS depreciation tables.)

Factors That Affect Depreciation

Four factors determine the amount of depreciation:

- The original cost of the asset.
- Estimated salvage value at the end of its useful life.
- Estimated useful life.
- Depreciation method used.

ESTIMATED SALVAGE VALUE

If, at the end of its useful life, you decide to sell an asset, how much is it worth? How much could you sell it for on the open market? That amount is called the *estimated salvage value.* Other terms for it are *scrap* or *residual value.* It's how much the company expects to recover when the asset can no longer be used. The estimated salvage value is subtracted from the asset's cost to determine the total depreciable amount.

DEPRECIABLE COST OF THE ASSET

The depreciable cost of the asset is the amount you can expense. Thus, the depreciable cost of the asset is the asset's original cost less salvage value. If you paid $10,000 for a piece of equipment, and its salvage value is $1,000, then the depreciable cost is $9,000 ($10,000 – $1,000).

ESTIMATED USEFUL LIFE

The term *useful life* refers to the period of time over which you expect to be able to use the item. A desk, for example, may have a useful life of seven years, an automobile, three years. How do you determine an asset's useful life? Often the manufacturer can tell you. For instance, if you buy a copy machine, the manufacturer can predict how many copies the machine can produce before it is no longer useful.

Several factors affect an asset's estimated life:

- Physical deterioration of the machine, which is the normal wear and tear that will take place no matter how carefully you maintain it. For example, an automobile will eventually wear out, no matter how often you have the oil changed or the engine tuned.
- Inadequacy of the asset. You may be using the asset in a way that it wasn't intended. Back to the copy machine example. If the machine is expected to handle 50,000 copies a year, but you make 100,000 copies a year, naturally it won't last as long as originally expected. The same thing may happen if you buy a piece of equipment that's less than your need requires. For instance, if you buy a handyman's version of a power drill, not the heavy-duty industrial model, and you use it in a factory, it will wear out much sooner than it would if it were used at home.

- Obsolescence. Almost everything becomes obsolete eventually. In the 1970s, for example, pocket calculators were the size of a paperback book, used batteries, and cost $100. These are now obsolete, having been replaced by the $4.99 model that runs on solar power and is the size of a credit card.

CONSISTENCY

Once you have determined a useful life of an asset, you need to stick with it. By changing the useful life, you could manipulate your net income by increasing or decreasing your depreciation expense. For that reason, if you do change an asset's useful life, you must disclose that on your financial statement as a "Change in Accounting Principle." (See Chapter 2.)

An example of when you might reduce the useful life of an asset would be if new technology made a piece of equipment outmoded, or if you used a piece of equipment more than anticipated, so it wore out faster.

WHAT IS THE STANDARD DEPRECIATION TIMETABLE?

The length of time over which you can depreciate an asset depends upon what is a *reasonable life* for that particular asset and is usually determined by corporate policy. Companies have various asset groupings in which they lump types of assets. These groupings might be titles such as building, furniture, computers and related peripherals, office equipment, machinery, and trucks and automobiles.

When a company has a new asset grouping, it typically reviews the useful life to determine over what period the firm will depreciate it. If it is an unusual asset, the company may look at industry standards.

In all cases, the reasonableness must be disclosed, which makes it possible to compare financial statements. You'll find that companies in similar businesses tend to follow the same guidelines; which creates a way to compare performances.

Differences in depreciation timing could make companies' results look quite different and portray an unrealistic picture of two businesses in the same industry. For example, if FedEx depreciates an airplane over a longer life than UPS, FedEx's earnings per share would be higher.

MANIPULATING DEPRECIATION TIMING

When a company goes to an extreme to extend the useful life of an asset, it can backfire. As we pointed out before, accounting issues always catch up. Extending the useful life increases maintenance and repair costs as the asset gets older. You may be passing up efficiencies of newer technologies just to depreciate your assets over a longer period of time.

METHODS OF DEPRECIATION

The four most common methods of depreciation are

- Straight-line.
- Units-of-production.
- Sum-of-the-years'-digits (SYD).
- Double-declining-balance (DDB).

You can choose to use any of these methods for keeping your books; however, whatever method you originally select should be the one you use throughout the asset's life. Choose the method that matches how you will use your equipment or assets.

STRAIGHT-LINE DEPRECIATION

The straight-line method of depreciation is the easiest and most widely used. It allocates equal portions of an asset's depreciable value to each accounting period.

The formula for straight-line depreciation is

$$\frac{\text{Asset cost} - \text{Estimated salvage value}}{\text{\# of accounting periods in estimated life}} = \text{Depreciation per period}$$

For example, assume you pay $2,100 for a desk with an estimated useful life of 7 years. At the end of 7 years the desk has no estimated salvage value. Using straight-line depreciation, you would figure annual depreciation as

$$\frac{\$2{,}100 - \$0}{7 \text{ years}} = \$300 \text{ annual depreciation}$$

Here's how it works with an asset that has salvage value. A piece of machinery costs $28,500 and has an estimated life of 10 years. Its estimated salvage value is $1,500. To figure the annual depreciation:

$$\frac{\$28{,}500 - \$1{,}500}{10 \text{ years}} = \$2{,}700$$

The straight-line method is most appropriate when you use the asset constantly over its estimated life and when obsolescence is not a factor.

UNITS-OF-PRODUCTION DEPRECIATION

Units-of-production depreciation, also known as the *output method,* depreciates an asset based on physical use rather than an estimated life. Therefore, you figure depreciation per units produced. You use units-of-production when usage is the major cause of the asset deterioration. The more you use it, the more of its value you receive, so the more of its cost you can depreciate.

In this example a piece of machinery costs $350,000, has no salvage value, and has a useful life of 20 years. The manufacturer estimates it will produce 15 million pieces of corrugated board.

The formula for figuring units-of-production depreciation is

$$\frac{\$350{,}000 - \$0}{15 \text{ million units over its useful life}} = .023 \text{ cents per unit}$$

If in one year you produced 150,000 units, the depreciation for the year would be 150,000 × .023 cents = $3,450.

Compare that with the depreciation you'd record for that same asset using the straight-line method:

$$\frac{\$350{,}000 - \$0}{20 \text{ years useful life}} = \$17{,}500$$

Because you didn't use the equipment to its maximum expected capacity in the first year, it would make more sense to use the units-of-production method.

SUM-OF-THE-YEARS'-DIGITS (SYD) AND DOUBLE-DECLINING-BALANCE (DDB) DEPRECIATION

The last two common methods of accounting for depreciation are *accelerated depreciation methods.* This means that you record more depreciation early in the asset's life than in its later life. The reasons to use one of these two methods are that:

- The value of the benefits received declines with age.
- The asset is subject to rapid obsolescence.
- Repairs substantially increase in the asset's later years.

Sum-of-the-Years'-Digits (SYD). Figuring SYD is a two-step process that uses a formula for each step.

In step 1, you calculate the SYD by adding all the digits for the useful life of the asset. So, if the estimated life is seven years, you add 1 + 2 + 3 + 4 + 5 + 6 + 7 for a total of 28. The easy formula for figuring it is

$$\frac{N(N+1)}{2} = \text{SYD}$$

where N=number of years. For an asset with a useful life of 7 years, that would be

$$\frac{7(7+1)}{2} \text{ or } \frac{56}{2} = 28$$

After you figure the SYD, you're ready for step 2, figuring the depreciation. The formula for SYD depreciation is

$$(\text{Asset cost}) - \text{Salvage value} \times \frac{\text{Remaining years}}{\text{SYD}} = \text{Depreciation}$$

Here's how that works. Let's look at each year for the first three years.

$$\text{Year 1} \rightarrow \frac{\text{7 years of remaining useful life}}{28}$$

$$\text{Year 2} \rightarrow \frac{\text{6 years of remaining useful life}}{28}$$

$$\text{Year 3} \rightarrow \frac{\text{5 years of remaining useful life}}{28}$$

From the fractions, you can see that you're depreciating more at the beginning of the asset's life than at the end.

Now, let's use the SYD method and plug in the numbers for the \$350,000 piece of equipment with a 20-year life with no salvage value:

$$SYD = \frac{20(21)}{2} = 210$$

Year 1

$$(\$350{,}000 - \$0) \times \frac{20}{210} = \$33{,}333$$

Year 2

$$(\$350{,}000 - \$0) \times \frac{19}{210} = \$31{,}667$$

Chart 6.1
\$10,000 Desk over 7 years
Salvage Value = \$1,000
SYD = 28

	Remaining Life SYD		**Depreciation Cost**	**Annual Depreciation**
Year 1	$\frac{7}{28}$	X	(10,000 – 1,000)	\$2,250
Year 2	$\frac{6}{28}$	X	9,000	\$1,929
Year 3	$\frac{5}{28}$	X	9,000	\$1,607
Year 4	$\frac{4}{28}$	X	9,000	\$1,286
Year 5	$\frac{3}{28}$	X	9,000	\$964
Year 6	$\frac{2}{28}$	X	9,000	\$643
Year 7	$\frac{1}{28}$	X	9,000	\$321
Total depreciation				\$9,000
Salvage value				\$1,000
Original cost of asset				\$10,000

Double-Declining-Balance (DDB). DDB is perhaps the most difficult depreciation method to understand. Simply, it allows you to depreciate your assets heavily in the first years. Figuring DDB is also a two-step process.

Step 1. Calculate the rate you would use for straight-line depreciation, then multiply it by 2. To compute the straight-line rate (SLR),

$$\frac{100\%}{\text{Estimated life}} = \text{SLR}$$

For example, an asset has a useful life of 7 years.

$$\text{SLR} = \frac{100\%}{7 \text{ years}} = 14\%$$

The straight-line rate is 14%.

Step 2. To compute the DDB method, the formula is

$$(2 \times \text{SLR}) \times (\text{Asset cost} - \text{Accumulated depreciation}) = \text{Depreciation expense}$$

Notice that you ignore the salvage value in the equation.

MACRS

The IRS uses DDB for tax depreciation, but calls it *MACRS* (pronounced may-kers) or *modified accelerated cost recovery system.* Typically, a company may use the straight-line method for book accounting and DDB for tax accounting. The advantage is that DDB, or MACRS, allows you to depreciate more of your assets in the early years. In other words, you pay less income tax in the early years!

ACCUMULATED DEPRECIATION

Accumulated depreciation is a separate line on the balance sheet located underneath fixed assets. It includes the sum total of all the depreciation expense from the past for assets you have on the books.

Why would you include all previous years? Because you determine the net value of your assets by taking the total value of your fixed assets minus the accumulated depreciation.

Chapter 7

INTANGIBLE ASSETS

Intangible assets are things that have no physical characteristics but have value to a company. There are two types of intangible assets:

- Goodwill.
- Legal rights or privileges.

GOODWILL

As it sounds, a company's goodwill signifies a positive intangible value that accompanies its name because of its reputation for

- Quality.
- Good management.
- Outstanding employees.
- Existing customer base, such as depositors at a bank.

Goodwill contributes to a company's ability to generate better than average financial results. You won't find a line for goodwill on most company financial statements. The only time goodwill appears is if the company has been purchased.

Suppose Grade A Paper Company purchases High Quality Paper company for $1 million. High Quality's assets are valued at only $900,000; however, Grade A is willing to pay the extra $100,000 because it believes High Quality can provide a good return on investment due to its reputation and customer base. The $100,000, or the difference between the fair market value and the amount paid, is goodwill. In this case, goodwill is shown on the books as $100,000.

What happens if you paid too much for a company? Too bad for you. You can't record a negative goodwill on the balance sheet!

LEGAL RIGHTS OR PRIVILEGES

Companies may enjoy certain legal rights that have been granted by the government or in a contract. These rights add value. For example, a soap company that owns the trademark *Tide* has more worth more than a generic brand. There are a number of intangible things—patents, copyrights, franchises, and trademarks, for example—that add value.

PATENTS

A company or individual may own the exclusive right to an invention and to the rights to manufacture, sell, or benefit in any way from the use of the patent. A patent might be for a unique method of processing wood or a design for a device such as a fax machine. The federal government grants exclusive rights in the form of patents. A patent lasts for some number of years as defined by the Patent and Trademark Office, after which the patent expires.

Just because you have a patent doesn't mean it's valuable. Value comes from the revenue the patent can generate and from its ability to create a competitive advantage.

If you buy a patent from another company, you record the value of the asset at the price you paid for it.

If you apply for the patent yourself, the costs you can include are

- Legal and registration.
- The cost of models and drawings that accompany the application.
- Successful legal defenses for protecting it.

Research and development costs are not included.

Patents are amortized over the shorter of the patent's economic or legal life (meaning the time assigned by the Patent and Trademark Office).

What could shorten its life?

- Technical advances.
- Similar products that do the same thing.
- Changes in consumer demand.
- Developments by competitors that are different enough to qualify for a separate patent.

Because of these potential threats to a patent's ability to generate income, you may want to amortize it over a shorter time if you anticipate something will shorten its economic life.

COPYRIGHTS

The government also grants protection for those who own a written work, literary production, photograph, or design. The copyright, designated by ©, ensures that no one reproduces the work without the owner's permission; people usually pay for the privilege of using the work. Like patents, a copyright lasts for a certain number of years and guarantees "exclusive" rights, which means that you can use it and you can legally stop anyone else from using it.

The cost included on the books for copyrights includes

- Legal and other registration fees if the material is internally developed.
- Acquisition price plus related expenses if the material is acquired.

Copyright costs are amortized over the economic life unless the economic life exceeds 40 years. In that case you amortize over 40 years. Typically, the life is much shorter unless the copyright is for something such as *Gone with the Wind,* which was first published in 1936.

FRANCHISES

A franchise is an agreement between two companies that gives one the right to use the name and other benefits associated with the other. For example, the hotel franchising company Rest Easy owns the Sleep Tight hotel brand. Rest Easy sells a franchise that allows a hotel owner or operator to use the name Sleep Tight and to gain from the existing reputation of the brand.

A franchise is a two-way street in that the franchisee (who receives the rights) must also abide by certain requirements. For example, the franchisee must follow Rest Easy guidelines for operating the hotel and using the brand name. The franchiser receives a fee for the right to use the company name and to benefit from its policies.

Franchise costs include:

- Cost of buying the franchise.
- Legal fees.

In a franchise agreement, the franchisee typically pays regular fees such as a percentage of monthly revenue to the franchiser. These costs are expensed as they are incurred.

TRADEMARKS

A trademark is a symbol or name associated with a company and its brands. Familiar trademarks are the McDonald's golden arches and the Coca-Cola swirl. When a company has registered its trademark with the federal government, it has the sole right to use that mark. Companies very jealously guard their trademarks because of the public awareness and expectation associated with the symbols, so great financial value can come from being affiliated with the company or brand. One of the benefits of buying a franchise is the opportunity to use the trademarks.

Companies are very cautious to make sure that their trademarks are used in consistent ways, because they want legal protection against imitators who might try to benefit from similar-looking marks. In addition, some companies have actually lost the legal right to a trade name because it was used as a generic term. An example is the word *aspirin*, which was once considered a brand name.

The costs that may be included in trademarks are

- Legal fees.
- Registration fees.
- Design.
- Acquisition.

Advertising expenses are not included.

Like copyrights, trademarks are amortized over the shorter of 40 years or its economic life. Because there are so many uncertainties that can affect a trademark's useful life, it's usually amortized over a much shorter period.

Trademarks are indicated by putting letters after a company's or product's name. Symbols are ® for registered mark, ™ for trademark, and ℠ for service mark. A company can lose its right to a trademark if the name is used in ways that are not registered or if the name is used without the accompanying symbol that indicates it's protected.

LEASEHOLDS

Leaseholds can be classified either as property, as plant and equipment, or as intangible assets.

A lease is a contract that gives you a right to use someone else's property for a specific period of time in exchange for fixed periodic payments called *rents.* The owner of the property is the *lessor,* and the person or company renting it is the *lessee.*

Sometimes the lessee makes improvements to the property. These are known as *leasehold improvements.*

For example, a company leasing a retail strip might want to revamp the landscaping or blacktop the parking lot. Although the lessee will benefit from the improvements for some time, at the end of the lease they become the property of the lessor.

The cost of these improvements should be amortized over the shorter of

- The lease term.
- The life of the property being improved.
- Forty years.

PREPAID EXPENSES

Companies sometimes prepay such as insurance, rent, and service fees. These prepayments are like money in the bank and, as such, are considered assets. For instance, when you prepay insurance, it is recorded as an asset because the term hasn't expired and you could get your money back. Each month, as the term expires, a portion of the prepayment should be expenses. The amount of expenses is equal to the prepayment amount divided by the number of months in the term. This is called *prorating.*

ORGANIZATION COSTS

When you set up a business, especially a corporation, there are costs involved. They include

- Legal fees for drafting the charter and bylaws.
- Legal fees for state registration.
- Promotional costs.
- Initial stock issuance costs, including legal fees and other miscellaneous costs.

The cost of setting up an organization is amortized over five years. (Naturally, this is a one-time cost. After the initial organization, no more organization costs occur.)

DEFERRED CHARGES

You'll find deferred charges either with or near intangible assets on the balance sheet.

Deferred charges is a broad term that describes different items with debit balances that don't fit anywhere else on the balance sheet. Examples of deferred charges include:

- Deferred income taxes.
- Plant rearrangement costs (such as rearranging equipment to make a process more efficient).

Deferred charges indicate money that's been spent but has not been expensed because it has an economic life longer than a year. It is usually amortized over the economic life of the asset.

SPECIAL EXPENSES

Research and development is considered a special expense, and is *not* capitalized on the balance sheet. You must expense R&D as costs are incurred, which can be a huge expense for, say, pharmaceutical and technology companies that must stay on the leading edge of research.

Elements of R&D costs are

- Materials, equipment, and facilities.
- Salaries, wages, and related expenses.
- Intangibles purchased from others, such as patents.
- Contract services.
- Indirect general and administrative costs.

AMORTIZATION

Economic assets that have a useful life over a year are considered long-term assets. You write off an equal portion of the cost of these assets in each accounting period. This is called *amortization* for intangible assets.

To amortize, you use the straight-line methodology just as you would in straight-line depreciation. For example, if you had organization costs of $300,000, you would write them off over a period of 60 months or five years. Monthly costs would be $5,000 ($300,000 ÷ 60), which means your annual amortization fee would be $60,000 (5,000 × 12).

ASSETS YOU WON'T FIND ON THE BALANCE SHEET

Some assets can't be valued in numerical terms so they never appear on the balance sheet. However, these intangible assets can often be more important to the ongoing operations of a company than the total value of its physical assets. Here are some, just to name a few:

- Management experience and ability.
- Loyal and committed employees.

- A good corporate culture.
- Intellectual property.

MANAGEMENT EXPERIENCE AND ABILITY

If you have the choice between a company with a terrific management team and a so-so product, versus a company with a so-so management team and a terrific product, which would you choose? As investors and employees, we would choose the terrific management team with the so-so product. Why?

A dynamite management team will win out every time over a dynamite product that isn't properly advertised, sold, or improved. A great management team adds value that can't be expressed in numbers, particularly when the entire team works well together and the leader is a visionary who knows how to motivate the other managers and employees.

Experience is also important. A great management team understands the industry it's working in. It understands the competition and the competition's management team. It knows the product and what the customer wants. It also knows how to give good customer service and how to get the employees to provide good customer service. A great management team working in the wrong industry may do well, but not as well as one working in its element. (No wonder stockholders don't mind paying those outrageous senior management salaries!)

LOYAL AND COMMITTED EMPLOYEES

We probably can't say enough about this almost extinct breed of employees. Over the past 20 years, mergers, downsizing, layoffs, and the myriad of corporate maneuverings have left employees with little or no certainty about their long-term future with any single company. The days of gold watches are gone. Employers have changed the rules about loyalty, and so have employees. In the old days, when an employee "job hopped," it was considered a mark of instability; today, it's the norm. Employees are looking for the best deal, knowing that security is a phantom quality.

No matter how bleak the picture looks, though, loyal and committed employees are out there. If they're willing to grow and change as business needs change, they're invaluable. While you may not be able to count on them being with you forever, you can benefit from their brain power and motivation. And if you're smart, you can also find performance rewards and other incentives that can convince them to stay.

Loyal and committed employees will find ways to solve problems. They will go beyond expectations to provide customer service. They will look for ways to save money. And they will be worth every penny you pay them.

But you know what? Most employees aren't given the chance to be loyal and committed. When they bring up a good idea, management brushes them off or ignores them. We can tell you that, as consultants, most of our implemented solutions are based upon suggestions from employees—suggestions that are often overlooked by the managers who hire us. Take a hint. Listen to your employees and treat them well.

A Good Corporate Culture

A healthy corporate culture is vital to a well-operated company because the culture often defines the business, the customers, the type of employees who are hired, and the type of employees who are successful.

What do we mean by culture? Culture is the "feel" of the company that results from a combination of elements, and, while it's seldom measured, there are obvious clues of a company's culture.

Culture blends factors such as how readily people respond to requests from co-workers, whether meetings start on time, and what happens to employees who take risks and fail. It might be clear in the fact that managers wear suits to corporate meetings even when the dress code is business casual or where there are no women or minorities in management.

Culture may be reminiscent of a frame from a "Dilbert" cartoon, or it could be an ideal environment that fosters individuality and recognizes performance. Southwest Airlines and Hewlett-Packard are frequently cited for their cultures, which nurture creativity and innovation.

In an everyday example, think about a law office. What image comes to mind? Serious, reserved, conservative. A law office uses this type of conservative appearance to project a professional image in hopes of gaining trust.

What comes to mind when you think about Disney World? Fun, clean-cut kids, laughter, Mickey Mouse, and Goofy. The law office and Disney World have different corporate cultures that suit their businesses. And their customers expect it. In fact, Disney customers pay high dollars to go to Disney for that very reason.

On another note, most company mergers and acquisitions either fail or take a long time to become profitable because this overlooked asset is often ignored. It's easy to merge balance sheets, income statements, and physical assets. But what about those other assets we just talked about: management teams and employees?

Corporate cultures often define the company. And if you put two distinctly different cultures together without a transition plan for a new culture, watch out! Fireworks inevitably go off!

INTELLECTUAL PROPERTY

Intellectual property is a bit difficult to define, but it involves employee and management experience, knowledge, creativity, and longevity. This asset is virtually created by the team working together to solve a problem or to invent a new product or service. It includes all the experiences and education the individual employee gained both before and after coming to work for the company. And it includes something elusive that's sometimes called *synergy* (a situation where the sum of the parts is greater than pure addition) when the entire team is working well together, gathering ideas, and brainstorming solutions.

In a well-managed company, you'll find all these assets. Investors look for them behind the scenes of financial statements and annual reports. But you'll never find them on the books.

Chapter 8

LIABILITIES

While companies may earn in the millions or billions of dollars, they may also have substantial liabilities on their balance sheets. A *liability* is something you're obligated to pay, whether it's money, a service, or a product. This means that someone has a claim against a portion of your assets, and they can sue to take those assets if you don't pay off your liabilities.

Who has a claim on a company's assets? Several groups:

- Creditors.
- Customers who have paid for products or services they haven't yet received.
- Owners, who are entitled to share in the profits of the company.

Like assets, liabilities are classified on the balance sheet in two categories:

1. Current liabilities (those due within a year).
2. Long-term liabilities (those due a year or more down the road).

CURRENT LIABILITIES

Current liabilities come in many shapes and sizes. They include

- Accounts payable, which is all the debts you owe for products or services rendered. This includes any of the invoices you've received but haven't paid.

- Short-term notes payable. These are financing arrangements that are due within a year.
- Accrued expenses, which are expenses recorded that haven't been paid yet.
- Wages payable, which are wages due to employees for hours worked but not yet paid.
- Unearned revenues (also known as advances, returnable deposits, or deferred revenues) that you've received from your customers, but you haven't done the work (or given them the product) yet.
- Dividends payable. This is recorded when dividends are declared but haven't been paid.

ACCOUNTS PAYABLE

Accounts payable (AP) are liabilities that come from acquiring goods or services to run the business. AP are usually due in 30 to 60 days, and companies don't have to pay interest on them.

SHORT-TERM NOTES PAYABLE

Short-term notes payable are financing arrangements you'll have to pay off within a year, and they usually involve interest. They may be liabilities such as

- A note that's paid off in less than a year (such as a credit card or a revolving credit line).
- The portion of a long-term debt that's paid within the year.

These notes might arise from borrowing money to pay operating expenses or buying assets. Sometimes, a company might use a short-term note to settle an accounts payable expense if it's having cash flow problems.

ACCRUED EXPENSES

Accrued expenses are expenses that have been incurred by your company, but you haven't yet received an invoice for them before the accounting close. You still need to record the expense if your company is accrual-based, even though you haven't gotten an invoice. Examples are federal and state income taxes, consultant fees, supplier invoices, pension or retirement benefits accrued to employees, and headquarters office allocations to operating units.

Unearned Revenues

Unearned revenues are amounts of money your company receives before the products are delivered or services rendered. Sometimes customers pay for products or services before they receive them. When this happens, the payments are considered liabilities to your company, because it's still obligated to provide the product or service owed (for example, magazine subscriptions and retainers).

Dividends Payable

When a company declares a stock dividend, it usually sets a price per share and establishes a payout date several months later. The dividend is recorded as a payable (hence, dividend payable) when it's declared, although the money hasn't been paid out. (Note: Dividends aren't considered an expense like other things paid, so it never goes to the P&L. Since it is money paid directly to stockholders, it reduces retained earnings on the balance sheet. Also, dividends paid cannot be deducted on your company's federal income tax return.)

Advances and Returnable Deposits

Advances are payments received as a pledge to a purchase contract. An example would be when someone has made a down payment on a contract and you haven't fulfilled the terms of the agreement yet.

Deposits are amounts paid by customers as a guarantee that the space or products they are renting will be returned to your company in good shape. For example, if someone has paid you a deposit that could be returned at some point, you don't record the deposit as revenue. It's a liability until the money officially becomes yours. For instance, if someone paid you a deposit equal to first and last month's rent on a building, the deposit you hold would not be yours until she vacated the building. Both advances and deposits are considered liabilities to your company because, at some point, you may have to pay the money back. For example, if your company cannot fulfill a customer's contract, it may be required to return the advance. Or, when a customer returns rented property to your company in good shape, he will expect to get his deposit back. If the money becomes yours free and clear, you reclassify it or move it to the P&L as revenue.

FUNDS COLLECTED FOR OTHER ENTITIES

When you collect money that must be forwarded to others, the money is considered a liability while your company has it because it isn't yours to keep. Examples include

- Sales tax.
- Federal income tax, FICA, and Medicare withheld from employees' checks—money that must be paid to the federal government on behalf of the employees.
- State income taxes withheld from employees' checks.
- Defined contribution plan payments withheld from employees' checks.

SALES TAX

Sales tax is collected on any item sold to the end user, sometimes even including services. The rules for what is subject to sales tax are regulated by each state. A company usually collects this tax and periodically sends it to the state with a sales tax return. Before the payment is made to the state, this is recorded in an account called "sales tax payable."

FEDERAL INCOME TAX, FICA, AND MEDICARE

These are withheld from an employee's paycheck and sent to the IRS periodically. How often depends on the dollar amount of payroll. Some companies can pay it quarterly, and others must do it as often as weekly. Before it's paid to the IRS, this money is recorded in a payable account.

STATE INCOME TAXES

Most states require an employer to collect state income tax from employees, similar to the IRS. Funds are remitted to the appropriate state periodically (the timing depends on the state's laws) on behalf of the employees. If a company operates in more than one state, it is required to follow each state's laws.

Sometimes a company operates in only one state, but its employees live in different states. (This is the case where we live. Memphis is located in the corner of the state of Tennessee, where it joins both Arkansas and Mississippi. Many people live in Arkansas or Mississippi and work in Memphis.)

The company is required to remit state income taxes to every state where its employees live. Until payments are made, the amounts are kept in a state income tax payable account.

RETIREMENT PAYMENTS

Some companies have defined contribution plans set up for their employees. Employees are allowed to have money from their paychecks go directly to the plan before income taxes are computed and withheld. The money withheld is paid to the retirement plan (through the plan trustee) periodically. Until it's paid, the amount is kept in a retirement payable account.

OTHER CURRENT TAX LIABILITIES

Besides state and federal income tax, there are three types of other current tax liabilities:

- Payroll taxes, which include the employer's part of FICA and Medicare paid to the IRS, and unemployment taxes (which are paid to both the federal and state governments).
- State franchise taxes.
- Property and real estate taxes.

PAYROLL TAXES

This is the employer's portion of FICA and Medicare, which is paid to the IRS for employees' Social Security benefits. FICA is a certain percentage of the salary or wage earned up to a certain limit that changes every few years. Medicare is a smaller percentage of salary and wages earned. (As of the date of this printing, the employer's portion of FICA is 6.2% of income, up to $76,200. The employer's portion of Medicare is 1.45% of income. There is no limit on earnings taxed for Medicare.)

What most employees don't understand is that they only have to pay half of FICA and Medicare obligations. The employer pays the other half. The total is sent with the federal payroll tax deposit. Self-employed people must pay both halves, and that's known as the *self-employment tax* (a total of 15.3% as of this printing).

Unemployment taxes are paid by companies to help defray the costs paid by the government to assist people who have been laid off. An employer pays a percentage of each employee's wage, up to a certain amount. The amount a company owes depends on its unemployment rate. If it lays off many people, the rate will be high, and vice versa. A portion of unemployment tax is paid to the state government, and the rest is paid to the federal government.

The Danger of Payroll Taxes. Perhaps the number one issue that gets small businesses in trouble with the IRS is related to not paying payroll taxes. Small employers can be tempted to delay paying their IRS payroll tax deposits because of cash flow problems. They feel it's more important to buy salable goods so they can increase revenue. This is a vicious circle and is one of the most dangerous things an employer can do. The IRS has no tolerance for this practice because the money you're using *is not your money.* It belongs to your employees, and you have a fiduciary responsibility to the employee to pay it on time.

If the IRS suspects you're doing this, it will take action, which could include

- Seizing your cash accounts.
- Closing your business.
- Putting personal liens on all of the owners' or officers' assets (even if the owners have no decision-making responsibilities). The IRS can do this even if you are incorporated. (Note: There are some circumstances when even bookkeepers are held liable for unpaid payroll taxes because they were responsible for writing and signing checks. We state this again: The IRS means serious business when it comes to remitting payroll taxes!)

If the IRS doesn't believe there is fraud involved, it will try to work out a payment plan with you, but if it does believe there is fraud, it will prosecute. *This is a federal offense with serious consequences!*

FEDERAL AND STATE INCOME TAXES

Every business entity (except passthrough entities such as partnerships, subchapter S companies, and some LLCs) must pay quarterly income tax on the income for the preceding quarter.

Accrual-based entities usually accrue this monthly, recording it in an account called *accrued federal income tax (FIT).* They make the payment with their quarterly deposits or by mail to the IRS. (Note: The IRS charges interest and penalties if you don't make quarterly tax deposits or even if the tax deposit is too low.)

For state income taxes, the same rules apply as for federal income tax, except state taxes may be paid annually instead of quarterly, depending on the state and the amount due.

PROPERTY AND REAL ESTATE TAXES

Companies pay these taxes for the privilege of doing business in their area. The tax is paid once a year, but if it is a large amount it is accrued throughout the year.

Real estate tax is computed based on appraised value of all real estate owned, even if it's not being used. Property taxes are paid on the tangible assets of the business. These would include

- Fixed assets.
- Capital leases.
- Office supplies.
- Inventory.

COMPENSATED ABSENCE LIABILITIES

If you grant employees paid sick leave and vacations, you must account for the amount of money it will take to pay them even when the employees have not used their time off. These are called *compensated absence liabilities.*

Compensated absence is typically accrued when the employee earns the right to take vacation or sick leave. Some companies accrue this each day, week, or month. Other companies require employees to work for a period of time (such as six months or a year), and then the employee can take vacation or sick leave. Thus, the method of accruing the liability is based on employee policies.

CURRENT MATURITIES OF LONG-TERM DEBT

By its very nature, your company's long-term debt is not all due today. Certain portions of your long-term debt, however, must be paid in the current accounting period. The amount of money you owe for this period is shown as a current liability.

LONG-TERM LIABILITIES

Long-term liabilities, or debts owed that are due in over one year, are used to finance the future operations of a business. Since they are considered "long-term," most companies use these funds for assets that will bring long-term value to the company, such as manufacturing equipment and buildings. This way the value provided by the asset will allow the company to pay back the debt owed. (Small business owners are tempted to use long-term debt to finance inventory and current-period operating costs. We caution against this because doing so may put the overall business operations at risk. It is better to use short-term financing for these situations.)

There are several types of long-term liabilities, with various lengths of maturity (durations of time after which the total loan or debt must be paid off):

- Credit lines.
- Notes payable.
- Mortgages.
- Bonds.

Each one has its purpose and can be used to leverage the value of the company to increase overall rates of return on the company's investments.

FINANCING TERMS AND EXPLANATIONS

Before we begin our discussion of each type of long-term liability, let's talk about common financing terms and their explanations to help you better understand the world of loans and debt. Each of these terms may be used repeatedly in the following sections on long-term liabilities. The terms include

- Loan agreement.
- Loan closing.
- Principal.
- Face or par value.
- Interest and interest rate.
- Simple interest.
- Compound interest.
- Effective annual interest rate.
- Prime rate.
- Maturity date.
- Secured debt.
- Collateral.
- Liens.
- Personal guarantee.
- Debt covenant.
- Unsecured debt.
- Loan amortization.
- Loan amortization schedule.
- Loan payoff.

LOAN AGREEMENT

The *loan agreement* is the legal document specifying all the terms and conditions of the loan, including

- Amount borrowed, or limit on amount borrowed.
- Interest rate.

- Payment terms.
- Maturity date.
- Collateral, if any.
- Personal guarantees, if any.
- Debt covenants.

A loan agreement is approved (signed) by both the lender and a company officer, or someone who is legally able to bind the company to financial agreements. (Note: Before signing a loan agreement, it's wise to review the wording carefully. This is a legally binding document that will be supported in court. If you are unsure of the legal terms, get an attorney to review it for you.)

LOAN CLOSING

Loan closing simply means the signing of the loan agreements. The *closing date* is the date that the agreement is signed by both the lender and the borrower, and the borrower receives the money loaned.

PRINCIPAL

Principal is the amount of money borrowed or the limit on the amount your company can borrow (as in the case of credit lines). For example, if your company borrows $50,000 for two years to finance new equipment, the principal is $50,000.

FACE OR PAR VALUE

The *face value* of a loan is the principal amount of the loan. *Face value* is also the term used to describe the bond principal value. For example, a $10,000 bond has a face value of $10,000. This is also known as the *par value* of the bond.

INTEREST AND INTEREST RATE

Interest is the fee charged for the use of money over time. Basically, it's a rental fee paid to a lender for using its money, just as facilities rent is a rental fee for the use of space. This is an expense to the company that borrows the money (but it's revenue to the lender).

The *interest rate* is the percentage rate charged (or paid) for use of money. In the U.S., interest rates are usually tied to the *prime rate* (which we discuss shortly). For example, the interest rate may be stated in a loan agreement as "the prime rate plus 1%" or "the prime rate plus 0.5%." The better your company's financial position and credit history, the closer to the prime rate it will pay for borrowing money.

The Interest Equation. The basic equation for figuring interest is

Interest = Principal x Interest rate x Time

For example, your company has borrowed $30,000 at 8% (or 0.08) for 5 years. The interest calculation is

Interest = 30,000 x 0.08 x 5 = $12,000

The $12,000 represents the total amount of interest paid on the loan if the $30,000 is repaid at the end of the 5 years. (See "Loan Amortization" in this chapter for information on interest on loans that are repaid during the life of the loan.)

SIMPLE INTEREST

Simple interest is interest calculated on the principal amount of the loan only. Therefore, interest isn't charged on the interest already due. (Sometimes interest is charged on interest due. See "Compound Interest" below for more information.) Any payments over the monthly payment are applied to the principal (i.e., they reduce the principal amount).

Mortgages or car loans are examples of simple interest loans. For example, normal car payments have an interest portion built into the monthly payments. The interest is calculated on the remaining car loan balance after it has been reduced for the principal included in the previous month's payment.

COMPOUND INTEREST

Some loans aren't simple interest loans. Instead, the interest is based on *compound interest,* which means your company may be paying interest on the interest due. (Wow! It's easy to see how some companies and individuals too get into credit problems with this type of debt.)

This is how it works. Initially, interest due (or payable) is calculated on the principal amount of the loan. If your company doesn't pay the interest due, it is added to the principal amount. (Yes, it increases the principal amount that your company owes.) When the next interest computation is made, interest due is calculated not only on the original principal, but also on the interest that was added to the principal.

Compound interest loans are becoming rare in the U.S. except with special financing companies that use "low monthly payments" as the bait for issuing loans to consumers and other entities (those entities that are poor credit risks and cannot borrow money elsewhere). Most loans are simple interest.

EFFECTIVE ANNUAL INTEREST RATE (EFAR)

The interest rate stated in the loan agreement may not be the interest rate that a company is actually charged. The interest rate charged actually depends upon the interest rate, the amount of principal that the borrower can access, and the time period of the loan. There are several ways that lenders can increase the *effective annual interest rate* (the interest rate a borrower actually pays) without adjusting the *stated interest rate* (the interest rate stated in the loan agreement):

- Limiting access to the principal.
- Making the total interest payment due on the first day of the loan.
- Requiring your company to maintain a *compensating balance* in another account held with the lender. (A compensating balance is a percentage of the principal required to be kept in another account while the loan is outstanding. It is called "compensating" because the lender has use of your company's funds for the period of the loan, and it isn't always required to pay interest on it. The amount of the compensating balance and the type of account it's kept in are negotiable.)

This may not make sense unless you look at it from the lender's point of view. Remember that the lender is in business to make money (interest revenue) on your company's loan. By somehow restricting your company's access to funds (in any of the three situations given above), it actually makes more than the stated interest rate of the loan. So, buyer, beware! The actual interest rate paid is the effective annual interest rate.

The calculation for the effective annual interest rate (EFAR) is

$$\text{EFAR} = \frac{\text{Interest paid}}{\text{Amount you can use}} \times \frac{12}{\text{\# months you've used the loan}}$$

Because of the truth in lending laws, lenders are required to disclose the effective annual interest rate before a loan is closed.

Example of a Lender Limiting Access to Principal. Your company borrows \$100,000 for 6 months at 5% annual interest. But it can only use \$90,000 of the \$100,000 principal. The effective annual interest rate would be calculated as

Interest paid = 100,000 × 0.05 × 6/12 = 2,500
(Interest = Principal × Interest rate × Time)

Amount you can use = 90,000

Number of months you've used the loan = 6

$$\text{EFAR} = \frac{\$2{,}500}{\$90{,}000} \times \frac{12}{6} = 0.0556 \text{ or } 5.56\%$$

Example of a Lender Requiring Up-Front Interest Payment. Paying the interest up front actually increases the cost of the loan. For example, your company borrows \$100,000 for 15 months at 9%. But instead of making an interest payment when it pays the loan back, your company is required to pay the interest of \$11,250 (\$100,000 × 0.09 × 15/12) at the beginning of the loan. Since your company doesn't have the cash (if it did, it wouldn't be borrowing money), the interest payment comes from the loan proceeds of \$100,000 (i.e., \$11,250 is paid back to the lender immediately after you receive the money). Your company can use \$88,750 (\$100,000 – \$11,250). The effective annual interest rate in this case is calculated as

Interest paid = \$11,250

Amount you can use = \$88,750

Number of months you've used the loan = 15

$$\text{EFAR} = \frac{\$11{,}250}{\$88{,}750} \times \frac{12}{15} = 0.1014 \text{ or } 10.14\%$$

Quite a difference from the stated 9% interest!

Example of a Lender Requiring Compensating Balance. Your company borrows $100,000 at 9% interest for 30 months. As part of the loan agreement, it is required to keep 12% of the principal on balance in another account at the bank so your company can only use $88,000 [$100,000 – ($100,000 × 0.12)]. The effective annual interest rate is calculated as

Interest paid = $100,000 × 0.09 × 30/12 = $22,500

Amount you can use = $88,000

Number of months you've used the loan = 30

$$\text{EFAR} = \frac{\$22{,}500}{\$88{,}000} \times \frac{12}{30} = 0.1023 \text{ or } 10.23\%$$

PRIME RATE

The *prime rate* of interest is the rate that a lending institution charges its best (or prime) customers. Each lending institution sets its own prime rate, but the rate tends to be based upon the prime rate charged by the largest New York banks. (These banks follow the prime rate set by Citibank.) The large banks link their prime rates to the "price of money in the open market," or the demand for short-term money and the supply available (which is affected by the U.S. Treasury's decision to issue treasury bills). All in all, the going interest rate is very much affected by the Federal Reserve and its fiscal monetary policies.

Most companies borrow at the prime rate plus a certain percentage. Only a few large, profitable companies are allowed to borrow at or below the prime rate.

MATURITY DATE

The *maturity date* of the loan is the date on which a loan becomes due and complete payment must be made. It is also known as the *termination date.* The maturity actually depends upon the wording of the loan agreement.

- *Payable on demand.* This means that the loan is due on the date decided by the lender.
- *Due on a stated date.* The loan agreement could specify that the loan is due on a stated date, meaning all payments must be made on or before the date of maturity specified in the agreement. (Note: You may be required to make periodic payments to repay the loan. It depends upon the lender's policies and the viability of your business.)

Maturity dates that fall on a weekend or national holiday are usually moved to the next business day.

SECURED DEBT

Secured debt is a note that has assets pledged to the debt in order to guarantee the loan repayment (also called a *mortgage).* For example, a building mortgage will have the building as security that the loan will be repaid by the company that borrowed the money to buy the building. The asset that secures the debt is called *collateral.* (See "Collateral" below for more detail.) If the company goes into *default on the loan* (cannot repay the debt), the lender can take the collateral and either use it or sell it. The company loses any equity (principal) that it has already repaid.

The company is not allowed to sell the property outright while the loan is in place. To make sure that any potential buyers are aware of this situation, the lender files a *lien* against the property (see "Lien" below for more information), making the debt a matter of public record.

COLLATERAL

As insurance for the lender, your company may be required to put up some form of collateral against the credit line. *Collateral* is something of value that your company pledges as security against a loan obligation. This gives the lender the right to take this "something of value" from your company if the loan isn't repaid on time.

Collateral can be either tangible assets (such as land, buildings, or equipment) or intangible assets (such as marketable securities of another company).

Usually, the lender will want collateral that can be easily converted to cash to pay off the loan (i.e., marketable securities or inventory). If you think about this, it makes sense. The lender is in the business of lending money, not in the business of selling fixed assets or leasing buildings.

LIENS

If your company has pledged collateral for a loan, the lender will probably file a *lien* against that property with the county register's office. All this means is that the lender has made it a public record that it has first priority to obtain the property used as collateral if your company is unable to pay its debts. The lender will show up on your company's credit reports as a *secured* lender.

PERSONAL GUARANTEE

If a small company has a short credit history or if it hasn't been in business for very long, the owner will be required to give a *personal guarantee* for the repayment of the loan. This means that the lender can come after the owner for loan repayment, even if the company is a limited-liability entity (such as a corporation or limited-liability corporation), whose owners' personal assets are protected from the liability of the entity.

DEBT COVENANT

A *debt covenant* is a binding promise that a company makes to the lender as part of the loan agreement. Debt covenants can commit a company to specific financial terms such as:

- Maintaining a certain level of cash in a bank account.
- Maintaining a specified accounts receivable aging limit, such as all accounts receivable must be collected within 90 days.
- Limiting the capital expenditures by specifying that no additional capital expenditures can be made once a certain amount is reached.
- Maintaining financial ratios, such as current ratio or debt-to-equity ratio, at a certain level.
- Limiting dividends by putting restrictions on dividend declarations and payouts.

If the debt covenant isn't kept by the borrowing company, the note comes due for complete payment unless the company gets a waiver from the lender. For this reason, companies usually review debt covenants each quarter or, at a minimum, once a year.

Public companies are required to disclose debt covenants in their annual reports. They must also disclose whether they have met the debt covenants. For example, this statement was taken from the 1998 Annual Report for Kmart Corporation, Note 6:

> The $2.5 billion Revolving Credit Agreement ("Revolver"), which expires in June 2000, includes commitment fees and interest rate spreads of 0.225% and LIBOR plus 75 basis points. *The Revolver also contains certain affirmative and negative covenants customary to these types of agreements. The Company is in compliance with all such covenants.* As of January 27, 1999, and January 28, 1998, there were no outstanding amounts under the Revolver. [Italics added.]

The italicized text represents the debt covenant disclosure.

UNSECURED DEBT

Unsecured debt is a note that is not supported by pledged assets (collateral). However, it may have personal guarantees. In the event of default, the lender has no specific claim to assets for repayment, but it does have a general claim against the borrowing company's assets.

LOAN AMORTIZATION

Loan amortization is similar to intangible asset amortization in that it specifies what portion of the loan repayment is an expense to the company (and therefore goes to the P&L). The expense portion represents interest expense to the company.

When a company borrows money, the loan is recorded on the balance sheet. With typical loans, a portion of the monthly payment represents a repayment of the principal and the rest is interest expense. So part of the payment reduces the liability on the balance sheet, and the rest is recorded as expense on the P&L. How much goes where is determined by the amortization of the loan, and it's calculated in an *amortization schedule.* (See "The Loan Amortization Schedule" section below for more detail.)

Loan Amortization Schedule. The *loan amortization schedule* shows, for each payment, how much of it reduces the loan principal (how much of the payment pays back the loan) and how much is really an interest payment. The schedule is used for simple interest loans. (See the earlier section "Simple Interest" for more detail.)

For example, your company has borrowed $15,000 at 12% for 2 years to pay for equipment. It is a simple interest loan and the monthly payment is $707. How much total interest will your company pay if it pays the monthly amount given?

If you use the basic interest formula of interest = principal × rate × time, interest expense would appear to be $3,600 ($15,000 × 0.12 × 2) for the 2 years. But this is assuming that your company is paying back the $15,000 at the maturity date. That means the total amount your company pays at maturity would be $18,600 ($15,000 + $3,600). But if your company is making monthly payments, is this really the amount paid?

If you multiply the number of monthly payments (24 months) by the monthly payment amount ($707), you'll find that the total amount paid is $16,968 (adjusted for rounding). As you can see, $16,968 is less than $18,600. Therefore, your company isn't paying as much interest as we calculated in the previous paragraph.

Two Ways to Calculate the Amount of Interest Paid

Method 1. Total all the payments (as we just did), then subtract the principal from the total payments: $16,968 – 15,000 = $1,968 in interest expense. This is fairly easy, and it's helpful in making quick decisions. But for accounting, you have to record the interest expense *each* month it is paid. For that you'll need a loan amortization schedule, as we next see in method 2.

Method 2. Use a loan amortization schedule (easily done in a spreadsheet like MS Excel or Lotus 123). Here is the loan amortization schedule for our example:

Principal = $15,000

Interest = 12% or 0.12

Time = 2 years with monthly payments (24 months)

Payment = $707

Loan Amortization Schedule I

	Monthly Payment	Interest Expense	Principal Repayment	Remaining Principal
At date of loan				$15,000
Month 1	$707	$150	$557	14,443
Month 2	707	144	563	13,880
Month 3	707	139	568	13,312
Month 4	707	133	574	12,738
Month 5	707	127	580	12,159
Month 6	707	122	585	11,573
Month 7	707	116	591	10,982
Month 8	707	110	597	10,385
Month 9	707	104	603	9,782
Month 10	707	98	609	9,173
Month 11	707	92	615	8,557
Month 12	707	86	621	7,936
Month 13	707	79	628	7,308
Month 14	707	73	634	6,674
Month 15	707	67	640	6,034
Month 16	707	60	647	5,387
Month 17	707	54	653	4,734
Month 18	707	47	660	4,075
Month 19	707	41	666	3,408
Month 20	707	34	673	2,735
Month 21	707	27	680	2,056
Month 22	707	21	686	1,369
Month 23	707	14	693	676
Month 24	683	7	676	(0)
Totals	16,944	1,944	15,000	

Each month's line is calculated as follows:

1. Monthly payment = the monthly payment determined by the lender.

2. Interest expense = the previous month's remaining principal × interest rate (0.12 ÷ 12). (Note: The interest rate is divided by 12, so you're using a monthly interest rate instead of an annual rate.)
3. Principal repayment = monthly payment ($707) – interest expense.
4. Remaining principal = last month's remaining principal – current month's principal repayment.

The neat thing about a simple interest loan is that your company can make additional payments with each monthly payment and pay off the loan much sooner than required. Let's see what happens when the company pays just $100 more each month:

Principal = 15,000

Interest = 12%, or 0.12

Time = 2 years with monthly payments (24 months)

Payment = $807

LOAN AMORTIZATION SCHEDULE 2

	Monthly Payment	Interest Expense	Principal Repayment	Remaining Principal
At date of loan				$15,000
Month 1	$807	$150	$657	14,343
Month 2	807	143	664	13,679
Month 3	807	137	670	13,009
Month 4	807	130	677	12,332
Month 5	807	123	684	11,649
Month 6	807	116	691	10,958
Month 7	807	110	697	10,261
Month 8	807	103	704	9,556
Month 9	807	96	711	8,845
Month 10	807	88	719	8,126
Month 11	807	81	726	7,401
Month 12	807	74	733	6,668
Month 13	807	67	740	5,927

(continued) . . .

	Monthly Payment	Interest Expense	Principal Repayment	Remaining Principal
Month 14	807	59	748	5,180
Month 15	807	52	755	4,424
Month 16	807	44	763	3,662
Month 17	807	37	770	2,891
Month 18	807	29	778	2,113
Month 19	807	21	786	1,327
Month 20	807	13	794	534
Month 21	539	5	534	(0)
TOTALS	16,679	16,679	15,000	

As you can see, with an additional $100 a month, the interest expense drops to a total of $1,679 (from $1,944) and the loan is paid off in 21 months.

Additional payments may not make much difference on a two-year or even a five-year loan. But they can make a substantial difference in paying off a 30-year mortgage, where the interest paid can exceed the principal several times over!

LOAN PAYOFF

The *loan payoff* is the amount that your company would have to pay the lender to completely pay off the loan at any given time. It includes the principal remaining (from our loan amortization schedules above) plus whatever interest has accrued for the loan from the last payment made. The formula is

Loan payoff = Principal remaining on the loan + Interest accrued to date

Calculating the Loan Payoff. Let's use the preceding Loan Amortization Schedule 1 as an example. Two weeks into month 19, your company decides to sell the equipment that it purchased with the loan. How can it determine the loan payoff amount?

At month 18, the principal remaining is $4,075. Since the company is going to pay off the loan two weeks after payment (14 days out of a 31-day month), the interest expense will be less than $41, the amount listed for month 19. We need to know the prorated amount of interest for 14 days. It is calculated as $41 × 14/31 = $19, which represents 14 days of interest. The loan payoff is calculated as

Principal remaining = $4,075

Interest = $19

Loan payoff = $4,075 + $19 = $4,094

CREDIT LINES

Credit lines are loans that have flexible borrowing capabilities. Your company can borrow any amount up to the credit line limit whenever it needs the money, and then make required payments to pay back the loan. Then it can borrow the amount again if it needs the money. (This is often called a *revolving credit line* because you can borrow and pay back as often as necessary within the term of the loan.)

Interest is charged on the outstanding loan balance each month. (See "Simple Interest.") So if your company pays down the loan, the interest expense also adjusts.

WHEN TO USE CREDIT LINES

Credit lines are often used when financial management has determined that there will be gaps of time where invoices must be paid, but revenues won't be received in time to pay them (because of normal accounts receivable aging). These are called *cash shortfalls* (i.e., cash will be "short" for a period of time).

Credit lines can be classified as either long-term or short-term debt, depending upon management's intention to pay back the loan. Typically, credit lines are used to finance short-term deficits in cash to pay operating expenses. Then when revenues are received, the amount borrowed is paid off. In this sense, the credit line supplements the company's *operating capital* (the money it uses to operate from day to day).

Credit lines can also be used to finance equipment purchases and other fixed assets. In this sense, the credit line could become long-term, particularly when management's intention is to pay off the loan over a number of years.

PERIOD OF TIME

Most credit lines are good for a defined period of time, specified by the loan agreement. The company is allowed to "draw" money against the credit line (borrow money from the lender), but it is required to pay back the loan amount before the termination (or end) date of the credit line.

At the termination date, your company may be given the option to either extend the credit line for a period of time or negotiate another credit line. At this time, if your company's credit history is good, it may be better to renegotiate the credit line for better interest terms.

PAYMENT TERMS

Credit lines work similar to credit cards. Usually, your company is required to make minimum payments that typically equal the interest due on the outstanding balance each month. At the end date of the credit line, your company will be required to pay off the outstanding balance of the loan. (This is known as a *balloon payment* because you are allowed to make small payments throughout the life of the loan and then one huge payment at the end.)

(Note: If your company draws against a credit line with no repayment for a period of time, expect a phone call from the lender. The lender will be concerned that your company is having financial difficulty if you continue to borrow and are making no efforts to make regular payments. The lender may even convert the credit line to a regular note payable, which forces your company to make specified monthly payments to pay off the loan amount.)

INTEREST TERMS

Interest terms on credit lines may be fixed (a fixed percentage over the life of the credit line) or adjustable (meaning the rate can increase and decrease over the term of the credit line). Typically interest terms are adjustable because of the flexible nature of the loan (and because the lender can earn more interest if the interest rates are expected to rise).

In adjustable interest terms, the interest rate is usually tied to another source rate, such as the prime rate of interest. (See this chapter's earlier section "Prime Rate.") The credit line agreement will specify how much "above prime rate" your company will be charged in interest. Again, the amount depends upon your company's financial position, the length of time your company has been in business, your company's credit history, and the lender's confidence in your business and management team.

NOTES PAYABLE

Notes payable is short for *promissory note,* which is an unconditional promise to pay a certain amount of money with interest at the due date of the note. Interest accrues on the principal amount until the note comes due. Then the borrowing company is required to pay the lender the principal plus interest.

A note payable is often transferable, meaning the lender can sell the note to another company and that company becomes the new lender. This is called *discounting* the note (similar to discounting accounts receivable).

A note can be written for many different purchases:

1. Inventory.
2. Accounts payables due (if the borrowing company cannot make timely payment of its payables to a vendor or supplier).
3. Fixed assets.

A company can have a note payable arise from dealings with suppliers, banks, or even individuals.

PERIOD OF TIME

Notes payable can be classified on the balance sheet as short-term (maturity in less than one year) or long-term (maturity in over one year), depending upon the circumstances.

PAYMENT TERMS

Typically, there are no payments made against a note payable until the maturity date of the note. Then the borrowing company is required to pay the lender the principal plus interest.

INTEREST TERMS

The interest rate is usually stated on the note payable as an annual rate, even though the payments may be monthly, quarterly, or semiannually.

DISHONORED NOTE

A *dishonored note* is one that the borrower failed to pay back by or at the maturity date of the loan (i.e., the borrowing company has defaulted on the loan). When this happens, the lender has several options:

1. If the note has collateral, the lender can seize the collateral and either use it or sell it.

2. The unpaid interest of the dishonored note can be added to the remaining principal of the note, and a new note can be issued at different terms and interest rate.

3. The lender can take the borrowing company to court for repayment.

(Note: Usually it's in the lender's best interest to renegotiate the terms for a longer period of time and for a higher interest rate because the borrowing company is trying to pay off the note. If the lender has to seize the collateral or take the borrowing company to court, legal fees and other expenses will have to be incurred in order to obtain repayment.)

MORTGAGES

A *mortgage* is a legal document that gives the lender possession of the property being financed if the borrower doesn't repay the loan according to the terms specified by the agreement. We usually think of mortgages as they apply to home ownership or building purchases; however, they also apply to equipment, automobiles, and so on. A mortgage is also known as a *secured note payable.*

The lender typically files a lien against the property to let the public know it has first rights to the property if the client happens to default. But there can also be second mortgages against the property if the borrower has any equity (ownership) in the property. *(Equity* is ownership of the property, earned either by paying down the principal or by the appreciation in value of the property itself. Appreciated values accrue to the property buyer as equity.) The second lender would also file a lien against the property, but it would be after the first lien filed. (The first mortgage would have to be paid before any proceeds could be paid to the second lender.)

PERIOD OF TIME

The time period for a mortgage depends upon the asset being financed. If the asset has a long life (as a building does), then the mortgage has a longer term (usually 15 to 40 years for a building, depending upon the lender). If the asset, such as a truck or car, has a shorter life, then the mortgage is also shorter (typically 3 to 5 years for a car).

Most people think the longer the term, the better because the monthly payments are lower. But this might not be a good thing. Yes, the payments are lower, but the interest paid will be much higher. On 30- and 40-year mortgages, the interest expense can be so high that you will pay for the building several times before the mortgage is actually paid for.

PAYMENT TERMS

A mortgage typically calls for equal monthly payments to be made over the term of the loan. Most mortgages are simple interest loans, so additional payments can reduce the remaining principal balance of the loan.

INTEREST TERMS

The interest rate is usually stated at an annual rate, although payments are typically made monthly. Each payment includes principal repayment and interest. The amount of interest is calculated as the remaining principal balance × interest for the month (annual interest rate ÷ 12 months). This is calculated first and deducted from the payment. Whatever remains is the repayment of principal. (See this chapter's sections "Loan Amortization" and "Loan Amortization Schedule" for more information.)

Traditional interest terms specify a fixed interest over the loan term. However, this concept of "fixed" interest over a long period of time is unique to the U.S. In European countries, fixed rates are rare except in specific cases (and even then they're only "fixed" for a short period of time). Most mortgages specify an adjustable interest rate. Even in the U.S., other terms are popular in times of high interest rates or when the economy is volatile. Other terms include

1. Point system mortgages.
2. Shared-appreciation mortgages.
3. Variable-rate (or adjustable-rate) mortgages.

Point System Mortgages. In the point system (which represents the majority of home mortgages), each point represents 1% of the face value of the note. The lender typically assesses a specified number of points with an interest rate. For each point paid, the borrower "buys down" (reduces) the interest rate. Therefore, each point actually increases the effective annual interest rate of the mortgage.

For example, your company purchases equipment for $1,000,000 with a $100,000 down payment and $900,000 mortgaged over 2 years. The stated interest rate is 9% with no points. But you can get an 8.25% interest rate with 2 points. You decide to pay the 2 points, which is $18,000 ($900,000 × 0.02). So the total amount of money your company pays for the $900,000 at the loan closing is $118,000 with $18,000 added to the loan value of $900,000. The effective rate of interest is calculated as

Interest paid = $918,000 × 0.0825 × 2 = $151,470

Amount you can use = $918,000 – 18,000 = $900,000

Number of months you've used the loan = 24

$$\text{EFAR} = \frac{151{,}470}{900{,}000} \times \frac{12}{24} = 0.0842 \text{ or } 8.42\%$$

So your company is effectively paying 8.42%, rather than the stated 8.25% interest rate. (See this chapter's section "Effective Annual Interest Rate" for specific information on the EFAR calculation.)

Shared-Appreciation Mortgages. The *shared-appreciation mortgage (SAM)* is more unusual. It allows the lender to share in the asset appreciation (but not share in asset depreciation or loss in value) rather than having the entire increase in value apply to the borrower's equity. The interest rate is typically lower than a normal mortgage with the same amount of perceived risk.

Variations on this include the lender's sharing of the profits from a project or having a specified ownership percentage in the asset.

Adjustable-Rate Mortgages. Instead of being fixed, the interest rate on *adjustable-rate mortgages* (also called *ARMs, variable-rate mortgages,* or *floating-rate mortgages)* goes up and down with the prime rate. The goal is to shift the risk of unstable interest rates from the lender to the borrower. In other words, when interest rates goes up, the borrower must pay more interest expense. The lender isn't locked into a situation where it could be earning more interest income elsewhere.

The floating interest rate is usually adjusted quarterly, semiannually, or annually. But it could be longer than that, too. Also, there is typically a specified period of time at the beginning of the loan during which the interest rate is fixed (for example, one year), and the borrower may be able to refinance the loan to a fixed-rate mortgage if interest rates become less volatile.

Why Use an Adjustable-Rate Mortgage?

There are several reasons to use an ARM:

1. An ARM often begins with a much lower stated interest rate than a fixed interest rate. If the company is having short-term cash flow problems, this may be a way to borrow money with the expectations that it can repay a higher amount (increased interest expense) later. Or, it may be able to lock in a fixed rate later on.
2. Interest rates may be high or very volatile. An ARM is a way for the company to borrow money at a slightly lower rate and then to possibly lock in a fixed rate when interest rates are lower than the current fixed rates.
3. The company may have credit problems, and an ARM is the only type it can qualify for.

BONDS

Bonds are negotiable debt securities that represent long-term notes payable. Each *bond certificate* shows a face value (stated principal amount) and a stated interest rate. Basically, the borrower is promising to pay the principal at maturity date and to make periodic interest payments determined by the stated interest rate.

Bonds are negotiable instruments and are usually issued as $1,000 bonds. For example, a company wanting to raise $200,000 would issue 200 bonds with the face value of $1,000. It probably wouldn't issue two $100,000 bonds. That's because it's easier to trade lower bond values than higher ones. (Of course, a company can issue bonds in any denomination it wants. But it will probably stick with common market terms.)

Usually bonds are issued through an investment firm or bank (called the *underwriter*), which often guarantees the company a fixed price for the bonds. In turn, the underwriter expects to make a profit for the bonds when they become available on the open bond market. The underwriter handles all the marketing costs of "getting the word out" that the bonds are available for purchase.

Since there are usually many bondholders, the issuing corporation may appoint a *trustee* (often a bank) to represent the interest of the bondholders. The trustee is responsible for making sure the company fulfills the terms of the bond agreement.

The contract or loan agreement for a bond issuance is called a *bond indenture.*

COMPARISON TO STOCK CERTIFICATES

Since bonds are negotiable, it's easy to compare them to stocks that can be traded as long as there are willing buyers and sellers. We compare them in the following chart:

Stock	Bond
Represents a unit of ownership so the stockholder is actually a company owner.	Represents a debt so the bondholder is actually a creditor of the company.
Remains outstanding indefinitely unless the company decides to retire it.	Has a defined life that is represented by the maturity date.
Has no fixed value (could go to zero).	Has a fixed face value.
Does not require dividend payments.	Requires interest payments at fixed amounts.
Paid dividends are not considered expense on the P&L. Instead, they are a return on the stockholders' investment.	Interest expense paid is considered another expense of the company. Therefore, it is recorded to the P&L.
Dividends are not deductible for income tax purposes.	Interest expense is deductible for income tax purposes.

WHY ISSUE BONDS?

Bonds are issued when a company (or government) needs to raise large amounts of money that a single lender wouldn't loan. For example, if a company needs to raise $10,000,000 to build a plant, and capital lending is tight, it may consider issuing bonds to raise the money.

TYPES OF BONDS

Bonds have two common characteristics:

1. They hold a promise to pay cash or other assets.
2. They have a maturity date.

Other characteristics are dependent on what type of bond has been issued. The common types are

1. Secured bonds. *Secured bonds* are bonds that have some type of collateral guaranteeing them.
2. Lien security bonds. *Lien security bonds* are bonds with liens already in place against certain types of property (marketable securities, buildings, equipment, etc.) as a guarantee for bond repayment.
3. Unsecured bonds. *Unsecured bonds* are bonds that have no collateral or guarantee.
4. Registered bonds. *Registered bonds* are bonds in which the owner's name appears on the bond certificate, and the issuing company (called the *registrar)* keeps a record of the bondholder. They may be registered as to face value or as to both face value and interest. They can be easily replaced if they are lost or destroyed.
5. Unregistered bonds (bearer bonds). With *unregistered bonds (bearer bonds),* there are no records kept on the owners, and the owners' names are not on the bond certificates. Instead, the person called the bearer who "holds" the bond owns it.
6. Coupon bonds. A *coupon bond* is a bond not registered as to interest. It has a detachable coupon that the bondholder presents (or mails) to the issuing company for interest payment.
7. Term bonds. A *term bond* is a bond that matures at the same time as all the other bonds from the same issuance (i.e., they all mature at the same date).

8. Serial bonds. *Serial bonds* mature in groups over the term of the bond issuance. For example, a fourth of the bonds may mature after three years, the next fourth after four years, the next fourth after five years, and so on.
9. Callable bonds. *Callable bonds* contain a provision to allow the issuing company to buy back (or to "call") the bonds before they mature. The company is required to pay a certain amount known as a *call premium* to the bondholder in order to obtain the bonds. Callable bonds are good if interest rates are high or volatile since they allow the company to stop making higher interest payments on the bonds by "calling them out."
10. Convertible bonds. *Convertible bonds* are bonds that can be exchanged for common stock at the bondholder's option. Usually they have specified conversion rates, such as 20 shares of common stock for a $1,000 bond. Any type of bond may be specified convertible, but it's more likely to happen if the company is risky or new. The convertible feature makes it more attractive to investors.
11. Bonds issued with stock warrants. A *stock warrant* allows the bondholder to purchase a certain number of common stock shares at a specified price. Stock warrants may be either detachable (the bondholder can purchase the common stock and keep the bond) or nondetachable (the bondholder must turn in the bond to purchase the stock, which is basically the same thing as a convertible bond).

PREMIUMS AND DISCOUNTS

Unlike stocks that are publicly traded, bonds have a fixed face value, a fixed interest rate, and a predetermined life. Thus, they seem fairly risk-free from an investment point-of-view. Who could turn down a guaranteed payment of a bond versus the unknown of a stock? But obviously, this isn't the case, or people wouldn't be investing in the stock market.

Although everything about a bond seems predetermined or fixed, investors have figured out a way to make sure the return on the bond is equivalent to a new issue of bonds at all times. This is done through bond premiums and discounts.

A *bond premium* is the amount an investor pays over the face value of the bond. For example, the face value of the bond is $1,000, but an investor pays $1,200 for it. The bond premium is $200.

A *bond discount* is the amount an investor pays less than the face value of the bond. For example, the face value of a bond is $1,000, but an investor pays only $900 for it. The bond discount is $100.

Why would an investor pay a bond premium? If the coupon rate (or stated interest rate) of the bond is above the market rate (meaning the going interest rate for similar types of bonds), then an investor may pay more for the increased return.

Why would a seller accept less than the face value for a bond (i.e., sell a bond at discount)? Because the coupon rate is lower than the market rate. In simpler terms, pretend that the bond is a car you are trying to sell. Its sticker price is $1,000. All other cars that have the exact same features and quality are priced at $800. Would you be willing to sell it at $1,000? Of course, you would. But would someone buy it for $1,000? Probably not. So you would mark the price down (discount it) to sell it. The same thing works with bond discounts.

Using the same example, let's say the car has a sticker price of $1,000, but cars of equivalent features and quality are selling for $1,500. Would someone pay you $1,000 for it? Of course. But you would probably mark the price up to the market price of $1,500. Or, you would charge a premium for the car. Again, it's the same principal that we just saw with bond premiums.

What's interesting about this is that bond premiums and discounts tend to make the bond value equal to the going market rate. In other words, the premium or discount changes the effective annual rate of interest to make it more equivalent to the market interest rates.

CAPITAL LEASING

A *lease* is a contract to rent property, whether that property is physical space, equipment, automobiles, or trucks. In accounting, there are two types of leases:

1. Capital leases.
2. Operating leases.

Capital leases are another way to finance the purchase of equipment or other property. The leased assets are treated as if the entity paying rent is the owner, and the leased assets are recorded as fixed assets and are depreciated. The lease payments are not expense on the P&L. They are treated as if they are repayment of a loan (i.e., they reduce a long-term liability).

Operating leases are truly rented property. The ownership of the property always belongs to the entity that receives the lease payments, and the lease payments are considered P&L expense to the entity paying the rent.

DETERMINING CAPITAL OR OPERATING LEASES

Accountants have specific conditions that determine whether a lease is a long-term liability (a capital lease) or an operating lease. The conditions are based on the lease terms rather than the characteristics of the asset itself. To qualify as a capital lease, the lease must meet only one of the four conditions:

1. The lease transfers ownership of the leased asset to the entity making lease payments by the end of the lease term.
2. The lease contains a bargain purchase option, which is a very low amount to purchase the leased asset (such as $1) at the end of the lease term.
3. The lease term equals 75% or more of the asset's useful life.
4. The present value of the lease payments at the beginning of the lease equals 90% or more of the market value of the leased asset.

If the lease doesn't meet one of these four conditions, it is considered an operating lease, and the lease payments are treated as expense on the P&L.

Accounting for capital leases is a little tricky because, although it is considered a lease, the accountant must treat it as a note payable with interest paid. Your accountant will determine a portion of each payment that is considered interest expense, and the rest of the payment will be recorded as a reduction to your long-term liability. There are several ways to determine how this is done, using present value formulas and other tools, but that discussion is technical from an accounting standpoint and outside the scope of this book.

Chapter 9

EQUITY

Equity simply means the portion of a company owned by stockholders, or owners, outright. In other words, it is the portion of the company's assets that an owner can lay claim to in a liquidation; thus, it is the assets that have no *leverage* (or creditor claims) against them.

For example, a homeowner who buys a house with a mortgage (loan) puts down a certain amount of money to buy the house. The homeowner owns that amount of equity in the house. The rest is leveraged with the mortgage (or someone else's money). As the homeowner pays monthly notes, she earns some amount of equity each month. The same is true for stockholders. They "put down" a portion of the entire value of the company as a down payment (or equity investment). The rest is financed with other peoples' (or other companies' such as banks') money. The only difference between a stockholder and a homeowner is that the stockholder doesn't make monthly payments. The company is expected to pay off its debt with net profits earned.

WHAT IS CAPITAL STOCK?

Capital stock is a transferrable unit of ownership of a company. It is recorded on stock certificates, which are legal documents much like receipts. They are printed or engraved and are evidence that a shareholder owns a certain number of shares. A *share* of stock is one piece worth a certain amount. If a person owns 1,000 shares, and the par value of each share is $5, he owns $5,000 of the company's book value.

STOCK CLASSIFICATIONS

Although we tend to use the word *stock* generically for the certificates (or units) of a company, there are actually several classes of stock. The two most recognized forms are common stock and preferred stock.

1. ***Common stock.*** Common stock is the class of stock for which rights are shared equally by all members of that class. It represents residual equity. (All other claims from lenders and preferred stockholders come before common stockholders' claims in bankruptcy.) Holding this type of stock entitles an owner to certain rights, such as voting in company meetings (to elect board members, approve a merger, or the like) and sharing in profits or the sale of the company.
2. ***Preferred stock.*** This stock offers different privileges from common stock. It is considered less risky because people who hold preferred stock are paid their portion of a company's dividends or sale before owners of common stock. They typically hold no voting privileges.

COMMON STOCK

Common stock can be valued on the books in two ways:

1. ***Par value.*** The value of a share is set when the company issues stock, and it is stated on the stock certificate. This is the stock's *par value,* and it has no relationship to the actual value of the company. Par value always stays the same. The total par value of all the stock is considered the *legal capital* of the company. Par value can be as low as $.001 per share or even less. It is an arbitrary amount set when a company is incorporated.
2. ***No par value.*** This is common stock to which the company has not assigned a value.

MARKET VALUE

The selling price of each share is unrelated to the par value, and it rises and falls with the stock market price. The total of all the outstanding shares of stock at the market price is the *market value.* There are two ways to look at market value: from the company's perspective or from the shareholders' perspective.

COMPANY'S PERSPECTIVE: COMPANY STOCK ISSUANCE OR INITIAL PUBLIC OFFERING (IPO)

A company might issue stock when it first becomes a public company, in an IPO, or at any time during the life of the company when it wants to raise money. In this case, the company actually receives the money raised on the stock market for the stock it sells. (Any subsequent issuance of stock is called a "second issuance," even if stock has been issued more than two times.)

When a company issues stock, the amount the company received will show on the books at market value. If par value is $1 and the company received $1.50 per share, it would be recorded as

Common stock par value	$100,000
Additional paid-in capital	$50,000
Total	$150,000

SHAREHOLDERS' PERSPECTIVE: TRADING BETWEEN SHAREHOLDERS

When stock is traded between shareholders in the stock exchange, it's not recorded on the company's books because the company never receives money. Stock certificates and monies paid are exchanged between buyers and sellers on the open stock market.

LEGAL CAPITAL

If a company goes out of business, the people who own stock are entitled to receive a payback for their investment, but only after the company's debts have been paid. For that reason, when the company issues dividends, it cannot distribute money that would deplete its worth to below the total par value or legal capital of the company.

For example, suppose a company issues 100,000 shares of common stock at $1 par value. The legal capital of the company is $100,000. If the equity section of the balance sheet shows $120,000, the most the company can pay out in dividends is $20,000. If the company paid out more than that, it would reduce its legal capital below $100,000, which is the amount of money common stock owners are entitled to.

PREFERRED STOCK

When a company is formed and needs to raise capital, it may face difficulty in obtaining funds. One easy way to raise cash is to sell preferred stock to shareholders who are willing to take a risk. In exchange for their willingness to take this risk, they earn certain rights and they give up certain privileges.

TYPES OF PREFERRED STOCK

Preferred stock may have one or more of the following features:

1. ***Cumulative.*** Cumulative stock is that which must be paid dividends in full before common stockholders receive any payment of dividends. Even when the company is unable to make dividend payments, the amount due the preferred stockholders accumulates until it is paid.
2. ***Preferred as to assets.*** If a company is liquidated, the stockholder will receive a liquidation value before any assets are distributed to common stockholders.
3. ***Preferred as to dividends.*** Holders of this type of stock are entitled to a specific dividend, spelled out as a dollar amount per share or as a percentage of par value.
4. ***Convertible.*** Preferred stock may, at the option of the holder, be exchanged for common stock.
5. ***Callable.*** Callable stock can be repurchased by the issuer for a certain amount, usually at a premium. This gives the issuer an opportunity to buy stock back when the interest rate is below the dividend return on the stock. The people who hold the shares have no say in this decision; the company has the power to call (buy back) stock at any time, as specified by the stock terms.
6. ***Preferred as to voting privileges.*** Owners of preferred stock may also have different voting privileges than common stock-

holders, depending upon what the company specifies. They may have double the voting privileges (two votes per share of stock owned), or they may have no voting privileges at all.

What Preferred Stockholders Receive

There are a number of stipulations (or preferences) a company can place on its preferred stock, meaning that the holders of preferred stock are treated differently than holders of common stock.

One stipulation frequently attached to preferred stock has to do with the priority order in which payments are made to shareholders if a company goes out of business. Its stockholders are entitled to be paid for their share of the ownership, but only after debts are paid. Holders of preferred stock are promised that they will be paid what they're entitled before holders of common stock (and after the creditors). In other words, their interests are *preferred* over those of the common stockholders. If the company doesn't have enough money to pay everyone, creditors will be paid first, and then the preferred stockholders will be paid.

The sequence of liquidation payments is

1. Secured lenders.
2. Unsecured lenders.
3. Preferred stockholders.
4. Common stockholders.

Another common requirement associated with preferred stock relates to the payment of dividends. Holders of preferred stock receive their dividend payments prior to common stockholders.

What Preferred Stockholders Give Up

Preferred stockholders agree to sacrifice certain privileges for preferential treatment. First, they may not have voting privileges to elect members of the board of directors or to vote on important matters such as mergers.

Second, the company may retain the right to buy back (or call) preferred stock at a time of its own choosing. For example, when the company becomes profitable, it may be required to pay out 6% in dividends to stockholders. If the loan interest rate is only 3%, the company can borrow the money to buy back the preferred stock at only 3% and save the difference between the 3% it pays and the 6% in dividends it would have to pay. This is a substantial financial advantage.

Why Issue Preferred Stock?

Companies issue preferred stock for several reasons:

- To avoid issuing bonds, which have more regulations and restrictions than stock. There are usually very tight debt covenants on bond issues, such as minimum debt-to-equity ratios. (This is defined specifically by debt covenants.) Each time the company issues a financial report, it must review all the covenants to ensure that the company is complying with them all. Preferred stock is more flexible than bonds. You can issue it with a "preference" in a number of areas, meaning you can define how it will reward shareholders. Bonds, on the other hand, are more rigid, and people expect interest payments.
- To avoid issuing more common stock, which dilutes the company's earnings per share (EPS), which is calculated only on the basis of common stock.
- To avoid diluting common stockholders' control; preferred stockholders may hold no or lesser voting privileges.

Preferred Stock versus Debt

Preferred stock is similar to bonds in that outside investors have invested expecting a specific return. Companies may be required to pay dividends on preferred stock, similar to debt interest payments, and preferred stock may be callable or convertible, just as bonds may be. However, bondholders' interests come before those of preferred stockholders (whose interests come before common stockholders) in the event of liquidation.

TREASURY STOCK

When a company buys back its stock, the stock is recorded on its books as *treasury stock*. The company may buy back its stock for several reasons:

- To hold the stock and sell it later at a higher price. (A company would do this if it views its stock as a good deal on the open stock market.)
- To reduce the number of shares outstanding so that price per share and EPS increase.
- To permanently retire the stock.
- To give the stock to employees.

PAID-IN CAPITAL

Common stock par value is the amount a company assigns to its stock when the company goes public. That is the amount recorded on the books, but you usually sell common stock for a price above par value. The amount that's above par value is called *paid-in capital.*

In an annual report, you will see a common stock line, and that's the stock's par value. This line will always have a footnote to indicate the number of shares authorized, the number of shares issued and outstanding, and the par value per share even if there is no par value. Any excess amount is shown on the paid-in capital line.

Shares Authorized

The number of shares authorized is defined by the corporation's charter. Very rarely does a company issue 100% of its authorized shares. A certain number are held back for bonuses to management, for issuing more stock, and so on. In fact, when a company gets close to having issued all its authorized shares, the board of directors will often increase the number of authorized shares. If the company is highly publicized or publicly traded, this will be reported in the press.

RETAINED EARNINGS

Retained earnings are the cumulative total of what the company has earned or lost since it was founded.

There are two things that can be included in earnings other than prior-year and current-year earnings:

- ***Dividends.*** Dividends reduce retained earnings because they are a return on the shareholders' investment. Obviously, this money is not available for reinvestment in other things because it has been paid to the stockholders. (Dividend payments are not deductible on a corporate tax return; however, they are considered taxable income to those who receive them.)
- ***Appropriations of and restrictions on retained earnings.*** Sometimes corporate management makes a decision to set aside corporate funds for a specific project or investment such as adding new products or services, opening new outlets, or building new facilities. To communicate this decision to investors, management sets aside a portion of retained earnings on a line called *appropriation of retained earnings.* This is basically a communications tool and may be used to explain to stockholders why dividends are lower than expected. This does not necessarily mean the funds will be used for that purpose; it simply means they've been reclassified.

Sometimes state law requires that a company put a restriction on retained earnings for the amount of treasury stock. This law protects creditors by preventing a substantial reduction in the company's equity.

PRIOR-YEAR AND CURRENT-YEAR EARNINGS

Companies also show their prior-year and current-year earnings as separate components of retained earnings. Prior-year earnings is the sum of all prior years' net incomes and losses. Current-year earnings is the net income or loss shown on the P&L.

SOME KEY TERMS

There are several other terms that are important to the subject of equity.

Market value of equity. This is the current price that all the stock can be sold for, or the total of all the stock in the company times the market price. For instance, if ABC stock is selling at $10 per share, its market value is $10. If there are 200,000 outstanding shares, sold at $10 apiece, the total market value is $2 million. This is also known as *market capitalization* of a company.

Book value. Book value of the company is the value of all assets, less depreciation, on a company's balance sheet. It bears no relationship to the market value of a company or the market value of its equity.

For example, the market capitalization (total value of outstanding stock on the open stock market) of a company could be $2 million. Book value only shows how much a company has paid for all of its assets, less depreciation and amortization. Book value is often less than market capitalization because market capitalization may reflect the current value of its assets and intangible assets you won't find on a company's balance sheet. (See Chapter 7.)

Liquidation value. When a company is being closed down or liquidated, its assets are sold and liabilities settled. The liquidation value is the amount of cash that could be generated as a result of selling all the assets collectively or individually in a "fire sale."

Redemption value. This is the amount to buy back a security (stocks, bonds, or mutual fund shares).

Chapter 10

STATEMENT OF INCOME

The statement of income (aka income statement, profit and loss statement, or P&L) is one of the first things management looks at to determine how well a company is doing. The P&L reports revenues and expenses for a given period of time, and management wants to know

- Is the company making money? (Is it profitable?)
- If so, is net income (and revenue) growing or shrinking? (Note: It's possible to make money through decreased sales and expenses.)
- How well is net income tracking P&L forecasts (or budgets)? (How far were we off in our estimates, and why?)

If the company is making money, revenues exceed expenses and the P&L has *net income.* If the company is losing money, expenses are greater than revenue and the P&L has a *net loss.*

As a manager, to understand how to find the answers to these questions, you need to understand the elements of a P&L statement. The two major elements are revenues and expenses (which we discuss in detail shortly). Within these are subelements—or smaller categories of items that, in total, make up revenues and expenses. On a real P&L, the headings may look like these:

- Revenues.
- Sales discounts and allowances.
- Net revenues.
- Cost of goods sold.

- Gross profit.
- General and administrative expenses.
- Net income before interest and taxes (aka earnings before interest and taxes or EBIT).
- Other income and expenses.
- Income taxes.
- Discontinued operations.
- Extraordinary items.
- Net income.
- Earnings per share.
- Diluted earnings per share.

REVENUES

Revenues (aka sales) are the income received for sales of products or services. Sometimes they are listed on a P&L before sales returns and discounts (so they're known as *gross revenues*). Other times, they are listed after sales returns and discounts (so they're known as *net revenues*).

Revenues include all the sales from the ongoing, main operations of the business. The types of sales differ depending upon the industry and business. In retail, wholesale, or manufacturing businesses, sales include tangible products that are sold to customers. (*Tangible* means something the customer can physically touch or see.)

In financial services businesses such as insurance, sales come from intangible products like life insurance or business insurance. Intangible products are more difficult to sell because customers have to buy an idea rather than something they can see. (For example, with insurance, customers are purchasing the idea of security in case of loss.)

In service businesses such as consulting or accounting firms, the product is really the people employed to provide the service to customers or clients. So these businesses charge for the hours worked or the project completed. This is a mixture of tangible and intangible because clients can often see or measure the results of the work (e.g., an income tax return), but they may not be able to see the actual "hours" they have paid for.

In all of these industries, the businesses have defined product lines, whether tangible or intangible, pertaining to the main operations of the business. The *gross revenue* line on the P&L includes all of these sales. But it doesn't include sales that don't relate to main operations, such as the sale of used manufacturing equipment, the sale of by-products and scrap, or even the sale of products from discontinued operations. Even though these sales are considered revenues, they are grouped separately on the P&L to help managers and investors read the financial statements. You'll find these items under categories called *other income and expenses.* (More detailed information is provided shortly.)

Sales Returns and Discounts

Sales returns are amounts given back to customers for items that have been returned to the company for whatever reason. This is a big issue for the retail industry, where consumers purchase many items based upon emotional needs and desires created by advertising. After the fact they may realize that their eyes were bigger than their pocketbooks, or maybe that purple sofa isn't so great looking after all. Result: They return the items to the store. Woe to the retailer.

Returns also occur in manufacturing and other industries, particularly if there have been defective materials used in creating the products. Sales returns are less common in the service industry, where labor is the key revenue generator for a business.

Sales discounts are markdowns off the original price of a product or service. For example, a department store may have a sale, marking down clothing 20%. The 20% is the sales discount. Usually sales discounts are given to motivate the buyer to purchase the product or service.

Tracking Discounts

Some businesses accumulate sales discounts in a separate account so managers know how many discounts were given and why. This information is helpful in pricing future products and services. The accounting staff records the sale at the original price on the P&L (gross revenues) and then records the discount as a negative number in a separate account known as "sales discounts."

NET REVENUES

After all the discounting and returning is said and done, the company will be left with *net revenues.* This describes gross revenues minus sales returns and/or sales discounts. This is the amount of profit available to pay for expenses.

EXPENSES

Unfortunately, as they say, most businesses have to spend money to make money. This is called expenses—all the costs incurred to bring in revenues. Since this is such a big category, accountants divide it into different sections:

- Expenses that are required for making products that are sold (called *cost of goods sold).*
- Expenses that are necessary but aren't required to make products (called *general and administrative expense* or *overhead expense).*

COST OF GOODS SOLD

Cost of goods sold (COGS), the second category found on a P&L, represents all the expenses directly related to the products that were sold. This includes purchasing products to be resold as well as actually manufacturing the products. You won't find COGS on the P&L of a service-based industry unless it also sells some type of product.

(Note: *Cost of goods sold* is the term typically used in merchandising industries, retail and wholesale. *Cost of goods manufactured* is the term used by manufacturers. They mean the same thing.)

MERCHANDISING INDUSTRIES (RETAILERS AND WHOLESALERS)

Retailers and wholesalers usually don't produce a product. They buy it from a company and then resell it at a higher price. They may also buy the product, repackage it, and then resell it at a higher price. So their COGS includes items such as

- Inventory purchases, including purchase discounts and purchase returns and allowances.
- Freight.
- Repackaging expenses.

Inventory purchases includes the cost of the products being resold. The formula to calculate how much inventory should be included in COGS is

> Inventory sold = Beginning inventory + (Purchases made during the period – Purchase discounts and/or allowances) – Ending inventory

Purchase discounts are simply special discounts received on the products or discounts taken by paying the invoices early. (In Chapter 4 see "Invoice Terms.") *Purchase allowances* is similar to discounts, but it relates to keeping products that can't be sold at retail or wholesale prices for some reason, such as the products being damaged in shipment or the wrong color or style.

Freight is the cost of shipping the product to your business.

Repackaging costs include labor, special packages, and equipment depreciation related to the cost of repackaging goods for sale.

COST OF GOODS MANUFACTURED

Manufacturers actually build products from raw materials or other sources, so their COGS contains costs such as

- Cost of inventory items.
- Labor and related expenses, such as employee taxes and benefits.
- Production management salaries and related expenses.
- Cost of facilities used to make the product, such as rent or building depreciation, maintenance, and utilities.
- Warehousing space for storing raw materials or work in progress.

- Machinery leases, depreciation, and maintenance contracts.
- Production supplies.
- Any other costs that are directly related to producing goods or services.

IN TWO WORDS: DIRECT AND INDIRECT

The term *directly related* is important in accounting. It means that the expense must occur in order to have a product. For example, raw materials, machinery, and the labor to run the machinery are absolutely essential to the product. So these costs are directly related to producing goods or services (called *direct costs),* and they are included in cost of goods manufactured.

Some expenses (for example, building depreciation and utilities) are important to manufacturing the product, but they can't be specifically identified to the manufacturing process. They are called *indirect costs.* A portion of these expenses is related to manufacturing, but the rest should really go in overhead expense. How do you divide them up?

Cost accountants spend a lot of time separating these costs, particularly when all staff is under one roof. Think about it. Building depreciation or rent, utilities, general supplies, and telephone expenses are all costs that must be split between cost of goods manufactured and G&A. Sometimes this is easy to identify. Most times it's not, and the cost accountants develop special mathematical formulas to split the costs between cost of goods manufactured and general and administrative expenses (G&A).

MANUFACTURING COST CATEGORIES

Manufacturing activities can be very complex, so measuring COGS is difficult, as we just explained. Each element of COGS could have its own complex computations to support the number that finally ends up on the P&L. Here is a general description of each.

Manufacturing costs include all costs associated with transforming raw materials into a finished product. There are three main types of cost:

1. Direct materials.
2. Direct labor.
3. Manufacturing overhead.

DIRECT MATERIALS

Direct materials includes all raw materials that make up a finished product. The term *raw materials* seems to imply natural resources (as we learned in elementary school), but that's not what it means in accounting. Raw materials could be anything used to make the finished good, including natural resources or subassemblies that are purchased from other companies. In fact, many companies produce finished goods that actually become raw materials for other companies that transform these into more finished goods. This cycle could be repeated several times before the final product ever reaches the end consumer. There could be one, two, or even more companies in the chain, depending upon the final product and the complexity of the manufacturing process.

A great example of this is the computer industry. Many small electrical components go into the finished computer or PC, but one company doesn't put all these components together to make the PC. One company takes silicon, gold, and other raw materials to make microchips as its finished product. The next company buys the microchips as its own raw materials, and combines them with other electrical components used to make up the printed circuit boards. The printed circuit boards become this company's finished product. Another company buys the printed circuit boards as its raw materials and puts them in cases with a bunch of other electrical components. And this becomes a computer, which is this company's finished product.

Not So All-in-One. Why doesn't one company make an entire product? Sometimes it does if the product is simple. But it makes sense to buy subassemblies from other companies because of three things that all add up to less cost:

1. Economies of scale.
2. Increased specialization.
3. Focus.

Economies of Scale. It's usually less expensive to make a lot of one item than it is to make small amounts of many different types of items. Therefore, it makes sense that an automobile manufacturing plant produces cars and trucks. It doesn't diversify its operations to build stoves and refrigerators on the same assembly lines because it costs too much to change the manufacturing process setup.

Increased Specialization. In this technical age, *increased specialization* has taken on new meaning. Admit it. Technology has invaded almost every aspect of our lives in the industrial world. And technology is rapidly changing. This means that manufacturing equipment used 10 years or even 5 years ago is probably outdated and inefficient.

To keep up with the competition, manufacturers must keep their equipment up-to-date. This can become very expensive, particularly if your business is involved in all aspects of the manufacturing process. Sometimes it is less expensive to let another company specialize (and stay current) in a particular part of the manufacturing process, rather than having one company do everything, especially if the equipment is expensive to replace or upgrade. For example, it's less expensive to let one company manufacture microchips for PCs and let another company assemble the final PC.

Focus. *Focus* simply means that a manufacturer can often become more efficient and effective in its manufacturing process if it concentrates on the products that it does well.

All three of these things mean less expense incurred in manufacturing products, which translates into a lower-priced product which is good for the consumer (and perhaps bad for the competition).

DIRECT LABOR

Direct labor means the wages and related expenses (e.g., payroll taxes, benefits) of the people who put the products together or who run the equipment that transforms raw materials into finished products. This includes only those who are directly responsible for producing whatever the company sells, such as assembly line workers and machine operators. These are the workers who produce so many products per hour, day, or week.

Direct labor doesn't include those who are involved in the manufacturing process indirectly (people known as *indirect labor*), such as supervisors, managers, janitors who clean the manufacturing floor, engineers, materials handlers, and buyers. This is because you can't trace their efforts back to specific units of production.

MANUFACTURING OVERHEAD

The easiest way to define *manufacturing overhead* is that it's all costs related to manufacturing products except direct materials and direct labor (not very profound, we know). This includes costs of indirect materials (e.g., supplies used by supervisors, managers, and their administrative staffs), indirect labor, utilities, building depreciation or rent, repairs, and maintenance and any other costs that are necessary to production but cannot be traced to specific unit production.

(Sometimes there are ways to trace the cost to products, but the work involved can be costly. For example, how would you measure the amount of electricity necessary to build one automobile? It could be done. But is it worth the effort? Probably not. This is what accountants weigh when they attempt to compute product cost. They look at how much the benefit would be compared with the cost of finding out.)

Manufacturing overhead is typically *allocated* to product groups based upon some predetermined formula, such as number of machine or labor hours. Whatever the formula used, there must be a logical reason for using it. (Note: *Allocated* means to divide up the cost and "give" it to another group.)

Conversion Costs

Conversion costs are all the costs necessary for converting raw materials into the finished product. The formula is

Conversion costs = Direct labor + Manufacturing overhead

Non-manufacturing Costs

The only costs included in manufacturing costs are everything related to the production process. After the product is finished, subsequent costs are considered nonmanufacturing. This includes advertising or marketing expenses, sales costs, buyers' salaries, and administrative expenses necessary to the overall business operations. These expenses are included in general and administrative expenses (G&A).

What Belongs in Cost of Goods Manufactured?

All this talk about what expenses go in cost of goods manufactured and what go in G&A can get confusing. For example, it would be easy to argue that cost of goods manufactured should include the salaries and related expenses for the buyers of raw materials and products. But it doesn't. Buyers' salaries are included in G&A. How do you know the difference?

The simplest way we can think of to help you determine what costs should go in cost of goods manufactured is to ask these questions:

1. Does the product need the (whatever the expense is) to exist? (For example, equipment and machinery to transform raw materials are vital to production, as is the building that contains them and the electricity that runs them. But the product doesn't need a financial accountant—who prepares the monthly financial statements—to exist.)
2. Does the expense occur before or after the product is ready for sale? (For example, storage costs for raw materials and work in progress occur before the product is complete, so they are included in cost of goods manufactured. But warehousing for finished goods occurs after the product is complete, so it isn't included.)
3. Does the expense "touch" the product in some way to get it ready for sale? (For example, a buyer may order product or raw material for resale, but he never actually "touches" the product to get it ready for sale.)

If the answer to any of these questions is yes, then the cost probably should be included in COGS. If the answer to all three questions is no, include the cost in G&A.

GROSS PROFIT

Gross profit is net revenues minus COGS. It represents the amount of money available to pay for other expenses such as G&A.

GENERAL AND ADMINISTRATIVE EXPENSES

General and administrative expenses (G&A) are all the other expenses that are incurred to run the business (and not included in COGS). They are also known as *overhead expenses.* They include

- Advertising.
- Administrative staff wages and related expenses.
- Accounting and finance staff salaries and related expenses.
- Business licenses.
- Depreciation on office equipment.
- Entertainment.
- Legal costs.
- Management salaries and related expenses.
- Market research.
- Office rent or building depreciation.
- Office equipment lease expense.
- Office supplies.
- Other office staff salaries and related expenses.
- Property and real estate taxes.
- Research and development.
- Sales and management bonuses.
- Sales and use tax.
- Sales expenses.
- Sales staff salaries and commissions.
- State franchise taxes.
- Storage of finished goods.
- Telephone and utilities.
- Training.
- Travel.

And the list goes on.

In a company, areas that do not directly produce revenue and that are considered overhead are often considered expendable. If you're in one of these areas, beware of high overhead. You may be subject to cost-cutting efforts.

NET INCOME BEFORE INTEREST AND TAX

Net income before interest and tax—aka earnings before interest and tax (EBIT) or net operating income—is the net income (or loss) from normal and recurring business operations. It doesn't include *Other Income and Other Expenses* or income taxes.

In financial calculations and analysis, EBIT is considered a "purer" representation of how well operations is doing than net income is. Therefore, it is often used in ROI computations and earnings analyses. It doesn't include other income and other expenses because these items (by definition) aren't related to operations. EBIT doesn't include income tax because it is based upon taxable income, not financial income.

OTHER INCOME AND OTHER EXPENSES

Other Income and Other Expenses are revenues and expenses that aren't related to the company's main business. Other income includes interest income on cash accounts, investments, or accounts receivable. It also includes gains on the sale of fixed assets (i.e., fixed assets are used in the business, but the business isn't a reseller of fixed assets) and revenues from selling scrap materials or manufacturing by-products. (Note: In some industries the sale of manufacturing by-products is so large that it may become a separate business unit in the company.)

Other expenses include interest expense on money borrowed for business operations or losses on the sale of assets.

INCOME TAXES

Income taxes include federal, state, and foreign income taxes. All other taxes are included in G&A.

For small, private companies, this is quite simple to compute. Taxes are equal to all the estimated income tax due on the income earned. But companies required to follow GAAP should watch out! The computation is more complex than computing the actual income tax (a chore in itself!). So we're not going to explain how to figure this line out. Suffice it to say that for accounting reasons, the AICPA has decided that it is more appropriate to make sure the tax assets and liabilities are correct than it is to take net income (or loss) and multiply it by the current effective tax rates. Therefore, if you added up the income taxes from all the company's income tax returns, it would probably never equal the amount on the P&L. Believe us when we tell you that unless you like to complicate your life, you should simply trust your CPAs on this one!

EXTRAORDINARY ITEMS

Once in a while, you may see a line on the P&L called *extraordinary items.* These are unusual and infrequent financial events that occur during a particular accounting period. They are separated from the rest of net income for a couple of reasons:

1. GAAP requires the items to be separated.
2. Financial management believes the event is significant enough to point it out separately in the P&L. For example, the event creates a large expense that would distort the normal net income. Such a separation is solely based upon financial management's professional judgment.

There are several items that are required by GAAP to be treated as extraordinary items, including

- Gains on restructuring debt.
- Gains and losses on paying off debt early.
- Most expropriations of property (such as the taking of corporate land to build a highway).
- Gains or losses from catastrophic events or major casualties (such as damage from hurricanes, tornadoes, or fires).
- Losses incurred because of events that are now prohibited under newly enacted laws.

In addition to these, the financial management may decide to treat a particular financial event as an extraordinary item because including it in net income would make it seem as if the company weren't really doing as well as it is. These are based upon management's professional judgment, but GAAP also gives these guidelines for making the decision to treat an event as extraordinary:

- The event must be material to the P&L (i.e., it must be large enough to significantly affect net income).
- The event must be significantly different than normal business activities.
- The event must not be expected to reoccur frequently.
- The event must not be normally considered in evaluating business results.

Some examples of this are merger or acquisition expenses; discontinuing operations of a product line, plant, or division; huge legal settlements; or the spin-off of a division as a separate publicly traded company. Since these may not be normal business expenses and since they could create inordinately large expenses, financial management may decide to separate them on the P&L to let managers and investors know that something unusual has affected net income. (Note: The unusual item could be expense or income.)

NET INCOME

Net income or *net loss* is net revenues minus expenses for all categories included on the P&L. It's known as the *bottom line*—that is, how much money the company made in any given period of time. (And this period of time must be stated on the financial statement so you know if you're looking at one month, one quarter, or one year.) If net revenues exceed all expenses incurred, the company made money and it's called *net income.* If the expenses incurred are more than net revenues, the company is losing money and it's called *net loss.*

For accrual-based companies (i.e., most middle and large-size companies), net income includes all revenues earned in that time frame and all expenses incurred to make the revenue. For cash-based companies (i.e., small companies), it includes all the revenues collected and all the expenses paid.

If the company didn't make money, the bottom line is called a *net loss.*

EARNINGS PER SHARE

Earnings per share (EPS) is the amount of net income theoretically available to be paid out to common stock owners in dividends. (We say "theoretically" because rarely does a company ever pay out the entire net income amount as dividends. Most companies reinvest the earnings to maintain or increase revenue growth. A portion may be paid out in dividends, but some companies don't pay out dividends at all.)

Simply stated, EPS equals net income divided by total outstanding shares of common stock. (*Outstanding* means held by other entities or individuals, not owned by the company.) This is the formula used if the company has only one class of stock—common stock. For public companies, this amount is the total number of shares that could be traded on the stock market. For private companies, this is the number of shares owned by private investors.

EPS CALCULATION

If a company has preferred stock and common stock outstanding, the formula becomes a little more complicated:

$$\text{EPS} = \frac{\text{Income} - \text{Dividend of nonconvertible preferred stock}}{\text{Weighted average number of outstanding shares of common stock}}$$

For example, ABC Corporation has net income of \$900,000. Dividends to nonconvertible preferred stockholders is \$20,000. The weighted average number of outstanding shares of common stock is 1,000,000 shares. The EPS calculation is

$$\text{EPS} = \frac{(\$900{,}000 - \$20{,}000)}{1{,}000{,}000} = \$0.88$$

Net income is reduced by the preferred stockholders' dividends because this money must be paid to the preferred stockholders. It isn't available to the common stockholders if all the earnings were paid out in dividends.

Weighted average number of outstanding shares of common stock sounds more complicated than it really is. Usually this is the number of outstanding shares of common stock at the beginning of the year. The number rarely changes throughout the year (as indicated by "weighted average"). It only changes if

1. The company issues more stock.
2. The company purchases stock back from its owners. (It then becomes known as treasury stock.)
3. The company announces a stock split.
4. A merger, acquisition, or division sale occurs in which stock is exchanged.

EPS AND THE STOCK MARKET

Senior management follows EPS closely because investors follow it closely. It is usually announced once a quarter with the quarterly results and again at year-end.

EPS is compared with the expected EPS for that period along with EPS for that quarter of the previous year. For example, a third-quarter EPS of $3.50 would be compared to last year's third-quarter EPS of $2.80 and the expected third-quarter EPS of $3.45. How do investors know about the expected EPS? Stock analysts talk with senior management to find out. Then they let the press know so investors will know.

Announcing an EPS that's lower than expected or even lower than in the previous year's quarter or year-end could have disastrous effects on the stock price of a company. It's like hitting the investors with a curve ball. They are surprised, and they don't like surprises, particularly if the surprise is bad. That's why senior management often has a press release to lower expectations of EPS before the actual results are released.

Unfortunately, a *higher-than-expected* EPS probably won't have the same upward effect on price. The stock price may go up a lot or it may go up a little, depending upon the mood of the investors. But like in real life, people tend to pay less attention to positive things than negative ones, and may shrug off a high EPS more than a lower-than-expected EPS.

Diluted Earnings per Share

Diluted earnings per share is a complex calculation of EPS that pretends that all convertible securities have been changed into common stock. (Convertible securities include convertible preferred stock and some types of bonds.) The SEC requires all publicly traded companies to compute this, so common stockholders know how much the EPS would go down if all convertible securities actually became common stock.

The basic formula remains the same:

$$\text{EPS} = \frac{\text{Income} - \text{Dividend of nonconvertible preferred stock}}{\text{Weighted average number of outstanding shares of common stock}}$$

But the denominator is calculated as if all convertible stock has been converted, so it becomes larger. For example, ABC Corporation has net income of $900,000. Dividends to nonconvertible preferred stockholders is $20,000. There are 1,000,000 shares of common stock outstanding and 300,000 shares of convertible preferred stock (that are converted at a 1:1 ratio). The undiluted EPS calculation is

$$\text{EPS} = \frac{(\$900{,}000 - \$20{,}000)}{1{,}000{,}000} = \$0.88$$

The diluted EPS calculation is

$$\text{EPS} = \frac{\$900{,}000 - \$20{,}000}{(1{,}000{,}000 + 300{,}000)} = \$0.68$$

Therefore, if all the convertible preferred stock were exchanged for common stock, EPS would go from $0.88 to $0.68.

It's important to remember that the real EPS is $0.88. If the preferred stockholders exchanged their stock for common stock after this EPS had been reported, it wouldn't affect this number. It would affect the next year's EPS. But the SEC requires companies to disclose diluted EPS so common stockholders know how EPS could erode if all conversions took place.

OTHER INFORMATION ABOUT THE P&L

- Net revenues = Gross revenues – (Sales discounts + Sales returns and Allowances).

- Net inventory purchases = Purchases – (Purchase discounts + Purchase returns and allowances).
- Cost of goods sold = Net purchases + Other related expenses.
- Gross profit = Net revenues – Cost of goods sold.
- Net income from operations = Gross profit – General and administrative expenses.
- Net income = Net income from operations + Other income – Other expenses.

COMPREHENSIVE INCOME

Recently, FASB has added a new section to the Statement of Income called *comprehensive income.* This new section is to show all of the "unrealized" gains and losses from the following items:

- Foreign currency translation adjustment.
- Changes in value of futures contracts or hedges.
- Adjustments due to defined benefit plans.
- Unrealized gains or losses on securities held for sale (i.e., stocks and bonds).

(Note: "Unrealized" simply means paper gains and losses that don't occur until a sale is made.)

FASB made these changes to help companies that have large international companies and their investors. These changes are very similar to international GAAP procedures.

Chapter 11

FINANCIAL REPORTING

Financial reporting is the term to describe the financial information reported to management and to the public about how a company is performing. Financial reporting involves a lot of complicated information; therefore, to make it easy for people reading them, the reports share similar formats for indicating common corporate financial results. The formats generally include the financial reports you typically see in annual and quarterly reports to investors.

There are two types of financial reporting:

1. Internal, or management, reporting, which is used by those inside the company to manage.
2. External, or market, reporting, which gives information to people outside the company.

MANAGEMENT REPORTING

Internal management needs more detailed reports than investors, because they need comprehensive information to help them make ongoing decisions about running the business. They may also need information presented in a different way. Management reports may be

- Familiar, generic reports (such as the profit and loss statement) used in every business.
- Reports that are specific to an industry, such as *revenue per available room,* a hotel industry measurement that allows a company to compare itself with a competitor.

- Reports that are devised by a manager to help manage the business better, such as a report on labor hours, machine hours, or something specific to the organization.

MARKET REPORTING

Market reporting is the information released to the public regarding the company's financial performance. It includes such items as

- Earnings per share.
- Increase over past quarter or past year.
- Comparison with what analysts predicted.

At times, the press release can affect a rise or drop in the price of the stock. For example, if the company reports unfavorable results, it might cause investors to lose faith in the company and sell shares, which makes the price decrease. For this reason, the SEC enforces strict rules about the timing of press releases about financial information or major company news that could affect the company's stock price.

WHY ARE YOU AUDITED?

The stock crash of 1929, though over 70 years ago, still affects the way we do things. Laws have been established to make sure that investors have the information they need to make good decisions, and that the information is presented in an easy to-read format. Thus, companies must report their financial performance. This practice is called financial reporting. The government, however, is not satisfied that all companies can be trusted (because of either integrity or capability) to report their financial performance accurately. For that reason, public companies must be audited by an external, objective group (called auditors) to verify that what they have reported is true.

THE SECURITIES AND EXCHANGE COMMISSION (SEC)

The historic instability of our financial system became disastrously evident in 1929 when the stock market crashed, devastating fortunes and ruining lives. In an attempt to restore some order to the system and to protect investors, in 1933 and 1934 two laws were passed that govern securities sold on exchanges or over the counter (OTC).

- The Securities Act of 1933 requires public companies to give investors accurate financial information and other pertinent data about a company.
- The Securities Exchange Act of 1934 established the Securities and Exchange Commission and expanded and clarified some of the regulations set out in the Securities Act of 1933.

SEC Organization

The SEC is an independent regulatory agency that safeguards investors. The commission governs not only the sale of securities, but also the disclosure of information that can affect the sale. Organizations that are affected by the SEC are public corporations, investment counselors, and people or organizations that sell securities.

Headquartered in Washington, D.C., the SEC has regional offices in 11 cities. Its five commissioners are appointed by the President of the United States, who names one of the commissioners as chairperson. Commissioners serve five-year terms, which are staggered and begin on June 5 each year.

Working with FASB

Because the SEC is very interested in the fair disclosure of information to investors, it is heavily involved with FASB, prescribing accounting practices and recommending what topics FASB should address.

Filing Financial Reports

The SEC requires that all public companies file with its agency reports describing their financial position and information that affects the company. These reports are available to anyone who requests them. The required reports are

1. ***10-K.*** This is an annual filing containing audited financial statements. Financial statements include the income statement, balance sheet, statement of changes in financial position, summary of operations, and auditor's report.

2. ***10-Q.*** This is a quarterly version of the 10-K, although the financial statements may be audited or unaudited. (Usually, public companies have auditors "review" the 10-Q information, and this process is less extensive than an audit.)

In addition to these formal required reports, public companies also publish an annual report, which is described later in this chapter.

EDGAR

EDGAR is the acronym for the Electronic Data Gathering, Analysis, and Retrieval system. Since 1996 EDGAR has allowed public companies to file required documents electronically, and the public can view these on the Internet.

What should be filed on EDGAR? Forms 10-K are required to be filed on EDGAR. Investment companies must also file their annual reports to shareholders on EDGAR, but other public companies are not required to do so.

THE ANNUAL REPORT

An annual report is a polished version of the 10-K, and it is sent to shareholders to inform them of the company's position and results. Because annual reports are intended not only to inform but also to impress, most annual reports include several sections of explanation, including a letter from the chairperson to shareholders describing the company's situation and outlook, and descriptions of the company's various business lines. Annual reports also contain the financial statements and an auditor's opinion. The auditor's opinion verifies that the information in the report has been fairly presented in accordance with GAAP or other stated guidelines.

THE AUDITOR'S REPORT

Any audited financial statement should have an auditor's report or auditor's opinion. This statement confirms that an outside auditing firm has reviewed the information included in the report and has verified that it has been fairly stated in accordance with GAAP or other guidelines. The auditor's report does not imply that the information is 100% correct or true, but only that the preparation of the information follows GAAP.

How to Read an Annual Report

Numbers are not meaningful in a vacuum. To fairly assess a company's performance, you must look at the relationships between several things. That is why an annual report includes more than one financial statement, often data for more than one year. In fact, it includes

- Income statement.
- Balance sheet.
- Cash flow statement.
- Changes in stockholders' equity.

(See Chapter 3 for more detailed discussion of financial statements and annual reports.) There are several types of financial statement analysis. Here are three key types:

- *Horizontal analysis* compares changes in each line item from one accounting period to another (i.e., from year to year or from quarter to quarter).
- *Vertical analysis* looks at a line item and the percentage it represents of the total financial statement.
- *Trend percentages* analyze the variances from one year to another, usually for several years.

See Table 11.1 on the following page.

Analyzing a Financial Statement

A financial statement only tells a story if you know what to look for. Remember, the company presents information in a way to make it look attractive and will not necessarily point a finger to things that are less than favorable.

Since a number of factors can affect the numbers, you must take everything into account to fairly judge what the numbers mean. For example, consider

- Inflation.
- Changes in markets' perception of the company's industry.
- Changes in company direction.

- Changes in management.
- Investor valuation.

In certain situations, companies may do something out of the ordinary to enhance their positions. For instance, *poison pills* are actions that companies take to make it less likely that others will carry out a corporate takeover. Taking on large debt or selling off profit-making interests are examples of poison pills.

TABLE 11.1

Consolidated Statement of Operations
For the years ended December 31
(in thousands, except per share amounts)

	1996	1997	1998
Revenues			
Franchise and management fees	$140,768	$185,546	$218,113
Owned hotel revenues	172,893	368,012	401,016
Leased hotel revenues	205,163	410,526	415,339
Purchasing and service fees	9,867	19,304	27,348
Other fees and income	31,522	54,623	45,473
Total revenue	560,213	1,038,011	1,107,289
Operating costs and expenses			
General and administrative expenses	62,638	79,249	80,429
Owned hotel expenses	105,146	224,052	248,990
Leased hotel expenses	190,797	362,681	367,176
Depreciation and amortization	36,276	73,127	79,254
Business combination expenses		115,000	28,065
Total operating costs and expenses	394,857	854,109	803,914
Net Operating income	165,356	183,902	303,375
Interest and dividend income	17,175	22,982	21,281
Interest expense	(36,647)	(72,027)	(61,917)
Gain on sale of real estate and securities	4,439	43,330	10,390
Income before income taxes and minority interest	150,323	178,187	273,129
Minority interest share of net income	(539)	(3,087)	(3,460)
Income before income taxes	149,784	175,100	269,669
Income tax expense	(59,126)	(79,664)	(115,581)
Net income	90,658	95,436	154,088
Net income per share:			
Basic	$1.25	$1.10	$1.79
Diluted	$1.23	$1.09	$1.78

A real-life example is what happened to Holiday Inn in the 1980s. A company was anxious to take over Holiday Inn because its real estate was undervalued on the balance sheet. The company wanted to use debt to buy out Holiday Inn so it could sell the real estate. Holiday Inn beat the company to it, taking on junk bonds (high-risk, nonsecured bonds) to make itself unattractive for takeover.

INVESTOR RELATIONS

Public corporations have one person or a group of people who manage all the activities that relate to the investors of the company. This activity is called *investor relations.*

Investor relations activities include planning the annual shareholder meeting, filing information with the SEC, publishing the annual report, and talking with financial analysts and stockholders about performance issues.

STOCKHOLDERS MEETINGS

Stockholders of public companies are not involved in the day-to-day management of business operations. Instead, company business takes place throughout the year overseen by the board of directors. Once a year, however, the company has an official shareholders meeting to take care of three types of business:

- To report financial and operating results.
- To elect board members.
- To discuss and vote on shareholder resolutions.

The SEC requires the company to notify all shareholders of the time, date, and location of the shareholders meeting. All shareholders are entitled to attend. Because shareholders reside in many different locations, many do not choose to attend the annual meeting. Instead, they voice their opinions by voting through proxy statements.

PROXY AND PROXY STATEMENT

Each shareholder is actually entitled to one vote per share owned. Since many shareholders cannot or will not attend the annual meeting, they need a way to cast absentee votes for directors and on other issues. They do this through a proxy, a written document on which they can record their votes. The proxy is, in effect, an absentee ballot.

The company sends out a proxy and proxy statement describing the issues to be discussed and voted upon. The shareholders return the proxy to the company with a record of their votes.

In truth, many shareholders have little opinion about the issues. The board usually makes decisions about how the company will be run.

THE ANNUAL MEETING

Once a year, the board of directors comes together to elect its members and to discuss what has taken place throughout the year. This meeting typically takes place after the annual report is issued. Timing depends on the fiscal year-end of the company.

ONGOING COMMUNICATION

In addition to the specific information a company must report to the SEC and its shareholders, there are additional issues that need to be communicated to the general public. To do this, companies issue press releases that are sent to the news media. These releases may contain several types of information:

- Financial results, including the issuing of dividends.
- Financial restructuring and other key financial events.
- Significant management changes.
- Decisions that will affect operations, such as closing divisions, company reorganization, and introducing new brands.

Not all press releases describe major events that will affect the stock price or the shareholders. Nevertheless, the company reports both positive and negative information that could affect the interests of its owners.

The SEC wants all investors to have equal, fair access to information because access to information can greatly affect how much stock people buy and sell and, as a result, the stock price. Therefore, corporate press release information is very carefully guarded in advance of a release and then given to all media simultaneously so that all parties receive it at the same time. Otherwise, someone who received the information before others could use the information unfairly to gain an advantage.

Often, to guard against the possibility of insider trading, companies will not allow their employees to buy or sell stock just before major announcements. This is particularly true if employees are in information-sensitive positions where they could have knowledge of something such as a potential merger, the sale of a division, or a major product announcement. (See the following section, Insider Information.")

Also, just because information is released at the same time doesn't mean investors get it at the same time. If investors trade on information in news stories on television or in the newspapers, it's too late to take advantage of the information.

Insider Information

Insider trading is a term for the illegal practice of using "inside" information about a company to gain an unfair advantage in the marketplace. For example, people who work at high levels in a company or in key finance positions typically have more information about its performance than others. Using information that's unavailable to the general public to buy or sell stock at an advantageous time is illegal and subject to very strict penalties. This practice by brokers, management, or others who have the inside scoop is called insider trading.

In the 1980s, instances of insider trading became so widely publicized that the federal government passed legislation creating tougher penalties for those convicted of such activity. The Insider Trading Sanctions Act of 1984 and Insider Trading and Securities Fraud Enforcement Act of 1988 strengthened the penalties, provided awards to informers, and let people damaged by the activity file suit.

Chapter 12

FINANCE

WHAT IS FINANCE?

Financial managers are both crystal ball readers and jugglers. Their main goal is to maximize the value of the corporation. They do that by

- Looking at information about the economic and market future using complex analysis and gut feeling resulting from experience and observation.
- Using the information and their own tools and savvy to increase the company's growth while minimizing its risk.

WHY IS FINANCE IMPORTANT?

While it's vitally important for a company to track where and how it gets and spends its money (accounting), it's critical that it also makes its money work for shareholders' benefit (finance). That takes planning. How does finance differ from accounting? Accounting professionals are the technical experts of the financial world. They understand the ins and outs of tracking transactions and meeting all requirements for providing accurate information in different report formats.

Finance professionals are not concerned with the nitty-gritty details of where and how the money comes and goes. They are focused more on managing the company's money to achieve a bigger picture: prosperity. As such, they are interested in a variety of things:

- ***Paying the bills.*** The financial manager forecasts how much money the company will need to pay its debts, and determines where the money will come from.
- ***Investing cash.*** The balancing act comes when a financial manager tries to make sure there is just enough cash to pay the bills, and that not too much cash is lying around unused. Excess cash should be invested in ways that contribute to building the company's strength, and the financial manager must decide where to put the money so that it will be used to the best advantage. Like Goldilocks, the financial manager is trying to make sure things are "just right."
- ***Getting money.*** By predicting a company's needs for money, a financial manager can determine whether there will be a shortfall or when the company will need large sums to invest in fixed assets. If this is the case, the financial manager will ensure that money is available for projects or other needs by finding appropriate ways to obtain financing.
- ***Budgeting.*** Budgeting is the process of projecting what a company's (or division's or department's) monetary needs are and allocating a limited amount of funds to certain areas, as well as then monitoring spending to see how it compares with the amount budgeted. Many managers find budgeting to be a frustrating process because the company asks them to project their needs for the next year, and then asks them to reduce their projected spending by a certain percentage. (Managers often ask, "Why don't they just tell me the number they have in their heads, and I'll allocate the money accordingly?" Good question.)
- ***Long-term forecasting of financial positions.*** To be prepared to handle a company's growth and to make sure it's using its money in the wisest way, financial managers look at what the company's financial position will be at various points in the future. This outlook will be based upon such factors as expected return on investments, potential expenses, the time value of money, and economic factors.

In short, financial managers are concerned about cash flow. Those simple descriptions, of course, merely hint at the complexity of the financial manager's job. The sum of responsibilities requires knowledge of a wide range of information as well as the willingness to have a corporation's financial health in their hands. An awesome task.

HOW FINANCE RELATES TO ACCOUNTING

A financial manager depends upon accountants to provide the facts and figures, both past and present, that express a company's position. She examines the facts, looks at trends, and makes recommendations and decisions based on that information. The accounting and finance teams, therefore, are interdependent to a great degree.

CAREER PATHS FOR FINANCE PROFESSIONALS

There are numerous finance specialties and positions both inside and outside corporations.

FINANCE POSITIONS

While accounting is technical and concentrates on what's happening now and in the past, finance focuses on the future, and is not bound by specific technical rules.

FINANCIAL ANALYST

An analyst looks at all the information an accountant has put together and uses it to analyze trends and make projections. The lines between accounting and analyst positions are often blurred. Analyst positions are often held by accountants, and sometimes this is a way for accountants to broaden their scope by working outside the realm of making journal entries and handling more technical details.

PLANNING STAFF

The staff consolidates all the budgets and long-range financial plans for review by the CFO and controller. They analyze new projects or new business opportunities to see if they're viable, using capital budgeting techniques. The staff presents information and can make recommendations, but usually doesn't make decisions.

BUDGET OR PLANNING MANAGER

This person manages the planning staff.

CASH MANAGEMENT DEPARTMENT

These are finance or accounting people who manage the company's cash inflows and outflows, matching needs with available funds. For example, if the company needs $1 million next month to pay for new equipment, and the company only expects to have $250,000 income, the cash management staff will figure out where to get the money needed to pay the $1 million or determine the best way to finance it.

This department also makes short-term investments of cash on hand. It usually reports to the treasurer.

TREASURER

This person accounts for all the cash in the company and how it's used, deciding how new projects should be funded. The treasurer also acquires long-term debt and issues or buys back stock. This is an officer position usually reporting to the CFO.

CHIEF FINANCIAL OFFICER (CFO)

The chief financial officer of a company is responsible for managing all the financial activities (including accounting) of a company as well as its relationships with shareholders and the investment community.

STOCK OR BOND BROKER (ALSO CALLED A REGISTERED REPRESENTATIVE)

A broker is an intermediary who brings together buyers and sellers of stocks or bonds. Brokers may be paid commissions based upon each trade they orchestrate. Stockbrokers must work for companies that belong to the National Association of Securities Dealers, which licenses brokers and regulates the way securities are sold.

FUND MANAGERS

These professionals oversee group investments in stock or bond funds, determining where to invest the money to achieve the desired return for the group, reporting results to investors, and working with brokers to buy and sell issues.

BANKER

Bankers are the cash intermediaries or cash distributors of funds who handle the transfer of money, pay interest on certain types of deposits, and loan money to individuals and to other institutions.

MARKET ANALYST

A market analyst watches a particular industry, talks with CEOs and presidents of companies to find out what their plans are, and reports back to stockbrokers, fund managers, and the public, giving his opinion about the company's performance and future.

CERTIFICATIONS

Finance experts can earn several certifications. Just as in accounting certifications, members must meet education, experience, ethics, and examination requirements. Following their licensing they may be required to update their skills by completing a minimum number of hours each year of continuing professional education (CPE) hours. They must also stay current with ever-changing rules and guidelines related to their field.

CERTIFIED FINANCIAL PLANNER (CFP)

This designation is administered by the Certified Financial Planner Board of Standards (CFP Board), an independent regulatory organization. To be certified, a person must have completed certain educational requirements either through a college curriculum or through a CFP Board-registered program. He must also pass a certification exam and have related work experience.

CHARTERED FINANCIAL ANALYST (CFA)

Investment advisors, security analysts, and other financial professionals may achieve a CFA designation. CFA is granted by the Association for Investment Management and Research (AIMR). CFA candidates must pass three difficult exams.

ACCREDITED PERSONAL FINANCIAL SPECIALIST (APFS)

The AICPA accredits CPAs as financial planners. They are required to pass an eight-hour exam.

CHARTERED FINANCIAL CONSULTANT (CHFC) AND CHARTERED LIFE UNDERWRITER (CLU)

These are both financial consulting designations issued by the American College. They're primarily for insurance agents.

STOCK OR BOND BROKERS

Aside from the jobs in accounting, banking, and finance, there are positions in professions related to financial matters such as stockbroker.

STOCKBROKER OR REGISTERED REPRESENTATIVE

Stockbrokers must be registered with the National Association of Securities Dealers (NASD) in order to sell stocks. To do that, they must be employed by a firm that is part of the NASD and must pass a comprehensive exam.

Chapter 13

FINANCE TOOLS

Will you have enough money to pay employees' salaries next month? Will you have excess cash in the bank? How are you investing your money to take best advantage of it? If you plan to build a new plant next year, how will you finance it?

While accounting tends to be historical, finance tends to be forward thinking. Financial analysts are concerned with a company's past performance, but their interest is primarily related to how the past will help predict the future and how to plan for expected (and unexpected) events.

Like accountants, finance specialists have a variety of tools that help them do their jobs.

PLANNING ENCOMPASSES MANY FACTORS

Being able to make a profit in today's operating environment is one thing. Being able to keep a company successful over time is quite another. Thus, running a successful company requires both operations savvy and the ability to accurately forecast the company's financial future.

Financial planners look at many variables that can affect a company's success as well as its financial needs or plans. They consider

- The current health of the business, its ability to pay its obligations, and the prospects for growth.
- The state of the financial business climate, whether the economy is in depression or recession, and other financial factors.

- Environmental and cultural factors that may affect the company's ability to do business.
- The competition.
- Customer expectations.
- Changes in financial, regulatory, or business environment issues.

Taking all of these factors into account, the financial professional can make some forecasts about potential income and other pertinent financial issues.

FORECASTING

Forecasting is the art of projecting the cash needs of the company to some point in the future. Needs may include personnel and technology, additional space needed for expansion, and increases in overhead due to inflation. There are a variety of ways to forecast.

CASH BUDGETS

Most companies manage through cash budgets, which are based on sales projections, showing the inflows and outflows of cash and their timing. This technique allows a manager to anticipate a surplus or deficit of cash, and to plan for financing ahead of time. For example, the cash budget allows the manager to say to a lender, "This is when we will be short of cash," or "This is when I can pay you back."

Because all forecasts have, by definition, a degree of uncertainty, companies look at comparative statements from the past, and give a projection based on what has happened before and what factors will affect results in the future. Then, managers can proceed with projects based on their degree of risk.

PRO FORMA FORECASTING

Forecasting can be done using ratios under the assumption that the ratios will be maintained. If the ratios are unstable, the forecaster must use a technique to plot the changes. There are two ways to do that:

- Simple regression analysis, which uses one dependent variable and one independent variable.
- Multiple regression which uses more than one dependent variable.

Fortunately, statistical software packages determine these numbers.

BUDGETING

Budgeting means allocating funds to various activities and determining when those activities will take place for a defined period of time.

Within a company, a budget serves several purposes:

1. It forces managers to think through their plans for a specified time period and to prioritize projects.
2. It provides a means for management to assess performance.
3. It creates discipline, requiring managers to live within certain financial parameters.
4. It acts as a benchmark to measure progress.

During budgeting, managers will determine the objectives of their department or division as well as the resources required to achieve those objectives. This requires them to think of overall corporate goals and how their departments support those goals. They predict various resources they will need to carry out their mission, such as

- Personnel (including wages and salaries, benefits, payroll taxes, space and equipment requirements).
- Operations space and equipment.
- Supplies.
- Technological needs.
- Outside help from temporary help or consultants.

- Travel and expenses.
- Dollars to fund projects.

Budgeting is a process that may take place at all levels of the company. At each higher level the considerations become more big-picture and less detailed. A supervisor or manager will determine projects and associated costs; a department head will take into account personnel-related expenses; the head of a department or division will consider the revenue and expense projections; and the president will review the financial strategy. The considerations of each lower group are rolled up into one overall budget for the company.

LONG-RANGE PLANNING

Long-range planning takes the next step. It looks at the more distant future, such as the next 5 to 10 years. The crystal ball that planners use may be fairly clear one year out, but it becomes a bit more hazy the farther away from today they go. As we said, interpretation and subjectivity play a big role in determining what long-range plans will include because outcomes are not as easy to predict.

Long-range plans are built on a foundation of assumptions. Since they deal with the future, they can't be based on fact, because you can't be 100% sure of what will happen in the future. Thus, you have to decide what you believe has the highest probability of happening and how it will affect your business.

There are quite a lot of areas that may affect a business, and you might make assumptions about all of the ones that will materially affect your operations or financial outlook. These could be factors directly related to your business or indirectly related to it through areas such as the economy and the political climate. They include

- Inflation rate.
- Cost-of-material increases.
- Cost of labor.
- New projects or products.

- Required head count.
- Sales.
- Competition.
- Customer demand.
- Potential government regulations.
- Changes in tax law.
- Life of assets.
- New purchases.
- Effectiveness of marketing and advertising plans on sales.

FINANCIAL MODELS

Because financial planning is based on a number of things that *could* happen, the financial analyst must consider more than one *what if.* If inflation goes up to 6%, how will that affect our business. If the price of oil drops $2 a barrel, how will that enhance our profits?

Businesses have complex financial arrangements so one decision may have a domino effect on every other aspect of the business. To consider all the possibilities is quite a complicated task. Fortunately for financial planners, the computer era allows them to rather painlessly generate a wide range of potential scenarios in a relatively short time. They do this through the use of *financial models,* using spreadsheets or data bases.

Financial models are a collection of information presented in a way that illustrates what would happen if certain circumstances exist. They can be simple, such as projecting revenue over the next five years by increasing each year's revenue by a fixed percentage. They can be complex, with many variables and outcomes, requiring multiple spreadsheets to be linked together, or used on a huge data base with statistical analysis.

By looking at various models, financial analysts can make recommendations of the most advantageous route to take to create financial well-being.

STATISTICAL ANALYSIS

Statistical analysis is used to determine what the probability is of something happening. For example, if there has been talk of new banking regulations, a banking institution would certainly consider that a factor in its plans. What is the likelihood of the proposed regulations becoming law? The company's plan would be based on the probability of that taking place.

ANALYTICAL VALIDITY

The quality of planning and the validity of analysis depends on the quality of the assumptions at the heart of the plan. This is why it is so very important to take every factor into consideration before planning and to anticipate the likelihood of certain events actually happening.

Managers must understand all of these variables in order to decide where and how to invest the company's money.

COST OF CAPITAL

Since most companies finance at least a portion of their assets through debt instruments, the interest rate they must pay is a very important factor in deciding which projects to do. To weigh various options, the company will compare the cost of capital (cost of financing) for various types of financing.

It might consider the possibilities of issuing stock, selling bonds, or taking out a loan, comparing what it must pay out and when as well as the overall costs.

FINANCIAL RATIOS

Financial ratios are comparisons that allow an analyst to evaluate how well a company is performing compared with

- Competition.
- Itself at a different time.
- Its industry average.

TIME VALUE OF MONEY

A dollar today is not worth the same as a dollar in 1940. And it may be worth more than a dollar 20 years from now. In order to more accurately evaluate investments and to compare one option with another, financial analysts use a formula for calculating what the investment is worth now compared with what the return on investment will be at some later time. For more details about the time value of money, see Chapter 15.

Chapter 14

FINANCIAL STATEMENT RATIOS

In 1471, John Fortescue, a British military historian, wrote, "Comparisons are odious." At about the same time (give or take 100 years), the Italians were perfecting the double-entry bookkeeping system, thus creating the foundation for numerous business comparisons. Fortescue must have flinched.

In accounting and finance, comparisons are essential to understanding the true meaning of numbers. You've heard the term *comparing apples to apples.* To be meaningful, a comparison must examine things that are the same. That's especially true in looking at financial statements because there can be such a variety of ways of interpreting numbers.

Ratios are the tools accountants and stock analysts use to make it easier to compare financial apples to apples.

WHAT IS A RATIO?

A ratio is a mathematical comparison of one thing to another. School children learn to compute very simple ratios when they learn how to work with fractions. Corporate performance ratios are almost as simple. They're all arrived at by using simple division formulas, and they are expressed in fractions.

For example, a company's price/earnings (PE) ratio describes how much the price of the stock is, compared with the company's earnings per share. If the stock costs $30 and the earnings per share is $5, then the price/earnings ratio is 30/5, or, as we normally express it, a PE of 6. In other words, the price of one share of stock is six times the amount of its earnings per share. By looking at that ratio and comparing it with another company's, you could begin to evaluate which company's stock was of greater value.

A ratio not only compares one number with another, but it also is a great equalizer, allowing you to compare things that are not necessarily equal. For example, you can't really compare the profits of a small computer manufacturing company with IBM. But you can measure profitability by using a ratio. The ratio evens the playing field.

RATIOS ARE MEANINGLESS OUT OF CONTEXT

To truly understand a number's meaning, you must put it in context. For example, if a firm has $1 million in net income, it's impossible to evaluate whether that is a favorable or an unfavorable result without knowing more about the situation. If a small manufacturing company had net income of $1 million, its owners might think that was a superb result. If IBM had a net income of $1 million, it would be considered a dismal failure.

Ratios allow you to put numbers in context. In this case, you might look at the ratio of revenues to net income. The small manufacturing company might have revenue of $5 million and net income of $1 million. By the same token, a large company with $50 million in revenue but only $1 million in net income might not be nearly as successful. You would only know by looking at the context.

TRENDS

Trends over time are also an important factor—in fact, perhaps the most important factor in evaluating a ratio. Take the small manufacturing company. If the firm made $1 million this year, you can't evaluate whether that's good or bad until you examine its record for the past several years. If it made $5 million last year and $7 million the year before, $1 million would not be a very favorable result. People who analyze financial results frequently compare ratios from several years or several different time frames to understand the company's trends.

HOW DO YOU USE RATIOS?

Ratios are the tool accountants and analysts use to put things in context. Ratios are useful tools for

- Comparing a company's performance at one time with its performance at another time.
- Comparing a company's performance with a competitor's.
- Comparing a company's performance with its industry's.
- Comparing a company's performance with the market's.

Which Ratios Count?

Every industry has ratios that are particularly relevant to their business. In banking, ROE (return on equity) is a standard measurement. In hotels, RevPAR (revenue per available room) is meaningful. Different companies emphasize different measurements.

GAAP doesn't specify which ratios are important or how they must be computed. Financial analysts decide which ratios are the best measures to help them evaluate a company's position and potential, and the ratios they use typically will become the standard for that industry.

Ratios are not necessarily etched in stone; they evolve, changing when business conditions change or when someone figures out a more effective way to measure performance.

Return On's

Eavesdrop on any corporate meeting and you're likely at least once to hear a question that begins, "What's our *return on . . .* ?" Many ratios involve the phrase *return on.* Return on investment (ROI), return on assets (ROA), and return on equity (ROE) are a few examples. That phrase, *return on*, indicates that you're going to weigh what you're getting back for what you put in.

Take the example of a company buying a new piece of equipment. The equipment costs $50,000. Someone would ask, "What's the ROI?" meaning, "Will we make enough money for it to be worth the $50,000 investment?"

Again, timing is also an important factor. Assuming that with the new equipment the company can generate an additional $50,000 in net income the first year, it would certainly be providing a good return on investment. If, on the other hand, it took 20 years to earn back the $50,000, the ROI would be questionable.

In a somewhat different way, you could apply the *return on* theory to an employee, who could wonder about the advisability of working overtime without pay. If there's no forthcoming promotion or other payback, then the ROI may not be sufficient to inspire a 50-hour week.

DETERMINING A "GOOD" RATIO

There is no such thing as a good ratio across the board. Is a ratio of 50/1 good? In some cases, yes. In others, no. For instance, if it costs you 50 times as much to produce a product as you can charge for it, a ratio of 50/1 would be unfavorable. But, if you turn the tables and say that you can charge 50 times as much for a product as it costs you to make, that would be extremely good news.

To decide whether a ratio is favorable or unfavorable, you must look at what is being measured. Ratios will also vary by industry. Generally an analyst will determine what an acceptable range is for certain ratios, but, of course, analysts may disagree.

Again, a ratio by itself means little. True value arises from looking at a ratio side by side with a competitor's or with an industry average.

WEAKNESS OF RATIOS

Most ratios have one or more shortcomings, and analysts don't always agree on which ratio is best. By looking at several ratios, an analyst can balance one result against another and overcome the flaws.

No ratio is an ironclad predictor. They are all merely guideposts that indicate a likely direction.

CATEGORIES OF FREQUENTLY USED RATIOS

There are four areas in which ratios are used to evaluate a company's performance:

- Liquidity.
- Activity.
- Profitability.
- Leverage.

LIQUIDITY RATIOS

Liquidity describes how much of your assets are quickly available to you as cash. For instance, cash is the most liquid asset you have; it's in hand. A building, on the other hand, is not liquid, because it cannot be sold quickly.

An investor or lender would want to know if they lend you money, whether you'll have the cash you need to pay your debts and theirs. Liquidity is a key factor in your ability to pay.

Two liquidity ratios are *current ratio* and *acid test* or *quick ratio.*

CURRENT RATIO

This ratio compares your current liabilities (debts due within a year) with your current assets (something you could turn to cash within a year). The formula for current ratio is

$$\frac{\text{Current assets}}{\text{Current liabilities}}$$

How do you tell if a current ratio is good or bad? The point of current ratio is to tell how well you could cover your debts if you had to. Therefore, you generally want a current ratio over 1.0 because this would mean that you could pay off all your liabilities with assets that are on hand. A very low current ratio indicates financial weakness, suggesting that you are not able to pay your debts.

At the same time, you don't want the ratio to be too high because that would mean you have a lot of cash left over after you paid your debts, and management isn't using its resources well.

Weakness of Current Ratio. The weakness inherent in current ratio is that inventory is considered a current asset, but it's not really easily converted to cash. In most cases, inventory is turned into a product and then sold within a year, so it's difficult to get rid of it quickly. Because of this weakness in the current ratio, analysts developed the acid test.

ACID TEST OR QUICK RATIO

$$\frac{\text{Current assets} - \text{Inventory}}{\text{Current liabilities}}$$

The acid test looks at all the assets that can be changed into cash within a matter of days or weeks, and examines if that amount is sufficient to cover all your current liabilities.

ACTIVITY RATIOS

Activity ratios are associated with how quickly your assets are turned into cash. Two common formulas used as activity ratios are

- *Inventory turnover,* which looks at your activity from the perspective of how quickly inventory can be converted to sales (i.e., cash).
- *Accounts receivable turnover,* which examines how quickly you collect cash from credit sales.

To have a clear picture of activity, you must look at both ratios. Consistency in how you compute and apply the ratio is the key because what you're looking for is trends.

Interpreting activity ratios is a bit tricky because they deal with the time it takes for an event to happen. In some cases, all the information you need won't be readily apparent. For example, seasonal sales or sales that don't occur evenly throughout the year may skew the ratio to look better or worse than it actually is.

INVENTORY TURNOVER

An *inventory turnover* ratio shows how often your inventory is being turned into a salable product and is being sold. Why is high turnover important? Because it means you earn money quickly.

Say you bought inventory to produce a product, and it takes 12 weeks to create the product and sell it. From the time you buy the inventory, until the time you collect your accounts receivable for the product, you are footing the bill. For that 12 weeks, you don't have the money you paid to buy the inventory to produce the product, and you don't have the money you expect to get when someone buys it. Therefore, the cost of buying the inventory and producing the product is totally on your shoulders; you're financing that activity somehow.

How are you financing it? In one of three ways:

- Cash.
- Equity.
- Liability (debt).

Now imagine that you could reduce the time from 12 weeks to 3 weeks. You're financing the activity for less time, which is positive. That's why it's good to have a high inventory turnover: You're financing your production costs for a shorter period of time.

A low inventory turnover is very negative, because it tends to indicate at least one of the following:

- Inefficient operating procedures.
- Poor inventory management.
- Poor sales management/forecasting.

There are two views on how to compute inventory turnover: one from the cost perspective and one from the sales perspective.

Inventory Turnover: The Cost Perspective. Accountants use COGS, which is the cost perspective, and finance people use the sales perspective. Why? Because COGS represents only how much the inventory cost you, or how much money you had tied up in inventory. The sales perspective has the profit built in, which means it's not as pure a number.

Look at the COGS version first. The formula is

$$\frac{\text{Cost of goods sold}}{\text{Inventory}}$$

The higher the number of times it turns over, the better, because it means you had less money invested in inventory at any given time. For example

$$\text{Inventory turnover} = \frac{\$100{,}000}{\$50{,}000} = 2$$

This shows that you were able to turn over all of your inventory two times in a year. So, at any time you had $50,000 tied up in inventory, even though you purchased $150,000 of inventory ($100,000 + $50,000).

Inventory Turnover: The Sales Perspective. Finance people use the sales perspective to gauge the effectiveness of inventory turnover. The formula is

$$\frac{\text{Sales (less sales discounts or returns)}}{\text{Inventory}}$$

Look at how different the sales perspective is from the cost perspective. The sales perspective says

$$\frac{\$1{,}000{,}000}{\$50{,}000} = 20 \text{ is the inventory turnover ratio}$$

From the finance perspective it might seem that you turned over your inventory 20 times in a year, but that's incorrect. It simply shows you what the return on your inventory investment is. That is, you invested an average amount of $50,000 in inventory and it returned 20 times that in sales.

Now compare that with the ratio of 2 that you computed in the COGS example. For the very same inventory, the ratio was 10 times as high, a clearly inflated picture of what happened. COGS represents the actual number of times inventory turned over, which is why accountants prefer this method.

ACCOUNTS RECEIVABLES TURNOVER

Receivables turnover demonstrates how quickly you turn credit sales into cash, or how fast you collect your money. The formula is

$$\frac{\text{Net credit sales for the period}}{\text{Average net receivables}}$$

For example, if your ratio is 4, it means you're collecting your total receivables four times a year or every three months.

That's the pure form of the ratio because you're only using credit sales, which means customers have bought your product on account. However, if you're looking at a company's annual report, it only lists total sales, which doesn't differentiate between cash and credit. As a result, you must use a modified formula, total sales divided by accounts receivable.

Either formula is acceptable as long as you use it consistently, meaning for that company and that industry.

What does the formula mean? Use this example: The total sales is $100,000, and accounts receivable is $20,000. Dividing $100,000 by $20,000 gives you an accounts receivable turnover ratio of 5. This tells you that you are collecting your total accounts receivables five times per year.

How is this interpreted? Ideally you would like for your turnover ratio to be 12, meaning your clients would be paying their accounts off every month. Naturally, that's a bit unlikely, but a number of 8 or above would be good because it would mean you don't have old accounts receivable. (Just how high the number should be depends on your terms for payment—for example, whether terms are 30, 60, or 90 days.)

PROFITABILITY RATIOS

Profitability ratios measure profit and loss performance. Here are the common profitability ratios:

- ***Gross profit margin (GPM).*** Formula: Gross profit divided by sales. GPM tells you how profitable your products are, or the return on the products themselves.
- ***Net profit margin (NPM).*** Formula: Operating income (profits after taxes) divided by net sales. Or, alternatively, *operating profit margin (OPM).* Formula: Operating profit divided by sales. Both measure the effectiveness of expense management.
- ***Return on assets (ROA).*** Formula: Net income for the current year divided by total assets from the previous year. ROA measures how effectively a company invests in its assets, which ultimately produce income.
- ***Return on equity (ROE).*** Formula: Net income for the current year divided by stockholders' equity from the previous year. ROE measures how much money the company is making on what its shareholders have invested.
- ***Return on sales (ROS).*** Formula: Net income divided by sales. ROS tells you what percentage of net income you can reinvest or return to shareholders from the revenues you've earned.
- ***Return on investment (ROI).*** Formula: Net income divided by average owners' equity. This is similar to ROE, and there is a good bit of discussion about what numbers should be used in this formula. One of the areas of difference centers around whether depreciable assets should be included at original cost, cost less accumulated depreciation, or current replacement cost. In any event, ROI includes income divided by investment, however the two terms are defined.

LEVERAGE RATIOS

Think of a *lever,* which enables you to move more weight than you could using your bare strength alone. *Leverage* in a financial sense means money you've borrowed from others, that is, you're able to do more because you have additional resources from others. Typically, when a businessperson refers to her leverage, she means how much money she's borrowed from others.

A *leverage* ratio measures your level or use of debt, that is, where you're putting your borrowed money and how it contributes to the growth or health of your company.

On a balance sheet, leverage is shown as *debt* or *liabilities.*

THREE COMMON LEVERAGE RATIOS

The three usual leverage ratios are debt to equity, debt to total assets, and times interest earned.

Debt to equity. Formula: Long-term debt divided by stockholders equity. The debt-to-equity ratio looks at the relationship between the long-term money provided by creditors and the money invested by owners. In the debt-to-equity formula, the smaller number is better because it means you have less debt than equity. Any number under 0.5 is favorable.

Chart 14.1
Debt-to-Equity Ratios for Selected Industrial Firms

Motorola	33.0%
Pfizer	41.6
Texaco, Inc.	59.9
Coca-Cola	82.7
Philip Morris	86.6
Union Carbide	100.6
IBM	144.2
Lockheed Martin	180.8

Source: *1999 Annual Reports.*

Debt to total assets. Formula: Debt divided by total assets. This ratio indicates what percentage of your assets is financed by creditors. The weakness of this ratio is that it doesn't distinguish between current and long-term assets. Firms with higher leverage ratios are considered more risky because they're based on using assets to pay back debt, rather than to reinvest in the company's products. If an asset declines in value rapidly, there will be less money to cover debt. Thus, a high leverage ratio would represent a risk to creditors and would be a risk indicator to creditors. (The weakness of both debt to equity and debt to total assets is that neither distinguishes between short-term and long-term debt.)

Times Interest Earned. Formula: Operating income, i.e., Interest before Interest and Tax divided by interest expense.

Times interest earned reflects your ability to cover your interest payments. A ratio of 2 would mean you have $2 left over from everything. Thus, if your interest expense was $3, you wouldn't have enough money to cover your interest. This is a very important ratio because if a company does not have the ability to service its debt, it could go bankrupt. When analysts detect a trend of this ratio declining, they see it as an early warning sign.

This ratio has two major weaknesses:

- It only indicates the ability to pay interest on the debt, not the ability to pay down long-term debt. (*Senior debt* means interest plus the pay down, both of which are paid first.)
- It doesn't show how you pay *subordinated debentures,* or secondary debt that gets paid off after you pay your senior debt.

(*Servicing debt* is common terminology that means keeping current on interest payments and the amount you pay down on your debt.)

There is a way to alter the calculation to take this into consideration. Use the formula

$$\frac{\text{Earnings before interest and taxes (EBIT)}}{\text{Senior debt service (or interest expense on senior debt)}}$$

This is how it works:

$$\frac{\text{EBIT}}{\text{Senior debt service}} = \frac{\$1{,}000}{\$400}\text{, ratio} = 2.5$$

You have \$600 (\$1,000 – \$400) left to service your subordinated debt. If the interest on your subordinated debt is \$200, you would record it this way:

$$\frac{\$600 \text{ (EBIT left after servicing senior debt)}}{\$200 \text{ (Interest on subordinated debt)}} = 3 = \text{ratio}$$

If you use the original formula of operating income divided by interest expense you would have

$$\frac{\$1{,}000}{(\$400 + \$200)} = \frac{\$1{,}000}{\$600} = 1.67 = \text{ratio}$$

The point of the exercise is to recognize that 1.67 is misleading. The ratio for subordinated debt is higher than the overall ratio, so the subordinated debt isn't as risky.

If a creditor getting ready to lend money only looked at the 1.67 ratio, this business would look riskier than it is.

RETURN ON INVESTMENT OR RETURN ON ASSETS

Return on investment (ROI) and return on equity (ROE) are essentially the same thing. They measure a company's earning power, showing how much the company will make on the amount it has invested.

CONSIDERING ALL FACTORS

It's almost impossible to say what a ratio means without looking at the bigger picture and other factors that may come into play. For example, if you have a high inventory turnover rate, combined with a current ratio of 1.0 to 1.5, the company is probably doing well. Why? Because the inventory is turning over quickly and is, therefore, liquid. In some industries the time it takes to turn inventory into products is fast, and that is more desirable than situations in which it's slow.

Another factor to consider is current liabilities. For example, are current liabilities typical, or are there unusual things affecting you, such as liability from a pending lawsuit?

Clearly, ratios, like other aspects of finance and accounting, have to be seen as a piece of a total picture. Standing alone, they represent an interesting fact. They only take on greater meaning when they're viewed with other key information.

Ratios That Investors Typically Use

- PE.
- Debt-to-equity.
- ROI.

Chapter 15

TIME VALUE OF MONEY

It's clear that the value of a dollar is different today than was 100 years ago. A company that made $1 million in 1900 would be worth more than a company that made $1 million in 2000. But why?

The foundation of the time value of money (TVM) is people's natural preference to have one dollar today rather than to be given one dollar tomorrow. Some of this may be because of greed and the desire to spend that dollar now, but most of it is based on the theory that you can put that dollar to work for you.

Think of money as an employee that goes out, works hard, and brings back more money in return. If someone gave you the choice of one dollar today or another comparable amount tomorrow, you would have to know how much that dollar could work for you (what amount could it earn) before you could make a good decision.

Let's go back to our example of the 1900 company that made $1 million. If you had that $1 million at that time, you could put it to work for you. Thirty years later with an annual rate of return of 10%, it would be worth $17.5 million. Fifty years later, it would be worth $117.4 million (also at 10%). Get the picture?

Similarly, the value of money changes over the life of a business project. To make sound decisions, management must take into account the time value of money, (how the value of money changes over time).

A number of factors (other than management's judgment) affect the time value of money. Here are the main ones:

- Inflation.
- Interest rates.

- Compounding.
- Risk.

INFLATION

Any physical asset, such as a building or a machine, deteriorates over time. Wood rots, bricks and mortar crumble, metal rusts. They seem permanent when they're new, but tiny microorganisms feed on them and eventually these structures are of very little value at all.

Inflation is like the tiny microorganisms, except it feeds on the value of money. In a sense, it is the disease that makes money rot away, much like wood rots over time.

In financial terms, inflation is the general rising of prices over time, which, in a sense, rots away the buying power of the dollar. It is caused by a number of things:

- Economic conditions.
- Employment rate.
- Interest rates.
- Consumers' attitudes toward spending.
- Employees' desires for greater income.
- Industry unions.
- Supply and demand for products and services.
- Economic outlook for the future, and the public's response (emotional attitude) toward the outlook.
- Economic health of foreign countries, and their financial interaction with our country.
- Political climate (such as coming election years and wars).

All these factors affect one another. For example, your employees want higher wages. They believe you aren't paying them what they could make elsewhere. You now have a decision to make. You can give them a raise, which will increase your P&L expenses and may cause you to increase your product prices. This makes it more expensive for your customers, who may have to raise their prices, and so on. Eventually, this gets back to us personally, and we request higher wages from our employers because we can't afford the higher prices in the marketplace.

You can choose not to give them a raise. If the unemployment rate is high (i.e., there aren't many open jobs available), you probably made a good choice. Your employees may earn less than elsewhere, but the probability of them finding another job is small because of the unemployment rate (there being too many people competing to get the higher-paying jobs). But if the unemployment rate is low (i.e., there are many open jobs and employers are bidding up wage rates to get good employees), you may have made a bad decision. You run the risk of losing good employees, and it may cost you more in the long run to replace them (e.g., higher wages, training costs). Either way, your costs may increase, causing you to eventually raise your product prices.

Any one of the factors mentioned above can trigger this cyclical decision to begin. It doesn't even have to be anything related to your business. If the banks begin to fail in Asia (as they did just recently) and our country's economy is so-so, the press could play up the problem and its effect on our country's economy. (Remember that negative news sells very well.) Then investors could get leery of putting their money in risky ventures, consumers could get frightened of spending money on new things, and overall demand for new products could plummet. This would probably affect the demand for your company's products, but your company did nothing to cause it.

Whatever the case, inflation is the erosion of the value of money over time.

Inflation Rate

The inflation rate is the percentage that prices are rising annually. You will hear people make statements such as "The inflation rate is 4%." This means that prices, as a whole, increased about 4% over the past year.

As we stated earlier, money has the potential to create value over time if you invest it. If you don't invest it, the value of money will actually decrease (or depreciate) because of inflation. (Note: Money that your company doesn't invest is called *idle cash*. You wouldn't stand for employees to sit around idle, would you? You shouldn't let your money sit around idle either!) Therefore, if the inflation rate is 4%, you must invest your cash in something that will return at least 4% just to break even! Otherwise, by doing nothing, you're losing money even though you aren't actually spending it.

INTEREST RATES

Interest is the amount paid to a company for the use of its money. For example, a bank will loan money to a company to undertake a project or to buy inventory, but it expects the company to pay interest in return for the loan. (From the bank's perspective, this is a simple way of putting "money" to work as an employee.)

The *interest rate* is the percentage rate charged (or paid) for use of the money. In our previous example, the interest rate represents the rate of return the bank gets on the loan.

In the U.S., interest rates are indirectly tied to the rates the federal government will pay on long-term, intermediate-term, and short-term debt. To understand this, it's helpful to understand the type of *debt instruments* sold by the U.S. Treasury. *Debt instrument* is an overall term to describe everything from marketable debt securities (bonds) to bank loans to credit agreements with your vendor. In this situation, it's a marketable debt security. It means the debt can be sold to a third party and there is a certificate or agreement that changes hands.

TREASURY BILLS

Treasury bills (T-bills) are short-term debt securities sold in denominations of $1,000 to $1,000,000. They mature in 3 to 12 months. Treasury bills have no stated amount of interest. Instead, they are sold at a discount (less than the par or face value of $10,000 to $1,000,000). When they mature, the full face value is paid out. So the investor earns the difference between the discounted purchase price and the face value paid on maturity.

For example, a buyer may purchase a $10,000 treasury bill that matures in six months for $9,600. At the end of six months, the buyer will receive $10,000. The difference, $400, represents the amount of money earned on the T-bill. The rate of return is calculated as 400/9600 × 100 = 4%. (Since this is a six-month bill, the annual percentage rate is double this, or 8%.)

Treasury bills can be purchased online from the U.S. Treasury and through Federal Reserve banks, commercial banks, and brokerage firms.

The U.S. Treasury initially auctions T-bills off to competitive and noncompetitive bidders. Then they are traded on the securities markets much like corporate bonds.

Treasury Notes and Bonds

Treasury notes are intermediate-term notes sold by the U.S. Treasury in denominations of $1,000 to over $100,000. They mature in more than one year and less than 10 years. They pay a fixed rate of interest to the note holder every six months. At maturity, the par or face value of the note is paid back to the note holder.

Treasury bonds are long-term bonds sold by the U.S. Treasury in denominations of $1,000 to $5,000,000. They mature in more than 10 years from date of issuance, and they pay a fixed rate of interest to the bondholder every six months. At maturity, the par or face value of the bond is returned to the bondholder.

There are two types of treasury notes and bonds:

- Fixed-principal.
- Inflation-indexed.

Fixed-principal treasury securities are the normal securities sold by the U.S. Treasury. The interest payment is based upon the face value of the security, calculated by a stated interest rate.

Inflation-indexed treasury securities are adjusted to the Consumer Price Index (CPI) to reflect the inflation rate in the interest paid on the face value of the note or bond. For example, if the semi-annual interest rate paid on a $10,000 treasury note is 3% and the inflation rate is 2%, the interest payment would be $306. This is calculated as (10,000 × 1.02) × .03 = $306. This is $6 higher than the fixed-principal interest payment of $300 (calculated as $10,000 × .03).

Like T-bills, both treasury notes and bonds can be purchased at auction or on the securities market at close to the face value.

How Treasury Securities Affect Interest Rates

Although treasury securities are sold by the U.S. Treasury to raise money to support the federal government, the Federal Reserve determines how many securities are sold. Since financial institutions indirectly link their commercial and consumer lending rates to these securities, when the interest rates on treasury securities go up, overall interest rates also go up. When the interest rates on treasury securities go down, overall interest rates also go down.

COMPOUNDING

Compounding simply means making money on the money you've just earned. It works like this:

- Your company invests money.
- The money earns a return.
- Your company reinvests the amount earned by adding it to the original amount, and the total amount earns more money.

For example, your company invests $10,000 in an interest-bearing savings account that yields (earns) 5% annually. At the end of one year, the investment is worth $10,500 (calculated as [10,000 x 0.05] + 10,000). If the extra $500 is left in the account, the investment will be worth $11,025 (calculated as [10,500 x 0.05] + 10,500) at the end of the second year. The extra $500 left in the account continued to earn 5 percent interest. This is called compounding.

TIMING OF COMPOUNDING

In the preceding example, we used an annual compounding factor in the calculation. This means the savings account earned interest only once a year. However, in most situations, compounding occurs more frequently: quarterly, monthly or even daily! This means that interest is added to the account at the time the compounding occurs, so it is available to earn more money. The more frequently the compounding occurs, the more money your company earns.

SIMPLE INTEREST

Simple interest is earning a rate of return on the principal only. So in this situation, interest isn't earned on the interest charged. The formula is

$$\text{Interest} = \text{Principal} \times \text{Interest rate} \times \text{Time period}$$

This is the case with most consumer loans, such as mortgages and car loans. For example, every car payment made has an element of interest. But the interest is only computed on the outstanding loan balance. Any additional payments (over the loan payment) reduce the principal amount of the loan rather than future interest payments. (See Chapter 8, "Long-Term Liabilities" for more information.)

RISK

Risk is inherent in the fact that the future is unknown and uncertain. When we talk about TVM, risk is the possibility that your money or investment will lose value rather than gain value as expected.

Three Types of Risk

From a business perspective, there are three types of risk that could affect business operations, projects, and investments:

- Market risk.
- Business risk.
- Financial risk.

Market risk is the risk associated with events that are external to the company or industry, such as war, inflation, recession, or high interest rates. Market risk is related to the general economic conditions, but it encompasses much more. It also includes natural occurrences that may or may not affect the economy, such as a volcano going off in the state of Washington or a huge hurricane hitting the coast of Japan. Market risk is considered to be uncontrollable, meaning you can't do much to get rid of it or to minimize it.

Business risk is the risk associated with the nature of the business. For example, let's say you're in the pharmaceutical industry. It usually takes many years, lots of labor, and tons of money to develop a new drug. The payoff for coming up with a new cure is tremendous. But there is no guarantee that a new drug will work, be approved by the FDA, or be accepted by doctors and the public in general. Sometimes a competitor may develop a comparable drug and get it to market more quickly than your firm. If your company succeeds in all these areas, there may still be long-term side effects of the drug that cause future law suits against the company that developed and marketed the new drug.

That's just one example of business risk. Other sources of business risk include changing technology and changing consumer preferences.

Financial risk is related to the amount of debt (or leverage) that a company uses to fund its operations. As with any loan, the creditors expect a normal rate or return on their money and repayment of the debt. Financial risk for a company is the risk that revenues won't be high enough to pay back the debt *and* return a good profit to its stockholders.

For example, some companies, such as banks or credit unions, must operate with a high degree of leverage because their depositors all represent liabilities. If anything causes severe changes in revenues, these companies could experience major problems because they can't pay back their debt. (This is exactly what happened in the "bank run" in the old movie, *It's A Wonderful Life.* Uncle Billy lost the loan payment, the loan got called, and the Bailey Building & Loan Association couldn't pay it. Depositors wanted their money—now!)

Controllable Risk

In both business and financial risk, there are elements that can be defined, understood, and controlled (or minimized). For example, an international firm may use hedges (see Chapter 25) to reduce the inherent risks associated with the fluctuating foreign currency markets. Or, a company may invest in long-term bonds to make sure it has enough cash coming in to cover its own interest payments on debt.

Some of the control comes from sound decision making, such as researching and understanding the costs and market for new product lines before investing in them. Control can come from having insurance to cover business losses due to plant fires or tornadoes. Controlling this risk is imperative to the continued success of a company.

Uncontrollable Risk

There are some types of risk that are completely unforeseeable. We'll call these *uncontrollable risks.* (After all, if you could have planned for them, you could have controlled or at least minimized your company's risk.)

Market risk is usually considered uncontrollable or (to put it in nicer terms) nondiversifiable. This just means there is a portion of risk that cannot be minimized, no matter how well you plan, how much you research, or how well you manage your business.

There are elements of uncontrollable risks in both business risk and financial risk. An uncontrollable element of business risk is due to human nature (i.e., your employees). As a manager, you can't control having half the department out on maternity leave at the same time or having back-to-back family emergencies. Nor can you control the fact that one employee is in the hospital due to an illness and another can't come in because of a sick child during the week of an important deadline.

Uncontrollable elements of financial risk, on the other hand, are more related to market conditions. But some of this can also be linked to human nature. For example, if one industry reports bad results, investors may decide to pull their money out of the market. At the same time, the Federal Reserve may decide to tighten credit and raise interest rates. And all this can occur in the same week! Every factor eventually affects your business operations.

How Does Risk Affect TVM?

Risk is everywhere. It's in every business, every investment, every action (even personal actions, such as driving your car during rush hour). How does risk affect the time value of money?

If investors expect an investment to be more risky, whether the risk is real or perceived, they want to be compensated more for the use of their money. (This is true whether your company is the one doing the investing or it's borrowing money from investors or creditors.) In other words, there's a high risk that the value of investors' money will decrease so there must also be a high potential payback. If not, investors can just take their money somewhere else where the returns are more reliable.

As such, the relationship between risk and return is said to be correlative. This means that as risk increases, so does the expected return on investment. If the investment is too risky for the return expected, companies will have a difficult time getting financing.

This directly affects you as a manager, too. If a project you are proposing has too much perceived risk for the return it will give the business, you will have a difficult time getting senior management to approve funding for it.

TVM FORMULAS

Calculating interest on a savings account that is compounded annually is simple. The basic formula is principal × interest rate = interest earned. Then add the interest earned to the original principal amount, as we did earlier in the compounding example, and that's what an investment will be worth at the end of one year. (An easier way to determine the total amount at the end of the year is to use this modified formula: principal × (1 + interest rate, using a decimal) = end-of-year investment value.)

On the other hand, things get really complicated when you get into compounding. Calculating the interest earned monthly or daily is a little more difficult if you try to use the basic formula. Or consider how tough it would be to work backwards. Let's say that in five years, your company needs $1,000,000. It can earn 15% compounded monthly. How much money does it need to invest today to have $1,000,000 in five years? YOW! How do you calculate that? You can see that trying to calculate by hand would be masochistic!

Fortunately, there are algebraic equations that financial analysts use to compute the future value and present value of money, using specific interest rates compounded at a given period of time. In the following sections, we'll use these abbreviations to define the equations:

- PV stands for present value.
- FV stands for future value.
- M stands for the lump sum amount invested.
- I stands for the annual interest rate.
- N stands for the number of years the money is invested.
- C stands for the number of compounding periods in one year (e.g., 1 for annually, 4 for quarterly, 12 for monthly).
- PMT stands for payment, meaning the amount of money you continue to invest every period. (In this chapter, we'll only discuss equal payments invested each period.)

Future Value of Money

The *future value* (FV) of money answers the question, "How much will my money be worth in *X* number of years if it's invested at *Y* percentage rate of return and I never pull out the earnings (i.e., I let the earnings make money, too)?"

There are a couple of ways to look at the equations:

- FV of a lump sum of money invested today.
- FV of a stream of equal payments invested periodically, with the investments made at the beginning of each period (called FV of an annuity due).
- FV of a stream of equal payments invested periodically, with the investments made at the end of each period (called FV of an ordinary annuity).

FUTURE VALUE OF A LUMP SUM

Let's start with the first one: the *FV of a lump sum of money* invested today. The premise of this formula is that your company invested in something at the beginning, and then after a number a years it expects to get a certain amount back. How much should it expect? It depends upon the rate of return it requires and the number of years invested.

The algebraic equation to compute FV with annually compounded interest is

$$FV = M \times (1 + I)^N$$

For example, your company has invested $20,000 in a joint venture project with another company. It expects to receive a 15% return on the investment in 5 years. How much will the $20,000 be worth in 5 years (or what is the FV)?

M = $20,000

I = 15% or 0.15

N = 5

$FV = \$20,000 \times (1 + 0.15)^5 = \$40,227$

The formula changes slightly if there is more than one compounding period in a year, such as with compounding monthly or daily:

$$FV = M \times (1 + I/C)^{(N \times C)}$$

Let's change the previous example to compound monthly, so

M = $20,000

I = 15% or 0.15

N = 5

C = 12

$FV = \$20{,}000 \times (1 + 0.15/12)^{5 \times 12} = \$42{,}144$

You can see that changing the number of times the investment compounds in a year from one to 12 increases the return by $1,917. This is almost 10% of the original investment of $20,000—quite a lot.

Future Value of an Annuity Due

The *FV of an annuity due* (payments are invested at the beginning of the period) are similar to making regular payments to a retirement plan or a savings account. The assumption is that the period amount is invested at the beginning of the period (such as the month for monthly payments). This basically gives you one more period of interest to be compounded over the period of time. The formula for this is

$$FV = PMT \times \left[\frac{(1 + I)^N - 1}{I} \right] \times (1 + I)$$

For example, suppose your company is investing $1,000,000 per year (with payments made at the beginning of the year) in a project expected to return 20% over the next 10 years. What is the FV of the project at the end of the 10 years?

PMT = $1,000,000

I = 20% or 0.20

N = 10 years

$$FV = (\$1{,}000{,}000 \times \left[\frac{(1 + 0.20)^{10} - 1}{0.20} \right] \times (1 + 0.20) = \$31{,}150{,}419$$

Again, the formula changes slightly if there is more than one compounding period in a year:

$$FV = PMT \times \left[\frac{(1 + I/C)^{(N \times C)}}{I/C} \right] \times (1 + I/C)$$

Let's change the previous example. Instead of making one investment of $1,000,000 at the beginning of each year, the company decides to make one payment of $83,333 ($1,000,000/12) at the beginning of each month. In this case, the rate of return is compounded monthly, and the FV becomes:

PMT = $83,333

I = 20% or 0.20

N = 10 years

C = 12

$$FV = \$83{,}333 \times \left[\frac{(1 + 0.20/12)^{10 \times 12} - 1}{0.20/12} \right] \times (1 + 0.20/12) = \$31{,}863{,}502$$

The difference between the two examples is $713,083. This is all due to monthly payments and compounding the interest each month.

FUTURE VALUE OF AN ORDINARY ANNUITY

The *FV of an ordinary annuity* (payments are made at the end of the period) are like making consistent payments to an investment (such as a retirement plan for the company's employees). This is called an ordinary annuity because it is the most common type. The formula for this is

$$FV = PMT \times \left[\frac{(1 + I)^{N} - 1}{I} \right]$$

For example, your company is contributing $1,000,000 a year for the employees' retirement plan. It makes the contribution at year's end so it can get a big tax write-off. The retirement plan earns 8% a year. In

15 years, several employees are expected to retire. What is the value of the company's contribution at that time (i.e., what is the FV of the annual contributions)?

PMT = $1,000,000

I = 8% or 0.08

N = 15 years

$$FV = \$1,000,000 \times \left[\frac{(1 + 0.08)^{15} - 1}{0.08} \right] = \$27,152,114$$

Compounding more than once a year changes the formula to

$$FV = PMT \times \left[\frac{(1 + I/C)^{(N \times C)} - 1}{I/C} \right]$$

So if your company made a monthly contribution of $83,333 ($1,000,000/12) at the end of every month, instead of an annual contribution, the FV of the retirement plan would be

PMT = $83,333

I = 8% or 0.08

N = 15 years

C = 12

$$FV = \$83,333 \times \left[\frac{(1 + 0.08/12)^{15 \times 12} - 1}{0.08/12} \right] = \$28,836,403$$

The difference between the two examples is $1,684,289. This is all due to monthly payments and compounding the interest each month.

EASIER WAYS TO COMPUTE FUTURE VALUE

The easiest way to compute the future value is to use a spreadsheet, such as MS Excel or Lotus 123, or a financial calculator. However, since we're writing this book for nonfinancial managers, we didn't assume that you have access to either of these things.

Before the days of spreadsheets and financial calculators, accountants and financial analysts used tables to look up the FV factors, and you can do the same thing. (We've included these charts in the appendix.) All you have to know are these four things:

- Is the payment a lump sum or a series of equal payments (an annuity)?
- What is the annual interest rate?
- What is the time period (number of years)?
- How often is the investment compounded?

Just follow these steps:

1. If the number of compounding periods is more than 1, you'll need to use these simple calculations to get the correct number of periods and the interest rate:
   - Number of years × number of compounding periods in one year = the number of periods to use on the chart.
   - Interest rate / number of compounding periods in one year = the interest rate to look up in the chart. (Note: The charts increase interest rates in increments of 0.5%. Either round up or round down to the nearest interest rate. The FV won't be exact, but it will be close enough.)
2. Look up the appropriate FV factor in the chart. If the payment is a lump sum, you'll use the chart labeled "Future Value of $1 at Compound Interest." If you're calculating the FV for an annuity, you'll use the chart labeled "Future Value of an Ordinary Annuity of $1 per Period." (You'll use the same chart for both FV of an annuity due and FV of an ordinary annuity.)
3. If you are calculating the FV of an annuity due, use this formula to convert the FV of an ordinary annuity factor:

   FV of an annuity due factor = FV of an ordinary annuity factor x (1 + interest rate, using a decimal)

4. Multiply the payment amount by the FV factor to get the future value.

PRESENT VALUE OF MONEY

The *present value of money* is what money is worth today. That seems fairly simple. If your company has $10,000 today, it is worth $10,000. Why would we use the term *present value?*

Let's think about it in a different way. If you knew that a customer could pay you $10,000 a year from now for a product, how would you know if you are getting a good deal? Without knowing what the future payment of $10,000 is worth today (its present value), you can't evaluate whether it's a worthwhile deal.

Or, if your company is going to receive installment payments for the purchase of a product, how would you know if the total value of the payments is enough to cover the product purchase price and earn you a decent rate of return on the money you've loaned? Again, you must know the present value of those payments.

There are several equations used to calculate the present value (PV) of money:

- PV of a lump sum of money to be received in the future.
- PV of a stream of equal payments received periodically, with the payment received at the beginning of each period (called PV of an annuity due).
- PV of a stream of equal payments received periodically, with the payments received at the end of each period (called PV of an ordinary annuity).

PRESENT VALUE OF A LUMP SUM

If your company is given the choice of receiving $10,000 today for a product or $12,000 in two years, which would you pick? Which option is the best answer for the company's profitability?

From a child's point of view, the $12,000 may seem better. After all, it's more money. But from a financial point of view, you need to know how much the $12,000 is worth today, in present-day dollars, given the interest rate you could earn on the $10,000 if you received it today and invested it for two years.

This calculation is known as the *present value of a lump sum.* The equation to compute this is

$$PV = M \times \left[\frac{1}{(1 + I)^N} \right]$$

Using this formula, let's see whether the $10,000 or the $12,000 is a better deal for the company. Before we can begin, we must know the rate of return we could earn on the $10,000. To be conservative, let's say it is 10% compounded annually. The PV calculation is

$$M = \$12,000$$

$$I = 10\% \text{ or } 0.10$$

$$N = 2 \text{ years}$$

$$PV = \$12,000 \times \left[\frac{1}{(1 + 0.10)^2} \right] = \$9,917$$

From this computation, we can easily see that receiving $10,000 today is much better for the company than receiving $12,000 in two years since the present value of $12,000 at 10% is only $9,917.

What happens if we can only earn 8% interest on the $10,000? The calculation is

$$M = \$12,000$$

$$I = 8\% \text{ or } 0.08$$

$$N = 2 \text{ years}$$

$$PV = \$12,000 \times \left[\frac{1}{(1 + 0.08)^2} \right] = \$10,288$$

If the company can earn only 8% on the $10,000, then it is a better decision to take the $12,000 in two years since the present value of $12,000 at 8% is $10,288.

Compounding more than once a year changes the equation to

$$PV = M \times \left[\frac{1}{(1 + I/C)^{(N \times C)}} \right]$$

Changing the previous example to a compounding period of 12, we get this result for a 10% rate of return:

M = \$12,000

I = 10% or 0.10

N = 2 years

C = 12

$$PV = \$12{,}000 \times \left[\frac{1}{(1 + 0.10/12)^{2 \times 12}} \right] = \$9{,}833$$

So compounding monthly makes the future payment of \$12,000 look even worse than receiving \$10,000 today.

What happens at 8% interest compounded monthly?

M = \$12,000

I = 8% or 0.08

N = 2 years

C = 12

$$PV = \$12{,}000 \times \left[\frac{1}{(1 + 0.08/12)^{2 \times 12}} \right] = \$10{,}231$$

This result is still better than receiving \$10,000 today.

PRESENT VALUE OF AN ANNUITY DUE

Very rarely do businesses run into situations of a lump sum payment at the end of a future period. More likely are situations where customers want to pay for a product over a period of time.

If a customer wants to pay a particular amount over a period of time, with payments given at the beginning of the period (similar to making the first payment when the product is delivered), you can use the *present value of annuity due* formula to determine whether the payments are better than receiving the full price at the purchase date. This equation is

$$PV = PMT \times \left[\frac{1 - \left[\frac{1}{(1 + I)N} \right]}{I} \right] \times (1 + I)$$

For example, your customer offers to pay $2,000 per year for 5 years for product worth $7,500. Your company could earn a 12% return on the $7,500 if it reinvested the money in the business. What should you do?

PMT = $2,000

I = 12% or 0.12

N = 5 years

$$PV = \$2{,}000 \times \left[\frac{1 - \left[\frac{1}{(1 + 0.12)^5} \right]}{0.12} \right] \times (1 + 0.12) = \$8{,}075$$

Since the present value of the $2,000 payments at 12% interest is $8,075 and the value of the equipment is $7,500, you should accept the customer's offer.

Compounding the interest for more than one period during the year changes the equation to

$$PV = PMT \times \left[\frac{1 - \left[\frac{1}{(1 + I/C)^{(N \times C)}} \right]}{I/C} \right] \times (1 + I/C)$$

For example, your company has the opportunity to purchase equipment worth $80,000 for $750 a month (with payments at the beginning of the month) for the next 15 years from a supplier. If you borrowed the money from the bank, you would pay 8% interest. Should you take the supplier's offer, or should you borrow the money from the bank?

PMT = $750

I = 8% or 0.08

N = 15 years

C = 12

$$PV = \$750 \times \left[\frac{1 - \left[\frac{1}{(1 + 0.08/12)^{(15 \times 12)}} \right]}{0.08/12} \right] \times (1 + 0.08/12) = \$79{,}003$$

The present value of the payments your company would make is $79,003 at 8% interest (the interest rate at the bank). Thus, it would be better for you to accept the supplier's offer. Since the present value of the equipment is really $80,000 (which is higher than the $79,003), you'll be paying less interest if you use the supplier's purchasing plan than if you borrowed the money from the bank.

(This example is a little more difficult to understand, but we used it because it is a common situation. To prove the answer, we calculated the payment to the bank on an $80,000 loan for 15 years at 8% interest, using a financial calculator. The monthly payment would be $765 per month.)

PRESENT VALUE OF AN ORDINARY ANNUITY

The *PV of an ordinary annuity* calculates the present value of a stream of payments made at the end of each period (i.e., at the end of each month). Because the payment is made after the period (or month) has occurred the payment includes that period's interest calculation. This is called an ordinary annuity because it is the most common type. The formula for this is

$$PV = PMT \times \left[\frac{1 - \left[\frac{1}{(1 + I)^{N}} \right]}{I} \right]$$

For example, your company has the opportunity to purchase a building for $500,000 today or to make end-of-the-year payments of

$100,000 for 6 years. Your company's rate of return (the rate of return your company can earn by reinvesting in its own operations), is 8%. Which is the better deal?

PMT = $100,000

I = 8% or 0.08

N = 6 years

$$PV = \$100{,}000 \times \left[\frac{1 - \left[\frac{1}{(1 + 0.08)^{6}}\right]}{0.08}\right] = \$462{,}288$$

Since the present value of the payments is $462,288 at your company's rate of return, it is more profitable for the company to make the $100,000 payments and reinvest the $500,000 in its business operations.

(To prove this, we've calculated the payments of a $500,000 loan at 8% interest using a financial calculator. The annual payments would be $108,158 versus the $100,000 the company has been offered.)

Compounding more than once a year changes the equation to

$$PV = PMT \times \left[\frac{1 - \left[\frac{1}{(1 + I/C)^{(N \times C)}}\right]}{I/C}\right]$$

For example, your company can either purchase equipment for $50,000 or make end-of-the-month payments of $850 for 7 years. Your company's rate of return is 12%. What should you do?

PMT = $850

I = 12% or 0.12

N = 7 years

C = 12

$$PV = \$850 \times \left[\frac{1 - \left[\frac{1}{(1 + 0.12/12)^{(7 \times 12)}}\right]}{0.12/12}\right] = \$48{,}151$$

Since the present value of the payments at 12% is $48,151 (which is less than the equipment's present value of $50,000), the company should use the payment plan to purchase the equipment.

(To prove this, we've calculated the payments of a $50,000 loan at 12% interest using a financial calculator. The monthly payments would be $883 versus the $850 the company has been offered. Basically, this means that the company could invest the $50,000 and receive $883 each month, which is more than enough to cover the cost of the $850 payment.)

EASIER WAYS TO COMPUTE PRESENT VALUE

Like future value, the easiest way to compute the present value is to use a spreadsheet or a financial calculator. If you don't have either of these available, you can use the charts for PV factors that we have provided in the appendix. To use the charts, you have to know these four things:

- Is the future payment a lump sum or a series of equal payments (an annuity)?
- What is the annual interest rate?
- What is the time period (number of years)?
- How often is the investment compounded?

Just follow these steps:

1. If the number of compounding periods is more than one, you'll need to use these simple calculations to get the correct number of periods and the interest rate:
    - Number of years × number of compounding periods in one year = the number of periods to use on the chart.
    - Interest rate ÷ number of compounding periods in one year = the interest rate to look up in the chart. (Note: The charts increase interest rates in increments of 0.5%. Either round up or round down to the nearest interest rate. The PV won't be exact, but it will be close enough.)
2. Look up the appropriate PV factor in the chart. If the payment is a lump sum, you'll use the chart labeled "Present Value of $1 at Compound Interest." If you're calculating the PV for an annuity, you'll use the chart labeled "Present Value of an Ordinary Annuity of $1 per Period." (You'll use the same chart for both PV of an annuity due and PV of an ordinary annuity.)

3. If you are calculating the PV of an annuity due, use this formula to convert the PV of an ordinary annuity factor:

   PV of an annuity due factor = PV of an ordinary annuity factor x (1 + interest rate, using a decimal)

4. Multiply the payment amount by the PV factor to get the future value.

Chapter 16

CAPITAL AND PROJECT BUDGETING

Capital budgeting is a way of determining how much your company is going to spend on capital assets. This is simple if your company has few or small purchases to make. But how does senior management decide to allocate millions of dollars to many different assets? And what if your company also has major (i.e., expensive) projects that are competing in-house for the same money?

A SCIENTIFIC APPROACH

You could use the "gut feel" method or the "fly by the seat of your pants" method that a lot of small business owners (and even some large companies' senior management teams) use. But we don't recommend it. The problem with these two common methods is that they are based on emotion or on some quick analysis that usually gets you into trouble when it's too late (i.e., after a major portion of the money has been spent). Of course, these methods do work for small projects and purchases, but for large or complex purchases, we suggest that you use what's known in the finance world as capital budgeting techniques.

THREE ESSENTIAL CONSIDERATIONS

The most challenging decisions involve the long-term effects of today's decisions. To alleviate some of the emotion involved in decision making, financial analysts uses mathematical formulas to determine the best way to allocate funds between capital assets and projects. These methods are called capital budgeting techniques.

Before we explain how each of these techniques work, and the pros and cons associated with them, we'll explain the following financial terms that are used in relation to these techniques:

1. Cost of capital.
2. Opportunity cost.
3. Breakeven point.

COST OF CAPITAL

In determining the potential value of projects, senior management wants to make sure the projects get some minimum return on its investment. This is usually the cost of borrowing funds to pay for the project, or the *cost of capital* (hurdle rate). (In other words, senior management wants the projects to earn more than the company is paying for project funding.) This is the lowest possible return rate management will consider.

If the company has cash on hand, it might consider another alternative. It would probably determine how much its money could earn if it were invested somewhere else. For example, how much could the company earn if it were invested in money in a CD (or other low-risk investment)? In this case, the cost of capital is the amount the cash could earn in another investment. If a capital asset or project won't return at least the cost of capital, management probably won't commit funds to it unless there are other redeeming factors. For example, if a capital asset or project lays the foundation for other long-term, business-building opportunities, a lower rate of return may be acceptable.

The cost of capital should consider the risk involved in the capital asset or project. If a project is considered high-risk, management might demand a higher rate of return than if the project has a relatively low risk.

OPPORTUNITY COST

Anytime a company chooses to spend money on one capital asset or project, it gives up the opportunity to spend it on another. In other words, there is a definite cost for taking advantage of one option over another. This is another consideration for management when it comes to capital budgeting.

For example, your company has the following capital project proposals:

- New software development for $10 million, risk is considered very high (because software development projects tend to run double or triple their projected budgets). The return is projected to be 55%.
- Plant expansion for $7 million, risk is considered low (because your company has done this before). The return is projected to be 15%.
- New product development for $3 million, risk is considered moderate (because you aren't sure if competitors are also working to get the product to market quickly). The return is projected to be 25%.

If your company only has $10 million to spend, senior management will take a long, hard look at whether to spend the money on the new software development project because the return is so high. However, it could do the plant expansion and new product development for lower returns but more stable results. If senior management decides to go with the plant expansion and new product development, the opportunity cost for the company would be the 55% return it *won't* make on the new software development.

Opportunity costs occur in almost every aspect of business (and in life). However, we are conditioned to ignore them even if they are great. For example, would taking a few business courses to help you earn a promotion be time well spent? Of course it would. Yet most employees prefer to relax in front of the television rather than expending the effort to gain knowledge. This is an opportunity cost, yet we hardly notice it.

Breakeven Point

Part of looking ahead is being able to determine what long-term and short-term projects your company should undertake to contribute to the growth and health of the company. This includes deciding when to do things, how to pay for them, and if your company is making the best use of its funds (to ultimately maximize shareholder wealth).

Management has a variety of ways of judging the value of a project; breakeven point is one method. Breakeven is the point at which sales equals costs, either as a whole or unit by unit.

When you undertake a project, you will incur two sorts of costs:

- ***Fixed costs.*** These are the investments such as rent, salaries, and insurance that will be the same no matter how much you produce.
- ***Variable costs.*** When you are producing a product, some costs will increase as you produce more. For example, the more cereal you produce, the more raw materials, such as corn, you will have to buy. The total variable costs, thus, increase or decrease depending on production level.

With fixed costs, the more you produce, the lower your cost per unit will be because you're dividing your cost by a higher number of units. Variable costs, on the other hand, are driven by production.

To compute breakeven cost, you must project the volume at which costs will equal sales. Therefore, the breakeven point is the point at which the return equals the investment made (revenues equal expenses).

The breakeven analysis has several weaknesses, including

- It relies on estimates, which may not be accurate.
- It doesn't take into account any changes in price or sales.

CAPITAL BUDGETING TECHNIQUES

Capital budgeting techniques (or *capital budgeting models*) are specific formulas for financial evaluation (with some subjectivity) that are used to determine how a company can best use its available cash. Some simple capital budgeting techniques that we've included in this text are

- Accounting rate of return.
- Payback period.
- Internal rate of return.
- Net present value.
- Equivalent annual benefit.

- Infinite net present value.
- Profitability index.
- Benefit-cost ratio.
- Total net present value.

We've discussed them in the order of our preference for using them (from least preferred to most preferred). Also, there are more sophisticated capital budgeting techniques available, such as the capital asset pricing model which we briefly discuss later, but they are beyond the scope of this book.

For each of these techniques, we've given you

- The algebraic equation.
- The standard of acceptability (i.e., if your result meets or exceeds this standard, then you should go forward with the project; if not, then scrap the project).
- The advantages of the technique.
- The disadvantages of the technique.
- An example.

We've included the advantages and disadvantages to help you understand what technique to use for the project or situation you've got. The techniques all have good and bad qualities. If you know what they are, you can make better decisions. (Plus, it may give you a "step up" with your boss if you really understand what makes one technique better than the other, given your project.)

Although you can calculate these by hand, we suggest that you use a spreadsheet or financial calculator to do a complete analysis. Calculating the formulas by hand is very tedious. Spreadsheets and financial calculators are designed to easily and quickly compute them.

Project Cash Flow Analysis

For all of the capital budgeting techniques described in this book, you must first determine

- The life of the project or capital asset to be purchased or built.

- The cash inflows from the project (through revenues or reduced ongoing expenses).
- The cash outflows from the project (expenses created by the project itself).

Simply stated, you need a cash flow analysis.

A project *cash flow analysis* is a forecast or projection of what the future cash flows will be over the life of the project. It includes the timing of expenses and revenues. Typically, a project will generate expenses in the early years or months. Later it will produce cost savings or additional revenue.

(Note: We use the term *project,* but this analysis and all the capital budgeting techniques apply to the purchase of fixed assets; building your own fixed assets, such as buildings or software; and new product development. We suggest that you use these techniques any time you're making a decision on spending a large amount of money for your company.)

A cash flow analysis is similar to a P&L: You begin with the items that generate more revenue or reduce expenses. You subtract from that all the expenses that will be incurred as a direct result of the project. And you end up with the *net cash flow* (cash inflow less cash outflows) from the project over its useful life.

As with any forecast or projection, it is vital that you document your assumptions. (If you want to look good to senior management, you'll compare actual results to the forecast and determine why variances occurred. And it doesn't matter if the variances are negative or positive. Most managers don't even think to go back and review actual compared with forecast, so you'll be ahead of the game just by taking the initiative to do this. However, you need good assumptions.)

Here is an example of a simple cash flow analysis for the development of a new toy:

ASSUMPTIONS

- The toy is being developed for the Christmas market. The target market is young girls, 5 to 7 years of age. It has an expected life of 10 years.
- Research and development costs for the first 6 months will be approximately $100,000.

- Production costs include a one-time $80,000 set-up fee.
- The first year's revenues will be only $50,000 because of the late entry into the Christmas market. The next 4 years, revenues are expected to grow at 75% each year (as documented by marketing research). However, after a peak in revenue at the fifth year, revenue will decrease each year by 35%.
- Production expenses will be approximately 45% of expected revenues.
- Marketing and advertising costs will average 25% of expected revenues generated for the first 3 years. Then they will drop to 20% of expected revenues for the remaining years.
- Packaging and shipping costs a minimum of $20,000 per year. For revenues over $100,000, packaging and shipping costs will be $20,000 plus 10% of revenues. (See the 10-year Cash Flow Analysis on the following page.)

Should you go forward with the new toy? It depends. The entire net cash flow from the new toy brings in $142,000 (calculated as the sum of all net cash flows for the 10 years). It doesn't break even until the fifth year. (Net cash flow for the first five years is $5,800.) However, there are some other things to consider before deciding whether to move forward on this:

- Does this toy produce an acceptable rate of return on the investment made?
- How does the company's cost of capital affect the return on the amount invested?
- Could the $180,000 (research and development of $100,000 plus production set-up costs of $80,000) be invested in something else that would bring more value to the company?

These are the types of questions that senior management will ask before approving any new product, project, or capital asset. You'll use capital budgeting techniques to have the answers ready for them.

(Note: We'll continue to use this cash flow analysis in the capital budgeting techniques to show you how they work.)

CASH FLOW ANALYSIS

	Year 1	Year 2	Year 3	Year 4	Year 5	Year 6	Year 7	Year 8	Year 9	Year 10
Expected revenues	50,000	87,500	153,100	267,900	468,800	304,700	198,100	128,800	83,700	54,400
Expenses:										
Research & development	100,000	-	-	-	-	-	-	-	-	-
Production set-up fee	80,000	-	-	-	-	-	-	-	-	-
Production costs	22,500	39,400	68,900	120,600	211,000	137,100	89,100	58,000	37,700	24,500
Marketing & advertising	12,500	21,900	38,300	53,600	93,800	60,900	39,600	25,800	16,700	10,900
Packaging & shipping	20,000	20,000	25,300	36,800	56,900	40,500	29,800	22,900	20,000	20,000
Expected cash outflows	235,000	81,300	132,500	211,000	361,700	238,500	158,500	106,700	74,400	55,400
Net cash flow	(185,000)	6,200	20,600	56,900	107,100	66,200	39,600	22,100	9,300	(1,000)

Accounting Rate of Return

The *accounting rate of return* (ARR) is the average rate of return on a project. Although it's very popular (probably because it's so easy to understand), it has some major drawbacks, and we suggest that you only use it for a guideline. For example, the computation doesn't consider your company's cost of capital, nor does it consider the risk of the project. These things are very important, particularly if you have limited resources and unlimited project possibilities (as most profitable companies do).

So use ARR as a guideline if you have to use it at all. And use one of the other capital budgeting techniques to make your decision.

FORMULA

$$ARR = \frac{\text{Average net income from the project}}{\text{Average investment in the project}} = \frac{(\text{sum of all } NI_T) \times (1/n)}{\left[\dfrac{(I + BV_n)}{2}\right]}$$

NI_T = the net income for each period

n = the number of periods considered in the calculation

I = the initial investment amount in the project

BV_n = the projected book value of the project at the end of its life (i.e., at n periods)

STANDARD OF ACCEPTABILITY

ARR is used over 50% of the time when a project return is calculated. However, there is no standard of acceptability, which means there is nothing to compare ARR with to determine whether you should go ahead with the project.

ADVANTAGES

- ARR fully incorporates the life of the project.
- It is easy to understand.
- It provides a unique solution.

DISADVANTAGES

- It doesn't consider the time value of money.
- There is no standard of acceptability.
- It doesn't consider the cash flows of the project.
- It assumes straight line depreciation.
- There is no adjustment for risk.
- You cannot compare projects with unequal lives.
- You cannot compare projects with different scales (i.e., different initial investment amounts).
- It has no value additivity (i.e., you cannot add ARRs of different projects together to determine the increase to stockholders' wealth).

EXAMPLE

Using the information from the cash flow analysis example above, let's treat the research and development costs ($100,000) and the production set-up costs ($80,000) as the investment amount. (Technically, this is correct because they represent the *sunk costs* of the project, the costs that could not be recouped if the project were halted after production began.)

Also, let's assume that the book value at the end of the new toy's NI_1 = -185,000; NI_2 = 6,200; NI_3 = 20,600; NI_4 = 56,900; NI_5 = 107,100; NI_6= 66,200; NI_7 = 39,600; NI_8 = 22,100; NI_9 = 9,300; NI_{10} = -1,000. The sum of all NI_T = – 185,000 + 6,200 + 20,600 + 56,900 + 107,100 + 66,200 + 39,600 + 22,100 + 9,300 – 1,000 = 142,000.

$$n = 10$$

$$I = 100{,}000 + 80{,}000 = 180{,}000$$

$$BV_n = 0$$

$$ARR = \frac{(142{,}000) \times (1/10)}{\left[\dfrac{(180{,}000 + 0)}{2}\right]} = 0.1578 \text{ or } 15.78\%$$

Since there is no standard to determine whether you should accept the new toy development, this is as far as you can go with the calculation. It simply represents the average rate of return from investment in the new toy.

(Note: NI is a little different than CF, or net cash flows, used in other capital budgeting techniques. NI includes expenses such as equipment depreciation that don't represent physical outlays of cash. For purposes of this example, we didn't include depreciation or other noncash expenses.)

PAYBACK PERIOD

Payback period (PP) is the length of time it will take to earn back your company's initial investment in a project. The payback period method is a simplistic capital budgeting technique that, like ARR, we only recommend as a baseline. However, it's one of the more popular methods so we've included it here. (Probably the best way to use this section on payback is to understand the advantages and disadvantages of the calculation, particularly if your company likes this technique.)

FORMULA

There are two different formulas for PP, depending on whether the net cash flow is equal each period (such as the interest received from a bond investment) or unequal (as in our cash flow analysis example).

PP Formula 1:

PP_E (equal net cash flows per period) = $I \div CF_E$

I = the initial investment amount

CF_E = the equal net cash flow received each period

PP Formula 2:

PP_U (unequal net cash flows per period) = all CF_T added together until the value is 0, where

CF_T = the cash flow for each period

(The PP_U formula is a bit difficult to explain. See the example for better information on how to calculate it.)

STANDARD OF ACCEPTABILITY

There is no standard of acceptability for PP, which means there is nothing to compare it with to decide whether you should go ahead with the project. Think of it more as a quick and dirty calculation of how soon you'll get the initial investment back.

ADVANTAGES

- It is easy to understand.
- It's a rough liquidity measurement.
- It's a rough risk measurement if you assume that time and risk are positively related.

DISADVANTAGES

- It doesn't consider the time value of money.
- It doesn't consider the life of the project.
- It doesn't consider any cash flows past the payback period.
- It assumes that the cash flows are evenly distributed throughout the year, instead of lump sum payments at the end of the year. (Note: This may be an advantage or disadvantage, depending on your project.)
- There is no adjustment for risk.
- It doesn't solve the capital rationing problem (i.e., it doesn't tell you which project to choose if you can only do one because of limited funding).
- You cannot compare projects with unequal lives.
- There is no standard of acceptability.

EXAMPLE

Like the ARR example, we'll treat the research and development costs ($100,000) and the production set-up costs ($80,000) as the initial investment amount.

$CF_1 = -185{,}000$; $CF_2 = 6{,}200$; $CF_3 = 20{,}600$; $CF_4 = 56{,}900$; $CF_5 = 107{,}100$; $CF_6 = 66{,}200$; $CF_7 = 39{,}600$; $CF_8 = 22{,}100$; $CF_9 = 9{,}300$; $CF_{10} = -1{,}000$

$I = 100{,}000 + 80{,}000 = 180{,}000$

$PP_U = -185{,}000 + 6{,}200 + 20{,}600 + 56{,}900 + 107{,}100 = 5{,}800$

We've added up all the cash flows through year 5; then we stopped because this is the first year's cash flow that makes our result positive. For example, if we add up the cash flows from year 1 to year 4, the result is –101,300. So we need more cash flow to get to 0.

Since there is a positive balance at the end of year 5, we can say that the PP is less than five years. If you need to be more specific, you can assume that the cash flows occur evenly throughout year 5 to find out exactly when the PP occurs in that year:

At the end of year 4, the sum of the cash flows is –101,300. This means we need 101,300 from year 5 to get to the PP. To get the exact PP, use this formula (Note: It assumes an evenly distributed cash flow within the period):

$$\text{Portion of year} = \frac{\text{Amount needed to get cash flow to 0}}{\text{Total cash flow from the period}}$$

Using our information, the portion of the year is calculated as

$$\text{Portion of year} = \frac{101{,}300}{107{,}100} = 0.95$$

Now add this to our four years, and we get a PP_U of 4.95 years.

There is no standard of acceptability, so you cannot tell by the PP whether to go forward with the new toy.

Internal Rate of Return

Internal rate of return (IRR) is the rate of return at which the present value of all cash inflows (revenues) equals the present value of all cash outflows (the initial investment amount plus any ongoing expenses). Said another way, it is the cost of capital that causes the net present value of a project to equal zero.

FORMULA

IRR is the value that makes the following statement true:

$$\text{The sum of all } \frac{CF_T}{(1 + IRR)^T} \text{ for all periods} = 0\text{, where}$$

- CF_T is the net cash flow for each period.
- T is the period (year 1, year 2, etc.).

IRR is very difficult to calculate by hand. Basically, it's a process of trial and error, searching for the correct value that makes the statement work. It's much easier to let a spreadsheet or financial calculator do the work for you.

STANDARD OF ACCEPTANCE

If the IRR is greater than the company's cost of capital, you should move forward with the project. If it is less than the cost of capital, you should look for other projects in which to invest the company's money.

ADVANTAGES

- IRR considers the time value of money.
- It considers the cash flow of the project.
- It's easy to understand because it's intuitive.
- It's well accepted.

DISADVANTAGES

- You cannot compare projects with unequal lives.
- You cannot compare projects with different scales (i.e., different initial investment amounts).
- There is no adjustment for risk other than what is inherent in the cost of capital.
- Multiple solutions to the formula are mathematically possible. (Note: Multiple solutions are created by using different, or unequal, amounts of cash flow each period. However, unequal cash flow amounts do not always cause multiple solutions.)

- It assumes a reinvestment rate of IRR, which may be too high.
- It has no value additivity (i.e., you cannot add IRRs of different projects together to determine the increase to stockholders' wealth).

EXAMPLE

Assuming a cost of capital of 12% for the original cash flow analysis presented, the IRR of the new toy would be 14.35%. To calculate this, we let a financial calculator compute IRR for us, using the following information: $CF_1 = -180{,}000$; $CF_2 = 6{,}200$; $CF_3 = 20{,}600$; $CF_4 = 56{,}900$; $CF_5 = 107{,}100$; $CF_6 = 66{,}200$; $CF_7 = 39{,}600$; $CF_8 = 22{,}100$; $CF_9 = 9{,}300$; $CF_{10} = -1{,}000$

Since the IRR calculated is higher than the cost of capital (14.35% > 12%), you should move forward with the new toy.

NET PRESENT VALUE

Net present value (NPV) is a capital budgeting technique in which all the cash flows of a project are discounted at either the required rate of return or the cost of capital to determine the present value of the cash flows from the project. Calculating NPV is similar to calculating the present value (see Chapter 15); however, it allows you to use unequal payment amounts (i.e., net cash flow) each period.

FORMULA

$$\text{NPV} = \text{The sum of all } \frac{CF_T}{(1 + CC)^T} \text{ for all periods, where}$$

- CF_T is the net cash flow for each period.
- T is the period (year 1, year 2, etc.).
- CC is the cost of capital, or the required rate of return on a project.

This means you calculate the formula above for each period (year 1, year 2, etc.), and you add them all together to get the NPV.

STANDARD FOR ACCEPTANCE

The standard for accepting a project is a positive NPV (an NPV greater than zero). If the NPV is less than zero, you should not do the project.

ADVANTAGES

- NPV considers the time value of money.
- It considers the reinvestment rate, which is the cost of capital.
- It uses the cash flow projections of a project.
- It provides a unique solution given a set of facts.
- It's well accepted.
- You can compare projects with different scales (different initial investment amounts).
- It fully incorporates the project life.
- It has value additivity (i.e., you can add NPVs of different projects together to determine the increase to stockholders' wealth).

DISADVANTAGES

- The concept is difficult to understand because NPV isn't intuitive.
- You can't use NPV to compare projects with unequal economic lives.
- There is no adjustment for risk other than what is inherent in the cost of capital.
- It doesn't solve the capital rationing problem (i.e., it doesn't tell you which project to choose if you can only do one because of limited funding).

EXAMPLE

Assuming a cost of capital of 12% for the original cash flow analysis presented, the NPV of the new toy would be calculated as CF_1 = –165,200; CF_2 = 6,200; CF_3 = 20,600; CF_4 = 56,900; CF_5 = 107,100; CF_6 = 66,200; CF_7 = 39,600; CF_8 = 22,100; CF_9 = 9,300; CF_{10} = –1,000; CC = 12%, or 0.12.

Year 0: This would be the initial investment amount for a project, but because the R&D and production costs occur throughout Year 1, we have assumed this to be 0 for this example.

Year 1: $-185{,}000 \div (1 + 0.12)^1$ = –165,200

Year 2:	$6{,}200 \div (1 + 0.12)^2$	=	4,900
Year 3:	$20{,}600 \div (1 + 0.12)^3$	=	14,700
Year 4:	$56{,}900 \div (1 + 0.12)^4$	=	36,200
Year 5:	$107{,}100 \div (1 + 0.12)^5$	=	60,800
Year 6:	$66{,}200 \div (1 + 0.12)^6$	=	33,500
Year 7:	$39{,}600 \div (1 + 0.12)^7$	=	17,900
Year 8:	$22{,}100 \div (1 + 0.12)^8$	=	8,900
Year 9:	$9{,}300 \div (1 + 0.12)^9$	=	3,400
Year 10:	$-1{,}000 \div (1 + 0.12)^{10}$	=	–300

Total NPV = –165,200 + 4,900 + 14,700 + 36,200 + 60,800 + 33,500 + 17,900 + 8,900 + 3,400 – 300 = $14,800.

(Note: All numbers were rounded to the nearest hundred in these computations.)

Since the NPV calculated is a positive number (14,800 > 0), you should move forward with the new toy. However, if you have an alternative project to compare with this one, you cannot tell which project to choose based on the NPV technique.

Equivalent Annual Benefit

Equivalent annual benefit (EAB), or annualized NPV, modifies the NPV calculation so you can compare projects with different lives. In effect, EAB converts the NPV into an annual annuity. This means you would either take the EAB amount (given in the calculation) as a payment each year or take the NPV amount in a lump sum now.

FORMULA

$$\text{EAB} = \frac{\text{NPV}}{\text{PV of an ordinary annuity factor}}$$

The PV of an ordinary annuity factor is discussed in detail in Chapter 15. You can look it up in the appendix tables.

STANDARD FOR ACCEPTANCE

The standard for accepting a project is a positive EAB (an EAB greater than zero). If the EAB is less than zero, you should not do the project.

ADVANTAGES

- EAB considers the time value of money.
- It considers the reinvestment rate, which is the cost of capital.
- It uses the cash flow projections of a project.
- It provides a unique solution given a set of facts.
- It's well accepted.
- You can compare projects with different scales (different initial investment amounts).
- It fully incorporates the project life.
- It has value additivity (i.e., you can add EABs of different projects together to determine the increase to stockholders' wealth).
- It allows you to compare projects with unequal economic lives.

DISADVANTAGES

- The concept is difficult to understand because EAB isn't intuitive.
- There is no adjustment for risk other than what is inherent in the cost of capital.
- It doesn't solve the capital rationing problem (i.e., it doesn't tell you which project to choose if you can only do one because of limited funding).

EXAMPLE

Using the NPV from the previous example, EAB for the new toy is calculated as

$$\text{NPV} = 14{,}800$$

PV of an ordinary annuity factor (for 12% interest at 10 years) = 5.65022

$$\text{EAB} = \frac{14{,}800}{5.65022} = 2{,}620$$

(Note: The EAB was rounded to the nearest ten.)

Since the EAB is positive (2,620 > 0), you should move forward with the new toy based on this computation. You can also compare the EAB of the new toy with EABs of other new products (with unequal economic lives) to determine which one you should do if you can only do one. You should choose the one with the highest EAB.

INFINITE NET PRESENT VALUE

Infinite net present value (INPV) modifies EAB to allow ranking of multiple projects with different lives. Using INPV, you can choose between two mutually exclusive projects (i.e., you have to choose between two; you can't do both because of limited resources). In ranking projects, you would choose the one with the highest INPV.

INPV also allows you to compare projects with different costs of capital, or different rates of return, so you know which will bring the highest value to the company. This is important because the projects you are considering may not have equal risk.

STANDARD FOR ACCEPTANCE

The standard for accepting a project is a positive INPV (an INPV greater than zero). If the INPV is less than zero, you should not do the project.

FORMULA

$$\text{INPV} = \frac{\text{EAB}}{\text{CC}}$$

(Note: The cost of capital used in this formula, CC, doesn't have to be the same cost of capital used in the EAB formula.)

ADVANTAGES

- INPV considers the time value of money.
- It considers the reinvestment rate, which is the cost of capital.
- It uses the cash flow projections of a project.
- It provides a unique solution given a set of facts.
- It's well accepted.

- You can compare projects with different scales (i.e., different initial investment amounts).
- It fully incorporates the project life.
- It has value additivity (i.e., you can add INPVs of different projects together to determine the increase to stockholders' wealth).
- It allows you to compare projects with unequal economic lives.
- It allows you to use different costs of capital.
- It can be used to rank mutually exclusive alternatives (i.e., you can tell what project to choose if you can only do one because of limited funding).

DISADVANTAGES

- The concept is difficult to understand because INPV isn't intuitive.
- There is no adjustment for risk other than what is inherent in the cost of capital.

EXAMPLE

Using a cost of capital of 15% to show more risk, the EAB from the previous example becomes an INPV for the new toy as

EAB = 2,620

CC = 15% or 0.15

$$\text{INPV} = \frac{2{,}620}{0.15} = 17{,}470$$

(Note: The INPV was rounded to the nearest ten.)

Since the INPV is positive (17,470 > 0), you should move forward with the new toy based on this computation. You can also compare the INPV of the new toy with other INPVs to rank projects according to the one that can bring the most value to the company. You should choose the project with the highest INPV.

(Note: If you are ranking projects with different costs of capital, use INPV. Using EAB could give you a result that disagrees with INPV.)

Profitability Index

The *profitability index* (PI) is an equalizing capital budgeting technique that allows you to rank projects with the same scale (the same initial investment amount).

FORMULA

$$PI = \frac{NPV + |I|}{|I|}$$

Where $|I|$ is the initial investment made, stated as a positive number.

STANDARD OF ACCEPTABILITY

The standard for accepting a project is a PI greater than 1.0. If you are ranking projects, rank them in the order of their PI, beginning with the highest PI and going to the lowest PI. (Note: You should choose the project with the highest PI.)

ADVANTAGES

- PI considers the time value of money.
- It considers the cash flows of the project.
- It fully incorporates the project life.
- It's well accepted.
- There is a unique solution, given a set of facts.
- It considers the reinvestment rate, which is the cost of capital.
- It's easy to understand because it's intuitive.
- It allows the ranking of projects.

DISADVANTAGES

- You cannot compare projects with unequal lives.
- You cannot compare projects with different scales (different initial investment amounts).
- There is no adjustment for risk other than what is inherent in the cost of capital.

- It doesn't solve the capital rationing problem (i.e., it doesn't tell you which project to choose if you can only do one because of limited funding).
- It has no value additivity (i.e., you cannot add PIs of different projects together to determine the increase to stockholders' wealth).
- It has an undefined result.

EXAMPLE

Using the new toy example, we'll treat the production set-up expense ($80,000) as the initial investment amount. (We've adjusted the NPV calculation, rounding to the nearest hundred, to take this change into account.)

$$NPV = 6{,}200$$

$$I = -80{,}000$$

$$PI = \frac{6{,}200 + |-80{,}000|}{|-80{,}000|} = \frac{6{,}200 + 80{,}000}{80{,}000} = 1.08$$

Since 1.08 is greater than 1.0, you should move forward with this project.

BENEFIT-COST RATIO

The *benefit-cost ratio* (BCR) is a capital budgeting technique that compares the present-day benefit of a project with the projected cost of a project. When the benefit exceeds the cost, it may be favorably viewed.

There are times when the benefit can't be quantified. For example, a company might launch an environmental campaign that will earn it positive public opinion. Although the company can't measure the benefit in dollars, it may project that its gain in ability to do business is worth the cost.

On occasion, there may be two or more projects competing for budget dollars. When that happens, management may prefer the one that provides the greatest potential benefit at the lowest cost.

FORMULA

$$BCR = \frac{\text{NPV of cash inflows}}{|\ \text{NPV of cash outflows}\ |}$$

When there is only one cash outflow, BCR is equal to PI, the profitability index.

STANDARD OF ACCEPTABILITY

The standard for accepting a project is whether the BCR is greater than 1.0. If the project's BCR is more than 1.0, the project is profitable. If the project's BCR is less than 1.0, the project is not profitable and you should reject moving forward with it.

ADVANTAGES

- BCR considers the time value of money.
- It considers the cash flows of the project.
- It fully incorporates the project life.
- It's well accepted.
- There is a unique solution, given a set of facts.
- It considers the reinvestment rate, which is the cost of capital.
- It's easy to understand because it's intuitive.
- It allows the ranking of projects.
- It solves the undefined result problem with PI.

DISADVANTAGES

- You cannot compare projects with unequal lives.
- You cannot compare projects with different scales (different initial investment amounts).
- There is no adjustment for risk other than what is inherent in the cost of capital.
- It doesn't solve the capital rationing problem (i.e., it doesn't tell you which project to choose if you can only do one because of limited funding).

- It has no value additivity (i.e., you cannot add BCRs of different projects together to determine the increase to stockholders' wealth).

EXAMPLE

Using the information from the cash flow analysis example with a cost of capital of 12%, we calculate the NPV of the cash inflows as

Year 1:	$50{,}000 \div (1 + 0.12)^1$	=	44,600
Year 2:	$87{,}500 \div (1 + 0.12)^2$	=	69,800
Year 3:	$153{,}100 \div (1 + 0.12)^3$	=	109,000
Year 4:	$267{,}900 \div (1 + 0.12)^4$	=	170,300
Year 5:	$468{,}800 \div (1 + 0.12)^5$	=	266,000
Year 6:	$304{,}700 \div (1 + 0.12)^6$	=	154,400
Year 7:	$198{,}100 \div (1 + 0.12)^7$	=	89,600
Year 8:	$128{,}800 \div (1 + 0.12)^8$	=	52,000
Year 9:	$83{,}700 \div (1 + 0.12)^9$	=	30,200
Year 10:	$54{,}400 \div (1 + 0.12)^{10}$	=	17,500

Total NPV of cash inflows = 44,600 + 69,800 + 109,000 + 170,300 + 266,000 + 154,400 + 89,600 + 52,000 + 30,200 + 17,500 = 1,003,400.

The NPV of the cash outflows is calculated as:

Year 1:	$-235{,}000 \div (1 + 0.12)^1$	=	–209,800
Year 2:	$-81{,}300 \div (1 + 0.12)^2$	=	–64,800
Year 3:	$-132{,}500 \div (1 + 0.12)^3$	=	–94,300
Year 4:	$-211{,}000 \div (1 + 0.12)^4$	=	–134,100
Year 5:	$-361{,}700 \div (1 + 0.12)^5$	=	–205,200
Year 6:	$-238{,}500 \div (1 + 0.12)^6$	=	–120,800
Year 7:	$-158{,}500 \div (1 + 0.12)^7$	=	–71,700
Year 8:	$-106{,}700 \div (1 + 0.12)^8$	=	–43,100
Year 9:	$-74{,}400 \div (1 + 0.12)^9$	=	–26,800
Year 10:	$-55{,}400 \div (1 + 0.12)^{10}$	=	–17,800

Total NPV of cash outflows = –209,800 – 64,800 – 94,300 – 134,100 – 205,200 – 120,800 – 71,700 – 43,100 – 26,800 – 17,800 = –988,400.

$$\text{BCR} = \frac{1{,}003{,}400}{|\,-988{,}400\,|} = \frac{1{,}003{,}400}{988{,}400} = 1.02$$

Since 1.02 is greater than 1.0, you should move forward with the new toy based on the BCR analysis.

Total Net Present Value

Total net present value (TNPV) is the sum of all projects your company is going to do. NPV is unique in that you can add different projects' NPVs together and determine how much total value will be added to the company.

FORMULA

The formula is the sum of all NPVs of the projects under consideration.

STANDARD OF ACCEPTANCE

Your goal with this is to maximize the value the company receives, which in turn maximizes stockholder value. So you would pick the projects that have the highest TNPV.

ADVANTAGES

- TNPV considers the time value of money.
- It considers the reinvestment rate, which is the cost of capital.
- It uses the cash flow projections of a project.
- It provides a unique solution given a set of facts.
- It's well accepted.
- You can compare projects with different scales (different initial investment amounts).
- It fully incorporates the project life.
- It has value additivity (i.e., you can add TNPVs of different groups of projects together to determine the increase to stockholders' wealth).
- It can be used to rank mutually exclusive alternatives (i.e., you can tell what project to choose if you can only do one because of limited funding).

DISADVANTAGES

- The concept is difficult to understand because TNPV isn't intuitive.
- You can't use TNPV to compare projects with unequal economic lives.
- There is no adjustment for risk other than what is inherent in the cost of capital.
- It assumes linearity.
- It violates the laws of diminishing returns to factors of production.
- It violates the law of diminishing returns to scale.

CAPITAL ASSET PRICING MODEL

The *capital asset pricing model* (CAPM) is a complex capital budgeting tool that introduces an external risk factor into the equation of capital budgeting. This technique is used to calculate the relationship between expected risk and expected return. It is based on the theory that investments with higher risk are expected to yield higher returns.

Although we're not going to discuss the model because of its complexity, the CAPM is a common capital budgeting tool in the finance world and we included it in case you run into the term.

TO LEASE OR NOT TO LEASE, THAT IS THE QUESTION!

The question of whether to lease a fixed asset or to purchase it is really a capital budgeting issue. You treat the lease of an asset like one project, and the purchase of an asset as another project. Then select a capital budgeting technique that allows you to compare mutually exclusive alternatives (such as INPV), figure the cash flow analysis for each scenario, and run the capital budgeting model. Then compare the results and determine which gives you the better decision for your company.

Here is an example:

Your company needs to get a piece of equipment worth $60,000. The equipment will generate $25,000 in revenues a year over its life of 8 years. It has a residual value at the end of its life of 0. In order to get it running, you have to pay $8,000 in set-up costs (a one-time fee). You'll also have to pay ongoing maintenance costs of $9,000 per year. The equipment distributor is willing to lease the equipment to you for 5 years for $10,680 per year ($890 per month), with an end-of-lease buyout of $20,000.

Should you borrow money to buy the equipment (8%, 3-year simple interest loan)? Or, should you lease it instead, and buy it out at the end of the lease (for cash, no loan)?

The monthly payments on a 3-year loan are $1,880 compared to monthly payments of $890 on the lease. If you were only thinking about the monthly payment, the lease may seem better. But the lease is over 5 years, and the loan is only 3 years. We'll use the NPV capital budgeting technique to make our decision.

SCENARIO 1: YOUR COMPANY BUYS THE EQUIPMENT

Here is the cash flow analysis for the purchase scenario. You'll notice that we don't include the effects of equipment depreciation because depreciation isn't a cash flow item. (And for simplicity's sake, we don't include the income tax consequences, although you probably should when you are doing this.)

	Year 0	Year 1	Year 2	Year 3	Year 4	Year 5	Year 6	Year 7	Year 8
Cash inflows		25,000	25,000	25,000	25,000	25,000	25,000	25,000	25,000
Set-up costs	8,000								
Maintenance		9,000	9,000	9,000	9,000	9,000	9,000	9,000	9,000
Principal repayment		18,426	19,955	21,619					
Interest expense		4,134	2,605	948					
Total cash outflow	8,000	31,560	31,560	31,567	9,000	9,000	9,000	9,000	9,000
Net cash flow	(8,000)	(6,560)	(6,560)	(6,567)	16,000	16,000	16,000	16,000	16,000

Looking at the cash flow analysis, years 1 through 3 don't look too good. We're running a large cash shortage for these years. But we pick up a lot of cash inflow in the later years. Will the income make up for the difference? Let's look at the NPV calculation: $CF_0 = -8{,}000$; $CF_1 = -6{,}560$; $CF_2 = -6{,}560$; $CF_3 = -6{,}567$; $CF_4 = 16{,}000$; $CF_5 = 16{,}000$; $CF_6 = 16{,}000$; $CF_7 = 16{,}000$; $CF_8 = 16{,}000$

CC = 8% or 0.08 (from our knowledge about the loan)

Year 0:	$-8{,}000 \div (1 + 0.08)^0$	=	–8,000
Year 1:	$-6{,}560 \div (1 + 0.08)^1$	=	–6,074
Year 2:	$-6{,}560 \div (1 + 0.08)^2$	=	–5,624
Year 3:	$-6{,}567 \div (1 + 0.08)^3$	=	–5,213
Year 4:	$16{,}000 \div (1 + 0.08)^4$	=	11,760
Year 5:	$16{,}000 \div (1 + 0.08)^5$	=	10,889
Year 6:	$16{,}000 \div (1 + 0.08)^6$	=	10,083
Year 7:	$16{,}000 \div (1 + 0.08)^7$	=	9,336
Year 8:	$16{,}000 \div (1 + 0.08)^8$	=	8,644

Total NPV = –8,000 – 6,074 – 5,624 – 5,213 + 11,760 + 10,889 + 10,083 + 9,336 + 8,644 = $25,801.

SCENARIO 2: YOUR COMPANY LEASES THE EQUIPMENT

Here is the cash flow analysis for the lease scenario. (Again, we haven't included the income tax consequences, although you probably should when you are doing this.)

	Year 0	Year 1	Year 2	Year 3	Year 4	Year 5	Year 6	Year 7	Year 8
Cash inflows		25,000	25,000	25,000	25,000	25,000	25,000	25,000	25,000
Set-up costs	8,000								
Maintenance		9,000	9,000	9,000	9,000	9,000	9,000	9,000	9,000
Principal repayment		10,680	10,680	10,680	10,680	10,680			
Interest expense						20,000			
Total cash outflow	8,000	19,680	19,680	19,680	19,680	39,680	9,000	9,000	9,000
Net cash flow	(8,000)	5,320	5,320	5,320	5,320	(14,680)	16,000	16,000	16,000

At first glance, this looks better than the purchase cash flow scenario because most of the years have a positive net cash flow, particularly at the beginning of the equipment's life. However, the sum of all the net cash flows (for all years) is $46,600 (-8,000 + 5,320 + 5,320 + 5,320 + 5,320 – 14,680 + 16,000 + 16,000 + 16,000). This is less than the sum of all net cash flows (for all years) of $52,313 (–8,000 – 6,560

– 6,560 – 6,567 + 16,000 + 16,000 + 16,000 + 16,000 + 16,000) for the purchase scenario. So now it looks like it may be better to purchase the equipment. Let's look at the lease scenario NPV to check this: CF_0 = –8,000; CF_1 = 5,320; CF_2 = 5,320; CF_3 = 5,320; CF_4 = 5,320; CF_5 = –14,680; CF_6 = 16,000; CF_7 = 16,000; CF_8 = 16,000; CC = 8%, or 0.08 (from our knowledge about the loan)

Year 0:	$-8,000 \div (1 + 0.08)^0$	=	–8,000
Year 1:	$5,320 \div (1 + 0.08)^1$	=	4,926
Year 2:	$5,320 \div (1 + 0.08)^2$	=	4,561
Year 3:	$5,320 \div (1 + 0.08)^3$	=	4,223
Year 4:	$5,320 \div (1 + 0.08)^4$	=	3,910
Year 5:	$-14,680 \div (1 + 0.08)^5$	=	–9,991
Year 6:	$16,000 \div (1 + 0.08)^6$	=	10,083
Year 7:	$16,000 \div (1 + 0.08)^7$	=	9,336
Year 8:	$16,000 \div (1 + 0.08)^8$	=	8,644

Total NPV = –8,000 + 4,926 + 4,561 + 4,223 + 3,910 – 9,991 + 10,083 + 9,336 + 8,644 = $27,692.

Wow! What happened? The NPV of the lease scenario is $27,692, and the NPV of the purchase scenario is $25,801. From this it appears that we should go with the lease because it brings a higher value to the company. But it doesn't make sense, does it? The net cash flows of the purchase scenario are higher than for the lease scenario.

Let's try EAB to see if we get the same results:

Scenario 1: EAB Calculation

NPV_P = 25,801

PV of an ordinary annuity factor (for 8% interest at 8 years) = 5.74664

$$EAB_P = \frac{25,801}{5.74664} = 4,490$$

Scenario 2: EAB Calculation

NPV_L = 27,692

PV of an ordinary annuity factor (for 8% interest at 8 years) = 5.74664

$$EAB_L = \frac{27{,}692}{5.74664} = 4{,}818$$

And we get the same result. The EAB for the lease scenario is a better value for the company than the EAB for the purchase scenario. Why did this happen?

The reason the lease scenario is a better value is simply because of the positive net cash flows in the earlier years of the lease. The company can invest this amount in something that returns at least 8%, which give the company more in the long run because of the great impact of time value of money.

In fact, we calculated the lease payment using 12%. In effect, your company was paying 12% for the $40,000 that it "borrowed" over 5 years (the lease terms). Then it bought the equipment outright in the fifth year for $20,000 cash. So it would seem that you are paying more for the lease (at 12%) than for borrowing the money for the purchase (8%). Not true. This cash payment at lease buyout makes a big difference because your company didn't finance it.

So the lease scenario is better for two reasons:

- There are positive cash flows at the beginning of the equipment life.
- Your company paid cash at the lease buyout rather than financing the $20,000.

See how the "real" financial results can differ from what your gut tells you? That's why it is so important to use capital budgeting techniques in your decision making.

Chapter 17

RESPONSIBILITIES OF NONFINANCIAL MANAGERS

No matter how far removed you may be from the finance and accounting department, if you manage a department you will have responsibility for something financial, if only your department's budget. We've included the following financial topics to help you with your financial management:

- P&L review.
- Steps to easy budgeting.
- Forecasting.
- Managing costs.
- Managing payroll and related expenses.
- Accruals and prepaid expenses.

P&L REVIEW

As a manager, it's up to you to support the financial goals of the corporation and to make sure your area contributes to the overall financial well-being of the company. Your area may be a cost center, meaning it doesn't generate revenue. If this is the case, your contribution is to make sure your spending is thoughtful and necessary. Cost centers usually operate on a fairly tight basis, and senior management often looks to them to cut costs.

If you are operating a profit center, you will of course want to make it more profitable by operating efficiently (controlling costs) and increasing revenue.

How do you accomplish these goals? First, you'll need to look at the P&L statement for your area to understand the categories of revenue and expense and what contributes to them. Most companies send a monthly P&L to each department for managers to review.

WHAT TO LOOK FOR ON YOUR P&L

Most departmental P&Ls show several important columns for each line item:

- Spending for this month.
- Year-to-date spending.
- Budgeted amount.
- Variance from budget (overspending or underspending compared to planned budget).

Your job is to compare what you expected to spend (i.e., your budget) with what you're actually spending and to ask yourself these questions:

- Are the budget variances significant?
- What were your budget assumptions, and what factors have caused deviation from those?
- In cases of overspending, how can it be brought in line?
- If it can't be brought in line, what other expenses can you control to offset the increases?
- Can your area generate additional revenue to overcome the deficit?
- What significant changes will occur in the next month (or quarter) that will affect your P&L numbers?

Budgets are generally based on a lot of unknowns, and it's not out of the ordinary for them to differ from actual results. Nevertheless, a company can't function effectively without a reasonable idea of where it's going and what it will cost. It relies on managers to do their part so that the overall totals resemble the plan. Keeping a close eye on your budget will allow you to avoid unexpected problems and to justify overages as they occur. Most bosses don't like surprises, and keeping yours appraised of spending issues gives you and the boss a chance to weigh options.

STEPS TO EASY BUDGETING

Preparing and gaining approval of a departmental or divisional budget is a bit like dancing to gunfire. It involves logic and is part guessing and part negotiating.

Imagine that you're a corporate manager who is charged with creating a budget for a department or division. Here are some easy steps to follow:

1. Review the corporate objectives for the coming year.
2. Determine what your department needs to do to support the corporate objectives including any special projects, purchases, and so on.
3. Review your P&L for the preceding and current year-to-date to establish baseline expenses.
4. Review each line item and determine what changes will occur next year that will affect expenses. Take into account any special projects or purchases determined in step 2. For example,
   - An administrative assistant is retiring, and the tight job market means you will have to pay a replacement more money.
   - Your product is petroleum-based, and the price per barrel of oil has gone up $1 this month.
   - The cost of paper is projected to increase 30%, and you print 5 million pieces of sales collateral each year.
   - You are launching a new ad campaign to support a new product to be released in the next year.
5. Develop assumptions based on changes you anticipate for the next year, and document them well. This step is extremely important

because it explains why you made certain decisions. As we all know, budgets are just guidelines, and they seldom end up where they began. For a variety of reasons, managers spend their departmental funds in different ways than planned. It might be because a new project came up, because an old one was cancelled, because budgets were cut midyear, or for a host of other reasons. At budget reviews at the end of each quarter, you may have to explain the variances. By looking at your assumptions and showing that reality did not line up with expectations, you can account for differences in your budget. When you develop your assumptions, look at trends that could affect your activities or need to spend funds. These might include factors such as

- A tight labor market causing you to need an outside recruiter, resulting in fees.
- An increasing inflation rate.
- Consumer trends contributing to changed marketing strategy. For example, in the fast food business, a growing trend toward eating at home or more expensive restaurants could affect business.

6. Translate your assumptions into numbers or formulas. (For example, if inflation is expected to increase at 1%, you would anticipate spending an additional 1% on any items that are ongoing expenses, such as supplies.) Then apply the formulas. Although it's not a by-the-book practice, most managers add a buffer to their budgets to cover unexpected overages. Your finance or accounting experts may frown on this, but you will find that it is a common practice in Corporate America.
7. Most often, senior management will ask you to reduce your budget from the first numbers you present. Typically, you would cut a portion to show good faith, but at the same time give solid justification for why the remaining amount is necessary to appropriately and effectively conduct business.

BUDGET ITEMS

As you think about your funding needs for the next year, review your previous year's P&L statement to identify key items that you'll need to include. Some things are predetermined, such as employee benefits as a percentage of wages and salaries. Here is a list of things that may be included in your budget:

- Small equipment purchases.
- Interest rates.
- Leases.
- Relocation fees.
- Head count changes.
- Recruiting fees.
- Customer demands.
- New product development and release costs.
- Research and development.
- Sales strategies.
- Advertising.
- Meals and entertainment.
- Depreciation expense.
- Bonuses.
- Special employee recognition.
- Training.
- Utilities.
- Telephones including cell phones.
- Long-distance charges.
- Computers.
- Technical consulting fees.
- Internet access.
- Subscriptions.
- Membership dues.
- Taxes.

- Fees.
- Certifications.
- Licenses.
- Patents.
- Gas and other auto expenses.
- Software.

FORECASTING

Forecasting is an important part of a manager's job. It means to predict financial information for some future period of time.

Companies use forecasting in two ways:

- ***Short-term forecast.*** This is a forecast usually done midyear to predict what the expenses and revenues will be for the remainder of the year. This allows a manager to evaluate how actual spending and income will compare with what was budgeted.
- ***Long-term forecast.*** This is a projection for three to five years and is intended to predict where the company is going and to anticipate the major things that will happen in the future.

The key to all forecasting is to document your assumptions well! If your spending and revenue vary from your estimates, management will want to know why your guesses were off-base.

SHORT-TERM FORECASTING METHODS

There are two ways to do a short-term forecast.

METHOD 1

The easiest method is to look at the expenses you've had to that point.

1. Look at each line item and see if your spending rate will continue.
2. If the spending rate puts you over budget, develop explanations. If they were approved budget variances, you should have no difficulty explaining them.

3. Review the remainder of the year from an overall perspective to anticipate what your other major expenses will be. To do this you may

   - Review your original budget assumptions to see if they are still valid.
   - Look for expenses that only occur once a year, and make sure you haven't included or excluded them from your estimate.
   - Think through things like leases or other recurring expenses to determine if they are likely to stay the same.

With this information, you should be able to fairly accurately predict your performance either in line with your budget or with good explanations for why you're out of line.

METHOD 2

Look at your expenses to date and prorate your budget for the remainder of the year. Again, if you will be over budget, you will need to come up with explanations for the variances.

Senior management will also review your area's expected capital expenditures for the short-term forecast. (Capital, in this instance, means fixed assets you might be purchasing.) Senior management wants to know this information so that it can determine cash flow needs and plan for any necessary financing.

Long-Term Forecasting Methods

Long-term forecasting is typically done when budgets are prepared for the coming year. This is a time to look around and look inside to determine what factors will be affecting your business several years out.

A good forecast is important to you because it is

- The basis for the next year's budget.
- A way to know what the company's growth and product development will be, and to understand how your department or division will support that.

Like budgeting, there are two basic methods for forecasting. The first method is much simpler than the second.

METHOD 1

Start with your base budget.

1. Determine an inflation rate. (This may be included in a set of assumptions given by your company's financial planning department.)
2. Determine increases or decreases in head count, and when they're likely to occur. Based upon what you expect, consider
   - Salary or payroll increases.
   - Bonuses.
   - Effect on payroll taxes.
   - Executive search firm fees for new employees.
   - Severance for employees who are terminated.
   - Equipment such as personal computers or other assets required.

Your financial planning department can assist with projected salaries, bonuses, and payroll tax effects. This information is simple to model in a spreadsheet application such as Excel or Lotus.

- Review your contracts with vendors to see if rates will increase and, if so, what the timing is likely to be.
- Review your unusual expenses to determine if they will occur again.
- Apply the inflation rate to all ordinary expenses that you believe will be ongoing. Since this is a forecast that will cover several years, you'll need to use a formula to figure each year. In other words,
  - Future Year 1: Expense = Base year's expense $\times$ (1 + Inflation %)
  - Future Year 2: Expense = Base year's expense $\times$ (1 + Inflation %)^2
  - Future Year 3: Expense = Base year's expense $\times$ (1 + Inflation %)^3

  And so on.

METHOD 2

If you're really good at statistics and math, you can use regression analysis; however, we suggest that the average person use a statistical package for this, because the explanation of regression analysis is too complex to cover in this text!

MANAGING COSTS

Managing costs is easier than you think. It's all summed up in a few words—buy smart. If you buy smart on the front end, you won't have budget "surprises" on the back end.

Buying smart means

- Understanding the product or services to be purchased.
- Understanding your company's needs.
- Understanding the wide variety in price and quality for those products or services.
- Understanding suppliers.
- Sending out requests for bids.
- And then making the decision.

Large corporations consolidate this activity into a department called Purchasing, where purchasing agents do nothing but keep up with this activity. However, there are times when you, as a manager, must understand this process in order to curtail your department's spending, particularly if you're buying an unusual product or service that the purchasing department isn't familiar with.

Medium and small companies may not have the luxury of paying a full-time staff to "buy smart." It doesn't matter. The same principles can be used by anyone who is willing to invest a little time *before* the purchase.

UNDERSTANDING THE PRODUCTS OR SERVICES

Often there are many different products or services available that do the same thing. The only way to know what product best meets your company's needs is to understand the available products or services. This means knowing the features, benefits, and weaknesses of each one so you can make a well-informed decision.

UNDERSTANDING YOUR COMPANY'S NEEDS

A little detective work will help you buy smart. The amount of work involved in this step depends upon the product or service your company is purchasing. If the product is supplies or anything purchased routinely, you'll need to know the annual volume and the average price your company is paying. If you use a software program for managing purchases, this may mean running a simple report on previous suppliers. If you don't, it means getting staff to review all invoices for a period of time to get an average volume for the year and average purchase price.

If the product or service is out of the ordinary (such as replacing worn equipment), you'll need to spend time with the users of the product (probably your staff) and management to find out what is important to each group. You may have to do some research to find out about technological advances or other new product or service features.

The bottom line is, the more you know what your company needs, the easier it will be to find a good product at a fair price.

UNDERSTANDING THE SUPPLIERS

Suppliers are in business to make money, but usually they are willing to lower their own profit margins to get more business from a customer. They know that they can increase their bottom line in two ways:

- Sell a few products at a high price.
- Sell a lot of products at a low price.

Look for suppliers who recognize the value of the second option—selling a greater volume at a lower price. And this is the best part: Once you understand the products and services available, the prices and quality available, and your company's needs, you can make the supplier do the rest of the work.

WHERE TO FIND SUPPLIERS

Finding a supplier for common products is relatively easy. Here are a few methods:

- Business associates, other department managers, or professional organizations. Asking someone who has used the product or service and has no vested interest in your company's purchase is often the best method. It works particularly well for high-priced products and for services, since you'll get referrals *and* personal evaluations.

- Government agencies (city, county, and state). This is a great place for getting low-cost product referrals since most government agencies are required to go through a strict bidding process, and they've done some of the homework already. Call the agency and ask for the person responsible for purchases or contract bids.
- Large companies. If your company has no purchasing department, then talk with the companies who do have experts. (Most people willingly share their knowledge with those who want to listen, as long as your company isn't a competitor.) Call the main telephone number and ask to speak with someone in Purchasing. Then ask for the purchasing agent who handles the product or service you are interested in. Be sure to tell them up front that you aren't trying to sell them anything and that you just want some help in locating a good supplier.
- The Internet. With the powerful search engines on the Internet, you may be able to find many suppliers who provide the products or services your company needs.
- Business libraries. This is the best source for all sorts of products. And the librarian will help you find exactly what you're looking for.
- The Yellow Pages. Letting "your fingers do the walking" may be easy, but it might not be the best method if there are pages of potential suppliers to contact.

LOCATING SPECIALIZED PRODUCTS AND SERVICES

The preceding methods work for most products and services, but what about specialized products? Suppliers for specialized products may be more difficult to find, but not impossible. The best places to start are professional organizations or companies that may use the same or similar products. For example, in searching for a special software package for a college or university, you may want to start with other universities of similar size and in similar locations.

HOW TO EVALUATE POTENTIAL SUPPLIERS

Once you've found a few suppliers, then you should make sure each one of them is suited to meet your company's needs by following these steps:

1. Contact the supplier by phone. Keep the call short (two or three minutes). Ask for a sales representative. Discuss the product you are looking for to make sure the supplier can provide it. Set an appointment to visit the supplier.
2. Visit the supplier's facility. Ask for a tour. If possible, ask to meet some of the management team. At this time, get a full understanding of the supplier's products, capabilities, pricing, practices, and so on. Limit the visit to one hour.
3. After the meeting, score each of the following areas on a scale of 1 to 10 to determine your gut feel about the supplier:
   - Pricing.
   - Service.
   - Products.
   - Working relationship.
   - Facilities.
   - Capabilities.
   - Reputation.

Visiting suppliers takes time. Of course, you can have them come to you, but there are some things you'll learn from a site visit that you couldn't find out any other way. These are the "observation-only" characteristics of a supplier. Here are some things you can learn by visiting:

- What is the manner of the front office staff? Are they courteous, willing to help you, and polite to callers on the phone?
- Is the environment relaxed and pleasant?
- Does everyone seem rushed or stressed out?
- Is the office well maintained, or is it disorganized?

All these things can tell you a lot about the management style of the supplier. You might not want to trust a supplier to meet an important deadline if the office staff seems harried or if the office is cluttered. In this case, a picture really can be worth a thousand words . . . or dollars!

UNDERSTANDING THE WIDE VARIETY OF PRICES AND QUALITY

Most people link "high quality" with "high price." Sometimes it's true; often it's not. And there are those times when you think you are getting a bargain, but you've purchased an inferior product that doesn't work, and later you end up buying the higher-priced item anyway. Ouch! That can get expensive, but not if you've done your "before-purchase" work.

After you've visited with each supplier, and you have several who could meet the needs of your company, ask yourself these questions:

1. What are the most important product or service features, characteristics, and so on to your company?
2. What are the "nice-to-have" functions?
3. What could the company really do without?
4. Are there any hidden costs? (For example, machinery and software purchases may have additional maintenance contracts. Or, the equipment might be inexpensive, while the supplies are outrageously priced. It's the little things that could eat up your budget quickly.)
5. If the purchase is for equipment, machinery, software, or another large-dollar item, can you and your team preview the supplier's products to see how easy the product is to maintain and run?
6. Can the product be purchased on the "aftermarket" (reconditioned or used markets)?

The amount of time you spend on these questions (and with the supplier) is obviously related to the relative value of the product. If you are going to purchase paper towels for the company kitchen, you wouldn't waste a lot of time. But if you're purchasing a million-dollar machine, you will want to clearly review all of your options.

MAKING THE SUPPLIERS DO THE REST OF THE WORK

The next step in the purchasing process is to send out bid requests (requests for bid or proposal; RFB or RFP) to each qualified vendor. This can be done with a form or a simple letter, but there are some key things to mention in the request for bids:

1. Specify the product (or services), the quantity needed, and the features you expect the product to have. If your company is looking for a contract, mention the period of time to be covered. For example, a request for proposal for paper may state:

   Product: 20 lb. white paper

   Approximate weekly volume: 10 cartons

2. Ask the supplier to present the pricing and quotes in writing.

3. Ask the supplier to present *any* ways that would allow your company to get better prices. (Sometimes there are volume discounts or other programs that a vendor can suggest that you may not mention in the request for proposal.)

4. Let the supplier know that other vendors are being asked for their best prices, and this will be the only opportunity to propose. There will be no further negotiations after all proposals are received. (This is important because it prompts the supplier to give its best pricing up front.)

5. Other things to note about the request for bid include

   - Put the request for bid in writing.
   - Be as specific as possible about the product or service needed.
   - Give a due date for the bid.
   - If the supplier is the company's current supplier, ask it to identify the savings.

MAKING THE DECISION

The last step is to promptly review all bids, and make a decision based upon the best product or service for the company. Remember that you have told each supplier that there is no more negotiation, so don't go back and ask for better pricing based upon the bids received.

Also, as a courtesy, send a letter to the suppliers that you didn't select, letting them know that a decision has been made and your company will be using a different vendor. You never know, they may be the supplier chosen the next time you take something to bid.

MANAGING PAYROLL AND RELATED EXPENSES

Typically, payroll and other related expenses (such as employee benefits) are the largest combined expenditures that a company will have on its P&L. When budget cuts need to be made, managers are often tempted to cut in this area because it has the largest impact on reducing costs.

However, keep in mind that cutting payroll and employee-related expenses may have some other effects that you need to consider before taking action. Here are a few:

- Trimming payroll, whether through staff layoffs, reduced raises, or reduced benefits is demoralizing to all employees who stay with the company. You may lose more staff than you want because of this effect. You certainly will lose some productivity.
- If you cut back on staff, you may need to review your processes to eliminate unnecessary tasks. Don't expect your staff to churn out the same amount of work with fewer people unless you are introducing new technology to help them or you are making their work more efficient. (If you are introducing new technology, expect resistance and learning curves.)
- Don't expect your staff to do anything that senior management isn't doing. In other words, if you expect your staff to forgo salary and wage increases this year because of budget cutbacks, you'd better make sure that all management is participating in this.

As we've said before, your employees are your company's most valuable assets. At the time of this writing, the unemployment rate is very low. In some fields it is difficult to find good employees. So, think smart. Treat them well.

ACCRUALS AND PREPAID EXPENSES

Managers may sometimes perform tricks with their accounting records to make everything come out where they want. In doing so, they may be misapplying accounting principles and may get questioned by the accounting staff.

Two types of accounting entries are prepaid expenses and accruals.

- ***Prepaid expenses.*** This is when you pay for a service or product before you receive it. A legitimate prepaid expense would be a payment for an insurance policy that will cover you for the next 12 months. You haven't received the benefit of the service, but you have paid for it. If you cancelled, you would receive a prorated refund. (Note: Prepaid expenses don't get recorded on the P&L until your company receives the benefit!)
- ***Accruals.*** An accrual is when you put a liability (or revenue) on the books before you've received it. This is when a service has already been delivered but you haven't received an invoice for it. This typically occurs at the end of a month when you simply haven't gotten your bill.

When and When Not to Accrue

We've often heard managers near the end of the year say they want to "spend the budget money this year, because otherwise we won't get the money next year." They ask vendors to send them a bill, thinking that it will be expenses in this year's income statement.

That is an incorrect accounting treatment. In other words, it makes the company accountants shake their fingers. Such an expense should actually be recorded as an asset rather than as an expense because you haven't yet received the benefit of it and the vendor "owes" the company something.

There are appropriate ways and times to do accruals: at the end of the quarter and at the end of the year. That's when reports are due to the SEC. If you're audited, that's what the auditors will focus on.

Chapter 18

PAYROLL CONCERNS

Paying employees is quite a complex process that involves much more than simply handing someone a paycheck. Keeping track of employees' earnings is an accounting specialty all its own, one that leaves no room for error. When you're dealing with people's livelihood, they don't tolerate even a penny's worth of mistake. In addition, there are a host of government requirements that companies must follow in relation to payroll. The U.S. Department of Labor web site at *www.dol.gov* is a good source for rules and regulations that result from laws regarding everything from child labor, employee safety, minimum wage, and retirement and benefit plans, to the many other issues associated with employment. Payroll is just one of the specific areas that is highly regulated.

FEDERAL WAGES AND HOURS LAW (FAIR LABOR STANDARDS ACT)

The Federal Wages and Hours Law is a foundation of payroll guidelines. It says that employers must pay employees.

- A minimum hourly wage established by the government.
- A minimum of 1½ times the hourly wage for hours worked beyond 40 hours a week.

As the cost of living increases, the amount considered a minimum wage changes to accommodate people's increased financial needs.

THE DIFFERENCE BETWEEN WAGES AND SALARIES

Although the terms are often used interchangeably, *wages* and *salaries* are actually two distinct terms:

- Wages are paid to employees who work by the hour and are considered *non-exempt,* which means they are subject to minimum wage and overtime pay requirements. These employees earn at least the minimum wage and are paid extra for any hours they work beyond 40 hours a week or eight hours a day, depending on the company's policy.
- Salaries are paid to *exempt* employees who work for a set annual amount and are not paid overtime for the time they work beyond a 40-hour week. These employees are described as *exempt,* because they are not subject to minimum wage requirements.

The law is very specific in defining which employees are paid a salary and are exempt from these rules.

GOVERNMENT CONTRACTS, GRANTS, AND FINANCIAL ASSISTANCE

Companies that participate in government contracts or receive grants or financial assistance under government programs are subject to additional rules about the required wage and benefit rates.

EMPLOYER PAYROLL REQUIREMENTS

Employers must

- Require employees to fill out a W-4 form when they're employed and indicate the number of exemptions they will take. (See this chapter's section "Exemptions and W-4 Forms.")
- Keep a record of all employee salaries and wages in detail by employee.

- Submit filings to the federal and state government.
- Make deposits for certain withholdings to federal depository banks, which are designated to receive the funds and pass them on to the appropriate agency.
- Provide a report to employees each year. This is a federal government form known as a W-2.

Record Keeping

Companies must keep scrupulous records of employees' earnings and related information. For this reason, they use a payroll journal that lists

- Regular and overtime hours worked.
- Vacation pay.
- Sick pay.
- Bonuses.
- Total earnings.
- Taxes paid by the company and the employee.
- Other deductions, such as retirement plan contributions, health and life insurance, disability insurance, cafeteria plans, credit union deposits, and company stock purchases.

Only the smallest businesses do this manually. Payroll computer software simplifies the process so that entries only have to be made once and the information appears in a variety of reports.

Payroll Bank Accounts

Many companies simplify the process of paying employees by keeping a separate bank account strictly for the purpose of writing paychecks. Each month they make a deposit into the payroll bank account sufficient to pay wages and salaries. Then they write checks from that account to employees.

UNION REQUIREMENTS

In addition to the regulations established by the government, companies must also abide by the conditions of union contracts that apply to their employees. These requirements may include

- Paying premiums for working certain times such as Sundays or holidays.
- Deducting union dues from paychecks and paying them to the union.

Contracts are negotiated facility-by-facility or union-by-union with the employers to cover a stipulated period of time.

PAYROLL TAXES AND DEDUCTIONS

There are a number of deductions shown on a paycheck (see Chart 18.1). Some are required by the government, some result from an employee's requests for deductions, and some are legal deductions (such as garnishments) that may affect an employee's paychecks.

There are two categories of deductions:

- ***Pre-tax.*** Certain deductions are taken out of an employee's gross earnings before taxes are computed and deducted. This would include certain types of retirement plans and cafeteria plans.
- ***After-tax.*** Some deductions are subtracted from employees' income after taxes are figured.

Basically, the difference between the two categories is that pre-tax deductions are paid with pre-tax dollars. (Thus they aren't subject to federal income tax, which lower's federal income tax a bit.) After-tax deductions are paid after federal income tax is paid, so they don't reduce an employee's taxable income.

CHART 18.1
PAYROLL—WHO PAYS

WHAT	WHO PAYS	HOW MUCH	WHEN	BENEFITS	TO DO'S
FICA (Social Security, Medicare)	Employer ½, employee ½	% of wages up to a salary limit	Every paycheck	Retirement family benefits after death	
FUTA, federal unemployment insurance (payroll tax)	Employer	% of wages up to a salary limit	Deposit within one month after quarter.	Pays admin. expenses and helps state.	Keep records. Deposit in federal depository bank. File tax return.
SUTA, state unemployment insurance (payroll tax)	Employer (sometimes employee)	% of wages up to a salary limit (merit rating for firms with few claims)	Tax return within one month after quarter	Pays unem-ployment. Operates facilities.	File tax return payroll records.
Federal tax withholding	Employee	Withholding allowances minus exemptions (W-4) on gross earnings	Every paycheck		File same report as for FICA. Give employee a W-2 by Jan. 31. Send forms to SSA.
City and state income tax	Employee	% of wages	Every paycheck		Depends on city and state laws
Union dues	Employee				

WHAT'S ON A PAYCHECK?

The deductions that may appear on paycheck stubs are

- Federal income tax withholding.
- Federal Insurance Contributions Act (FICA) deductions, which include two elements:
    - Medicare. (Required deductions are not subject to annual limits.)
    - Retirement. (Required deductions are subject to annual limits.)
- Benefit plan contributions.
- Savings plan contributions.
- Retirement plan contributions.
- Cafeteria plan elements (such as plans for child care expenses) and health-related expenses (such as prescriptions) not covered by insurance.
- Union dues.
- Credit union payments or contributions.
- Charitable contributions.
- Garnishments (such as for child support or court-ordered repayment of debt).

FEDERAL AND STATE INCOME TAXES

The government requires that employers withhold from employees' paychecks the estimated amount of federal tax owed on their gross earnings (total earnings less pre-tax deductions). In states where there is an income tax, the state may also require tax to be withheld.

Federal income taxes withheld are deposited in a federal depository bank, which then sends the amount to the Internal Revenue Service. State income taxes are sent directly to the appropriate state.

EXEMPTIONS AND W-4 FORMS

Employees are allowed to deduct set amounts from their taxable income based on the number of exemptions (dependents) they claim.

Exemptions may include yourself, your spouse, and your direct dependents (including children and legally adopted children) and family members who are solely dependent upon you for their support because of their age or infirmity or because they are studying at a college or university and haven't achieved a certain age.

When you are hired, an employer will require that you fill out a W-4 form, which is a government form stating how many exemptions you will take. The more exemptions you take, the less money that is withheld from your paycheck (because the less taxable income you will have).

The odd thing about exemptions is that you can claim more exemptions than you actually have, at least at the front end. Many people take the maximum number of exemptions allowed, because it means that they will have a bigger paycheck each pay period. Withholding less money from their paychecks, however, may mean they have to make a large tax payment at the end of the year. (It doesn't make you owe more; you still owe the same amount, but it may be more difficult to pay in one large lump sum.)

Federal Insurance Contributions Act (FICA)

The Federal Insurance Contributions Act was passed in 1935 to provide benefits to retired people and various others who are unable to support themselves. FICA is also known as the Social Security tax.

The employer must deduct a percentage of gross earnings from every employee's paycheck for FICA; this is the Medicare and retirement deduction. There is a cap on the amount of retirement money withheld, so that when a person's earnings exceed a certain level, the employer no longer deducts that portion of FICA. (This level may change annually.) There is no annual limit on the amount of income subject to Medicare withholding.

Social Security Credits

Any work you do is tracked under your Social Security number, because Social Security is an earned benefit that accrues with the amount of time you work, the amount of money you make, and the FICA you pay. Each year, you can earn up to four credits (one credit for every quarter worked) toward being eligible for collecting Social Security benefits when you retire. Most people need 40 credits (10 years) to be eligible for retirement benefits, but younger people may also qualify if they are disabled or if a parent or spouse dies.

Some jobs are not covered by Social Security and rely upon other types of retirement or disability plans. They include

- Federal employees hired before 1984.
- Some state and local government employees.
- Railroad employees who have more than 10 years of service.
- Children under 21 who work for their parents.
- Ministers of religious organizations who elect not to pay Social Security tax.
- Retired military personnel.

SELF-EMPLOYED VERSUS OTHER EMPLOYED

If you work for a company, you pay one-half of your Social Security tax, and your employer pays the other half. If you work for yourself (for example, as a sole proprietorship or partner in a partnership), you must pay the full amount yourself. This is known as self-employment tax.

SOCIAL SECURITY BENEFITS

There are five types of benefits which are paid for through Social Security:

- ***Retirement.*** By paying into the Social Security system, you earn the right to receive a percentage of your normal income when you retire. (Although people for a long time have viewed Social Security as a way to fund their retirement years, we have recently come to understand that this is an unrealistic expectation. Social Security serves only as a supplement to other retirement or pension plans and investments.)
- ***Disability.*** If you become physically or mentally disabled, or if you have a life-threatening condition, you may be eligible for disability benefits.

- ***Family benefits.*** Family members also sometimes share in benefits for retirement or disability.
- ***Survivors benefits.*** A person who dies may have family members who can receive benefits. These would include the spouse as well as children under a certain age or still in school.
- ***Health insurance.*** A part of the FICA deduction represents payments to Medicare, the national health insurance plan that provides medical benefits for retired and disabled individuals.

Federal and State Unemployment Tax

The Federal Unemployment Tax Act (FUTA) set up a joint effort by the government and companies to provide for people who are unemployed. This law requires employers to contribute to a federal fund that is set up to pay unemployment benefits to people who are terminated or laid off. The amount the company is required to pay depends upon its track record.

The state also requires companies to pay unemployment taxes (SUTA). If a company has a history of not laying off large numbers of employees, it may earn a merit rating from the state, which reduces its FUTA owed.

Employee Benefits and Other Deductions

Employees who participate in company-sponsored benefits plans may also have money withheld for

- Health and welfare plans, such as health, disability, or life insurance.
- Retirement plans to which they make a contribution.
- Employee stock ownership plans (ESOP).
- Credit union contributions or loan payments.
- Union dues.
- Charitable funds endorsed by the company, such as United Way.

Garnishments

There are times when a creditor sues to legally force a debtor to pay. In cases where the debtor is entitled to money from a paycheck or other sources, the employer may be required to hand it over to satisfy the debt. This is called a *garnishment.*

When an employee has a legal judgment requiring him or her to pay debts such as child support or obligations to creditors, the employer will be required by law to subtract the amount required from the employee's paycheck. Another instance in which a garnishment might be ordered is when a person files for bankruptcy and is required to make payments to satisfy the negotiated amount owed.

OTHER EMPLOYEE COMPENSATION

Companies have a number of ways of rewarding employees for special achievements, for having attained a certain job level, or as a way of contributing to the employee's future. Usually, companies benefit from tax breaks associated with providing this additional compensation called supplemental wages.

Supplemental wages include bonuses, overtime, commissions, and special awards and they are subject to both federal income tax and FICA withholding. If these are paid with normal wages, withholding is computed as normal on the entire amount paid to the employee (regular wages plus supplemental wage). Alternatively, the employer may withhold a flat 28% (rather than the normal FICA and federal income tax percentages) from the supplemental wage if it's paid separately to the employee.

Other contributions to employees might include

- ***Bonuses.*** These may be paid at random for achievement or may be awarded at the end of the year based on company performance.
- ***Commissions.*** These may be paid on a percentage-of-sales basis to employees who are directly responsible for selling products or services.
- ***Stock options.*** (See Chapter 19 for more information.) One way to secure an employee's interest in the company's well-being is to create actual ownership through stock. Stock options give employees the right (but not the obligation) to buy company stock at a set price until some predetermined point in the future.

Plans of this type usually include a vesting period. The value of stock options is not included in an employee's income until the employee exercises the stock options.

- ***Restricted stock.*** Another way a company may allow employees to own stock is to give them restricted stock, which allows them to buy stock at a reduced price if they meet certain conditions or restrictions. These conditions might include a length of employment or the achievement of some company earnings growth or other performance measurement. When a company gives restricted stock, the company incurs costs. For this reason, many companies are giving more stock options (which the employee pays for), because it reduces the amount the company must pay. At first glance, options may seem like a good deal to the employees (because they get stock), but the true winner is the company, which puts up no money for stock options and gets all the benefits of employee ownership.

INDEPENDENT CONTRACTORS

When companies hire independent contractors, they aren't required to keep payroll records because these contractors are not technically employees. There are several IRS rules that govern whether a person who works for you is an independent contractor or an employee. She is an employee if

- You provide the workplace,
- You control the hours worked, and
- You supervise the work regularly.

The person's work must meet all three requirements for her to be considered an employee. Thus, professionals who work as consultants for you, even on a regular basis, are not considered employees unless all three criteria apply.

1099 INFORMATION

WHAT'S A 1099?

Even though independent contractors don't work for you as employees, you must still report the money you paid them, as long as you paid them more than a certain amount (at this printing, $600 per year). At the end of the year, instead of sending them a W-2 form, you may be required to send them a 1099, which shows the total amount of money you paid them in the preceding year, depending on whether you paid the consultant directly or you paid the company he works for.

A copy of all your 1099 forms also goes to the federal government. Form 1099 is an information report sent to both the IRS and to independent contractors. It reports service fees paid to these vendors (see below for qualifications). The 1099 form allows the IRS to track revenue reported on a vendor's income tax return.

NON-1099 VENDORS

These are vendors to whom you are not required to send a 1099:

- Corporations. (Inc., Incorporated, Corp. or Corporation generally end their names.)
- Professional corporations (PCs) with the exception of legal and medical vendors.
- Schools.
- Colleges and universities.
- Hospitals.
- Foundations.
- Government entities.
- Not-for-profit organizations.
- Societies (e.g., American Society of Family Practitioners).
- Associations (e.g., American Heart Association).
- Vendors with foreign addresses.
- Vendors supplying goods and/or tangible products.

You also need not file a 1099 for employment candidates' expense reimbursements.

1099 VENDORS

These are vendors to whom you must send a 1099:

- Individuals.
- Companies.
- Associates.
- Partnerships.
- Limited liability corporations (LLCs).
- Limited liability partnerships (LLPs).
- Professional corporations (PCs) that are legal or medical vendors.
- Limited (Ltd) companies.
- Foreign limited partnerships (FLPs).

INFORMATION REQUIRED FOR 1099 VENDORS

To process a 1099, you will need the following information:

- Tax ID or Social Security number.
- Complete mailing address.

1099 PAYMENT TYPES

Forms 1099 must be sent to 1099 vendors for the following types of payments:

- Consulting fees.
- Contracting fees.
- Service fees (all types).
- Medical payments.
- Legal payments.
- Legal settlements.

Chapter 19

EMPLOYEE COMPENSATION AND BENEFITS

The days of the gold watch are gone, replaced—or at least supplemented—with a wave of innovative methods of paying, rewarding, and recognizing employees. Under the heading of compensation and benefits are a host of financial and nonfinancial rewards.

Why the change? For several reasons:

- Employees today seek a more balanced life than they did in the past and aren't always lured by promises of higher and higher wages and salaries. They are looking for situations that offer a work environment that supports a flexible, healthy lifestyle.
- Low unemployment rates have made the competition for employees fierce, and employers can't compete cost-effectively for employees by offering higher and higher pay. Employees are often just as interested in the additional things an employer offers as they are the amount of their day-to-day pay.
- As companies merge, divest divisions, reorganize, and re-engineer themselves, employees are left without the security they used to enjoy in the "gold watch" days when they stayed with a company for 25 years and then collected their pensions. This lack of loyalty is a two-way street: Employees no longer feel compelled to stay with the same company long-term. A majority may change positions every few years, looking for better and better deals. (No longer are such job-hoppers seen as unreliable. On the contrary, anyone who stays in the same position more than a few years may be viewed as rigid, unable to handle change, or without greater potential. In short, they are considered stuck.) To retain top-notch

professionals, companies must offer unique incentives that make sticking around more attractive (personally or professionally profitable) than going.

- Regulatory practices are growing tighter, requiring employers to live up to certain standards.

The result of all these changes is that employers are using both traditional and nontraditional means of compensating employees, finding creative ways to make them happy, and throwing some interesting benefits into the mix. Companies provide a variety of incentives that reward performance and longevity, in hopes that they will be able to attract the cream of the crop and retain these outstanding performers.

This chapter describes some types of employee compensation and benefits plans. This is an area that is heavily regulated and extremely complex. While we here offer an overview, if you need specific details you should consult a CPA or a corporate benefits specialist. Because of the complexity of the subject, there are a number of companies that specialize in this field.

SOCIAL SECURITY

Before we discuss employer-provided compensation and benefits, let's talk briefly about Social Security.

Everyone who is employed in the U.S. must have a Social Security number, which allows the government to track their earnings no matter where or how long they work.

Workers pay a certain percentage of their wages in Social Security tax to the federal government, and their employers match that amount. If you're self-employed, you pay both parts.

As you work, you earn credits that entitle you to Social Security benefits in the future. The level of benefits you receive is based on the amount you earned, up to a certain limit. For instance, you can earn up to 4 points per year, and you need 40 points to be eligible for retirement benefits.

Social Security Benefits

Social Security is intended to provide several types of benefits, all dependent upon the person having earned enough credits to be eligible:

- ***Retirement benefits.*** Workers are eligible at age 65, with reduced benefits as early as 62.
- ***Disability benefits.*** When a person is physically or mentally unable to work, he may receive SS benefits.
- ***Family benefits.*** A spouse or dependent children receive benefits when the employee retires.
- ***Survivor benefits.*** The spouse or children may be eligible for benefits when a person dies.
- ***Medicare.*** Hospital and medical insurance is available under certain conditions.

Supplementing Social Security

There is a good bit of discussion today about the future of the Social Security program and the inadequacy of benefits for retirees. Proponents of the plan say it was designed to supplement, rather than replace, your own savings and investments. In and of itself, the government-sponsored program may be insufficient to provide adequate healthcare or retirement benefits.

EMPLOYER-RELATED COMPENSATION AND BENEFITS

Luckily, most people don't have to depend solely on Social Security. In addition to the pay an employer provides in an employee's regular paycheck, there are two types of pluses an employee may receive:

- Health benefits.
- Retirement plans.

CAFETERIA PLANS

Cafeteria plans do just what they sound like they would: They give employees a choice—a choice between certain benefits. In a cafeteria plan, if the employee chooses to "buy" benefits, the benefits are paid with pre-tax (income tax and FICA) dollars, which reduces the employee's taxable income. The employee has a number of benefits options that she can select according to her needs.

EMPLOYEE RETIREMENT INCOME SECURITY ACT (ERISA)

The *Employee Retirement Income Security Act (ERISA)* of 1974 is a federal law governing employee benefit and retirement plans. ERISA has very strict rules about

- Reporting to the U.S. Department of Labor and the Internal Revenue Service.
- Disclosing comprehensive plan information to participants.
- Having a process for handling benefits claims.

As a part of the ERISA requirements, companies must provide participants with information on a timely basis. Most companies must publish an annual report to employees of their benefits.

HEALTH BENEFITS

Health benefits may include a variety of options ranging from hospitalization coverage to dental plans to vision plans. While these are an important part of an employee's benefits, they are not strictly related to finance and accounting. If you need information about these areas, check with a corporate benefits specialist.

RETIREMENT PLANS

Employers provide compensation for the work employees do by paying them hourly wages and overtime pay, or annual salaries, as well as bonuses and commissions. Besides paying wages and salaries, companies help their employees save money and prepare for their retirement by offering savings plans. See Chart 19.1 at the end of the chapter for choices in retirement plans.

Restrictions on Company Plans

PRE-TAX DOLLARS

There are a variety of retirement investment options that allow you to put money aside before you pay any federal, state, or local income tax on it. This is an extremely beneficial way to save, because it lowers the income you pay tax on, and it gives you a return on your money as well.

EMPLOYER MATCHING CONTRIBUTION PLANS

In some types of retirement or investment plans, the employer will allow the employee to contribute and will match the employee's contributions to some degree, such as 25 cents to the dollar, up to a certain percentage of the employee's salary. (Some employers even match dollar for dollar!) For example, if an employee makes $40,000 and is allowed to contribute 6% of income, the employee would contribute $2,400 annually. The employer might match that dollar for dollar, which doubles the amount invested.

PROFIT SHARING

When an employer meets certain financial objectives, management may decide to share a portion of the proceeds with employees as a way of saying thanks and of demonstrating to employees that their work makes a difference. Such *profit sharing plans* may have several features. They could define the reward in terms of a percentage of an employee's salary, they may be for a set amount, or they may be given based on certain individual objectives, such as a bonus for job performance. These terms are all defined by the employer.

VESTING

In any savings and retirement plan, employees always "own" the money that they have invested, but they must earn the ownership of the portion contributed by the employer. Thus, they become entitled to, or *vested in,* the amount the company has contributed over time. This means that they are only entitled to a certain percentage of what the company has given them for each year they work there.

For instance, if the company has given an employee 100 shares of stock, after one year, the employee can leave and take 20% of the shares. After two years, the number of shares increases. Under current laws, companies are required to give an employee full vesting either after five years of service or between the third and seventh years. Thus, it may take as many as seven years for an employee to become fully vested, that is, to be entitled to 100% of the dollars or stock.

The idea of vesting means that the company wants something back for its investment; it wants employees to be more loyal.

401(k) Plans

A very popular employee retirement/savings plan is the *401(k),* which allows employees to make tax-deductible contributions to the fund. The company usually makes a contribution as well.

These plans place the employee's money in various investment accounts, and the employee usually has options about what type of investment to select:

- Company stock.
- Other investments.

A 401(k) reduces taxable income in the year the contributions are made, and the employee doesn't pay taxes on the interest until withdrawing the money.

INVESTMENT RISK

When employees participate in a 401(k) plan, they can usually choose to invest their money in one or several of a range of high-to-low-risk funds. The employee may choose to put all the money in one fund or to split the money among one or more.

Suppose the employee invests 6% of salary. He might choose to put 2% in company stock (which is considered the highest risk), 2% in a medium-risk plan, and 2% in a lower-risk plan such as a guaranteed investment contract.

403(b) Plans

A 403(b) plan is just like a 401(k), but it is for people who work for tax-exempt organizations such as churches, universities, and charitable organizations. Like a 401(k), it reduces taxable income in the year you make contributions. You don't pay any taxes on the interest until you withdraw the money.

EMPLOYEE STOCK OWNERSHIP PLANS (ESOPS)

Companies sometimes help fund a retirement plan through plans that include stock. Pronounced like the fabled Aesop, *ESOPs* provide a way for employees to own a part of the company. Employers consider sharing ownership to be a good way to accomplish two things:

- It encourages employees to work more actively for the benefit of the company, offering suggestions and finding ways to do their jobs better.
- It is an incentive to stay with a company, rather than job-hopping.

Although the plans operate somewhat differently, both public and private companies may set up ESOPs for their employees.

STOCK AS INCENTIVES

In employer-provided plans, the company gives the employee a certain amount of stock, which serves as an incentive to the employee to work toward the betterment of the company. ESOPs also provide tax incentives to the company.

The employer usually has some formula for determining how many shares are given to employees on a graduated basis.

- ***Time with the company.*** Employees may receive more shares depending upon their length of service.
- ***Job status.*** The higher the job title, the greater the number of shares.
- ***Performance.*** Accomplishment of certain goals may serve as a reason for extra distributions.

When an employee leaves the company, she may take the stock with her.

STOCK PURCHASE PLANS

In addition to the stock that an employer may give employees, the company may make it easy for employees to invest in company stock by buying it themselves. Although this is not a "retirement"or savings plan, it is a convenient way for an employee to make an investment.

EMPLOYEE STOCK PURCHASE PLANS (ESPPS)

Employee stock purchase plans allow employees to buy company stock at a certain price. They usually do this without paying a commission and with the added convenience of payroll deduction.

STOCK OPTIONS

Stock options, as we described in Chapter 18, are the right to buy or sell stock at a certain pre-established price. A company may give its employees stock options as a form of giving ownership or providing a potential investment, and may absorb the cost of any commissions.

Stock options require that the employee be vested before he can exercise the option. When an employee vests, there are a couple of things he should consider:

- Does it make sense to exercise the options? (If the stock price on the market is at or above the option price, it may be profitable to exercise it. If the stock price on the market is below the option price, why exercise it? You can buy it cheaper on the open stock market.) If you exercise the option, the difference between the market and option prices is included in income.
- Should you buy the stock and hold it, or take the difference between the market and option price in cash? You can choose either one. Again, the difference between market and option prices equals income. (Note: You may be required to write the company a check for income taxes due if you choose to buy the stock.)

ROLLOVERS

When you leave your job, what happens to the money you've invested in an employer plan? You have several options:

- You can leave the money where it is.
- You can take it with you and put it in your new employer's qualified retirement plan if the new employer's plan allows it.
- You can roll the money over to an IRA on a tax-free basis.

There is a time limit for transferring the money, and you can only do this once a year.

PERQUISITES (PERKS)

Nonfinancial rewards called *perks* also add to compensation. These might include things that accompany a person's position (such as automobile allowances, membership in country clubs, tickets to events, and trips) as well as general perks that might be available to all employees (such as the ability to buy products at reduced rates through a company store).

Perks may result from activities that are required as a result of the job. For example, salespeople enjoy dinner with clients at the company's expense. Other perks may result from the level of the position: Vice presidents could benefit from the use of the company plane. High-tech companies are especially competitive for employees and have taken the lead in creating extremely innovative perks, such as free dry cleaning.

These perks may not technically be "financial," but they certainly are nice!

REPORTING

Companies are required to keep extensive records of all types of employee benefits and compensation transactions (such as stock purchases or sales and bonuses paid) for purposes including tracking tax payments or taxes required. In addition, employees are always entitled to know where they stand in regard to their benefits and compensation programs.

At the same time, employees are responsible for filing the appropriate tax documents associated with any taxable income they receive as a result of company plans.

RETIREMENT PLANS FOR THE SELF-EMPLOYED

People who work for themselves don't have the luxury of an employer who will match their investments or offer stock options and other ways to amass retirement income. They do, however, have other methods of putting money aside in a tax-deferred, tax-deductible plan. Here are two plans that benefit self-employed people:

- ***Keogh.*** Self-employed people can set aside a percentage of their income in savings in a Keogh plan where all contributions and earnings are tax-free until they retire.
- ***Simplified Employee Pension (SEP).*** A SEP account is a special type of Keogh/IRA that lets the self-employed person and his employees make contributions to the plan.

Both the Keogh and the SEP have limits on the amount of money that can be contributed each year.

Chart 19.1
The Choices in Retirement Plans

Plan type	Major source of funding	Usual form of benefits	Where invested	Remarks
Defined-benefit pension	Employer	Annuity	Diversified among stocks, bonds, cash and sometimes real estate	Benefits depend on salary and length of service
Money-purchase pension	Employer; employee contributions sometimes allowed	Lump sum or installments	Same as defined-benefit pension	Benefits depend on size of contributions and investment performance of pension fund
Profit-sharing plan	Employer; employee contributions usually optional*	Lump sum	Usually employee's choice of diversified stock fund, fixed-income account, or company stock	Company contributions depend on size of company profits
Savings plan	Employee*, company usually matches a portion of employee contributions	Lump sum	Same as profit-sharing plan	Employees may be permitted to borrow a portion of vested benefits
Employee stock-ownership plan (ESOP)	Employer	Single payment of stock shares	Company stock	Starting at age 55, employees must be given a choice of other investments for a portion of their account balance
Tax-sheltered annuity (TSA or 403[b] plan)	Employee**; employer may contribute in some plans	Employee's choice of lump sum or annuity	Usually employee's choice of mutual funds or insurance company annuities	Offered only by schools and nonprofit institutions
IRA	Any salary or wage earner	Lump sum or periodic withdrawals	Account with bank, brokerage, insurance company, mutual fund, credit union, savings and loan, or trustee	Contributions are tax-deductible for some IRA holders+
Keogh plan	Self-employed people	Same as IRA	Same as IRA	Contributions are tax deductible
Simplified employee pension (SEP)	Company; employee contributions may be optional++	Same as IRA	Same as IRA	Designed for small businesses

*Employee contributions are tax-deductible if the plan is set up as a 401(k).

**Employee contributions are tax-deductible.

+Those not covered by a company retirement or Keogh plan or who have adjusted gross income less than $25,000 ($40,000 for married couples).

++Employee contributions are deductible in some SEPs.

Chapter 20

BUSINESS OWNERSHIP AND ORGANIZATION

Times have changed since Mom and Pop opened their corner grocery store. Business is now a complex proposition fraught with financial mazes, legal pitfalls, and tax strategies that can make or break a new business.

How a business is organized affects its responsibilities and liabilities, the types of reporting it's required to do, fees it will pay, taxes due, and so on. Before forming a business, it's a good idea to understand all the choices, because changing your mind down the road can have numerous implications in terms of time, money, and energy.

TYPES OF BUSINESS ORGANIZATION

There are a number of ways business can be organized:

- Sole proprietorship.
- Partnership.
- Corporation.
- Limited liability corporation.

Depending on the nature of the business and its owners, one form of organization may be more advantageous than others. Each type offers benefits and drawbacks.

SOLE PROPRIETORSHIP

This form of ownership is the simplest in terms of organization, accounting, and reporting. In a sole proprietorship one person owns the company (basically, that person *is* the company). While a sole proprietor may need a business license from the local and/or county government, there is no need to file for registration with the state or to create a separate legal entity.

Although sole proprietorships operate in an essentially informal fashion, there are some important financial considerations that apply:

- ***Co-mingling of funds.*** Clear record keeping is important no matter how the business is organized. Eventually, all money goes in the same pocket, and for tax purposes there's no distinction between personal funds and business funds. It's best, however, to keep separate records of the business and all its income and expenses, maintaining a separate checking account and/or savings account.
- ***Tax implications.*** If profitable for tax purposes, sole proprietorships are usually required to pay income taxes quarterly. This requires some estimating of annual income and planning to make sure the funds are available each quarter to pay taxes.

PARTNERSHIP

A partnership is comprised of two or more owners who are liable for issues associated with the company. Like a sole proprietorship, a partnership can be formed with no involvement on the part of government agencies. (Think of a partnership like a marriage. The same problems exist, except you may not know your business partner as well as your spouse! Many friendships are ruined when friends become partners.) To enter a partnership, people simply have to agree to be partners and, hopefully, draw up a legal contract stipulating such things as

- Percentage of ownership for each partner.
- Contribution of assets.
- How income and expenses will be divided.
- How debts will be divided.

- How disputes between partners will be settled.
- What happens if a partner dies.
- Rules of dissolution.

TYPES OF PARTNERSHIP

There are two types of partnership:

- ***General partnership (GP).*** In this arrangement, the partners are involved in managing the business. They must pay self-employment tax on their income.
- ***Limited partnership (LP).*** These partners are investors only, and they cannot legally bind the entity in any way. They can give input into the management decisions, but only as advice and not as decisions. They do not pay self-employment tax on their earnings. You must have at least one general partner in an LP.

MUTUAL AGENCY

Every general partner is an *agent* of the company, which means they can enter into and bind the company to agreements. All the partners are held responsible for these agreements, even though only one person may have decided to enter the contract. Of course, the agreements should be integrally related to the purpose of the business and in the best interest of the company. For example, a marketing company partner can engage the services of a graphic designer or hire a printer to produce materials. You would certainly hope that the person wouldn't go out and buy a speed boat with company funds or create some obligation that will not further the purpose of the business. Sometimes, however, this kind of monkey business does happen; so the more clearly the partners' responsibilities and limitations are defined, the better.

LIABILITY

In a partnership, all general partners are personally liable for any partnership debts, and if the company doesn't have enough assets to pay the bills, creditors can go after the partners' personal assets. If one partner can't pay her share, the other partners may be responsible for the full debt.

TAXATION

Partnerships aren't considered separate legal entities for federal income tax purposes. They are just an extension of the partners themselves. Therefore, partnerships don't pay federal income tax (although they are required to file an information return). The taxable income (or loss) from partnerships is included on the partners' individual tax returns, in the percentages specified by the partnership agreements. This is considered "earned income" to the general partners and therefore is subject to self-employment tax if the partner is a person.

(Note: Corporations can also be partners. Also, limited partners aren't subject to self-employment tax because the income is considered "passive." The catch is that the partner may end up paying income taxes on money he never received if the partnership doesn't distribute its earnings.)

LIMITED LIFE

Every partnership has a limited life. Here are some events that could end the partnership.

- Death of one of the partners or any other physical health circumstance that makes him unable to enter a contract.
- Bankruptcy.
- A contract specification that defines the length of the contract.
- The completion of the business for which the partnership was formed.
- A decision by any of the partners to terminate the agreement.
- The partnership agreement specifing a termination date.

LIMITED PARTNERSHIP

A limited partnership has one or more partners who never have exposure for more losses than the amount of capital they have invested. At least one of the partners must be a general partner who is personally liable for the business losses or debts.

Corporation

A corporation is a legal entity separate and apart from its owners. It is considered to have a life of its own.

There are two types of corporations:

- Privately held.
- Publicly held.

Privately held corporations are not traded on a stock market. Publicly held companies have issued stock that can be traded on the open market.

GOAL OF A CORPORATION

The goal of a corporation is to maximize shareholder wealth. This means that the entity itself is interested in decisions that are for the good of the shareholders but not necessarily of the company itself. Most times, the shareholders' and company's best interests are the same; however, sometimes the best interest of the shareholders is to sell the company, merge with another company, or otherwise end the life of the company as a separate legal entity. The point is, decisions are made only to maximize shareholder wealth, not to maximize the well-being of the corporation, management, or employees.

THE PROCESS OF INCORPORATION

The process of becoming a corporation is called *incorporating,* and it consists of various legal filings with the state. Incorporation laws are governed at the state level, so corporate charters and letters of incorporation must be filed according to state rules.

Companies have the option of incorporating in the state where they're located or in another state. In the state where it's located, a company is called a *domestic* company. In other states it's called a *foreign* company.

Because some states have more advantageous tax laws, companies might tend to organize there. Usually companies that do business in a number of states will choose to incorporate in the state that offers the most tax advantages (lowest tax rates).

CORPORATE CHARTER

A charter is a legal agreement between the state and the company's owners to make the corporation a separate legal entity.

ARTICLES OF INCORPORATION

The articles of incorporation are a company's application for a corporate charter. Each state requires different information, but the articles generally include

- Corporate name.
- Location of main office.
- Business purposes.
- Number of shares authorized.
- Classes of stock.
- Voting and dividend rights of each class.
- Total original capital contribution.
- Limitations on the authority of management and owners.

WHO OWNS A CORPORATION?

The people who own a corporation are called *shareholders* or *stockholders* because they own shares of stock that entitle them to a piece of the company. Shareholders have certain rights depending on the type of stock they own. While they don't usually get involved in the day-to-day operation of a company, the shareholders do vote on major company decisions and elect the members of the board of directors.

HOW A CORPORATION IS GOVERNED

A corporation is governed by a board of directors elected by the shareholders to act in their best interest. The members formulate broad policies and the vision or direction of the corporation. They also authorize large contracts, declare dividends, set executives' salaries, and authorize the borrowing of money.

Board members may be a part of company management or may be managers in other companies that offer expertise to the organization. Usually, boards comprise a number of both.

The bylaws are the set of regulations that govern the conduct of corporate affairs. They must be adopted by the board of directors. Bylaws typically include

- Place and date of the stockholders meeting and how the meeting will be announced.
- Number of directors and how they're elected.
- Responsibility and powers of directors.
- Method of selecting officers.

Officers are the top management team of the company. The president of the company reports to the board of directors, who report to the shareholders. All other officers report to the president.

The boards of directors of major corporations tend to meet quarterly to review performance and to vote on decisions. In some circumstances there may be a special board meeting called to take action on issues such as a crisis in the company, removal of the president, a proposed merger or acquisition, or other out-of-the-ordinary business.

The actions of the board are recorded in the meeting minutes, which must be kept on file according to state regulations. Decisions must be documented in resolutions. Outside auditors may request to look at the minutes, because board meetings are often the source of large transactions that the auditors need to review.

PUBLICLY HELD CORPORATIONS

When companies *go public,* it means they sell portions of their ownership in an open stock market.

There are several good reasons for a company to go public:

- It's easy to transfer ownership. Shareholders are widely dispersed, and have little interest in who owns the stock. Conversely, in a partnership, owners must work together and usually are quite concerned that other owners share their point of view. (Note: Some partnerships are publicly traded. And some corporations are not widely traded, so it's difficult to sell when you want to.)
- Limited liability. In a partnership or sole proprietorship, the general partners (or owner) are personally liable for the debts of the

organization. In a corporation, the most a shareholder can lose is the initial investment (money used to buy the stock). (In small corporations, banks or other financing institutions sometimes require owners to personally guarantee debt by securing their personal assets or being held personally accountable for the debt. This changes some of the limitations on liability.)

- Continuous existence. Ownership may be passed from one person to another at the death of the owner.
- Professional management.
- Separation of owners and entity. Individual owners can't bind the corporation to a legal contract; only corporate officers can do that. In addition, there is no requirement for mutual agreement of all owners to make a business contract. There are agents of the corporation who can act on everyone's behalf.

DISADVANTAGES OF A CORPORATION

There are five main disadvantages of a corporation:

1. ***Agency problem.*** The goal of a corporation is to maximize shareholder wealth. The goal of management is to maximize personal wealth. Obviously, there may be a conflict of interest in those two goals. This is called the agency problem. What corporations sometimes do to overcome this obstacle is to offer the management team stock options or restricted stock as a performance incentive. Thus, management becomes a part of the ownership team and supposedly shares the interest of other owners. There can, however, be negative side effects from these incentives, as well. When top management owns a large percentage of the shares, they can make business decisions that maximize their own wealth at the risk of the corporation or other shareholders' wealth.
2. ***Double taxation.*** Corporations are taxed on their net income by both federal and state governments. If they pay dividends, the owners are also taxed by the federal government and by most states on that same income.
3. ***Government regulation.*** Because they are a separate legal entity, corporations are subject to greater restrictions and control than partnerships or sole proprietorships.

4. ***Inefficient management.*** Poor management may stay in control because it has the power to use corporate funds to solicit shareholder votes. Shareholders may be geographically scattered and not aware of what's going on. The logistics issue might also make it hard for shareholders to organize and oppose existing management.
5. ***Limited ability to finance.*** If the corporation can't pay its debts, creditors cannot look beyond the corporate entity to the owners to collect. This may make it more difficult to get financing, particularly for small corporations.

TYPES OF CORPORATIONS

There are two types of corporations for federal income tax purposes:

- Subchapter C, called a C corp.
- Subchapter S, called an S corp.

Note: "Subchapter" just means a particular section of the U.S. Tax Code.

Subchapter C Corporation. "Subchapter C" means the corporation is taxed as a separate legal entity by the federal and state governments. Therefore, it is subject to restrictions on recognizing income and on taking deductions, as specified by the tax code.

Although this tax structure is a benefit to large corporations, there are some drawbacks to being taxed as a C corporation, namely:

- If the corporation pays dividends to its shareholders, its net income is taxed twice: at the corporate level and at the individual level (dividends are considered income to the shareholder).
- In some circumstances, the corporate tax rates are higher than individual tax rates.

Subchapter S Corporation. S corps offer liability protection to the owners like C corps, yet the income isn't taxed twice. Instead of being taxed as a separate legal entity, its net income is included in the taxable income of the shareholders. Therefore, an S corp's net income is taxed at the individual tax rates.

S corps have very complex tax rules. More and more businesses are moving toward limited liability corporation (LLC) status to get the same benefit as an S corp instead.

LIMITED LIABILITY CORPORATION (LLC)

A limited liability corporation is not really a corporation, but is instead a crossbreed: part partnership, part corporation. It's similar to a partnership in its formation requirements, but it gives owners protection from personal liability (i.e., it doesn't put an owner's personal assets at risk), which is similar to normal corporations.
An LLC does has three basic characteristics in common with a corporation:

1. Limited liability.
2. Central management.
3. Interest that is easily transferred.

An LLC is similar to a partnership in that it has a limited life.

This type of corporation is particularly advantageous for small businesses for two reasons:

- You don't have to go through all the documentation required of a corporation on an ongoing basis.
- You can elect to be treated as a partnership or a C corp under federal and state income tax rules, depending on which type provides the best tax solution in your situation.

In some states, partnerships are taxed differently than corporations, making it advantageous even for a large company to convert to an LLC.

In an LLC, owners can receive a salary or share profits.

- If the LLC is treated as a corporation for tax purposes, you pay a salary and Federal tax and FICA are withheld.
- If it's treated as a partnership for tax purposes, you pay distributions of profits, and the general partners are subject to self-employment tax on their portion of net taxable income (which may be different from the distribution amount).

Requirements for an LLC include articles of incorporation and registration documents. An LLC must be registered with the state. Requirements differ from state to state.

MEMBERS OF AN LLC

Owners are called members, and there is usually a chief member who functions like a president of a corporation. Some states restrict LLCs to two or more owners, but some states do allow single owners.

OTHER INFORMATION

Pass-Through Entities

Partnerships, S corps, and LLCs that have elected to be treated as partnerships are called *pass-through* entities. This means the entity is not required to pay income tax. Instead, the income is included in the owner's federal income tax return.

Pass-through entities are required to file an information return; they just don't pay tax.

Initial Public Offering (IPO)

When a privately held company decides to go public, it notifies the Securities and Exchange Commission that it wants to sell shares to the public. The SEC examines the accuracy of the information submitted and then grants or denies the right to trade shares of the company's stock.

The SEC requires companies to send potential buyers a *prospectus,* which is like a business plan. It includes financial information and other data about the company that could affect its potential and could therefore influence an investor's decision to buy.

To determine what price the stock should sell for, the company seeks an outside appraisal of its worth. Usually all available shares are pre-sold at a specified price. These pre-sold shares are called *subscription shares.* The investors who buy these early shares take a huge risk, because there is no way to know whether the IPO will be successful or whether the company will fail. To compensate these risk takers, the company releases the stock to the public at a higher price than they paid for the shares. Thus, people who have put their faith in the company are rewarded.

PIERCING THE CORPORATE VEIL

Under the law, a legal corporate entity can't be thrown out in order to reach owners to satisfy debt. In some rare circumstances, however, the courts have "pierced the corporate veil" when there was fraud or another significant unusual event contributing to the debt. (This usually occurs if owners are treating corporate assets like personal assets and mixing the two. Then the courts can truly state the corporation isn't a separate entity but only an extension of the owners.) Such a situation usually would relate to a private company rather than a public one.

INVESTING IN A PUBLIC COMPANY

Investors buy shares of ownership in a public company with the intention that they will make money over the long term. Their goal is to buy a stock that has the potential to increase in price. When the price climbs, the stockholder may sell it and enjoy a profit of the difference between the price paid and the price received. Thus, the oversimplified (and facetious) advice, "Buy low, sell high."

Strangely enough, whenever someone wants to sell a widely traded stock, there is usually a buyer.

RETURN ON INVESTMENT: TWO POINTS OF VIEW

You can consider return on investment (ROI) from two different perspectives that have no correlation to each other:

- *Company perspective.* The company's ROI may be from an overall evaluation of how the company is doing (i.e., its earnings) or from the point of view of ROI on individual projects. How the company performs (its ROI) can affect the market price of its stock; however, the company does not get any direct money from the increase in stock price.
- *Shareholder's perspective.* A shareholder purchases the stock on the open market at a certain price. The payback for that purchase

may be dividends paid by the company or an increase in the price of the stock, which thereby increases the value of the stock to the shareholder. Thus, the shareholder's ROI is dividends and capital appreciation.

Two Ways to Reward Shareholders

A corporation may reward its shareholders in two ways:

- Short-term, through the payment of stock dividends.
- Long-term, through reinvestment that results in their stock being higher valued.

(Some shareholders would prefer not to receive dividends, because they are considered regular income and are taxed at a higher tax rate than capital gains.)

DIVIDENDS

One way a company shares its success with owners is by paying dividends. On a quarterly basis, the board of directors evaluates the company's performance and decides, based on management's recommendation, whether to issue a dividend. The decision is based on how well the company is performing financially. If the company is enjoying profits, it usually shares a portion of them with the owners, agreeing to pay a certain amount of money per share to anyone who held the stock on the *record date.*

The *payout date* is the day the actual dividend is paid.

A dividend is paid per share owned. For example, if a company declares a $.50 dividend, the owner will receive $.50 for every share she owns on the record date.

If a company is not doing well, it may bypass paying a dividend for that quarter and possibly for several quarters.

(Note: A company that usually pays dividends will think long and hard before decreasing dividends or not declaring them at all, because this has a long-term adverse affect on the stock price.)

CAPITAL APPRECIATION

Another reason for not paying a dividend is that the company may reinvest the money in the company, with the goal of increasing the value of its stock long-term. This is another way of rewarding shareholders, who will benefit from the increased stock price. When the money is reinvested and the value increases, this is called *capital appreciation.*

There are times when the company doesn't pay dividends, but the stock price also does not go up. If that situation continues over some period of time, stockholders will probably not look favorably on the strategy.

Chapter 21

TYPES OF INVESTMENT

Investing is using money to make money. Investors today have a wide range of choices to use to increase their wealth. Some people choose to invest in tangible things, such as real estate or antiques, assets that they expect will increase in value. Others choose assets such as securities, which are a means of having ownership in a company or extending credit to a company.

There are many types of securities, including stocks, bonds, and mutual funds. Some types of securities, including stock, offer a degree of involvement in the company's operation, such as voting privileges, whereas other investments represent a more passive form of ownership.

This chapter is intended as an overview of information about investing only. It is not to be considered an endorsement of any investment philosophy or method. Opinions vary dramatically with regard to the advisability of any investment, and we do not recommend any particular investment stance.

TYPES OF PAYBACK

Why do people invest in securities? To increase their wealth. For the payback. Average investors can potentially earn a payback on their investment in one of three ways:

- Dividends.
- Interest.
- Capital appreciation.

DIVIDENDS

Dividends are payments made to stockholders from a corporation's earnings or profits. Dividends may be prescribed to be paid at certain times, often quarterly, as with preferred stock.

If a company is doing well, the board of directors, at its discretion, may decide to pay a dividend to common stockholders based on the profit of the company. How much each shareholder receives depends upon the number of shares he owns because dividends are paid as a certain amount per share outstanding (for example, $0.05 per share).

FOUR KEY DIVIDEND DATES

There are four key dates associated with the issuing and payment of dividends:

1. ***Declaration date.*** This is the date on which the dividend is announced.
2. ***Record date.*** The shareholders of record, that is, all those who own stock on this day, are the ones who will receive the dividend payment.
3. ***Ex-dividend date.*** This is the time between the announcement and the payment of the next dividend. Anyone who buys stock during this time will probably pay a higher price for the stock because of the dividend he will receive.
4. ***Payment date.*** This is the day on which the dividend is actually paid, usually several weeks after the record date.

The board may choose not to issue a dividend. Instead, it may choose to reinvest the earnings or profits in the company rather than pay dividends to shareholders. This decision, hopefully, will increase the value of the shareholders' investment over time by strengthening the company.

INTEREST

Interest is a set percentage that is paid based on the amount of an investment (for a credit security such as a bond). There are two types of interest:

- Simple interest.
- Compound interest.

SIMPLE INTEREST

With *simple interest,* you're only paid a percentage on the principal you've invested. For example, if you invest $10,000 at 10% interest annually, you would earn $1,000 in a year.

COMPOUND INTEREST

If you invest the interest in the security (which you can do with mutual funds), you'll receive interest on the principal plus the interest that you've reinvested. This is called *compound interest.*

To figure compound interest, you must know two things:

- The interest rate being paid.
- How often the interest is computed and added to your account.

For example, if you invest $1,000 at 10% interest compounded *daily,* then every day your interest would be added to your account. Therefore, the first day you would earn $0.27 ($1,000 × 0.10 ÷ 365 days), and your account balance becomes $1,000.27. The second day, you would earn $0.28 ($1,000.27 × 0.10 ÷ 365 days).

If you invest $1,000 at 10% interest compounded *quarterly,* you would earn $25 the first quarter ($1,000 × 0.10 ÷ 4 quarters), $25.63 the second quarter ($1,025 × 0.10 ÷ 4 quarters), $26.27 the third quarter ($1,050.63 × 0.10 ÷ 4 quarters), and $26.92 the fourth quarter ($1,076.90 × 0.10 ÷ 4 quarters). The value of your investment at the end of one year would be $1,103.82, which is your original investment with the addition of the interest you earned each quarter.

CAPITAL APPRECIATION

The third way to profit from an investment is from the increased value over time. (Note: The only way to benefit is to actually sell the asset.) Capital appreciation occurs when you sell something for a higher price than you paid for it. For instance, if you buy 100 shares of stock at $25 per share and you sell them at $35 per share, you have then earned capital gains of $1,000 [100 shares × ($35 – $25)], the difference between what you paid for it and your selling price.

INVESTMENT STRATEGIES

If you decide to invest in securities, the first step to take is to decide what kind of payback you require, because that will determine what type of securities you purchase. For example, if you're a younger person saving for retirement, you have a long time over which to accumulate retirement income, so you can afford to take a fairly aggressive strategy. And if you're older (and, therefore, closer to retirement) you might need to take a more conservative (less risky) approach, so you don't lose the money you've already saved. As you can see, your goals will dictate your strategy. (Risk means your potential to lose money.)

Naturally, retirement isn't the only reason people want to make money. Other reasons include saving for a new home, putting kids through college, and just accumulating wealth. Circumstances dictate what type of payback the investor needs to achieve, and then guide the investor with the selection of investments for

- Low risk and low income.
- Medium risk and slightly higher income.
- High risk with potentially even greater income.

MARKET TIMING VERSUS BUY-AND-HOLD

Investors tend to use one of two market strategies regarding their philosophy of investing. One is an active stance, in which the investor participates and manages the investments. The other is a more passive stance, in which the investor prefers to have less involvement in the investment activities.

1. ***Market timing.*** Some people might see investing in stocks or other securities as a way to get rich quickly. They try to time their buying and selling of stocks to take advantage of rises and falls of the market (i.e., buy low, sell high).
2. ***Buy-and-hold.*** Others believe that while the market may rise and fall short-term, over the long term it will provide adequate returns. Therefore, rather than buying and selling stocks quickly, they maintain their investments despite short-term results. (Note: One method of practicing this philosophy is to allocate a certain

amount of money each month to buy a stock, no matter what the price is. When the price is low, the investor gets more shares; when it's high, fewer shares. This practice is called *dollar cost averaging* or *constant dollar plan.)*

FACTORS IN SELECTING AN INVESTMENT

When you've determined what type of strategy you want to pursue, you can then take these other factors into consideration.

- ***Price.*** There are investments to suit every pocketbook. Very-low-price stocks can become stars. Those who bought Microsoft, FedEx, and IBM in the early days were certainly rewarded for their faith in the unknown. Those stocks today are high-ticket stocks, and, while established firms like these tend to offer a steady payback, the opportunity for huge gains is less likely than with start-up companies or younger organizations. However, these "cheap" investments could also carry huge risks.
- ***Minimum investment.*** Some financial instruments, such as mutual funds, require a minimum front-end investment. If you have limited cash, you'll have to select one that has no such requirements.
- ***Interest or yield.*** There is a wide range of potential return on your investment depending on the type of securities you buy. Typically, the safer the investment, the lower the rate of interest or yield. People looking for high returns will usually have to assume a higher risk. On the other hand, safer bets tend to provide low but steady gains.
- ***Risk.*** As we said above, generally speaking, the investments with the highest level of risk also offer the highest potential return (with heavy emphasis on the word *potential* because risk implies no guarantees). (Note: By observing a person's investing patterns, chances are you have a clue to his personality: high rollers versus the risk averse!)
- ***Timing.*** Investments tie up money for varying degrees of time, from days to years, and some have penalties for early withdrawal.

The date an investment comes due, expires, or becomes available to the investor is called its *maturity date.* This factor will weigh heavily with an investor who wants to maintain quick access to assets. Also, timing can affect your investment because of inflation. You must weigh the investment return with the potential inflation rate over the period of time. If prices are rising at a higher rate than your investment, you're losing money.

- ***Tax incentives or liabilities.*** Different types of investments have different requirements in terms of tax reporting and payment. For instance, some municipal bonds are tax-free. To weigh the real value of an investment, you must take into consideration your own tax position and how the investment return—or lack thereof—will affect your financial position in regard to paying taxes.

PORTFOLIOS

The combination of an investor's investments (securities, real estate, and cash) are called the *portfolio.* Frequently, advisors recommend having a diversified portfolio, meaning a balance of high-, medium-, and low-risk investments, a variety of stocks and bonds, or a combination of stocks from different industries that are not all dependent on the same factors for their success. This diversified approach is intended to reduce the risk associated with putting all your eggs in one basket.

STOCKS

Stocks are segments of ownership of public companies. An investor may buy a share of stock for a price, in hopes that the price will ultimately increase. Stocks are somewhat risky, because there is no guarantee the stock price will increase. In fact, there is always the possibility that it will decrease below the price the investor paid. When that happens, the investor could take a loss if he sells the stock at that point. If the investor holds the stock, the price could rise later.

Stock Splits

When a stock price rises, a company's board of directors may decide that it is too high-priced to be affordable for investors. As a result, the board may declare a *stock split* and give existing shareholders more than one share of stock for every share owned. The total value of all their shares does not change; only the number of shares does. For example, if the board declares a 2-for-1 split, a stockholder with 100 shares would now own 200 shares. If the stockholder paid $100 per share for the 100 original shares, the original purchase price of the 200 shares becomes $50 per share.

The board can declare any type of split it wants: 2-for 2, 3-for-1, or even 4-for-1. A stock split reduces the price of the stock proportionately, enabling more people to buy shares. This, in turn, pushes the stock price back up.

Historically, when a stock splits, the price begins to rise again soon, which can make it attractive to buy immediately after a split, before the price goes up.

Reverse Stock Splits

There are also times when the board believes that a company's stock is selling too cheaply. If so, the board may declare a *reverse stock split,* which cuts the number of shares each person owns. The result is that the stock price rises. For example, in a 1-for-2 split, a stockholder with 100 shares would now own 50 shares. If he originally paid $30 per share, the original purchase price of the 50 shares becomes $60 per share (i.e., the amount of money invested doesn't change, but the number of shares is reduced).

Dividend Reinvestment Plans

Some companies offer dividend reinvestment plans (DRIPs). A DRIP allows a stockholder to take dividends paid and automatically use them to purchase additional shares of the same stock.

Frequently, the company will absorb the brokerage fees or even sell the stock at a discount to the market price. To take advantage of such a savings, you must buy a share of the stock in your own name (not the brokerage or street name) and take delivery of your stock certificate.

COMMODITIES

Commodities are mining or agricultural products that are sold in large quantities. This includes items such as corn, coffee, sugar, gold, silver, and cotton. They are sold in segments called *contracts.*

Commodities are traded through markets similar to stock exchanges. Two of the largest U. S. markets are the Chicago Board of Trade and the Commodity Exchange in New York.

BONDS

When an organization wants to raise a large amount of money, it may sell bonds in small increments to many investors. Bonds do not give the buyer any ownership in the organization; instead, they are a type of loan with a specified date of maturity. Maturity dates are often as long as 10 or 15 years from the date of issuance. Organizations that issue bonds include the federal government, municipalities, and public companies.

A bond issuer makes two promises to the people who buy its bonds:

- It promises to pay the face value of the bond at the maturity date.
- It promises to pay a stated interest or interest rate at certain intervals during the life of the bond.

Bonds are often seen as more stable investments than stocks because their value is more guaranteed and because they have set interest payments. Don't forget, though, that organizations do go out of business without paying all their debts. Nothing is 100% certain.

There are several potential drawbacks in purchasing bonds:

- The interest rate may be lower than for other investments. Once again, in most instances, the greater the security of the investment, the lower the return.
- The bond may be callable, which means the organization that issued it can repay the loan in full at any time. (This is most likely to happen when the stated interest rate is higher than the market bond rate.) This essentially cuts off your potential for growth over the long term.

- Bond holders may actually be adversely affected by strong economic conditions or by inflation, because bonds are usually held over a long period of time. For example, if you purchase a bond that will pay a 10% return, and inflation is high, your payback may be eaten away by the increased cost of living. In other words, the time value of money will work against you.

Most bond trading is done over the counter. When the issuing company pays back the bonds, it is called a *redemption.*

Value of a Bond

There are several terms to describe the value of a bond: *principal, face value,* and *par value.* They all mean the stated amount on the bond that will be paid at maturity.

Commercial Paper

Companies with a need for short-term capital may issue *commercial paper.* These are fairly high-priced notes that mature in 30 to 270 days. Usually, commercial paper is expensive and is purchased primarily by mutual funds or institutional investors.

The Indenture

The legal document that describes the terms of a bond or commercial paper is called the *indenture.* This document prescribes the requirements made of the company in order to live up to the promises made to the investors. It includes a description of any property used as collateral for the loan as well as specifications about the interest payments and other features. It may also describe conditions that restrict the company's ability to take on other debt, and other factors that could affect its ability to pay what it owes to the bond owners.

Default

If the issuer of a bond doesn't meet one or all of the stipulations in the indenture, the company is considered in default, and the entire loan comes due immediately. We're accustomed to hearing of default if people don't pay their interest or principal. In the case of bonds it may have nothing to do with payments. It can mean that the company has failed to do something associated with the indenture or else has done something prohibited, such as taking on other debt when that is forbidden.

TYPES OF BONDS

There are quite a variety of bonds:

- *Treasuries* (T-bills, T-bonds, and T-notes issued by the federal government). These are debts to the U. S. government. They are considered more stable than other types of bonds because they are backed by the U. S. government. The differences in the three are maturity times, timing of interest payments, and minimum investment requirements.
- *Savings bonds.* These are sold at a discount and at maturity can be redeemed for their face value. For instance, a $100 bond might be sold at $25 and redeemed in 20 years for its $100 face value.
- *Zero-coupon bonds.* These bonds are also sold at a discount and don't pay interest annually. Their interest accrues and is paid all at once at the maturity date.
- *Certificates of deposit (CDs).* These are receipts issued by a bank for investments in increments of $1,000 or $10,000, for which the bank pays a set rate of interest for a set period of time. When you buy a CD, you agree to give the bank the money for a certain period of time, usually no less than 60 days and ranging up to five years. The longer you agree to leave the money untouched, the higher the interest rate. If you choose to withdraw the money before its maturity date, you sacrifice a portion of your interest earned as a penalty for early withdrawal. *Jumbo CDs* are sold in increments of $100,000.
- *Municipal bonds* (local or state government). Municipal bonds are debt issued by the local or state government, typically to fund a specific project. These bonds pay interest, and the proceeds are tax-exempt from federal income tax.
- *Asset-backed securities.* These are securities backed by collateral such as mortgages or car loans. The most familiar asset-backed securities are Ginny Maes and Fannie Maes (real estate) and Sallie Maes (student loans).
- *Corporate bonds.* Corporate bonds are issued by corporations and pay interest also.

Yield

Part of deciding what type of investment to purchase lies in evaluating its true return. Bonds have a life over a relatively long period of time, so you must compute their value not only today but also in terms of what they will be worth when they mature. There are, thus, three measures of a bond's worth:

- ***Coupon rate.*** For a bond, the annual interest rate at which it is sold is called its coupon rate. The coupon rate does not change over the life of a bond.
- ***Current yield.*** Current yield takes into account the bond's price (at a premium or discount to face value) as well as the stated interest rate. To figure yield, divide the annual interest payment by the price of the bond. If the bond is for $1,000, the annual return at 5% interest is $50. The yield is 0.05, or 5% ($50 ÷ $1,000). If the same bond price was only $900 (i.e., it was sold at a $100 discount to its face value of $1,000), the yield is 0.056, (5.6%). Note: When the bond is sold at face value, the yield always equals the stated interest rate.
- ***Yield to maturity (YTM).*** YTM is the annual return assuming the bond is held until its maturity date, and taking into consideration the interest payments and any price premiums or discounts. (For more information on premiums and discounts, see Chapter 8, "Long-Term Liabilities.")

Trustees

A company typically appoints an outside source, called a trustee, to manage its bonds, communicate with owners, and make sure that the interest payments are made and funds are appropriately disbursed. The trustee takes action on behalf of the bond owners if the company defaults on the bond. A trustee is usually a bank.

Bond Ratings

How can an investor know whether a bond is a good investment? There are several firms such as Standard & Poor's and Moody's that rate bonds according to their value, safety, and potential for return. When bonds are issued, they are ranked on a scale ranging from highest quality, AAA (triple-A), to lowest, C. The lowest-quality bonds are called *junk bonds,* and they carry a high return and high risk.

CONVERTIBLE BONDS

Convertible bonds are those that can be swapped for shares of stock of the issuing corporation. The bondholder can choose to convert at any time at a predetermined rate of exchange. For example, if the bond is worth $1,000 and the conversion rate is $50 per share, the bondholder would receive 20 shares of stock in exchange for the bonds. Some high-risk bonds include a convertible feature to make them more attractive.

OPTIONS (OR DERIVATIVES)

Options are opportunities to buy and sell any assets, including stock, at specified prices for a payment (called a premium). If an investor has an option, that means he *may* buy or sell the stock at a price that's locked in until a specified date, but he is not required to buy it.

Options are traded on options markets, just like stocks. As such, they are known as a derivative of the underlying stock. Options prices move up and down with the price of the underlying stock; however, they are more risky than the stock because they have an expiration date. The value of the option naturally declines as it gets closer to the expiration date.

There are four things you can do with options:

- Exercise your option at maturity. If you hold an option until the stated time of maturity, you can buy it at the price you were quoted, even if the price has gone up.
- Exercise your option before maturity. If you exercise the option before maturity, you buy the stock at the option price, which may be higher or lower than the market price of the stock.
- Let the option expire. If the option matures and the price is unfavorable, you don't have to buy it at all; however, once it has matured, your contract expires and you no longer have the right to buy the stock.

- Sell the option before maturity. Since options are traded, you may be able to sell the option for a higher price than what you paid for it.

Calls and Puts

- ***Call option.*** This is the right to buy *x* shares of stock at a specified price.
- ***Put option.*** This is the right to sell *x* shares of stock at a specified price.

Both call and put options are sold in contracts of 100 shares per contract. Thus, 10 contracts is the equivalent of 1,000 shares of stock.

The price of an option is its *premium.* It's the price an investor pays in order to hold the option.

Executive Stock Option Plans

Companies frequently give executives stock options for their own company to accomplish one or several of four things:

- To motivate an executive to come to work for the organization.
- To compensate executives for performance.
- To create a sense of ownership, which serves as an incentive to the executive to help the company improve its performance.
- To encourage the executive to remain at the company. Usually, if the person leaves the company, the options are forfeited.

Companies have found that stock options are an effective way to attract and retain management personnel.

Futures Contracts

A futures contract is a type of option that you might purchase for stock, foreign currency or commodities. In most instances, buyers who deal with commodities don't ever intend to take ownership of what they've purchased. They speculate on what the price of a commodity may be at a later date, and then they purchase a contract based on the speculative price. This is called buying a *futures contract* or *buying futures.*

Buying futures is a high-risk investment because when you buy or sell a futures contract, you are essentially betting on the price of the commodity going up or down by a certain date. Many futures rely upon highly unpredictable factors such as weather, which can adversely affect the future value of a commodity. For example, if the South has a long rainy season followed by a drought, the cotton crop might be adversely affected, which would subsequently raise the future price of cotton.

OPTIONS CLEARING CORPORATION (OCC)

The Options Clearing Corporation (OCC) is the only official clearinghouse for options contracts in the United States. The OCC is approved by the SEC.

MONEY MARKETS

Money market investments are like savings accounts and are good for short-term investment (due in one year) purposes. They usually require some minimum level of deposit, and they limit the number of times each month you can perform transactions. While they offer low returns, they are also highly secure. Some companies use money markets as overnight investments for their excess cash.

INVESTMENT FUNDS

Some investments may be too expensive for the smaller investor (the person with a small amount of money to invest.) That's where investment funds become useful. Investment funds are companies that buy diverse investments in large volume. These may include stocks, bonds, options, futures, currencies, or money market securities.

Investment funds allow small investors to own a more diverse group of investments than they might be able to on their own with limited funds.

Money managers are the people who oversee investment funds, deciding to buy or sell investments in the best interest of the overall group. There are quite a number of companies that sell funds. Some of the most widely known are Fidelity, Vanguard, Dreyfus, and Janus.

Fund Goals

Investment funds are like pot luck: they combine a variety of high- and low-risk investments in the same group of ownership. A fund will tend to follow one of three types of investment philosophies:

- ***Aggressive growth.*** These funds invest in companies that have the highest growth over time.
- ***Growth.*** These funds are more conservative and invest in steady, blue-chip types of stocks.
- ***Growth and income.*** These funds balance a desire for investments that provide stability with the desire to take a risk to earn higher dividends.

Anyone considering investing in a fund should select one that matches their own investment goals and risk tolerance.

Cash-to-Assets Ratio

Like individuals who invest for themselves, various fund managers have different investing philosophies as well. Investment funds include both cash and securities. The fund manager may invest more or less money in cash instruments depending on his view of the stock market. Typically, a fund manager who is bullish (believes the market is healthy) will invest more in stocks than in cash instruments if the fund guidelines allow him to, because he thinks stock or bond prices will rise. A fund manager whose stand is bearish (who has less faith in the market's stability) will safeguard more money in cash.

In reviewing a fund's position, some people like to look at its cash-to-assets ratio. This compares the amount of money the manager has invested in cash with the amount invested in stock. When a manager has more than 10% invested in cash, that is considered a large cash position.

Two Types of Investment Funds

CLOSED-END MUTUAL FUNDS

Closed-end funds are funds that have a designated number of shares of stock and amount of debt that do not increase. A closed-end fund has a limited number of shares so when all the stock and debt is owned, no one else can invest unless one of the owners is willing to sell a portion. The price of closed-end funds fluctuates much like stock because of this supply-and-demand issue. Therefore, the price may not reflect the value of the fund.

OPEN-END MUTUAL FUNDS

Open-end funds are similar to closed-end mutual funds in that they also invest in a diverse group of securities. One major difference, however, is that they allow investors to buy in at any time. The company receives the investor's money and then purchases stock or bonds with those funds. The "buy-in" price of the open-end fund depends on

- Value of the fund.
- How many investors want to take their money out.

An open fund manager may have to liquidate some of the funds' positions if many investors want out of the fund, because the fund pays the investors their money. Therefore, open funds can grow in assets or shrink depending upon market conditions and investor expectations.

INVESTMENT FUND FEES

There may be several types of fees charged for investment funds:

- ***12b fees,*** known also as management fees.
- ***Loads,*** or commissions on the purchase or sale of fund shares. A *no-load fund* is a fund that simply charges no fee for purchasing or selling the fund.

FUND RETURNS

There are several ways in which funds provide a return:

- ***Dividends.*** These result from income paid by the investments. Dividends may be paid monthly, quarterly, or annually.
- ***Interest.***
- ***Capital appreciation.*** When the fund manager sells units of the fund at a higher value than the purchase price, the owners benefit.

However, owners can also receive losses if the fund manager is forced to sell at a bad time. This might happen if investors want to leave the fund and the manager is obligated to give them their money.

The investment fund manager reinvests interest and funds from capital appreciation in the fund, and investors pay income tax on the returns.

Investment Company Institute (ICI)

This is the largest mutual fund trade group. Each month, the ICI publishes the cash-to-assets ratio for every mutual fund group.

INDEX SHARES OR EXCHANGE-TRADED FUNDS

An increasingly popular investment option is index shares. These are another type of derivative on stocks, but they are similar to investment funds.

Index shares work like mutual funds, but they are traded like stocks. They are priced constantly, and they can be bought and sold anytime during the day.

For example, an investor who buys SPDR, called "spider" (the Standard & Poor's Depositary Receipt), buys a tiny portion of the stocks that comprise Standard and Poor's 500 stocks.

Other index shares that are widely known are

- Diamonds from Dow Jones Industrial Average.
- QQQs (or cubes) from the NASDAQ 100.
- HOLDRs (Holding Company Depository Receipts) from Merrill Lynch.
- VIPERs (Vanguard Index Participation Equity Receipts).

Obviously, their names come from the indices they represent.

Index Fund Listings

Index shares are traded on the stock market just like stock, and they have similar symbols. Here are some major index shares:

DJX—Dow Jones Industrial

SPX—S&P 500

OEX—S&P 100

RUT—Russell 200

NDX—NASDAQ 100

MSH—high tech index

XCI—hardware index

CWX—software index

SOX—semiconductor index

NWX—networking computer index

INX—Internet index

BIX—banking index

XBD—brokerage index

IUX—insurance index

RLX—retail index

DRG—drug index

HCX—healthcare index

XAL—airline index

OIX—oil and gas index

XAU—gold and silver index

Chapter 22

STOCK EXCHANGES AND RATING AGENCIES

STOCK MARKETS

The stock exchanges are like trading posts, where buyers and sellers come together to dicker for goods. People who want to invest in securities go through one of several stock markets, using brokers to buy and sell corporate stocks and bonds for them. The stock exchange itself doesn't own the stock; it merely serves as a venue for transactions to take place. Corporations list their stocks with these stock markets, and the brokers serve as intermediaries.

HOW STOCK EXCHANGES WORK

Some stock markets still consist of a huge open floor where brokers yell out their buy and sell bids to representatives of companies that issue stocks and bonds. In some exchanges, however, this in-person, frantic auction activity is being replaced by an electronic trading process where buying and selling happen lightning fast and don't depend upon a broker's lung power and tenacity.

MARKET SECURITY

Because the trading of stock is a highly regulated business, stock exchanges are under constant surveillance for abuses. Much of the surveillance activity is conducted by the exchanges themselves. They carefully monitor unusual trading patterns or significant price or volume changes because these can be warning signals of abuse.

TRADING TIMES

Stock exchanges are open at different times, but the American Exchange (AMEX) and New York Stock Exchange (NYSE), the two largest exchanges, operate on Eastern time, and are open Monday through Friday from 9:30 A.M. to 4:00 P.M. The exchanges recognize the standard U.S. holidays, but vary in their specific observance schedules. One might be open for a partial day, until 1 P.M., while the other might be closed for the entire day.

There are unusual instances when a company's stock might not be traded because of a serious event that could have drastic consequences for its stockholders—for example, a company disaster such as a fire, a lawsuit being filed, or the company president being in a fatal accident. The company might ask that trading of its stock be suspended until a press release could be issued giving the facts of the situation. In the absence of official information, stockholders could be making decisions about buying and selling that would be ill-advised.

In other rare instances, the SEC might stipulate that the company suspend trading of its stock because it has not followed the SEC regulations in some way. This might involve not filing required reports or not disclosing pertinent information in a timely way, or there might be evidence of insider trading.

There are special circumstances when the markets close early because of extreme events that could dramatically affect the trading of stocks—for example, an outbreak of war or other major civil disturbance, or the assassination of the U.S. President.

STOCK EXCHANGE MEMBERSHIP

The U.S. stock market is the world's largest, and there are a number of major companies that serve as listing agencies and places to exchange or sell stocks. Some of the top U.S. exchanges are

1. NYSE
2. AMEX
3. Boston Stock Exchange (BSE)
4. Cincinnati Stock Exchange (CSE)

5. Chicago Stock Exchange (CHX)
6. Pacific Exchange: stock and options (PCX)
7. Philadelphia Stock Exchange (PHLX)
8. NASDAQ Stock Market

(Although separate, the NASDAQ and AMEX are a part of one corporate organization.)

To be listed on a stock exchange, a company must buy a *seat,* or place, on the stock exchange floor and must meet certain minimum standards regarding its

- Number of shares publicly held.
- Market value of the shares.
- Number of stockholders.
- Net income level.
- Asset book value.

A stock may be listed on more than one exchange.

New York Stock Exchange (NYSE)

The New York Stock Exchange is far and away the largest securities exchange in the world. Founded in 1792, the exchange lists thousands of publicly traded stocks.

The first company listed on the NYSE was the Bank of New York. The company with the longest listing history is Con Edison, which was first listed in 1824 as the New York Gas Light Company.

American Stock Exchange (AMEX)

The first firm to go public on the American Stock Exchange was Donaldson, Lufkin & Jenrette in 1970. The AMEX lists middle- to small-size companies.

NASDAQ

Founded in 1971, the National Association of Securities Dealers Automated Quota System was the world's first electronic stock market. Rather than trade on a giant trading floor, NASDAQ is a giant network that trades over-the-counter stocks.

NASDAQ was formed as a result of an SEC review that began in 1963 and subsequently found weaknesses in the over-the-counter securities market. To make trading more consistent and stable, the SEC recommended an automated system and charged the NASD with creating it. In 1998, the NASD and the American Stock Exchange (AMEX) entered a partnership to provide such a service.

OVER-THE-COUNTER (OTC)

The over-the-counter (OTC) market comprises mostly stocks of small companies and companies that don't meet the minimum requirements of the major exchanges. Some OTC stock is not traded every day, which means you won't necessarily find a buyer when you're ready to sell.

STOCK LISTINGS

Most daily newspapers show stock listings in their business section each day for the preceding day. (Because the markets aren't open on weekends, there are no listings on Sunday and Monday.) These listings represent every publicly traded stock in a consolidated listing for all the stock exchanges.

Listings include

- The company's ticker symbol (stock trading symbol). For example, the symbol for American Express is AXP. Stocks listed on the NYSE and AMEX have three-letter symbols; those on NASDAQ have four-letter symbols.
- The 52-week high and low selling prices.
- The price at the close of the market the preceding day.
- The amount the price changed the preceding day and over the week. The amount of change is shown in $\frac{1}{32}$, $\frac{1}{16}$, $\frac{1}{8}$, $\frac{1}{4}$, $\frac{1}{2}$, and whole number increments.(For instance, a stock price that went from $23\frac{1}{8}$ to $24\frac{1}{16}$ would be shown as $+\frac{15}{16}$.) Note: Currently the stock exchanges are converting to a decimal system.
- The percentage that a stock price has changed for the year to date.

RATING AGENCIES

Few investors have the time or resources to examine all of the pertinent information about a company or investment fund that might influence their decisions about investing. For that reason, there are a number of rating agencies that do research and report on their findings. For example, companies collect information about corporations such as their debt level, whether they pay their bills on time and their historical financial performance to determine whether they believe the company is a good investment or a good risk. Dun & Bradstreet is one rating company that is widely known. You may hear someone say, "Let's buy a D&B," meaning they will hire Dun & Bradstreet to research the company's background and deliver a detailed report.

Some ratings companies specialize in one industry, such as insurance. Others may specialize in types of investments. Morningstar Mutual Funds and Wiesenburger are two that address the mutual fund industry, and AM Best deals with insurance companies.

INDUSTRY DESIGNATIONS

For the purpose of taxation, census information, and other government concerns, the U.S. Department of Commerce for many years assigned Standard Industrial Classification codes (numbers) to types of businesses. Since 1997, however, there has been a new system called the North American Industry Classification System (NAICS). This system is standard for Canada, the U.S., and Mexico, which allows analysis of statistics from all three areas.

THE SIX-DIGIT CODE

The six-digit NAICS code is divided into several sections:

- First two digits: a major economic sector.
- Third digit: economic subsector.
- Fourth digit: industry group.
- Fifth digit: industry.

- Sixth digit: May be specific to the country's needs for additional classification. (Note: Not all countries use six digits.)

The NAICS is also compatible with an international system, the International Standard Industrial Classification System (ISIC), under the auspices of the United Nations.

(The National Technical Information Service of the U.S. Department of Commerce can provide more information.)

As described by the NAICS, there are three types of business:

- ***Service.*** A company provides a service for a price. Service companies include medical organizations, law firms, hotels and airlines, and accounting or financial management firms.
- ***Merchandising.*** A company buys products and resells them either to another company or to a customer. Merchandisers are companies such as retail clothing stores and auto dealers. Within the general category of merchandising, there are two subcategories: distributors, who don't pay sales tax, and retailers, who do.
- ***Manufacturing.*** A company buys raw materials and manufactures a product and sells it either to another business or to a customer. These include, for example, cereal companies, furniture manufacturers, and computer hardware firms.

FOLLOWING THE MARKETS

The securities market is of major interest to a great number of people who try to predict, quantify, and participate in what happens with various stocks and bonds. There are a number of indices, publications, and services that follow the markets, thereby serving as bellwethers for what's happening to the economy as a whole.

Chapter 23

TRADING

PEOPLE WHO TRADE SECURITIES

You can buy securities from different types of organizations that charge a myriad of fees and offer a wide range of service levels. Because the securities industry is strictly regulated, some of the people who participate must be registered. (See Chapter 12 for qualifications and requirements.)

FULL-SERVICE BROKERS AND BROKER-DEALERS

Full-service brokers are professional stock traders who negotiate the buying and selling of stock at a profit or for a commission. The broker's job is to bring together buyers and sellers, acting as a registered agent (certified) to facilitate the sale.

A broker-dealer purchases inventory and then resells it to the customer. Unlike a broker, a dealer actually buys the stock and runs the risk of not being able to sell it.

You have certainly heard these familiar names in the brokerage industry: Smith Barney, Merrill Lynch, and Prudential.

FULL-SERVICE DISCOUNT BROKERS

These brokers offer limited services to investors at a reduced fee. While they provide the services of bringing together buyers and sellers, they often don't do the research and recommendations that a full-service broker would. You might choose a discount broker for one of several reasons:

- If you're a small investor, you may not want or be able to afford the higher commissions/fees charged by full-service brokers.
- If you're an educated investor, you may feel that you're capable of selecting the securities yourself without the advice of a broker.

Some of the better known discount brokers are Charles Schwab, Fidelity Investments, and Quick and Reilly.

COMMISSIONS AND FEES

Brokers and planners earn their money in any of several ways:

1. ***Commissions.*** Brokers may be paid a percentage based on the products an investor buys or sells. In these cases, they may not charge anything for planning, but only for what you buy and sell.
2. ***Fee-only.*** Brokers who work on a fee-only basis may be paid a percentage fee based on your portfolio amount or an hourly fee for work done.
3. ***Fee and commission.*** These brokers charge a fee for a plan and make a commission on products.
4. ***Salary.*** When brokers work for a bank, credit union, or other financial institution, they are usually paid a salary.
5. ***Maintenance fees.*** These are fees for handling your account.
6. ***Postage and handling.***
7. ***Inactivity fees.*** Some companies charge a fee when you don't generate a minimum amount of commissions over a certain period of time.
8. ***Telephone switching fees.*** In the case of mutual funds, you can sometimes change from one fund to another in a family of funds just by picking up the phone. There may be a fee for this service.

ONLINE OR E-TRADING

With the popularity of the Internet, a number of investors are participating in electronic trading (e-trading) or buying and selling stocks online. These do-it-yourselfers put in their orders to buy and sell stock, monitoring their own portfolios and buying and selling on their own judgment.

In some cases, they use a discount broker such as Charles Schwab, which has a lower fee and fewer services than a traditional broker. Prices vary considerably among those brokers who are considered discount brokers who happen to be online, and among online brokers such as E*trade. (For information about a host of brokers, try the Internet site *www.gomezadvisors.com* under Brokers.)

People who choose to trade online find several benefits:

- Ability to place an order 24 hours a day (although the order may only be executed during normal exchange hours).
- Access to timely information.
- Quick access to prices, company information, and other research data.

DAY TRADING

The advent of the Internet also has spawned a technique known as *day trading.* Day traders are nonprofessional traders who use Internet services that allow them to pursue a fast-paced technique of buying and selling stock in the same day. The high risk of day trading is that traders must be in and out of investments in the same day, which means that no matter what the price is at the end of the day, they must pay up or sell. It's not unusual to see very high gains and losses in day trading (but typically losses are greater than gains).

INSTITUTIONAL BUYERS

Large firms may invest huge amounts of money in the securities market. These institutional buyers may represent mutual funds, insurance companies, investment groups, pension plans, or other major investors. In today's market, it is not unusual for institutional investors to hold the largest portion of a company's stock. The largest institutional investors are insurance companies and pension plans.

INVESTMENT CLUBS

As "civilians" become more comfortable with the concept of investing, investment clubs have been developed to allow the casual investor to participate and learn more about stocks and the process of investing. These investment clubs meet regularly, pooling their resources to buy larger blocks of stocks than an individual might. Some use a full-service broker to trade for them. In fact, as online investing becomes more popular, a number of investment clubs are using discount brokers merely to buy and sell, and they do their research themselves.

Clubs form a legitimate partnership business entity, open bank accounts for the purpose of investing, and keep records like any business. At the end of the year, the treasurer is responsible for sending members a statement of earnings for tax filing purposes.

The National Association of Investment Clubs has created a number of tools to help clubs get started, including a start-up kit and research instruments that allow groups to investigate and evaluate stocks.

BUYING AND SELLING STOCK

The process of buying and selling stock is rather complex for the beginner. You need to understand the jargon if you want a head start.

Bid Price and Ask Price

For every stock transaction, a price is negotiated between a buyer and seller. A buyer will determine at what price he wants to purchase a stock (bid price), and a seller will determine at what price she will sell the stock (ask price).

Stock purchases don't actually take place the minute an order is placed. Thus, you won't know the exact price you paid for the stock until after the trade has been placed.

Market Makers

In a typical stock transaction, there are four parties:

- Buyer
- Seller
- Broker
- Market maker

The market maker is a middleman who facilitates the deal. In a transaction, the buyer or seller initiates the deal through a broker, and the market maker matches them up, taking the difference between the ask price and bid price (called the *spread)* as his profit.

Round Lots and Odd Lots

Stocks are most often purchased in round lots (or lots of 100 shares). Stocks can also be sold in *odd lots,* that is, fewer than 100 shares. And in any event, you can always buy shares one at a time.

Some investors cannot afford to buy the requisite 100 shares. To avoid this, they put their money into a *fund,* which pools the money from smaller investors and buys securities for them as a group.

Discretionary Accounts

Some clients put their faith in the professionals who manage their portfolios, and they give the advisor the authority to make investment decisions without their knowledge or approval. Their accounts are called *discretionary accounts.*

Stock Orders

There are three types of orders you can place:

- Market orders
- Limit orders
- Stop loss orders

Each type of order may be an order to purchase or an order to sell.

MARKET ORDERS

Market orders tell the broker to buy or sell a stock at the going ask or bid price (market price). The broker places the market order. On the trading floor the market maker will entertain offers to buy and sell stock at the *bid price,* which is what someone is willing to pay, or the *ask price,* which is the amount at which someone is willing to sell. The market maker will match up the buyers and sellers.

LIMIT ORDERS

Limit orders allow a buyer or seller to set a price limit at which he wants to buy or sell a stock.

Limit Order to Purchase. A buyer may place a limit purchase order if she believes the stock will fall to a certain level before rising again. The limit purchase order is triggered when the ask price reaches the price limit on the order, with no involvement from the buyer.

Limit Order to Sell. A seller may place a limit sell order if he believes the price is going to rise to a certain level and then fall. When the bid price reaches the price limit on the sell order, the limit sell order is triggered automatically.

STOP ORDERS

A stop order allows investors to limit their potential losses by selling when the price falls. It also allows investors to purchase when the ask price falls to a certain level. If the stock price hits the amount specified on a stop loss order, a market order is triggered.

How does this provide insurance against loss? It reduces the amount of risk. For example, suppose an investor buys a stock at $100 per share. The price rises to $150 per share. The investor believes that the stock may have peaked and could begin to fall. He might place a stop loss order to sell at $145 per share. This could still give him a $45 per share gain, even if the price falls. (A stop order doesn't guarantee a sell price of $145. It only ensures that a market order will be placed if the stock price falls to this level. Therefore, the stock could be sold at a price much lower than $145, if the market is dropping quickly.)

By the same token, suppose a well-respected stock is selling at $100 per share, and an investor doesn't want to pay that much for it. However, the stock price begins to decrease, and the investor wants to take advantage of that situation to buy the stock at what he considers a bargain price. He might place a stop order to buy the stock at $80 per share. What he anticipates, of course, is that the decrease is only temporary, and that the stock will ultimately go back up to its more normal value.

The key to remember is that a stop order triggers a market order, so the investor may or may not buy at the stop price on the order. This is different than a limit order, which only places an order *at* the price limit (rather than market).

WAYS TO PAY FOR SECURITIES

When a broker purchases a security for a buyer, the broker sends the buyer a confirmation that affirms the stock bought, the price, the number of units bought, and the total amount due. The buyer has three to five business days to pay the broker.

BUYING ON MARGIN

The broker may also allow a buyer to purchase a security *on margin,* which means on credit. The investor borrows money from the broker to pay for the security, and the broker will charge the buyer interest on the margin plus the normal commission on the purchase.

Buying on margin is more than just a convenience for the investor; it can actually increase the investor's gain. How? The investor doesn't have to pay up front, and if the security increases in value, the investor makes money on the amount borrowed. However, the investor is often required to maintain a specified cash balance in the account (say 30 to 50% of the margin), which ties up the investor's cash.

TAKING DELIVERY OF SECURITIES

An investor may decide to take delivery of securities or to leave them in the broker's care. If the investor doesn't take delivery, the securities will be registered in the broker's name, which is also known as the *street name.* The broker will send monthly statements summarizing the buyer's transactions. Here are advantages and disadvantages of each.

When taking delivery,

- The investor has control of securities.
- The investor can ensure the safekeeping of investments.

When leaving securities with broker,

- Securities can be bought and sold easily without the need for delivering them back and forth.
- The broker has the responsibility for keeping the documents safe and keeping track of transactions.

Chapter 24

MARKET MEASUREMENTS

When it comes to opinions about the performance of the stock market, they're a dime a dozen.

BULLS AND BEARS

You may hear people refer to a bull market or a bear market. These terms are used to indicate the condition of the market.

- In a *bull market,* stock price trends are going up, backed by strong economic growth and high consumer expectations.
- In a *bear market,* stock price trends are going down along with slowing or declining economic growth and falling consumer optimism.

STOCK INDEXES

An assortment of stock indexes mark the activity of various numbers of stocks. The best known are

- Dow Jones Industrial Average.
- Standard and Poor's 500.
- New York Stock Exchange Index.

Some indexes, such as the New York Stock Exchange Index, are weighted according to the market value of the stocks. The most widely reported index is the Dow Jones Industrial Average, which is not weighted.

DOW JONES INDUSTRIAL AVERAGE (DJIA)

Dow Jones is a publishing business that distributes some of the world's most influential business and financial news reports. Its most widely recognized publication is *The Wall Street Journal,* a daily newspaper. In addition, Dow Jones business extends to magazines, electronic media, and international publications.

The Dow Jones Industrial Average (DJIA) is an index used as an indicator of general trends in stock performance across the board. Since 1928 the DJIA has included 30 companies, selected by *The Wall Street Journal* editors and known as *blue chip stocks,* that are noted for their stability in growth and great management and products. The stocks in the composite change infrequently.

Originally, to compute the average, the editors simply added up the prices of the stocks and divided by the number of stocks included. Today, they sometimes adjust the computation for unusual events such as a stock split, which, if not considered, could skew the average.

The DJIA is the index cited most often, but there are also indexes for transportation and utilities companies. In fact, the first index, which was started in 1884, was composed of railroad stocks.

STANDARD AND POOR'S 500 INDEX

Standard and Poor's (S&P) is a company that publishes financial indices, rates securities and provides other services that provide information about corporations. The S&P 500, an index of 500 stocks, is intended to be a barometer of stock price fluctuations. The index includes industrials, utilities, transportation, and financial stocks. Although the DJIA is the most recognized index, S&P is sometimes considered more comprehensive because it is more diversified.

NYSE

NYSE publishes a composite index of all the stocks listed on its exchange.

NASDAQ

NASDAQ publishes an index of approximately 5,000 over-the-counter stocks as well as other specialized industry indices.

INDICES AS PREDICTORS

Indexes are historical; they show where the market has been, and they indicate trends over time. As such, they are not predictors of future performance. Considering that the goal of a corporation is to maximize shareholder value, how a company's stock is performing in relation to the indices is a very important measure of how well its management is performing.

MARKET RATIOS

Besides the obvious rewards of dividends, a company may exhibit its success through performance of its stock. There are several ways to interpret stock performance.

STOCK PRICE

The simplest way to evaluate stock is by looking at how its price is changing and at what rate in comparison with its industry and the overall market.

EARNINGS PER SHARE (EPS)

The EPS tells investors how much the company is earning for every share of stock that owners have. The way to compute EPS is to divide net income for the year by the average number of common shares outstanding.

There are two types of EPS calculations:

- ***Primary.*** This divides net income by the number of shares of common stock and common stock equivalents outstanding.
- ***Fully diluted EPS.*** This formula computes the EPS using the average number of shares of common stock computed as if all convertible securities were translated into shares of common stock.

PRICE/EARNINGS (PE)

A company's price/earnings ratio describes the relationship between how much the stock is selling for and how much it is earning. The formula for PE is current market price per share divided by EPS.

Analysts can judge how a company is doing by looking at its PE ratio. A PE higher than 18 to 20 has historically meant that the stock is overpriced. In start-up companies, however, a high PE may mean that investors are taking into account its potential rather than its actual performance.

WHEN IS A STOCK OVERPRICED?

There are certainly many opinions about ways to evaluate how much a stock is worth, but one way to begin to analyze its value is to look at the annual report, particularly the P&L. Check to see how much revenue the company generates. Now look at the total market value of the company. Is the amount of revenue worth the stock price? In some cases, a new company that has just gone public may be in the red (running at a loss) but have a high PE, indicating a potential for increased income. However, investors should take a very close look at the stock price.

With fast-tracking stocks becoming increasingly widespread, investors may be looking at potential future income versus existing income. They ask, "How much risk can I bear? And how long will it be until the company begins to achieve its potential?" The investor may decide the company is worth an investment because its future is bright. This has been true for some Internet companies that were perhaps losing money while making huge gains in stock price. Investors have counted on the companies' ability to recoup losses in the future.

PRICE FLUCTUATIONS

There is risk inherent in purchasing stocks and bonds. To mitigate risk, astute investors usually diversify (invest in a number of types of stocks and bonds). Risk that can be avoided through diversification is called "diversifiable" or "company-specific" risk. This simply means that you can eliminate a certain amount of risk by investing in various things that are not affected by the same factors.

For example, technology is not affected by the events that affect commodities. Adverse weather conditions, an orange grove fungus, or other disastrous things that would dramatically affect a commodity would have little or no effect on a technology stock. Thus, if you buy a little of each, you cut your potential risks.

Market Risk

In the securities market, there is a great degree of risk that you cannot avoid. This is because the market is dependent on too many factors outside your control—for example, weather, foreign wars, international policy, and interstate policies. These are all issues outside the scope of what you can manipulate. This is known as *market risk* or *nondiversifiable risk.*

RISK MEASUREMENTS

Investment almost always involves some elements of risk. There are several types of risk associated with an investment portfolio.

- ***Systematic risk.*** Security prices in general rise and fall, and the risk associated with that inevitable flow is called systematic risk.
- ***Unsystematic risk.*** Risks that are unique to a firm or an industry are called unsystematic. For example, if the building industry is affected by shortages of bricks, that is an unsystematic risk.

Beta Coefficients

Because most investors don't have the time, expertise, or desire to analyze every stock, financial analysts have developed a concept to help them understand the risk of a stock compared with other stocks in the market. One way of measuring systematic risk is to compare how a company's stock price changes compared with changes of the market in general. To find out the comparison, you divide the percentage of change in a price index in the market by the percentage of change in the price of the stock. This is called a *beta coefficient* or simply *beta.*

A beta coefficient measures a stock's relative volatility against a market index such as the Dow Jones Industrial Average. Indices such as the Dow are given a beta of 1.0, which is the average for all stocks. If a stock rises or falls at the same rate as the index, its beta is 1.0. If it rises or falls at a rate twice that of the index, it has a beta of 2. This shows how risky a stock is in relation to the market. Most stocks have a beta in the range of 0.5 to 1.5.

By looking at the beta, an investor can determine if she prefers a more or less volatile stock. Once again, as in all investments, the more volatile the stock, the greater the possibility of large gains . . . or losses.

Betas are calculated and published by companies such as Merrill Lynch, Value Line, and other investment organizations.

In an arena where totally accurate measurement is impossible, betas are considered as good a measurement as there is.

MARKET INVESTMENT ASSUMPTIONS

People who know how to invest operate under certain general assumptions:

- The market is efficient. When prices are not fair, the market will adjust rapidly.
- There is enough information in the market for people to make right decisions; therefore, the price is fair.
- Some securities are undervalued or overvalued.

THE EFFICIENT MARKET

The theory of the market being efficient stems from two beliefs:

- Stock prices reflect all the current information available about companies.
- It's impossible for an investor to consistently beat the market. All investors have access to information, and, when things are out of kilter, the market adjusts almost immediately to new information. Therefore, it's impossible to find bargains in the market. (This theory excludes instances of insider trading.)

BARGAINS OR NO BARGAINS?

Analysts understand that the theory of not beating the market generally holds true; however, there are bargains to be found because

- There truly is more information available to some people than others.

- Some people who have the information don't understand how to use it wisely.
- Small investors can move faster than institutional investors.

FUND MANAGERS AND THE EFFICIENT MARKET

Fund managers for institutional investors can seriously affect the market because they buy and sell such large blocks of stock. When they buy or sell a stock, it tends to create a snowball effect. Therefore, they usually go about their transactions gradually.

Nevertheless, their participation can have a dramatic effect. At a particular time, a stock may be low or high, but over a period of time it will even out.

EVALUATING STOCK

Some people consider investing in the stock market to be a form of legalized gambling because the variables that affect a stock are many and uncontrollable. So is there such a thing as a *wise* stock market investment?

Like frequent gamblers, many people who invest in the market have their own favorite formula for winning. There are seemingly unlimited ways to evaluate a stock and to determine when it's a good idea to buy and when to sell. In his book *A Random Walk down Wall Street,* Burton G. Malkiel describes several theories, from firm-foundation to castles-in-the-air. In short form, here are his ideas:

People who support the Dow theory look at the combination of the Dow Jones Industrial Average and the Dow Jones Transportation Average, noting when the two exceed their normal range and anticipating a major upswing or downturn as a result.

Random walk theorists say that you cannot predict short-term changes in stocks, and that anyone selecting stocks at random will do as well as someone who studies the market.

Firm foundation believers espouse the theory that every stock has intrinsic value that you can estimate based on present conditions and future potential.

Castles-in-the-air theorists say that since the price of stock is largely a matter of supply and demand, the most important factor to take into account is psychological (What investments will people be attracted to?) because that is what determines price.

Perhaps if you desire to invest, you will want to explore the numerous theories and decide which one feels most comfortable to you. Or perhaps you will prefer to hire an expert to do your research and your buying and selling. In any case, here are some things that can influence your judgment of a stock's value:

- ***Price.*** What can your pocketbook allow? And what is a stock worth?
- ***Price/earnings ratio.*** This measure, which we described earlier in this chapter, compares the share price and earnings per share. You may not want to buy a stock with a high PE because it's selling at too many times its earnings.
- ***History.*** How has the company performed over time, in good times and bad? Where is a company headed, where is it in the business life cycle, and will it continue to perform as it has in the past?

Chapter 25

INTERNATIONAL FINANCE

Neither of this book's authors is an international expert; however, because of the growing impact of the Internet on today's global economy, we wanted to include some financial terms that you'll probably run across if your company is involved in international business.

The Internet has rapidly changed the view of world markets and global economies. In the not too distant past, business people recognized the opportunity of increased product and service demands because of international markets, but not many companies ventured into this seemingly strange world. Today, companies of every size—from Mom and Pop businesses to Fortune 500 companies—are setting up their "international shops" by setting up web sites through which anyone with access to the Internet can purchase their products and services.

This great expansion of local markets into the "wild unknown" is just on the verge of exploding. Whether it occurs 2 years or 10 years from now, only time will tell. All we can do is stand on the sidelines and shout, "It's coming! It's coming!"

Never has our society lived in a period of such wealth. And never has civilization been on the edge of such unlimited opportunity. This is a wonderful, exciting time to be living. It's also scary and volatile.

The point is that, whether or not your company is now involved in international trade or has plans to be involved, you will need to understand the basics of international trade and finance. In fact, even if your company has no plans whatsoever to be involved in international business, you will still need to understand the effects of international trade on your business. The world is growing smaller and your next competitor may be the one living on the opposite side of the globe, trying to figure how to get your market share.

INTERNATIONAL FINANCE TERMINOLOGY

Our goal in this chapter is not to tell you how to financially manage an international firm. It's only to introduce key terms and ideas that you may need to know about international finance in the future. To do this we briefly describe some international finance terms, beginning with the big picture and then working our way down to company-level issues. Specifically we'll look at

- International Monetary Fund.
- World Bank.
- Foreign exchange.
- International trade.
- Reporting international operations in U.S. financial statements.

INTERNATIONAL MONETARY FUND

The International Monetary Fund (IMF) is a cooperative group of member countries that was formed over 50 years ago to stabilize the international financial markets. It has no authority over domestic economic policies. It can only encourage its members to follow agreed-upon policies determined by the members themselves.

The foreign exchange policies are lenient, allowing each country to determine how its own currency will be valued. The only requirements are that the currency value cannot be based on gold, and that the country must let all other members know how it determines the value of its currency.

The currency valuation methods range from allowing the currency value to fluctuate on the open market (like stock and bond values do) to linking the currency value to another, more stable currency. The U.S. and other wealthy countries, such as Japan and the U.K., allow their currencies to be valued at market.

The IMF also allows member countries to borrow money from the fund during times of economic crisis. For example, just recently the IMF loaned money to the Asian countries to help stop bank failures. The normal repayment period is three to five years, and the fees paid include service charges, commitment fees, and interest. Also, the member must effectively demonstrate its willingness to change economic policies to help the economy, its commitment to repayment, and its ability to repay (much like our consumer loans!).

IMF History

The IMF began as a result of the Great Depression that affected all economies in the late 1920s and early 1930s. The destruction associated with this worldwide depression was not only evident in bank failures and soup lines, but it also fueled a lack of confidence in paper currencies because of soaring inflation (the erosion of the value of currency). Some countries recorded inflation rates in the thousands! Prices for consumer goods increased without warning. And people who had quantities of money socked away suddenly found themselves almost penniless.

At this time, the major world currencies were on the gold standard, meaning their currency values were backed by gold. At any time, someone could turn in the paper currency and receive a specified amount of gold. That specified amount of gold rarely changed because, when it did, it completely disrupted local economies.

The gold standard also gave foreign exchanges (exchanges trading one paper currency for another country's paper currency) a way to value different currencies in terms of other currencies. For example, a U.S. dollar might be equivalent in value to 1.5 Canadian dollars. Or four French francs could equal one U.S. dollar. Since each paper currency was backed by gold, and its gold value rarely changed, the foreign exchange market had an easy way to value currency exchanges and the foreign exchange markets were fairly stable.

However, lack of confidence in the paper currency and in countries' inability to provide gold on demand (i.e., their gold stores weren't high enough) forced many countries to go off the gold standard. Because currencies no longer had a common valuator (gold), foreign exchanges went haywire. There was no consistent, stable way to value foreign currencies in terms of other currencies.

So a cooperative organization called the International Monetary Fund was developed with the U.S. and the U.K. as leaders. In July 1944, the organization was established with 44 member countries.

IMF Membership and Quotas

As of this date, there are over 180 member countries in the IMF. Membership is open to all countries that have a foreign trade policy and are willing to follow the IMF charter rights and obligations. Members can leave the IMF at any time. All major countries are members of IMF.

When a country joins the IMF, it contributes an amount of money, called a *quota subscription,* as its membership fee. This is paid once and is held "on deposit," almost like a payment of money to a credit union.

Quotas are based on each country's wealth and economic performance. The U.S. pays the highest quota, over 18% of the fund. (The next largest quotas only represent just over 5% of the fund.) Quotas are reviewed every five years, when they can be raised or lowered, depending on the financial circumstances of each country.

There are three purposes for quotas:

1. To provide a pool of funds that the IMF can loan members during financial difficulties.
2. To form a basis for determining how much a member can borrow from the IMF.
3. To determine the voting rights of each member country. (The premise is that the wealthiest countries, whose economies depend on foreign trade, should have a greater say in the policies set forth.)

WORLD BANK

The *World Bank* is the world's largest lending institution to developing countries. Its loans total almost $30 billion a year, and its purpose is to help develop stable, sustainable growth in countries that don't have necessary resources, knowledge, and/or experience.

The World Bank focuses on assisting the poorest countries, helping them develop:

- Government strength to help policy and decision making at the highest level.
- Health and education systems to promote knowledge at the individual level.
- Investment and long-range planning for economic growth.
- Private business ventures.
- Environmental protection.
- Poverty-reduction plans.

The World Bank begins at the foundations—teaching leaders how to reform their overall economy and to strengthen their banking systems.

Two Sources of Lending

Much of the World Bank's aid comes through financial loans made to developing countries. There are two major organizations within the World Bank involved in lending activities:

- International Bank for Reconstruction and Development (IBRD).
- International Development Association (IDA).

INTERNATIONAL BANK FOR RECONSTRUCTION AND DEVELOPMENT

The *International Bank for Reconstruction and Development* accounts for about 75% of the annual loans made to developing countries. It obtains its funds by issuing AAA-rated bonds and other debt securities to pension funds, insurance companies, corporations, banks, and individual investors around the world. Interest is based upon its own cost of borrowing, and it expects repayment within 15 to 20 years, depending upon the loan. Usually, the borrowing nation has a 3-to-5-year grace period, during which only interest payments are made. There has never been a default on a World Bank loan.

INTERNATIONAL DEVELOPMENT ASSOCIATION

The *International Development Association (IDA)* was established in 1960 to help countries that are too poor to borrow at commercial interest rates. It promotes growth and development in the same way as the IBDR, but its loans are interest-free. It accounts for approximately 25% of the World Bank's annual loans.

Borrowing countries pay a servicing fee of less than 1% of the loan to cover administrative charges. They are required to repay the loan within 35 to 40 years. They typically have a grace period of 10 years, during which they do not have to make principal payments.

The IDA obtains its funds through contributions from almost 40 countries. The contributing countries include industrialized nations (such as the United States, the United Kingdom, Germany, Japan, and France); as well as developing nations that may have received the IDA's assistance (for example, Argentina, Brazil, Hungary, Korea, Russia, and Turkey). The IDA's funds are replenished by contributing countries every three years.

FOREIGN EXCHANGE

Foreign exchange is the exchange of one country's currency for another country's currency at a specified exchange rate. The *exchange rate* is the relative value of the currency stated in terms of another currency.

For example, the exchange rate for U.S. dollars to Japanese yen is 107.69 at the time of this writing. This means that $1 equals 107.69 yen. Alternatively, the exchange rate for Japanese yen to U.S. dollars is 0.009286, which is 1/107.69. This means 1 yen equals $0.009286.

The current exchange rates are listed in the financial section of most newspapers in terms of $1 (i.e., $1 equals a specific amount of the foreign currency). To get one unit of the foreign currency in terms of U.S. dollars (as we did in the previous example), take the inverse of the exchange rate (1 ÷ the exchange rate).

It is difficult to exchange currencies at the market exchange rate listed in the newspaper (unless your company is a financial institution that deals in foreign currencies) because most financial institutions charge an increased rate as revenue for exchanging currencies. (In other words, a bank will keep the difference between what it pays for foreign currency and what it charges you for the exchange. This is called the *spread.*)

Most national banks located in large cities will exchange dollars for foreign currency; however, they typically charge among the highest exchange rates. Credit cards, on the other hand, will also allow you to purchase with foreign currencies, but their exchange rates tend to be lower than the banks'. Also, if you are planning to travel abroad, you can purchase American Express Travelers Cheques in some foreign denominations, sometimes at a much lower exchange rate.

HEDGING FOREIGN EXCHANGE RATES

Hedging is a strategy used to minimize the risk of changes in the foreign exchange rates. It's like an insurance policy that guards companies against loss from the devaluing of their country's currency.

Hedging works like this: When a company sells its product in a foreign currency, it bears the risk that the foreign currency value may appreciate compared to its own currency. To *hedge* (or mitigate) the foreign exchange risk, the company will purchase a forward foreign currency contract at the time of sale (or before payment is made). The contract allows the company to convert the foreign dollars to its own currency at a set exchange rate. So if the foreign exchange rates move against the selling company's favor, it can use the contract to exchange the foreign currency it receives in payment. If the exchange rates are better, the company can allow the contract to expire without taking any action.

See the Foreign Currency Units table that follows.

FOREIGN CURRENCY UNITS

Country	Unit	Currency Country	Currency Unit
Afghanistan	afghani	Costa Rica	colon
Albania	lek	Croatia	kuma
Algeria	dinar	Cuba	peso
Angola	kwanza	Cyprus	pound
Argentina	peso	Czech Republic	koruna
Aruba	guilder (aka florin or gulden)	Denmark	krone (pl. koner)
Australia	dollar	Dominica	dollar
Austria	schilling	Ecuador	sucre
Azerbaijan	manat	Egypt	pound
Bahamas	dollar	El Salvador	colon
Bangladesh	taka	Estonia	kroon (pl. krooni)
Belgium	franc	Ethiopia	birr
Belize	dollar	Europe	euro
Bermuda	dollar	Falkland Islands	pound
Bolivia	boliviano	Fiji	dollar
Boznia-Herzegovina	convertible mark	Finland	markka (pl. markkaa)
Brazil	real	France	franc
Bulgaria	leva	Germany	deutsche mark
Cambodia	new riel	Ghana	new cedi
Canada	dollar	Greece	drachma
Cayman Islands	dollar	Grenada	dollar
Chad	franc	Guatemala	quetzal
Chile	peso	Guyana	dollar
China	yuan renminbi	Haiti	gourde
Columbia	peso	Honduras	lempira

continued . . .

Country	Unit	Currency Country	Currency Unit
Hong Kong	dollar	Mauritius	rupee
Hungary	forint	Mexico	peso
Iceland	krona	Morocco	dirham
India	rupee	Mozambique	metical
Indonesia	rupiah	Nepal	rupee
Iran	rial	Netherlands	guilder (aka florin or gulden)
Iraq	dinar	New Zealand	dollar
Ireland	punt or pound	Nicaragua	gold cordoba
Israel	new shekel	Nigeria	naira
Italy	lira (pl. lire)	Norway	krone (pl. kroner)
Jamaica	dollar	Oman	rial
Japan	yen	Pakistan	rupee
Jordan	dinar	Paraguay	guarani
Kenya	shilling	Peru	new sol
Korea	won	Philippines	peso
Kuwait	dinar	Poland	zloty
Lebanon Liberia	pound (livre) dollar	Portugal	escudo
Libya	dinar	PRC	renminbi
Lithuania	litas (pl. litai)	Russia	ruble
Madagascar	ariayry = 5 francs	Saudi Arabia	riyal
Malaysia	ringgit	Singapore	dollar

continued . . .

Country	Unit	Currency Country	Currency Unit
Taiwan	new dollar	Uruguay	peso
Tanzania	shilling	Uzbekistan	som
Thailand	baht	Venezuela	bolivar
Trinidad & Tobago	dollar	Viet Nam	new dong
Tunisia	dinar	Yemen	rial
Turkey	lira	Yugoslavia	dinar
Uganda	shilling	Zaire	new zaire
Ukraine	Hryvnia	Zambia	kwacha
United Arab Emirates	dirham	Zimbabwe	dollar
United Kingdom	pound		
United States of America Guam Panama Canal Zone Puerto Rico Samoa Turks & Caicos Islands Virgin Islands	dollar		

INTERNATIONAL TRADE

International trade is discussed in terms of imports and exports. *Imports* are the goods that are produced by a foreign country, such as Mexico, and sold to the domestic country, in our case the U.S. For example, British wools are imported into the U.S.

Exports are the products manufactured within one country, such as the U.S., and sold within another country, such as France. For example, the U.S. manufactures automobiles and exports them to Europe and Asia.

Terms of Sale

The terms of sale (the point at which the property ownership transfers from seller to buyer) are a little different for international sales than the ones we describe for domestic U.S. sales. They include the following

- C.I.F.
- F.A.S.
- F.O.B.
- EX

C.I.F. stands for "cost, marine insurance, freight." It means the seller is responsible for all costs up to the port of final destination. It is used with a named port of import. (Marine insurance is an insurance policy that covers the product while it is being shipped on the sea or ocean. The owner is compensated if something happens during shipping.)

F.A.S. stands for "free alongside a ship." It means the seller will pay for the product until it reaches a ship at a port of export. After that, the buyer is responsible for the costs. It is used with a named port of export.

F.O.B. stands for "free on board," which is similar to F.A.S. except the seller also pays for the vessel-loading costs of the product.

EX (such as EX-warehouse or EX-factory) means the seller will pay all costs to get the goods to a specified delivery point.

Documents Used in International Trade

International trade involves a slew of new documents that may or may not be required in order to ship products to foreign countries. Here are some of the more common documents for shipping and payment:

CERTIFICATE OF ORIGIN

A *certificate of origin* is a document that is typically issued by the local chamber of commerce and certifies that the product was produced in a specified location and country. Some countries require that certificates or origin have a visa stamped on them by the resident consul at the port of export.

Countries may receive "most-favored country" designation, which results in their receiving preferential treatment in trade agreements. This status is used to encourage nations to continue to do business with the country that's issuing the status, and usually means they enjoy lower taxes or duties. Certificates of origin are often required in order to receive these preferential rates on import duties (see later under "Taxes").

An officer or other responsible person of the company must sign certificates of origin. The signature of a salesperson or manager won't be accepted.

COMMERCIAL INVOICE

A *commercial invoice* is an invoice that conforms exactly to the agreement made between the buyer and seller. The commercial invoice should

- Itemize the product by price per unit and total.
- Specify any marks or numbers on the packages.
- Clearly specify any additional charges.
- Clearly document the terms of payment.

CONSULAR INVOICE

A *consular invoice* is an invoice obtained from the commercial attaché or through the consular office of the country of export (located at the port of export). It is issued in addition to the commercial invoice and must conform exactly to the terms and conditions written on the commercial invoice. However, it isn't always required for payment.

(Note: A *commercial attaché* is a commercial expert who is a part of the diplomatic staff at your country's embassy.)

CERTIFICATE OF MANUFACTURE

A *certificate of manufacture* is a document that certifies to the buyer that the products ordered have been produced and are ready for shipment. A certificate of manufacture may be sent to a buyer who has only made a down payment against the product. Usually, it is sent to the buyer with the commercial invoice and copies of packing lists.

INSURANCE CERTIFICATES

Insurance certificates are documents that provide evidence of coverage. They may be a stipulation of a purchase contract or commercial invoice in order to receive payment. An insurance certificate specifies

- Type of coverage.
- Insured amount.
- Description of packages.
- Identifying marks on the packages.

(Note: This information must agree with other documents.)

INSPECTION CERTIFICATES

Inspection certificates are affidavits, usually by an independent firm, that the products being shipped are in good condition, or meet specified conditions, before shipment. Buyers sometimes require them as protection against fraud, error, or product quality problems.

SHIPPERS EXPORT DECLARATION

A *shippers export declaration* is a data collection document that is completed by either the exporter or freight company and forwarded to the U.S. government. It is required for all exports valued at over $2,500. It provides statistical information to the U.S. Bureau of the Census, and it indicates proper authorization to export goods.

The shipper export declaration requires information about the shipment, including

- Description of products shipped.
- Value of products shipped.
- Net weight.
- Gross weight.
- Relevant license information.

BILLS OF LADING

Bills of lading for international shipments are similar to shipments within the U.S. A *straight bill of lading* is a non-negotiable bill of lading that consigns products to the company listed on the bill. When using a straight bill of lading, the seller's bank loses title control over the goods because they will be delivered to anyone identified as the consignee (i.e., the products shipped cannot be used as collateral for letters of credit).

An *order bill of lading* is a negotiable bill. The order represents title to the products shipped, and it means that the title doesn't pass until it has been presented with appropriate approvals. The products shipped can be used as collateral.

When the freight carrier arrives at a port of import, it will inspect the packages shipped and stamp the bill of lading with "clean on board" or "foul bill." *Clean on board* means there was no damage to the products during shipment. *Foul bill* indicates some type of damage that is typically noted on the bill of lading.

BANK DRAFTS

Bank drafts are bills of exchange, or written orders that allow payments at a specified date. (The date could be the current date or a future date.) In simpler terms, a bank draft is similar to a check written on a checking account. Bank drafts are typically used when the customer must provide foreign currencies to a bank in a distant location.

There are several documents that must accompany a bank draft in order to obtain payment from a bank:

- Negotiable bills of lading.
- Insurance certificates.
- Commercial invoices.

LETTER OF CREDIT

A *letter of credit* is a document stating that the buyer's bank guarantees that if all documents are presented in exact conformity with the terms (as stated in the letter of credit), the bank will make payment. (In other countries, the term *document credits* may be used instead of *letter of credit.*)

Letters of credit are the most common forms of payment for goods shipped between countries. They are simple to use, and most traders around the world accept them. They are usually specified in accordance with the Uniform Customs and Practice for Documentary Credits of the International Chamber of Commerce, a code of practice that is recognized in world trade.

The documents that are required to be presented with the letter of credit vary, but will almost always include

- Negotiable bills of lading.
- Insurance certificates.
- Commercial invoices.

Currency Clearinghouses

Currency clearinghouses are large financial institutions located in the major financial markets (New York, London, Tokyo) that accept payment in one currency and exchange it for another currency to make payment on behalf of a company or legal entity. In effect, the financial institution acts as an intermediary, purchasing foreign currencies as needed by its account holders.

For example, your company has major divisions all over the world, and money flows between the divisions on a frequent basis. Instead of purchasing a foreign bank draft for all the currency transactions, your company could set up an account with a currency clearinghouse to take payments in the division's local currency (via a wire transfer), then exchange it for the currency to be paid, and make the payment on that division's behalf.

The currency clearinghouses make their fees on the difference between the exchange rate they pay to purchase funds and the exchange rate they charge their customers.

Taxes

Taxes on international trade are very complex and involve confusing terms. A few of the most common terms are

- *Duties.*
- *Tariffs.*
- *Value-added tax.*

Duties are taxes imposed on imports and exports. Countries use them either to deter or to encourage the international trade of specific products or industries.

Tariffs is the overall term used to describe either

- A schedule of rates or charges, usually regarding freight.
- The tax on products that cross a country's borders.

Revenue tariffs are used to raise revenue for the country imposing the tax.

Protective tariffs are used to protect domestic industries within a country.

Value-added tax (VAT) is a consumption tax imposed on manufactured products at every stage of production as well as at the time of sale to the end consumer. It is used in European countries as a major source of revenue. It actually represents a form of sales tax.

REPORTING INTERNATIONAL OPERATIONS IN U.S. FINANCIAL STATEMENTS

GAAP requires all financial statements of U.S. companies to be presented in U.S. dollars. This creates some complexity when international trade companies such as FedEx Corporation and Pfizer Inc. report on operations located all over the world. This is known as *translating* financial statements into U.S. dollars.

OTHER INTERNATIONAL INFORMATION

BALANCE OF PAYMENTS

The *balance of payments* represents the relationship between all cash paid to a country and all cash paid by the same country (to other countries) for exports and imports. In a sense, it's like having a huge international "cash flow statement" for the entire country. That would include

- The government's international cash flow.
- Businesses' international cash flow.
- Individuals' international cash flow.

Related to the balance of trade, the goal of balance of payments is to have the same amount of money coming in as going out. (Many countries, however, have adopted the idea that it is economically better to have more money paid into the country than is paid out from the country. But of course, it's impossible for everyone to achieve this. Someone will always have a deficit.)

Balance of Trade

The *balance of trade* is the relationship between the values of a country's exports and its imports. At one time, economists believed that a country's exports should be more than its imports to promote its economic health, and this notion is still widely held. However, if you think about the world as a local economy and each country as a business, there will always be businesses that need more goods than others. And there will be businesses that provide those goods. The amount of a country's imports and exports may never be equal. Therefore, it may not be possible to have a balance of trade.

U. S. Trade Deficit

The U.S. has been in a trade deficit for at least 20 years, meaning the value of its exports is less than the value of its imports. This has caused many discussions between the U.S. government and other governments, such as Japan's and China's.

Some of this deficit is caused by our booming economy. However, much is caused by foreign government policies on import controls (or limits) in their countries, trade policies, or simply high foreign duties and taxes on U.S. goods.

Sometimes the reasons are due more to culture than to government import controls. For example, in Japan, electronics stores are owned or operated by the manufacturer, rather than being a separate retail entity whose interest is to provide variety. To purchase Sony electronics, you go to the Sony store. This is very different from what we find in the U.S. So U.S. electronics manufacturers may complain about not being able to sell their products in Japan, when the real problem is that they can't find a market for their product without opening their own store.

World Trade Centers

World trade centers are nonpolitical organizations that are set up to help companies and individuals with international trade. They house all the services a company would need for importing and exporting. Their services include trade information, trade education, communication services, clubs, and display facilities.

World trade centers are located in almost every major trade center in the world. There are over 170 offices, and they sponsor worldwide trade shows and international conferences for importers and exporters.

Foreign Corrupt Practices Act

The Foreign Corrupt Practices Act of 1977 makes it illegal for companies to bribe foreign officials, candidates, or political parties. This includes making payments or gifts in order to get a contract. The penalties include a five-year jail sentence and fines of up to $10,000.

North American Free Trade Agreement

The *North American Free Trade Agreement (NAFTA)* includes Canada, the United States, Central America (including Mexico) and South America. Effective January 1, 1994, NAFTA offers preferential tariff treatment for business trading within this specified area. It offers

- Elimination of tariffs between the U.S. and Canada.
- Phase-out of duties between U.S. and Canadian trade with Mexico within 15 years.
- Elimination of agricultural tariffs and subsidies.

- Elimination of custom user fees.
- Elimination of import quotas (unless grandfathered in).
- Prevention of third-party intruders through certificates of origin.
- Prevention of product standards as a barrier to trade.
- Expansion of government procurement markets.
- Elimination of discriminatory laws directed at services.

Chapter 26

FEDERAL RESERVE SYSTEM

News reports covering financial issues, interest rates, and other monetary policies often refer to "the Fed." That's short for the Federal Reserve System, which determines the financial policies of the U.S.

The Fed was born in 1913 after panics had put the nation in a financial uproar. Its purpose was to stabilize the nation's financial system.

The Fed operates independently of Congress and the White House as an interesting cross between a government agency and a private enterprise. This balance, according to the Fed, makes for an extremely effectivc operation.

PURPOSE

The Fed meets several times a week for four main purposes:

- To develop and implement the nation's monetary policy.
- To regulate banking and protect consumers.
- To ensure the stability of our financial system.
- To deliver certain financial services.

All national banks must be members of the Fed.

The Fed buys and sells government securities and controls the level of short-term interest rates to keep the economy stable. The two key interest rates the Fed controls:

1. The discount rate, the rate the Fed charges banks for loans it provides.
2. The federal funds rate, the rate Federal Reserve member banks pay to each other to borrow money overnight.

ORGANIZATION AND GOVERNING BODY

The Fed is a three-part organization. It includes

- The Board of Governors.
- The Reserve Banks.
- The Federal Open Market Committee.

THE BOARD OF GOVERNORS

The Fed is governed by a seven-member Board of Governors, all of whom are appointed by the president with the approval of the Senate. The president appoints one of the governors to serve as chairman.

The Board of Governors is charged with keeping our economy sound. To do that, it examines economic issues and trends, and solicits feedback from the Reserve banks about regional concerns that could ultimately affect the national economy. Its participation in the Federal Open Market Committee is essential in setting economic policy for the nation.

Another key role the governors play is in supervising member banks to make certain they abide by regulations and protect consumers through sound practices.

CHAIRMAN OF THE FED

The chairman of the Fed is a very high profile and powerful person who is looked to for indications of the economy's progress and whose comments about trends are taken very seriously. In fact, a simple word from the chairman can significantly influence investors and generate activity, both positive and negative, in the financial market as well as in corporate board rooms. An awesome responsibility, to say the least.

The chairman reports twice a year to Congress and is regularly consulted for guidance by key policy formulators. He works closely with the secretary of the treasury and is a trusted presidential advisor.

TERMS OF OFFICE

The chairman of the Federal Reserve's Board of Governors serves a four-year term. Other members of the board each serve one 14-year term. When the president selects board members, only one may be from one of the 12 Federal Reserve Districts. The goal is to establish fair representation according to factors such as geographical area and business interest.

Federal Reserve Banks

The 12 Federal Reserve banks provide a vital link between the local communities and regions and the national Board of Governors. Their perspective on issues of importance to the economy, feedback on how policies are working, and business outlook give the Fed a well-rounded picture of what is happening in the country.

The Reserve banks are also the workhorses of the Fed system. These banks

- Serve as the "banker's bank," storing cash and coins and lending to member banks whose reserves fall short. They charge the banks a low interest rate, called the *discount rate*, for money they borrow.
- Examine member banks' policies and processes to make sure they are sound.
- Research economic issues at the local and regional levels in order to provide input to the Federal Open Market Committee (FOMC), which we'll discuss shortly.
- Process the U.S. Treasury's payments and manage its cash.

RESERVE BANK BOARDS

The Reserve banks operate under the auspices of the Board of Governors. Each bank has a nine-member board of directors with six representing the public and three representing banking. Once again, this balance of the public and private involvement is intended to provide a clear perspective.

RESERVE BANK RESPONSIBILITIES

The Reserve banks are independent of the government and are operated as separate business entities. Although they are money-making ventures, they are not operated for profit; their revenues pay operating expenses, and any excess is returned to the U.S. Treasury.

The Reserve banks' responsibilities include

- Supervising the activities of member banks. This includes examining bank practices to make sure that they are solid financial institutions, and making sure that they adhere to established government policies.
- Loaning money to other banks.
- Transferring funds.
- Collecting data from member banks for analyzing trends and performance.
- Conducting research and analysis of regional information to contribute to the Beige Book, a report which is used for FOMC discussions.

LOCATIONS

The 12 Federal Reserve banks are located in

- Boston
- New York
- Philadelphia
- Richmond
- Atlanta
- Chicago
- St. Louis
- Minneapolis
- Kansas City
- Dallas
- San Francisco
- Cleveland

Federal Open Market Committee (FOMC)

What should we do about the economy? That's the question the FOMC answers eight times each year in meetings in Washington, D.C. This body has the major role in determining whether there will be a little or a lot of money available to lend. (This is called the money supply.) The growth of the money supply is a crucial factor in keeping inflation rates low, which contributes to economic growth.

The Federal Open Market Committee has three primary responsibilities:

1. To determine the discount rate, which is the interest rate that banks must pay to borrow money from the Fed. (This is the only interest rate the Fed actually controls.)
2. To decide how much money banks must hold on reserve with the Fed for their deposits. This is a percentage of their deposits.
3. To buy and sell treasury securities on the open market.

Their decisions about those three areas substantially influence economic trends and contribute to how much money banks will lend.

To make such decisions, of course, the FOMC needs vast amounts of information, which it gets from the Board of Governors and Reserve banks. Armed with research and analysis supplied by these sources, members of the FOMC decide whether to increase or decrease the money supply. Their decisions are intended to maintain a healthy economy.

The FOMC has 19 members:

- The seven people on the Fed's Board of Governors.
- The 12 Reserve bank presidents.

Only 12 of the 19 members vote. They are

- The Board of Governors.
- The president of the Federal Reserve Bank of New York.
- Four other Reserve bank presidents.

GLOSSARY

401(k) plan is a tax-deferred retirement plan to which employees may contribute pre-tax dollars. In some cases, an employer has an option to match the employee's contribution or not. The money contributed is put into an investment fund comprised of a variety of securities. There are restrictions on when an employee may withdraw his own or the company's portion of the funds.

403(b) plan is a tax-sheltered retirement plan for people who work for tax-exempt organizations such as churches, universities, or charitable organizations.

Account is an accounting record of all the financial transactions and activities that take place related to a particular line item reported on financial statements. It shows increases and decreases to an item in chronological order.

Accounting is a system of recording, verifying, and reporting information about financial transactions.

Accounting close describes the activity that occurs at the end of an accounting period, so financial statements can be reported and released. It occurs at the end of each month, with greater emphasis (and therefore more activity) at the end of quarters and years.

Accounting period is a unit of time for which revenues and expenses are recorded and reported. Examples include months, quarters, and years.

Accounting Principles Board (APB) was an arm of the AICPA that existed from 1959 to 1973 to define a theoretical foundation of accounting and to issue pronouncements on current issues. The APB issued a number of opinions regarding accounting methods, but they have since been replaced by Generally Accepted Accounting Principles (GAAP) which are issued by the FASB.

Accounts payable is the amounts your company owes to other companies and individuals for goods and services you have received.

Accounts receivable is the amounts owed to your company for goods and services delivered.

Accounts receivable turnover is a ratio used to measure the number of times during an accounting period you receive the money owed to you in your accounts receivable portfolio. It is equal to total credit sales divided by the average accounts receivable balance.

Accrual means recording income or expense when it's earned or incurred rather than when you receive money or make a payment.

Accrual basis accounting is the type of accounting required by GAAP and the IRS for corporations and other businesses with more than $5 million in gross receipts for the past three years. It means to record financial transactions when they occur (when revenue is earned or expense is incurred), rather than when money is exchanged.

Accumulated depreciation represents the cumulative total of depreciation expenses for those items listed on the balance sheet in Property, plant and equipment (PPE). It is the total of prior-year and current-year expense.

Acid test ratio. See *quick ratio.*

Activity ratios are ratios that show how quickly your accounts receivable and inventory are turned into cash. Two common formulas used to create activity ratios are *inventory turnover* (which looks at your activity from the perspective of how much it costs you to sell your product) and *accounts receivable* (which examines how much you gain from a sales perspective).

Adjustable rate mortgages (ARMs) are variable-rate mortgages that have predetermined interest rate increases included in the loan agreement. Interest rates may or may not be fixed for a specified period of time.

Aging report tells you the amounts of your outstanding invoices and at what stage in the payment cycle they are. The aging report also shows patterns of payment delinquency and where collection efforts should be focused.

Allocated means to divide up the cost and assign it to different groups, departments, or divisions. It is based upon a logical and explainable formula for dividing costs, such as man-hours or machine-hours.

American Accounting Association (**AAA**) is a group of accounting educators who research principles and publish reports and opinions.

American Institute of Certified Public Accountants (**AICPA**) is an organization that certifies CPAs and governs the practices they use. The AICPA was instrumental in creating the Financial Accounting Standards Board, the father of Generally Accepted Accounting Principles (GAAP), which continues to issue FASB statements.

American Stock Exchange (**AMEX**) is a U.S. stock exchange that trades stocks, bonds, options, and derivatives of small to medium-size companies.

Amortization is an accounting technique used to reduce an intangible asset's value over time through expensing a portion of the cost each period. *Depreciation* and *depletion* are two other terms for amortization. *Amortization* also refers to the portion of periodic payments that reduces the principal balance of a loan.

Annual report is a year-end description in words and financial statements of the preceding year's activities. It includes a description of the company's operations, the balance sheet, the income statement, and the auditor's opinion. The Securities and Exchange Commission requires all public companies to send their annual reports to all shareholders once a year.

Annuities are instruments through which you make or receive regular payments into or from a fund.

Asset-backed securities are bonds or notes payable backed by collateral such as mortgages or car loans.

Assets are things a company owns that are used to produce income.

Ask price is the price at which a marketable security is held for sale.

Audit is an objective, third-party examination of financial statements and supporting documents to ensure that the records and reports are fair and consistent and that they conform to GAAP.

Average cost inventory method (weighted average) is a method of valuing inventory by using the average cost or weighted average cost for one unit. The formula for calculating inventory cost is the number of units available for sale multiplied by the average item cost.

Bad-debt expense (writing it off) is the expense recorded on the P&L to reflect accounts receivable that are uncollectible.

Balance of payments is the relationship between all cash paid between countries for government, business, and individual funds during a specified period of time.

Balance sheet is a financial statement or report that lists everything a company owns (its assets), everything it owes (its liabilities), and the difference between the two (owners equity). It is based on the basic accounting model: assets = liabilities + owners equity. It is formally known as the *statement of financial position,* and it is presented as of a specific date.

Basic accounting model is assets = liabilities + equity.

Basis point is a measurement used in quoting yields on securities and equals one-hundredth of one percentage point (0.01%) of yield.

Bear market is a prolonged period of falling stock prices.

Bearer bonds are bonds that are owned by the individual or entity that "holds" the bond certificate (the bearer). They are difficult to replace if lost or stolen because no record of ownership is kept by the issuing company.

Benefit-cost return is a capital budgeting technique that compares the benefit determined by the NPV of cash inflows from a project with the cost, or NPV of cash outflows, of a project.

Beta coefficient, also known as **beta**, measures a stock's relative volatility against a market index such as the Dow Jones Industrial Average. It is also a measure of a stock's relative risk compared to market. The market's beta is 1.0.

Bid price is the price a buyer is willing to pay for a marketable security.

Blue chip stocks are those stocks that are noted for their stability in profit growth and high-quality management teams and products.

Bond certificate is the actual receipt that defines the terms of the bond.

Bond discount is the face value of the bond less the amount an investor pays.

Bond premium is the amount an investor pays over the face value of the bond.

Bonds are a type of interest-bearing loan made to a company or government agency, with a specific date of maturity. They are negotiable debt securities that can be purchased and sold on the open securities market.

Book value is the value of an asset shown on the balance sheet. It is equal to the asset's cost less amortization (or depreciation) or any other recognized decline in value.

Bottom line refers to how much money a company makes (net income or loss) in any given period of time.

Breakeven point is the point at which sales equals cost, either as a whole or unit by unit.

Brokers are professional stock and bond traders who buy and sell stock or bonds at a profit or for a commission.

Budgeting is the financial term used to describe determining the estimated revenues and expenses for a given period of time, such as a year.

Bull market is a prolonged period of increasing stock prices.

Business risk is the risk associated with the nature of the business.

Buying on margin is the same as buying securities on credit, and often requires a minimum cash balance for the duration of the margin loan.

Call is an option to buy.

Call option is the right to purchase a specific number of stock shares (in lots of 100) at a specific price before a certain date (called the *expiration date*).

Call premium is the amount a buyer must pay to acquire a call option.

Callable bond a bond issued with the right of the issuing organization to buy it back (to call it) before the bond's maturity date.

Capital appreciation is the increased value of an asset or investment over its purchase price.

Capital asset is an asset on the balance sheet of a company.

Capital budgeting is a way of determining how much your company is going to spend on capital assets.

Capital gains are computed as the excess of the selling price over the purchase price for a capital asset.

Capital lease is lease classified as a financing arrangement by GAAP.

Capital stock is a transferable unit of ownership of a company.

Capitalize means to record an item on the balance sheet as an asset and expense it in portions to the P&L over time.

Capitalizing the cost means to include something as an asset on the balance sheet.

Cash flow statement is a financial statement that describes where a company's money came from and where it is going. It is formally known as the *statement of cash receipts and disbursements* as of a period of time.

Cash on hand is any currency or coins not deposited into the company's bank account.

Cash shortfalls occur when there are gaps of time where invoices must be paid, but revenues won't be received in time to pay them off.

Certificates of deposit (CDs) are interest-bearing debt instruments issued by banks. They are issued in $1,000 or $10,000 increments.

Closed-end investment funds are funds that have a certain number of shares issued to investors. To invest, a buyer must find a willing seller on the open fund market.

Collateral is something of value that your company pledges as security against a loan obligation.

Commercial paper signifies fairly high-priced notes that are usually issued by companies with a need for short-term capital.

Commodities are mining, agricultural, or food products that are sold in large quantities on a commodities exchange.

Common stock is a unit of corporate ownership that typically has voting and dividend rights. Claims of creditors and preferred stockholders come before common stockholders' claims in the event of corporate liquidation.

Compensated absence liabilities refers to the accrued amount for employee sick leave and vacations.

Compensating balance refers to the percentage of the principal required to be kept in another account while the loan is outstanding. It increases the effective annual interest rate on the loan.

Compensation is defined as the hourly wages and overtime pay, or annual salaries paid, as well as bonuses.

Compound interest is interest paid on the principal and on interest you've already earned.

Compounding simply means making money on the money you've just earned.

Constraint is an accounting term that refers a financial limitation due to the cost involved.

Contra accounts are accounts that have a normal balance that is contrary (opposite) to what you might think. For example, contra asset accounts have a normal credit balance, rather than a debit balance which the normal for asset accounts.

Convertible bonds are those that can be exchanged for shares of stock of the issuing corporation, as specified by the bond certificate.

Corporate bonds are interest-bearing bonds issued by corporations.

Corporation is a legal entity that is separate and apart from its owners. It has three distinct characteristics: limited liability for the owners, easy transfer of ownership through the sale of stocks, and a continuing existence.

Cost of capital is the interest rate at which a company can generate funds (through stock or debt issuance) to finance capital assets.

Cost of goods sold (COGS) is a line item on a P&L that refers to the cost of products sold during an accounting period.

Coupon bond is a bond issued with detachable coupons that are presented to the paying authority in order to receive interest payments.

CPA firm (certified public accounting firm) (also known as **public accounting firm**) is an independent accounting organization that is registered with state boards of accountancy and focuses on three main areas: auditing (looking at a company's financial statements objectively to give an opinion about whether they are presented according to GAAP), tax, and management advisory or consulting.

Certified public accountant (CPA) is an accountant who has the certifications and credentials to perform accounting services for others. A CPA works inside companies and other organizations (as a private accountant) and in public accounting firms (as a public accountant).

Credit is an accounting term that describes a decrease in assets and expenses, or an increase in liabilities, owner's equity and revenues. It also describes short-term financing, such as financing extended by suppliers or vendors.

Credit risk describes the risk involved with the likelihood of a debtor being able to repay a debt or a note owed. To determine credit risk, a rating agency takes into account factors such as financial stability and history of credit.

Credit lines are loans that have flexible borrowing capabilities.

Current assets are assets that will be converted to cash within a year.

Current liabilities are debts that must be paid within a year.

Current ratio is a liquidity ratio that determines whether a company has enough liquid assets (assets easily converted to cash) to cover current liabilities. The formula is current assets divided by current liabilities. Its weakness is that inventories are included in current assets, but inventories may not be as easily converted to cash as marketable securities or accounts receivable.

Current yield is the annual interest on a bond divided by its current market price. It represents the effect of annual interest rate earned on the bond.

Day traders are nonprofessional traders who use online brokerages (a fast-paced technique of buying and selling securities in the same day). The goal of day traders is to be completely out of all positions by the time the market closes.

Debit is an accounting entry that describes an increase in assets and expenses, or a decrease in liabilities, owner's equity, and revenues.

Debt covenant is a binding promise that a company makes to a lender as part of a loan agreement. Debt covenants commit a company to specific financial terms. If the company doesn't meet the terms, the debt comes due immediately unless the company can receive a waiver from the lender.

Default on loan means the company cannot repay the debt.

Deferred charges is a broad term that describes different items with debit balances that don't fit anywhere else on the balance sheet.

Depreciation is the amount of a fixed asset's value that is expensed on the P&L. The expense amount is determined by a defined depreciation method, such as straight-line or double-declining balance, and it represents a reduction in value.

Direct costs are costs directly related to producing goods and services.

Direct labor means the wage and related expenses of the people who either assemble components to build finished products or run the equipment that transforms raw materials into finished products.

Direct materials include all raw materials that make up a finished product.

Discount brokers are brokers who offer limited services to investors at a reduced fee or commission.

Discounted bond is a bond that sells for less than its face value.

Discretionary accounts provide brokers with the authority to make investment decisions without the clients' knowledge or approval.

Dishonored note is one that the borrower failed to pay back by or at the maturity date of the loan (i.e., the borrowing company has defaulted on the loan).

Dividend reinvestment program (DRIP) is a plan offered by some companies that allows investors to automatically reinvest their dividends in the same stock, often without broker fees and sometimes at a discount.

Dividends are payments made to shareholders from a corporation's earnings or profits. They represent a return on the shareholders' investment.

Double-declining balance (DDB), also known as 200% declining balance, is an accelerated depreciation method that allows a company to take more depreciation earlier in a fixed asset's life. It is also an approved method of depreciation for federal income tax.

Double-entry bookkeeping is the practice of using two methods (debits = credits and assets = liabilities + owners' equity) to make sure financial transactions are accurately recorded in journal entries.

Dow Jones is a publishing business that distributes some of the world's most influential business and financial new reports.

Dow Jones Industrial Average (DJIA) is a price-weighted average of 30 actively traded blue chip stocks. It is used as an indicator of general trends in the stock market.

Due on the stated date means that all payments must be made on or before the date of maturity specified in the agreement.

EDGAR (Electronic Data Gathering, Analysis and Retrieval System) allows public companies to file required documents electronically with the SEC, and gives the public a way to view the filings online through the Internet.

ERISA (the Employee Retirement Income Security Act) was passed in 1974 to regulate employee benefits and retirement plans.

Earnings before interest and taxes (EBIT) is net income (or loss) before adding interest income or deducting interest expense and income taxes. It is also known as net operating income (or loss).

Earnings per share (EPS) tells investors how much the company is earning for every share of stock that owners have. It is calculated as the net income divided by average number of outstanding shares.

Economies of scale is the reduction in the cost of producing one unit of goods due to mass production technologies and efficiencies. In other words, it's usually less expensive to make a lot of one item than it is to make small amounts of many different types of items.

Effective annual interest rate is the interest rate that a borrower actually pays, which may be higher than the stated interest on a loan.

Employee stock ownership plan (ESOP) is a way for an employee to own a portion of the company. Some employers give stock to employees, with provisions about their remaining with the company. In other cases, the employer may make it easy and attractive for employees to buy company stock with brokers' fees reduced or eliminated.

Equity is the portion of ownership in property, whether in the assets of a company or in individual assets.

E-trading, also known as **electronic trading,** is the buying and selling of securities over the Internet through an online brokerage.

Expense it means to record it as an expense on the profit and loss statement.

External auditors are CPAs who work for a public accounting firm. After analyzing a company's financial statements to make sure they are following Generally Accepted Accounting Principles (GAAP), they issue opinions.

FASB (pronounced *faz-bee*) **(Financial Accounting Standards Board)** is an independent nongovernment board that outlines accounting practices and Generally Accepted Accounting Principles (GAAP).

Face value of a loan is the principal amount of the loan.

Federal Insurance Contributions Act (FICA) is the federal law that requires employers to withhold a percentage of an employee's wages and pay them into a government trust fund. This act created what we know as Social Security, and the fund pays for retirement, disability, and other benefits.

Federal Reserve is the national banking authority that regulates the U.S. money supply, oversees national monetary policies, and makes sure that national banks are adhering to those policies.

Federal Unemployment Tax Act (FUTA) is a federal law that requires employers to contribute to a government fund that in turn pays unemployment benefits to people who are terminated or laid off.

Finance is a science that involves interpreting the information compiled in accounting, predicting outcomes, and planning to achieve favorable financial results.

Financial ratios are comparisons that allow an analyst or investor to evaluate how well a company is performing compared to the competition, to itself at a different time, and to its industry average.

Financial risk is related to the amount of debt (or leverage) that a company uses to fund its operations.

Financial statements are standardized formats for reporting financial information. Examples include the balance sheet, income statement, and statement of cash flow.

Finished goods are inventory products that are ready to be sold.

First-in, first-out (FIFO) is an inventory valuation method that treats the oldest item in your inventory as the first one sold.

Fixed costs are expenses such as rent, utilities, and salaries that will continue to be the same no matter how much a company produces.

Float is the difference between the time a check is written and mailed, and the time it clears the bank.

F.O.B. (free on board) shipping point designates that the title of goods passes when the seller delivers the goods to the shipper.

F.O.B. destination designates that the title of goods passes when the goods arrive at the customer's site.

Focus, in business terms, simply means that a manufacturer can often become more efficient and effective in its manufacturing process if it concentrates on the products that it does well.

Forecasting is the finance tool used to project revenues, expenses, and major capital expenditures of a company at some point in the future. It is used to manage cash flow expectations and to make other management decisions.

Future value is what today's money is worth at some time in the future.

Future contract is an agreement to buy or sell an investment at a specified price by a specified future date.

GAAP (Generally Accepted Accounting Principles) are the rules governing accounting for financial transactions and reporting them.

Garnishment is a legal situation in which a creditor (first party) asks the court to require a third party to collect funds from a debtor (second party). We hear of this often when an employer is required by the court to withhold an amount from an employee's check to repay a creditor.

General and administrative expenses (G&A) are expenses that are not included in cost of goods sold.

General journal is a diary of all the financial events or transactions (debits and credits) that happen in a month and are recorded in order by date.

General ledger is the collection of all an entity's accounts.

Goal of a corporation is to increase shareholder wealth.

Goodwill refers to intangible characteristics of a company (such as its good reputation, established brand names, and loyal customers) that result in its profits being higher than would be expected simply from its products or services.

Horizontal analysis is a method of analyzing financial statements that compares changes in each line item from one accounting period to another.

Hurdle rate is the lowest possible return on investment that management will consider for new products or projects.

IRA rollover is the reinvestment of a lump-sum distribution from a company-sponsored or other federal-government-approved retirement plan to an individual retirement account (IRA).

Idle cash is money that isn't earning anything because it hasn't been invested.

In the black means that the company has net income.

In the red means that the company has net loss.

Income statement is a financial statement that depicts a company's revenues and expenses for a defined period of time, such as one month, quarter, or year. It is formally known as the **statement of income** as of a period in time.

Indenture is the legal agreement that describes the terms of the bond. It's also called a **deed of trust**.

Index shares are stocks that represent small ownership percentages of all stocks listed on a defined index, such as the S&P 100 or the Dow Jones Industrial Average. They can be traded on stock exchanges like normal stocks.

Indirect costs are costs that can't be specifically linked to manufacturing a product, such as building depreciation or utilities.

Indirect labor refers to labor costs that are not directly involved in the manufacturing process, such as salaries, wages, and related expenses for supervisors, managers, janitors who clean the manufacturing floor, and engineers.

Individual retirement account (IRA) is a savings accounts to which the federal government allows an investor to contribute a certain amount of pre-tax or after-tax dollars. The earnings aren't taxed until the investor receives distributions at retirement. If an investor pulls the money out before a specified retirement age, the distributions may be subject to federal income tax and early withdrawal penalties.

Infinite net present value is a capital budgeting technique that is the equivalent annual benefit (EAB) divided by the cost of capital.

Inflation is the general rising of prices over time.

Inflation rate is the percentage increase that prices are rising over period of time.

Initial public offering (IPO) is the legal process a corporation goes through to make its stock available for sale to the public.

Insider trading is the term for the illegal practice of using "inside" information about a company to gain an unfair advantage in the stock market.

Institutional buyers are large firms that invest huge amounts of money in securities markets.

Intangible assets are company assets that are listed on the balance sheet, but do not have physical characteristics that can be perceived by the senses. Examples include reputation and patents.

Interest is the amount paid to a lender for the use of its money.

Interest rate is the percentage rate charged (or paid) for use of money.

Internal auditor is a CPA who works for a company to review its policies and accounting practices to make sure it maintains appropriate internal controls to prevent fraud and promote good operations, and to ensure that the company is following GAAP.

International Monetary Fund (IMF) is a group of member countries that work together to stabilize the world economy by developing foreign exchange and domestic currency policies.

Inventory is the dollar value of the goods you have on hand for resale to customers. It includes raw materials, work in process, and finished products.

Investment clubs are legitimate partnership business entities that allow the casual investor to participate and learn more about stocks and the process of investing.

Investment funds are large entities that allow small investors to diversify by pooling their funds to purchase stocks in large volumes. They are managed by a professional investing team and governed by the stated investing strategies.

Journal entry is an accounting term used to describe the recording of financial transactions in the general journal with debits and credits.

Junk bonds are high-risk investments that are rated as the lowest-quality bonds. They may also be called "high-yield" or "non-investment-grade" bonds.

Keogh is a tax-deferred retirement account for unincorporated businesses and individuals.

Kiting is a form of fraud where an employee cashes an accounts receivable check, pockets the money, and covers the shortage on the company's books by recording other accounts receivable checks in its place.

Last-in, first-out (LIFO) is an inventory valuation method that treats the last item purchased as the first item sold.

Lease is a contract to rent property.

Leasehold is the property that is leased.

Legal capital is the total par value of common stock.

Leverage ratios are ratios that measure your company's level or use of debt.

Liabilities are the amounts a company owes to other businesses or individuals.

Lien is public record that a lender has first priority to obtain the property used as collateral if the company is unable to pay its debts.

Limit order requires a broker or dealer to buy or sell a security only at a specified price (the limit) or better.

Limited liability corporation (LLC) is a cross between a partnership and a corporation. It allows the members to be protected from liability for debts incurred by the entity, but it doesn't have the extensive reporting requirements of a corporation. Like a partnership, it has a limited life.

Line item refers to an individual account on any financial statement.

Liquid assets are assets that can be quickly converted to cash.

Liquidation value is the amount of cash that could be generated as a result of selling all the assets of a company at a "fire sale."

Liquidity ratios are ratios that reflect a company's ability to pay its current debt. The two liquidity ratios are *current ratio* (current assets divided by current liabilities) and *acid test* or *quick ratio* (quick assets inventory divided by current liabilities).

Loan agreement is the legal contract specifying all the terms and conditions of the loan.

Loan amortization is similar to intangible asset amortization in that it specifies what portion of the loan repayment is an expense (interest expense) to the company.

Loan amortization schedule is a spreadsheet or financial statement that shows, for each loan payment, how much of the payment is actually reducing the loan principal (paying back the loan) and how much is the interest payment.

Loan closing refers to the signing of the loan agreements by both the lender and the borrower.

Loan payoff is the amount that your company has to pay the lender to completely pay off a loan at any given time. It includes the remaining principal and interest due.

Long-term assets are assets that generate revenues and have an estimated useful life of more than one year.

Long-term forecast is a projection of revenues and expenses for three to five years and is intended to predict where the company is going and to anticipate the major financial events that will occur.

Long-term liabilities are liabilities that come due in over one year.

Lower of cost or market (LCM) is a GAAP rule that states if your inventory value decreases below market value or replacement cost, inventory must be written down to the depreciated value.

MACRS (Modified Accelerated Cost Recovery System) is an accelerated tax depreciation method approved by the IRS.

Manufacturing overhead is all costs related to manufacturing products except direct materials and direct labor.

Market order is an order to buy or sell a security at the market price as soon as the order reaches the marketplace.

Market risk is the risk associated with events that are external to the company or industry, such as war, inflation, recession, or high interest rates.

Market value of equity is the current market price for all of the outstanding stock, or the total number of outstanding shares multiplied by the market price.

Matching principle states that a company should match revenues earned with the expenses incurred to generate the revenue, even if the cash is not yet received or paid.

Maturity date (also known as **termination date**) of the loan is the date on which a loan becomes due and complete payment must be made.

Money market investments are short-term investments that are similar to interest-bearing savings accounts. They are often used to invest idle cash overnight.

Mortgage is a legal document that gives the lender a lien on the property being financed. If the borrower doesn't repay the loan according to the terms specified by the agreement, the lender can take the property and the borrower will lose all equity. Mortgages apply to real estate and other types of property held for collateral. They are also known as secured debt.

Municipal bonds are interest-bearing debt issued by local or state governments, usually to pay for a specific project. The interest is exempt from federal income tax.

Mutual funds are investment funds that include a combination of cash and securities, and are directed by a fund manager who buys and sells on behalf of a group of investors.

NASDAQ (National Association of Securities Dealers Automated Quota System) is owned by the National Association of Securities Dealers, and is a computerized system that provides price quotations for over-the-counter stocks and some NYSE-listed stocks.

National Association of Securities Dealers (NASD) is an association of securities dealers who work under the guidance of the SEC to oversee the practices associated with investment banking houses and over-the-counter (OTC) trading.

Net income is the result of revenues exceeding expenses incurred to generate the revenues.

Net loss is the result of expenses exceeding revenues.

Net present value (NPV) is a capital budgeting technique that determines the present value of an unequal flow of cash payments. It is used to determine whether new projects and capital assets will bring a required rate of return.

Net revenues describes gross revenues less sales returns and/or sales discounts.

New York Stock Exchange (NYSE) is the largest stock exchange in the United States.

No-load fund is a fund that charges no commission for purchasing or selling fund shares.

No par value is common stock that was not assigned a legal value when a corporation was formed.

Noncallable bond is a bond issued without the right of the organization to buy it back before its redemption date.

Normal balance means the balance under normal circumstances. For example, assets have a normal debit balance; liabilities and owners' equity have a normal credit balance.

Notes payable is short for **promissory note**, which is an unconditional promise to pay a certain amount of money with interest at the due date of the note.

Odd lot refers to stock sold in blocks of less than 100 shares.

Online trading, also known as **e-trading**, is the buying or selling of stock over the Internet through an online brokerage.

Open-end investment funds are mutual funds that allow unlimited numbers of investors to participate in them.

Operating capital is the money a company uses to operate from day to day.

Opportunity cost is the cost (or net income lost) of taking advantage of one investment option instead of an alternative. Its relevance is due to limited resources or funding for projects and new products.

Option is the right to buy and sell assets at a certain price before a specified date.

Options Clearing Corporation (OCC) is the largest clearinghouse for options contracts in the U.S.

Outstanding stock is stock held by other entities or individuals outside the issuing organization.

Over-the-counter (OTC) **stock** is stock that isn't listed on an organized stock exchange, probably because the company cannot meet exchange listing requirements.

Overhead expenses. See general and administrative expenses.

Owners' equity is the same as stockholders' equity; however, this term usually applies to sole proprietorships, whereas stockholders' equity applies to corporations.

Paid-in capital is the amount above par value that common stock is sold for.

Par value, also known as **face value**, is the stated value or principal of a security as it appears on the certificate.

Partnership is comprised of two or more owners who are equally liable for issues associated with the company. There are two types of partnerships: general partnerships and limited partnerships.

Pass-through entities are entities that are not considered separate legal entities for federal income tax purposes. They are required to file information returns with the IRS, but their taxable incomes are included in the owners' income tax returns (and the owners pay the income tax owed). Examples include partnerships, Subchapter S corporations, and limited liability corporations that have elected to be treated as partnerships.

Payable on demand means that the loan is due on a date decided by the lender.

Payback period is the length of time it will take for management to earn back its initial investment in a project.

Payroll bank account is an account used by an employer exclusively for the payment of employee wages and salaries.

Payroll taxes are the employer's portion of FICA and Medicare that are paid to the Social Security Administration for their employees' Social Security benefits.

Penny stocks are stocks that used to be valued at pennies, but are now available at $5 or less per share.

Pension plan is a systematic accumulation and investment of money for the purpose of providing retirement benefits for employees.

Periodic inventory system is an inventory tracking system in which employees count inventory items periodically in physical inventories. Accountants value inventory on the balance sheet by adjusting it to the actual counts multiplied by a specified cost.

Perks (perquisites) are benefits that accompany a person's position. Examples are automobile allowances, membership in country clubs, tickets to events, and trips.

Perpetual inventory system is an inventory tracking system that counts and values inventory as sales are made.

Personal guarantee is a company owner's guarantee that a debt will be repaid, even if the company goes into default. The lender can come after the owner for loan repayment, even if the company is a limited liability entity, such as a corporation or limited liability company, whose owners' personal assets are usually protected from the liability of the entity.

Petty cash is a small amount of cash, perhaps $100 to $500, that a company (or department) keeps on hand to buy miscellaneous items.

Portfolio is a collection of investments including cash, real estate, securities, and other investments.

Posting is the act of recording general journal transactions into the general ledger.

Preferred stock is a class of stock that defines one or more preferences over common stock, such as a right to be paid dividends before common stockholders.

Prepaid expenses are expenses that have been paid in advance of receiving the benefit of the goods or services. For example, insurance premiums paid in advance are prepaid expenses, which are refunded if the service is discontinued before the expiration of the paid period.

Present value is what a future amount of money is worth today.

Price/earnings ratio (PE) is a ratio that describes the relationship between how much the stock is selling for and how much it is earning. The formula for PE is current market price per share divided by EPS.

Prime rate is the interest rate that a lending institution charges its best customers.

Principal is the amount of money borrowed or the limit on the amount your company can borrow (as in the case of credit lines). It is also the stated value (or face value) of a bond.

Private accounting is an accounting term used to describe the work performed by an accountant or CPA who works for a company or an organization other than a public accounting firm.

Profit and loss statement (P&L) is the income statement of a company.

Profit-sharing plan is a savings plan in which the company shares its profits with employees by making discretionary contributions into a tax-deferred employee retirement account.

Profitability ratios are ratios that measure performance as indicated by a company's return on sales or assets. The common profitability ratios are *gross profit margin (GPM), net profit margin (NPM), return on assets (ROA), return on equity (ROE), return on sales (ROS),* and *return on investment (ROI).*

Property and real estate taxes are taxes paid to local and/or county governments as a privilege to do business in their area.

Proxy and proxy statement is an absentee ballot that a shareholder uses to vote on company decisions if she is unable to attend the annual stockholders' meeting.

Publicly held corporations are companies that sell portions of their ownership (stock) in an open stock market.

Put is an option to sell.

Put option is the right to sell a specific number of stock shares (in lots of 100) at a specific price before a certain date (called the expiration date).

Quick assets are assets that are easily converted to cash, such as cash equivalents, marketable securities, and accounts receivable. It is equal to current assets less inventory.

Quick ratio is a liquidity ratio used to determine if a company has enough liquid assets (those easily converted to cash) to cover current liabilities. It is computed as quick assets divided by current liabilities. It is also known as an **acid test ratio**.

Raw materials are inventory items that must be processed before they can be sold to customers.

Reconcile an account means to compare an account balance with an independent source, such as a bank statement, to locate errors and adjustments.

Redemption date is the date on which a bond matures or will be redeemed by the issuing corporation.

Redemption value is the amount needed to buy back securities (stocks, bonds or mutual fund shares). For bonds, it is typically the face value.

Registered bonds are bonds in which the owner's name appears on the bond certificate. The issuing company (called the registrar) keeps a record of ownership, making registered bonds easy to replace if they are lost or stolen.

Retained earnings refers to the cumulative total of what the company has earned or lost since it was founded. It includes all prior-year net income (or losses) and current-year net income (or loss).

Revenues (also known as **sales**) are the income received for sales of products or services.

Reverse stock split is the issuing of fewer stock shares in exchange for the current amount that is outstanding. This may happen when the board of directors feels its stock is underpriced. Each shareholder's number of shares is reduced by the amount specified in the split. The investment is worth the same amount of money, but each share of stock has a higher proportionate value.

Risk is the potential loss in value caused by controllable and uncontrollable events. It is inherent in all financial transactions and is caused by the fact that the future is unknown and uncertain.

Round lot refers to stock sold in blocks of 100 shares.

Salaries are money paid to employees who work for a set amount per period and are not paid overtime.

Sales discounts are markdowns off the original price of a product or service.

Sales returns are amounts given back to customers for items that have been returned to the company for whatever reason.

Sales tax is a tax collected on a product (or service sometimes) sold to the end user.

Securities and Exchange Commission (SEC) is a government agency that administers policies governing the sale of securities.

Secured bonds are bonds that have some type of collateral guaranteeing them.

Secured debt (also called a **mortgage**) is a note that has assets pledged to the debt (collateral) to guarantee that the loan will be paid.

Security is an investment instrument that represents an ownership or credit interest in a company or with the federal, state, or local government.

Securities Act of 1933 requires public companies to give investors accurate financial information and other pertinent data about a company.

Securities Exchange Act of 1934 established the Securities and Exchange Commission and expanded and clarified some regulations set out in the Securities Act of 1933.

Serial bonds are bonds that mature in groups at different maturity dates over the term of the bond issuance.

Servicing debt means keeping current on interest payment and the current amount due to repay principal.

Share (of stock) is one unit of ownership.

Shared-appreciation mortgage (SAM) allows the lender to share in the asset appreciation (but not share in asset depreciation or loss in value), rather than having the entire increase in value apply to the borrower's equity.

Shareholders, also known as **stockholders**, are individuals or legal entities that own stock in a company.

Short-term forecast is a forecast usually done midyear to predict what the expenses and revenues will be for the remainder of the year.

Short-term investments are stocks, bonds, or commercial paper that the company intends to sell within one year of the financial statement date.

Simple interest is interest calculated on the principal amount of the loan only. It is calculated as principal × interest × time.

Simplified employee pension (SEP) is a type of IRA, Keogh, or 401(k) plan for self-employed persons.

Social Security Act was passed by Congress in 1935 and created two national social insurance programs that provided old age benefits and unemployment insurance.

Sole proprietorship is a business entity in which one person owns the company. (For federal income tax purposes, that one person is the business entity.)

Specific identification is an inventory valuation method that requires you to value each item sold according to what the company specifically paid for it.

Standard & Poor's 500 Index (S&P 500) is a market-value-weighted index showing the change in aggregate market value of 500 stocks relative to their market values in a base period (1941-43).

State Unemployment Tax Act (SUTA) is a state law that requires employers to contribute to a state government fund that pays unemployment benefits to people who are terminated or laid off.

Stated interest rate is the interest rate stated in the loan agreement or a bond certificate.

Stock certificates are printed or engraved documents that are evidence that a shareholder owns a certain number of shares.

Stock option is the right to purchase or sell a stock at a specified price before a stated date.

Stock splits increase the number of outstanding shares of stock, thereby reducing the per share price and enabling more people to afford to buy shares. The total value of an investor's stock doesn't change because of a stock split.

Stock warrant allows a bondholder to purchase a certain number of common stock shares at a specific price.

Stockholders, also known as **shareholders**, are individuals or legal entities that own stock in a company.

Stockholders' equity, also known as **shareholders' equity**, is the portion of a company's assets that is owned by the stockholders.

Stocks are ownership of a corporation represented by shares.

Straight-line is a depreciation method that allocates equal portions of an asset's cost to each accounting period.

Subchapter S corporation (**S Corp**) is a federal income tax classification that allows corporate earnings to be taxed on the owners' income tax return, thereby eliminating the problem of double taxation.

Sum-of-the-years' digits (**SYD**) is an accelerated depreciation method that allows a company to record more depreciation early in a fixed asset's life than later in its life.

Supplemental executive retirement plan (**SERP**), otherwise known as a **top hat plan**, is a nonqualified retirement plan that can only be offered to key management.

Sweep account is a cash management tool used by companies that automatically "sweeps" idle cash into interest-bearing accounts for a specified period of time (often overnight). They are also used by large corporations to remove excess cash from bank accounts of divisions or operating units.

T-account is an accounting tool used to chart financial transactions.

Tangible assets are assets you can see and touch, such as buildings or office furniture.

Term bond is a bond that matures at the same time as all the other bonds from the same issuance.

Time value of money is the concept that the real value of money depends on when it is received.

Transfer journal voucher is a journal entry made between companies that are owned by the same holding company.

Treasury bills (T-bills) are short-term debt securities that are sold in denominations of $1,000 to $1,000,000 that mature in 12 months and have no stated amount of interest.

Treasury bonds are long-term bonds sold by the U.S. Treasury in denominations of $1,000 to $5,000,000 that mature in more than 10 years from the date of issuance, and pay a fixed rate of interest to the bondholder every six months. At maturity, the par or face value of the bond is returned to the bondholder.

Treasury notes are intermediate-term notes sold by the U.S. Treasury in denominations of $1,000 to over $100,000 that mature in more than one year but less than 10 years and pay a fixed rate of interest to the note holder every six months. At maturity, the par or face value of the note is paid back to the note holder.

Treasury stock is the stock that a company buys back from stockholders.

Trustee is an entity (often a bank) that represents the interest of the bondholders, ensuring that the issuing company meets the terms specified by the bond indenture.

Uncontrollable risks are risks that are completely unforeseeable and cannot be controlled or minimized by a company.

Underwriter refers to an investment firm or bank that guarantees the company a fixed price for issuance of stocks or bonds.

Unearned revenues are monies your company receives before you have delivered the goods or services.

Uniform Commercial Code (UCC) provides rules about when the title to goods passes from one entity to another.

Units of production, also know as the **output method**, is a depreciation method based on physical use rather than an estimated life.

Unregistered bonds (bearer bonds) are bonds in which the owner's name does not appear on the bond certificate, and there are no records kept on ownership.

Unsecured bonds are bonds that have no collateral or guarantee.

Unsecured debt is a note that is not supported by pledged assets (or collateral).

Useful life refers to the time you expect to be able to use an asset.

Variable costs are those that increase or decrease depending on the level of production.

Vertical analysis is a method of analyzing financial statements that looks at a line item and the percentage it represents of the total financial statement.

Vested benefits are pension benefits that belong to an employee independent of his future employment. An employee becomes partially "vested," that is, earns the right to a partial amount of the money for each year that he is employed. Companies are required to give employees full (100%) vesting in three to five years.

Wages refers to the money paid to employees who work by the hour.

Work in progress, also known as **work in process**, refers to partially completed manufactured products.

World Bank is the world's largest lending institution to developing countries.

Write down means to decrease an account balance.

Write up means to increase an account balance.

Yield is the percentage return on an investment.

Yield-to-maturity is a measurement that compares the total amount earned over the life of an investment to the price paid for it.

Zero-coupon bonds are those that do not pay periodic interest payments.

APPENDIX

TABLE I

Modified Accelerated Cost Recovery System
Applicable Depreciation Method: 200 or 150%
Declining Balance Switching to Straight Line
Applicable Recovery Periods: 3, 5, 7, 10, 15, 20 years
Applicable Convention: Half-Year

If the recovery year is	and the recovery period is 3 years	5 years	7 years	10 years	15 years	20 years
1	33.33	20.00	14.29	10.00	5.00	3.750
2	44.45	32.00	24.49	18.00	9.50	7.219
3	14.81	19.20	17.49	14.40	8.55	6.677
4	7.41	11.52	12.49	11.52	7.70	6.177
5		11.52	8.93	9.22	6.93	5.713
6		5.76	8.92	7.37	6.23	5.285
7			8.93	6.55	5.90	4.888
8			4.46	6.55	5.90	4.522
9				6.56	5.91	4.462
10				6.55	5.90	4.461
11				3.28	5.91	4.462
12					5.90	4.461
13					5.91	4.462
14					5.90	4.461
15					5.91	4.462
16					2.95	4.461
17						4.462
18						4.461
19						4.462
20						4.461
21						2.231

TABLE 2

Future Value of an Ordinary Annuity of $1 per Period, 0.5–20%

Period	0.5%	1.0%	1.5%	2.0%	2.5%	3.0%	3.5%	4.0%	4.5%	5.0%	5.5%
1	1.00000	1.00000	1.00000	1.00000	1.00000	1.00000	1.00000	1.00000	1.00000	1.00000	1.00000
2	2.00500	2.01000	2.01500	2.02000	2.02500	2.03000	2.03500	2.04000	2.04500	2.05000	2.05500
3	3.01502	3.03010	3.04522	3.06040	3.07563	3.09090	3.10622	3.12160	3.13703	3.15250	3.16803
4	4.03010	4.06040	4.09090	4.12161	4.15252	4.18363	4.21494	4.24646	4.27819	4.31013	4.34227
5	5.05025	5.10101	5.15227	5.20404	5.25633	5.30914	5.36247	5.41632	5.47071	5.52563	5.58109
6	6.07550	6.15202	6.22955	6.30812	6.38774	6.46841	6.55015	6.63298	6.71689	6.80191	6.88805
7	7.10588	7.21354	7.32299	7.43428	7.54743	7.66246	7.77941	7.89829	8.01915	8.14201	8.26689
8	8.14141	8.28567	8.43284	8.58297	8.73612	8.89234	9.05169	9.21423	9.38001	9.54911	9.72157
9	9.18212	9.36853	9.55933	9.75463	9.95452	10.15911	10.36850	10.58280	10.80211	11.02656	11.25626
10	10.22803	10.46221	10.70272	10.94972	11.20338	11.46388	11.73139	12.00611	12.28821	12.57789	12.87535
11	11.27917	11.56683	11.86326	12.16872	12.48347	12.80780	13.14199	13.48635	13.84118	14.20679	14.58350
12	12.33556	12.68250	13.04121	13.41209	13.79555	14.19203	14.60196	15.02581	15.46403	15.91713	16.38559
13	13.39724	13.80933	14.23683	14.68033	15.14044	15.61779	16.11303	16.62684	17.15991	17.71298	18.28680
14	14.46423	14.94742	15.45038	15.97394	16.51895	17.08632	17.67699	18.29191	18.93211	19.59863	20.29257
15	15.53655	16.09690	16.68214	17.29342	17.93193	18.59891	19.29568	20.02359	20.78405	21.57856	22.40866
16	16.61423	17.25786	17.93237	18.63929	19.38022	20.15688	20.97103	21.82453	22.71934	23.65749	24.64114
17	17.69730	18.43044	19.20136	20.01207	20.86473	21.76159	22.70502	23.69751	24.74171	25.84037	26.99640
18	18.78579	19.61475	20.48938	21.41231	22.38635	23.41444	24.49969	25.64541	26.85508	28.13238	29.48120
19	19.87972	20.81090	21.79672	22.84056	23.94601	25.11687	26.35718	27.67123	29.06356	30.53900	32.10267
20	20.97912	22.01900	23.12367	24.29737	25.54466	26.87037	28.27968	29.77808	31.37142	33.06595	34.86832
21	22.08401	23.23919	24.47052	25.78332	27.18327	28.67649	30.26947	31.96920	33.78314	35.71925	37.78608
22	23.19443	24.47159	25.83758	27.29898	28.86286	30.53678	32.32890	34.24797	36.30338	38.50521	40.86431
23	24.31040	25.71630	27.22514	28.84496	30.58443	32.45288	34.46041	36.61789	38.93703	41.43048	44.11185
24	25.43196	26.97346	28.63352	30.42186	32.34904	34.42647	36.66653	39.08260	41.68920	44.50200	47.53800
25	26.55912	28.24320	30.06302	32.03030	34.15776	36.45926	38.94986	41.64591	44.56521	47.72710	51.15259
26	27.69191	29.52563	31.51397	33.67091	36.01171	38.55304	41.31310	44.31174	47.57064	51.11345	54.96598
27	28.83037	30.82089	32.98668	35.34432	37.91200	40.70963	43.75906	47.08421	50.71132	54.66913	58.98911
28	29.97452	32.12910	34.48148	37.05121	39.85980	42.93092	46.29063	49.96758	53.99333	58.40258	63.23351
29	31.12439	33.45039	35.99870	38.79223	41.85630	45.21885	48.91080	52.96629	57.42303	62.32271	67.71135
30	32.28002	34.78489	37.53868	40.56808	43.90270	47.57542	51.62268	56.08494	61.00707	66.43885	72.43548

TABLE 2 *(Continued)*

Future Value of an Ordinary Annuity of $1 per Period, 0.5–20%

Period	6.0%	6.5%	7.0%	7.5%	8.0%	8.5%	9.0%	9.5%	10.0%
1	1.00000	1.00000	1.00000	1.00000	1.00000	1.00000	1.00000	1.00000	1.00000
2	2.06000	2.06500	2.07000	2.07500	2.08000	2.08500	2.09000	2.09500	2.10000
3	3.18360	3.19923	3.21490	3.23063	3.24640	3.26223	3.27810	3.29403	3.31000
4	4.37462	4.40717	4.43994	4.47292	4.50611	4.53951	4.57313	4.60696	4.64100
5	5.63709	5.69364	5.75074	5.80839	5.86660	5.92537	5.98471	6.04462	6.10510
6	6.97532	7.06373	7.15329	7.24402	7.33593	7.42903	7.52333	7.61886	7.71561
7	8.39384	8.52287	8.65402	8.78732	8.92280	9.06050	9.20043	9.34265	9.48717
8	9.89747	10.07686	10.25980	10.44637	10.63663	10.83064	11.02847	11.23020	11.43589
9	11.49132	11.73185	11.97799	12.22985	12.48756	12.75124	13.02104	13.29707	13.57948
10	13.18079	13.49442	13.81645	14.14709	14.48656	14.83510	15.19293	15.56029	15.93742
11	14.97164	15.37156	15.78360	16.20812	16.64549	17.09608	17.56029	18.03852	18.53117
12	16.86994	17.37071	17.88845	18.42373	18.97713	19.54925	20.14072	20.75218	21.38428
13	18.88214	19.49981	20.14064	20.80551	21.49530	22.21094	22.95338	23.72363	24.52271
14	21.01507	21.76730	22.55049	23.36592	24.21492	25.09887	26.01919	26.97738	27.97498
15	23.27597	24.18217	25.12902	26.11836	27.15211	28.23227	29.36092	30.54023	31.77248
16	25.67253	26.75401	27.88805	29.07724	30.32428	31.63201	33.00340	34.44155	35.94973
17	28.21288	29.49302	30.84022	32.25804	33.75023	35.32073	36.97370	38.71350	40.54470
18	30.90565	32.41007	33.99903	35.67739	37.45024	39.32300	41.30134	43.39128	45.59917
19	33.75999	35.51672	37.37896	39.35319	41.44626	43.66545	46.01846	48.51345	51.15909
20	36.78559	38.82531	40.99549	43.30468	45.76196	48.37701	51.16012	54.12223	57.27500
21	39.99273	42.34895	44.86518	47.55253	50.42292	53.48906	56.76453	60.26384	64.00250
22	43.39229	46.10164	49.00574	52.11897	55.45676	59.03563	62.87334	66.98891	71.40275
23	46.99583	50.09824	53.43614	57.02790	60.89330	65.05366	69.53194	74.35286	79.54302
24	50.81558	54.35463	58.17667	62.30499	66.76476	71.58322	76.78981	82.41638	88.49733
25	54.86451	58.88768	63.24904	67.97786	73.10594	78.66779	84.70090	91.24593	98.34706
26	59.15638	63.71538	68.67647	74.07620	79.95442	86.35455	93.32398	100.91430	109.18177
27	63.70577	68.85688	74.48382	80.63192	87.35077	94.69469	102.72313	111.50116	121.09994
28	68.52811	74.33257	80.69769	87.67931	95.33883	103.74374	112.96822	123.09377	134.20994
29	73.63980	80.16419	87.34653	95.25526	103.96594	113.56196	124.13536	135.78767	148.63093
30	79.05819	86.37486	94.46079	103.39940	113.28321	124.21473	136.30754	149.68750	164.49402

TABLE 2 *(Continued)*

Future Value of an Ordinary Annuity of $1 per Period, 0.5–20%

Period	10.5%	11.0%	11.5%	12.0%	12.5%	13.0%	13.5%	14.0%	14.5%	15.0%
1	1.00000	1.00000	1.00000	1.00000	1.00000	1.00000	1.00000	1.00000	1.00000	1.00000
2	2.10500	2.11000	2.11500	2.12000	2.12500	2.13000	2.13500	2.14000	2.14500	2.15000
3	3.32603	3.34210	3.35823	3.37440	3.39063	3.40690	3.42323	3.43960	3.45603	3.47250
4	4.67526	4.70973	4.74442	4.77933	4.81445	4.84980	4.88536	4.92114	4.95715	4.99338
5	6.16616	6.22780	6.29003	6.35285	6.41626	6.48027	6.54488	6.61010	6.67594	6.74238
6	7.81361	7.91286	8.01338	8.11519	8.21829	8.32271	8.42844	8.53552	8.64395	8.75374
7	9.63404	9.78327	9.93492	10.08901	10.24558	10.40466	10.56628	10.73049	10.89732	11.06680
8	11.64561	11.85943	12.07744	12.29969	12.52628	12.75726	12.99273	13.23276	13.47743	13.72682
9	13.86840	14.16397	14.46634	14.77566	15.09206	15.41571	15.74675	16.08535	16.43166	16.78584
10	16.32458	16.72201	17.12997	17.54874	17.97857	18.41975	18.87256	19.33730	19.81425	20.30372
11	19.03866	19.56143	20.09992	20.65458	21.22589	21.81432	22.42036	23.04452	23.68731	24.34928
12	22.03772	22.71319	23.41141	24.13313	24.87913	25.65018	26.44711	27.27075	28.12197	29.00167
13	25.35168	26.21164	27.10372	28.02911	28.98902	29.98470	31.01746	32.08865	33.19966	34.35192
14	29.01361	30.09492	31.22065	32.39260	33.61264	34.88271	36.20482	37.58107	39.01361	40.50471
15	33.06004	34.40536	35.81102	37.27971	38.81422	40.41746	42.09247	43.84241	45.67058	47.58041
16	37.53134	39.18995	40.92929	42.75328	44.66600	46.67173	48.77496	50.98035	53.29282	55.71747
17	42.47213	44.50084	46.63616	48.88367	51.24925	53.73906	56.35958	59.11760	62.02027	65.07509
18	47.93170	50.39594	52.99932	55.74971	58.65541	61.72514	64.96812	68.39407	72.01321	75.83636
19	53.96453	56.93949	60.09424	63.43968	66.98733	70.74941	74.73882	78.96923	83.45513	88.21181
20	60.63081	64.20283	68.00508	72.05244	76.36075	80.94683	85.82856	91.02493	96.55612	102.44358
21	67.99704	72.26514	76.82566	81.69874	86.90584	92.46992	98.41541	104.76842	111.55676	118.81012
22	76.13673	81.21431	86.66062	92.50258	98.76908	105.49101	112.70149	120.43600	128.73249	137.63164
23	85.13109	91.14788	97.62659	104.60289	112.11521	120.20484	128.91619	138.29704	148.39871	159.27638
24	95.06985	102.17415	109.85364	118.15524	127.12961	136.83147	147.31988	158.65862	170.91652	184.16784
25	106.05219	114.41331	123.48681	133.33387	144.02081	155.61956	168.20806	181.87083	196.69941	212.79302
26	118.18767	127.99877	138.68780	150.33393	163.02341	176.85010	191.91615	208.33274	226.22083	245.71197
27	131.59737	143.07864	155.63589	169.37401	184.40134	200.84061	218.82483	238.49933	260.02285	283.56877
28	146.41510	159.81729	174.53513	190.69889	208.45151	227.94989	249.36618	272.88923	298.72616	327.10408
29	162.78868	178.39719	195.60668	214.58275	235.50795	258.58338	284.03062	312.09373	343.04145	377.16969
30	180.88149	199.02088	219.10144	241.33268	265.94644	293.19922	323.37475	356.78685	393.78246	434.74515

TABLE 2 *(Continued)*

Future Value of an Ordinary Annuity of $1 per Period, 0.5–20%

Period	15.5%	16.0%	16.5%	17.0%	17.5%	18.0%	18.5%	19.0%	19.5%	20.0%
1	1.00000	1.00000	1.00000	1.00000	1.00000	1.00000	1.00000	1.00000	1.00000	1.00000
2	2.15500	2.16000	2.16500	2.17000	2.17500	2.18000	2.18500	2.19000	2.19500	2.20000
3	3.48903	3.50560	3.52223	3.53890	3.55563	3.57240	3.58923	3.60610	3.62303	3.64000
4	5.02982	5.06650	5.10339	5.14051	5.17786	5.21543	5.25323	5.29126	5.32951	5.36800
5	6.80945	6.87714	6.94545	7.01440	7.08398	7.15421	7.22508	7.29660	7.36877	7.44160
6	8.86491	8.97748	9.09145	9.20685	9.32368	9.44197	9.56172	9.68295	9.80568	9.92992
7	11.23897	11.41387	11.59154	11.77201	11.95533	12.14152	12.33064	12.52271	12.71779	12.91590
8	13.98101	14.24009	14.50415	14.77325	15.04751	15.32700	15.61181	15.90203	16.19776	16.49908
9	17.14807	17.51851	17.89733	18.28471	18.68082	19.08585	19.49999	19.92341	20.35632	20.79890
10	20.80602	21.32147	21.85039	22.39311	22.94997	23.52131	24.10749	24.70886	25.32580	25.95868
11	25.03095	25.73290	26.45570	27.19994	27.96621	28.75514	29.56737	30.40355	31.26433	32.15042
12	29.91075	30.85017	31.82089	32.82393	33.86030	34.93107	36.03734	37.18022	38.36088	39.58050
13	35.54692	36.78620	38.07134	39.40399	40.78585	42.21866	43.70424	45.24446	46.84125	48.49660
14	42.05669	43.67199	45.35311	47.10267	48.92337	50.81802	52.78953	54.84091	56.97529	59.19592
15	49.57548	51.65951	53.83638	56.11013	58.48496	60.96527	63.55559	66.26068	69.08547	72.03511
16	58.25968	60.92503	63.71938	66.64885	69.71983	72.93901	76.31338	79.85021	83.55714	87.44213
17	68.28993	71.67303	75.23307	78.97915	82.92080	87.06804	91.43135	96.02175	100.85079	105.93056
18	79.87486	84.14072	88.64653	93.40561	98.43194	103.74028	109.34615	115.26588	121.51669	128.11667
19	93.25547	98.60323	104.27321	110.28456	116.65753	123.41353	130.57519	138.16640	146.21244	154.74000
20	108.71007	115.37975	122.47829	130.03294	138.07260	146.62797	155.73160	165.41802	175.72387	186.68800
21	126.56013	134.84051	143.68721	153.13854	163.23531	174.02100	185.54194	197.84744	210.99002	225.02560
22	147.17695	157.41499	168.39560	180.17209	192.80149	206.34479	220.86720	236.43846	253.13308	271.03072
23	170.98937	183.60138	197.18087	211.80134	227.54175	244.48685	262.72763	282.36176	303.49403	326.23686
24	198.49272	213.97761	230.71571	248.80757	268.36155	289.49448	312.33225	337.01050	363.67536	392.48424
25	230.25910	249.21402	269.78381	292.10486	316.32482	342.60349	371.11371	402.04249	435.59206	471.98108
26	266.94926	290.08827	315.29813	342.76268	372.68167	405.27211	440.76975	479.43056	521.53251	567.37730
27	309.32639	337.50239	368.32233	402.03234	438.90096	479.22109	523.31215	571.52237	624.23135	681.85276
28	358.27198	392.50277	430.09551	471.37783	516.70863	566.48089	621.12490	681.11162	746.95647	819.22331
29	414.80414	456.30322	502.06127	552.51207	608.13264	669.44745	737.03300	811.52283	893.61298	984.06797
30	480.09878	530.31173	585.90138	647.43912	715.55585	790.94799	874.38411	966.71217	1068.86751	1181.88157

TABLE 3

Present Value of $1 at Compound Interest, 0.5–7%

Period	0.5%	1.0%	1.5%	2.0%	2.5%	3.0%	3.5%	4.0%	4.5%	5.0%	5.5%	6.0%	6.5%	7.0%
1	0.99502	0.99010	0.98522	0.98039	0.97561	0.97087	0.96618	0.96154	0.95694	0.95238	0.94787	0.94340	0.93897	0.93458
2	0.99007	0.98030	0.97066	0.96117	0.95181	0.94260	0.93351	0.92456	0.91573	0.90703	0.89845	0.89000	0.88166	0.87344
3	0.98515	0.97059	0.95632	0.94232	0.92860	0.91514	0.90194	0.88900	0.87630	0.86384	0.85161	0.83962	0.82785	0.81630
4	0.98025	0.96098	0.94218	0.92385	0.90595	0.88849	0.87144	0.85480	0.83856	0.82270	0.80722	0.79209	0.77732	0.76290
5	0.97537	0.95147	0.92826	0.90573	0.88385	0.86261	0.84197	0.82193	0.80245	0.78353	0.76513	0.74726	0.72988	0.71299
6	0.97052	0.94205	0.91454	0.88797	0.86230	0.83748	0.81350	0.79031	0.76790	0.74622	0.72525	0.70496	0.68533	0.66634
7	0.96569	0.93272	0.90103	0.87056	0.84127	0.81309	0.78599	0.75992	0.73483	0.71068	0.68744	0.66506	0.64351	0.62275
8	0.96089	0.92348	0.88771	0.85349	0.82075	0.78941	0.75941	0.73069	0.70319	0.67684	0.65160	0.62741	0.60423	0.58201
9	0.95610	0.91434	0.87459	0.83676	0.80073	0.76642	0.73373	0.70259	0.67290	0.64461	0.61763	0.59190	0.56735	0.54393
10	0.95135	0.90529	0.86167	0.82035	0.78120	0.74409	0.70892	0.67556	0.64393	0.61391	0.58543	0.55839	0.53273	0.50835
11	0.94661	0.89632	0.84893	0.80426	0.76214	0.72242	0.68495	0.64958	0.61620	0.58468	0.55491	0.52679	0.50021	0.47509
12	0.94191	0.88745	0.83639	0.78849	0.74356	0.70138	0.66178	0.62460	0.58966	0.55684	0.52598	0.49697	0.46968	0.44401
13	0.93722	0.87866	0.82403	0.77303	0.72542	0.68095	0.63940	0.60057	0.56427	0.53032	0.49856	0.46884	0.44102	0.41496
14	0.93256	0.86996	0.81185	0.75788	0.70773	0.66112	0.61778	0.57748	0.53997	0.50507	0.47257	0.44230	0.41410	0.38782
15	0.92792	0.86135	0.79985	0.74301	0.69047	0.64186	0.59689	0.55526	0.51672	0.48102	0.44793	0.41727	0.38883	0.36245
16	0.92330	0.85282	0.78803	0.72845	0.67362	0.62317	0.57671	0.53391	0.49447	0.45811	0.42458	0.39365	0.36510	0.33873
17	0.91871	0.84438	0.77639	0.71416	0.65720	0.60502	0.55720	0.51337	0.47318	0.43630	0.40245	0.37136	0.34281	0.31657
18	0.91414	0.83602	0.76491	0.70016	0.64117	0.58739	0.53836	0.49363	0.45280	0.41552	0.38147	0.35034	0.32189	0.29586
19	0.90959	0.82774	0.75361	0.68643	0.62553	0.57029	0.52016	0.47464	0.43330	0.39573	0.36158	0.33051	0.30224	0.27651
20	0.90506	0.81954	0.74247	0.67297	0.61027	0.55368	0.50257	0.45639	0.41464	0.37689	0.34273	0.31180	0.28380	0.25842
21	0.90056	0.81143	0.73150	0.65978	0.59539	0.53755	0.48557	0.43883	0.39679	0.35894	0.32486	0.29416	0.26648	0.24151
22	0.89608	0.80340	0.72069	0.64684	0.58086	0.52189	0.46915	0.42196	0.37970	0.34185	0.30793	0.27751	0.25021	0.22571
23	0.89162	0.79544	0.71004	0.63416	0.56670	0.50669	0.45329	0.40573	0.36335	0.32557	0.29187	0.26180	0.23494	0.21095
24	0.88719	0.78757	0.69954	0.62172	0.55288	0.49193	0.43796	0.39012	0.34770	0.31007	0.27666	0.24698	0.22060	0.19715
25	0.88277	0.77977	0.68921	0.60953	0.53939	0.47761	0.42315	0.37512	0.33273	0.29530	0.26223	0.23300	0.20714	0.18425
26	0.87838	0.77205	0.67902	0.59758	0.52623	0.46369	0.40884	0.36069	0.31840	0.28124	0.24856	0.21981	0.19450	0.17220
27	0.87401	0.76440	0.66899	0.58586	0.51340	0.45019	0.39501	0.34682	0.30469	0.26785	0.23560	0.20737	0.18263	0.16093
28	0.86966	0.75684	0.65910	0.57437	0.50088	0.43708	0.38165	0.33348	0.29157	0.25509	0.22332	0.19563	0.17148	0.15040
29	0.86533	0.74934	0.64936	0.56311	0.48866	0.42435	0.36875	0.32065	0.27902	0.24295	0.21168	0.18456	0.16101	0.14056
30	0.86103	0.74192	0.63976	0.55207	0.47674	0.41199	0.35628	0.30832	0.26700	0.23138	0.20064	0.17411	0.15119	0.13137

TABLE 3 *(Continued)*

Present Value of $1 at Compound Interest, 0.5–7%

Period	0.5%	1.0%	1.5%	2.0%	2.5%	3.0%	3.5%	4.0%	4.5%	5.0%	5.5%	6.0%	6.5%	7.0%
31	0.85675	0.73458	0.63031	0.54125	0.46511	0.39999	0.34423	0.29646	0.25550	0.22036	0.19018	0.16425	0.14196	0.12277
32	0.85248	0.72730	0.62099	0.53063	0.45377	0.38834	0.33259	0.28506	0.24450	0.20987	0.18027	0.15496	0.13329	0.11474
33	0.84824	0.72010	0.61182	0.52023	0.44270	0.37703	0.32134	0.27409	0.23397	0.19987	0.17087	0.14619	0.12516	0.10723
34	0.84402	0.71297	0.60277	0.51003	0.43191	0.36604	0.31048	0.26355	0.22390	0.19035	0.16196	0.13791	0.11752	0.10022
35	0.83982	0.70591	0.59387	0.50003	0.42137	0.35538	0.29998	0.25342	0.21425	0.18129	0.15352	0.13011	0.11035	0.09366
36	0.83564	0.69892	0.58509	0.49022	0.41109	0.34503	0.28983	0.24367	0.20503	0.17266	0.14552	0.12274	0.10361	0.08754
37	0.83149	0.69200	0.57644	0.48061	0.40107	0.33498	0.28003	0.23430	0.19620	0.16444	0.13793	0.11579	0.09729	0.08181
38	0.82735	0.68515	0.56792	0.47119	0.39128	0.32523	0.27056	0.22529	0.18775	0.15661	0.13074	0.10924	0.09135	0.07646
39	0.82323	0.67837	0.55953	0.46195	0.38174	0.31575	0.26141	0.21662	0.17967	0.14915	0.12392	0.10306	0.08578	0.07146
40	0.81914	0.67165	0.55126	0.45289	0.37243	0.30656	0.25257	0.20829	0.17193	0.14205	0.11746	0.09722	0.08054	0.06678
41	0.81506	0.66500	0.54312	0.44401	0.36335	0.29763	0.24403	0.20028	0.16453	0.13528	0.11134	0.09172	0.07563	0.06241
42	0.81101	0.65842	0.53509	0.43530	0.35448	0.28896	0.23578	0.19257	0.15744	0.12884	0.10554	0.08653	0.07101	0.05833
43	0.80697	0.65190	0.52718	0.42677	0.34584	0.28054	0.22781	0.18517	0.15066	0.12270	0.10003	0.08163	0.06668	0.05451
44	0.80296	0.64545	0.51939	0.41840	0.33740	0.27237	0.22010	0.17805	0.14417	0.11686	0.09482	0.07701	0.06261	0.05095
45	0.79896	0.63905	0.51171	0.41020	0.32917	0.26444	0.21266	0.17120	0.13796	0.11130	0.08988	0.07265	0.05879	0.04761
46	0.79499	0.63273	0.50415	0.40215	0.32115	0.25674	0.20547	0.16461	0.13202	0.10600	0.08519	0.06854	0.05520	0.04450
47	0.79103	0.62646	0.49670	0.39427	0.31331	0.24926	0.19852	0.15828	0.12634	0.10095	0.08075	0.06466	0.05183	0.04159
48	0.78710	0.62026	0.48936	0.38654	0.30567	0.24200	0.19181	0.15219	0.12090	0.09614	0.07654	0.06100	0.04867	0.03887
49	0.78318	0.61412	0.48213	0.37896	0.29822	0.23495	0.18532	0.14634	0.11569	0.09156	0.07255	0.05755	0.04570	0.03632
50	0.77929	0.60804	0.47500	0.37153	0.29094	0.22811	0.17905	0.14071	0.11071	0.08720	0.06877	0.05429	0.04291	0.03395
51	0.77541	0.60202	0.46798	0.36424	0.28385	0.22146	0.17300	0.13530	0.10594	0.08305	0.06518	0.05122	0.04029	0.03173
52	0.77155	0.59606	0.46107	0.35710	0.27692	0.21501	0.16715	0.13010	0.10138	0.07910	0.06178	0.04832	0.03783	0.02965
53	0.76771	0.59016	0.45426	0.35010	0.27017	0.20875	0.16150	0.12509	0.09701	0.07533	0.05856	0.04558	0.03552	0.02771
54	0.76389	0.58431	0.44754	0.34323	0.26358	0.20267	0.15603	0.12028	0.09284	0.07174	0.05551	0.04300	0.03335	0.02590
55	0.76009	0.57853	0.44093	0.33650	0.25715	0.19677	0.15076	0.11566	0.08884	0.06833	0.05262	0.04057	0.03132	0.02420
56	0.75631	0.57280	0.43441	0.32991	0.25088	0.19104	0.14566	0.11121	0.08501	0.06507	0.04987	0.03827	0.02941	0.02262
57	0.75255	0.56713	0.42799	0.32344	0.24476	0.18547	0.14073	0.10693	0.08135	0.06197	0.04727	0.03610	0.02761	0.02114
58	0.74880	0.56151	0.42167	0.31710	0.23879	0.18007	0.13598	0.10282	0.07785	0.05902	0.04481	0.03406	0.02593	0.01976
59	0.74508	0.55595	0.41544	0.31088	0.23297	0.17483	0.13138	0.09886	0.07450	0.05621	0.04247	0.03213	0.02434	0.01847
60	0.74137	0.55045	0.40930	0.30478	0.22728	0.16973	0.12693	0.09506	0.07129	0.05354	0.04026	0.03031	0.02286	0.01726
61	0.73768	0.54500	0.40325	0.29881	0.22174	0.16479	0.12264	0.09140	0.06822	0.05099	0.03816	0.02860	0.02146	0.01613

TABLE 3 *(Continued)*

Present Value of $1 at Compound Interest, 0.5–7%

Period	0.5%	1.0%	1.5%	2.0%	2.5%	3.0%	3.5%	4.0%	4.5%	5.0%	5.5%	6.0%	6.5%	7.0%
62	0.73401	0.53960	0.39729	0.29295	0.21633	0.15999	0.11849	0.08789	0.06528	0.04856	0.03617	0.02698	0.02015	0.01507
63	0.73036	0.53426	0.39142	0.28720	0.21106	0.15533	0.11449	0.08451	0.06247	0.04625	0.03428	0.02545	0.01892	0.01409
64	0.72673	0.52897	0.38563	0.28157	0.20591	0.15081	0.11062	0.08126	0.05978	0.04404	0.03250	0.02401	0.01777	0.01317
65	0.72311	0.52373	0.37993	0.27605	0.20089	0.14641	0.10688	0.07813	0.05721	0.04195	0.03080	0.02265	0.01668	0.01230
66	0.71952	0.51855	0.37432	0.27064	0.19599	0.14215	0.10326	0.07513	0.05474	0.03995	0.02920	0.02137	0.01566	0.01150
67	0.71594	0.51341	0.36879	0.26533	0.19121	0.13801	0.09977	0.07224	0.05239	0.03805	0.02767	0.02016	0.01471	0.01075
68	0.71237	0.50833	0.36334	0.26013	0.18654	0.13399	0.09640	0.06946	0.05013	0.03623	0.02623	0.01902	0.01381	0.01004
69	0.70883	0.50330	0.35797	0.25503	0.18199	0.13009	0.09314	0.06679	0.04797	0.03451	0.02486	0.01794	0.01297	0.00939
70	0.70530	0.49831	0.35268	0.25003	0.17755	0.12630	0.08999	0.06422	0.04590	0.03287	0.02357	0.01693	0.01218	0.00877
71	0.70179	0.49338	0.34746	0.24513	0.17322	0.12262	0.08694	0.06175	0.04393	0.03130	0.02234	0.01597	0.01143	0.00820
72	0.69830	0.48850	0.34233	0.24032	0.16900	0.11905	0.08400	0.05937	0.04204	0.02981	0.02117	0.01507	0.01074	0.00766
73	0.69483	0.48366	0.33727	0.23561	0.16488	0.11558	0.08116	0.05709	0.04023	0.02839	0.02007	0.01421	0.01008	0.00716
74	0.69137	0.47887	0.33229	0.23099	0.16085	0.11221	0.07842	0.05490	0.03849	0.02704	0.01902	0.01341	0.00947	0.00669
75	0.68793	0.47413	0.32738	0.22646	0.15693	0.10895	0.07577	0.05278	0.03684	0.02575	0.01803	0.01265	0.00889	0.00625
76	0.68451	0.46944	0.32254	0.22202	0.15310	0.10577	0.07320	0.05075	0.03525	0.02453	0.01709	0.01193	0.00835	0.00585
77	0.68110	0.46479	0.31777	0.21766	0.14937	0.10269	0.07073	0.04880	0.03373	0.02336	0.01620	0.01126	0.00784	0.00546
78	0.67772	0.46019	0.31308	0.21340	0.14573	0.09970	0.06834	0.04692	0.03228	0.02225	0.01536	0.01062	0.00736	0.00511
79	0.67434	0.45563	0.30845	0.20921	0.14217	0.09680	0.06603	0.04512	0.03089	0.02119	0.01456	0.01002	0.00691	0.00477
80	0.67099	0.45112	0.30389	0.20511	0.13870	0.09398	0.06379	0.04338	0.02956	0.02018	0.01380	0.00945	0.00649	0.00446
81	0.66765	0.44665	0.29940	0.20109	0.13532	0.09124	0.06164	0.04172	0.02829	0.01922	0.01308	0.00892	0.00609	0.00417
82	0.66433	0.44223	0.29497	0.19715	0.13202	0.08858	0.05955	0.04011	0.02707	0.01830	0.01240	0.00841	0.00572	0.00390
83	0.66102	0.43785	0.29062	0.19328	0.12880	0.08600	0.05754	0.03857	0.02590	0.01743	0.01175	0.00794	0.00537	0.00364
84	0.65773	0.43352	0.28632	0.18949	0.12566	0.08350	0.05559	0.03709	0.02479	0.01660	0.01114	0.00749	0.00504	0.00340
85	0.65446	0.42922	0.28209	0.18577	0.12259	0.08107	0.05371	0.03566	0.02372	0.01581	0.01056	0.00706	0.00473	0.00318
86	0.65121	0.42497	0.27792	0.18213	0.11960	0.07870	0.05190	0.03429	0.02270	0.01506	0.01001	0.00666	0.00445	0.00297
87	0.64797	0.42077	0.27381	0.17856	0.11669	0.07641	0.05014	0.03297	0.02172	0.01434	0.00948	0.00629	0.00417	0.00278
88	0.64474	0.41660	0.26977	0.17506	0.11384	0.07419	0.04845	0.03170	0.02079	0.01366	0.00899	0.00593	0.00392	0.00260
89	0.64154	0.41248	0.26578	0.17163	0.11106	0.07203	0.04681	0.03048	0.01989	0.01301	0.00852	0.00559	0.00368	0.00243
90	0.63834	0.40839	0.26185	0.16826	0.10836	0.06993	0.04522	0.02931	0.01903	0.01239	0.00808	0.00528	0.00346	0.00227
91	0.63517	0.40435	0.25798	0.16496	0.10571	0.06789	0.04369	0.02818	0.01821	0.01180	0.00766	0.00498	0.00324	0.00212
92	0.63201	0.40034	0.25417	0.16173	0.10313	0.06591	0.04222	0.02710	0.01743	0.01124	0.00726	0.00470	0.00305	0.00198

TABLE 3 *(Continued)*

Present Value of $1 at Compound Interest, 0.5–7%

Period	0.5%	1.0%	1.5%	2.0%	2.5%	3.0%	3.5%	4.0%	4.5%	5.0%	5.5%	6.0%	6.5%	7.0%
93	0.62886	0.39638	0.25041	0.15856	0.10062	0.06399	0.04079	0.02606	0.01668	0.01070	0.00688	0.00443	0.00286	0.00185
94	0.62573	0.39246	0.24671	0.15545	0.09816	0.06213	0.03941	0.02505	0.01596	0.01019	0.00652	0.00418	0.00269	0.00173
95	0.62262	0.38857	0.24307	0.15240	0.09577	0.06032	0.03808	0.02409	0.01527	0.00971	0.00618	0.00394	0.00252	0.00162
96	0.61952	0.38472	0.23947	0.14941	0.09343	0.05856	0.03679	0.02316	0.01462	0.00924	0.00586	0.00372	0.00237	0.00151
97	0.61644	0.38091	0.23594	0.14648	0.09116	0.05686	0.03555	0.02227	0.01399	0.00880	0.00555	0.00351	0.00222	0.00141
98	0.61337	0.37714	0.23245	0.14361	0.08893	0.05520	0.03434	0.02142	0.01338	0.00838	0.00526	0.00331	0.00209	0.00132
99	0.61032	0.37341	0.22901	0.14079	0.08676	0.05359	0.03318	0.02059	0.01281	0.00798	0.00499	0.00312	0.00196	0.00123
100	0.60729	0.36971	0.22563	0.13803	0.08465	0.05203	0.03206	0.01980	0.01226	0.00760	0.00473	0.00295	0.00184	0.00115
101	0.60427	0.36605	0.22230	0.13533	0.08258	0.05052	0.03098	0.01904	0.01173	0.00724	0.00448	0.00278	0.00173	0.00108
102	0.60126	0.36243	0.21901	0.13267	0.08057	0.04905	0.02993	0.01831	0.01122	0.00690	0.00425	0.00262	0.00162	0.00101
103	0.59827	0.35884	0.21577	0.13007	0.07860	0.04762	0.02892	0.01760	0.01074	0.00657	0.00403	0.00247	0.00152	0.00094
104	0.59529	0.35529	0.21258	0.12752	0.07669	0.04623	0.02794	0.01693	0.01028	0.00626	0.00382	0.00233	0.00143	0.00088
105	0.59233	0.35177	0.20944	0.12502	0.07482	0.04488	0.02699	0.01627	0.00984	0.00596	0.00362	0.00220	0.00134	0.00082
106	0.58938	0.34828	0.20635	0.12257	0.07299	0.04358	0.02608	0.01565	0.00941	0.00567	0.00343	0.00208	0.00126	0.00077
107	0.58645	0.34484	0.20330	0.12017	0.07121	0.04231	0.02520	0.01505	0.00901	0.00540	0.00325	0.00196	0.00118	0.00072
108	0.58353	0.34142	0.20029	0.11781	0.06947	0.04108	0.02435	0.01447	0.00862	0.00515	0.00308	0.00185	0.00111	0.00067
109	0.58063	0.33804	0.19733	0.11550	0.06778	0.03988	0.02352	0.01391	0.00825	0.00490	0.00292	0.00174	0.00104	0.00063
110	0.57774	0.33469	0.19442	0.11324	0.06613	0.03872	0.02273	0.01338	0.00789	0.00467	0.00277	0.00165	0.00098	0.00059
111	0.57487	0.33138	0.19154	0.11101	0.06451	0.03759	0.02196	0.01286	0.00755	0.00445	0.00262	0.00155	0.00092	0.00055
112	0.57201	0.32810	0.18871	0.10884	0.06294	0.03649	0.02122	0.01237	0.00723	0.00423	0.00249	0.00146	0.00086	0.00051
113	0.56916	0.32485	0.18592	0.10670	0.06140	0.03543	0.02050	0.01189	0.00692	0.00403	0.00236	0.00138	0.00081	0.00048
114	0.56633	0.32164	0.18318	0.10461	0.05991	0.03440	0.01981	0.01143	0.00662	0.00384	0.00223	0.00130	0.00076	0.00045
115	0.56351	0.31845	0.18047	0.10256	0.05845	0.03340	0.01914	0.01099	0.00633	0.00366	0.00212	0.00123	0.00072	0.00042
116	0.56071	0.31530	0.17780	0.10055	0.05702	0.03243	0.01849	0.01057	0.00606	0.00348	0.00201	0.00116	0.00067	0.00039
117	0.55792	0.31218	0.17518	0.09858	0.05563	0.03148	0.01786	0.01016	0.00580	0.00332	0.00190	0.00109	0.00063	0.00036
118	0.55514	0.30908	0.17259	0.09665	0.05427	0.03056	0.01726	0.00977	0.00555	0.00316	0.00180	0.00103	0.00059	0.00034
119	0.55238	0.30602	0.17004	0.09475	0.05295	0.02967	0.01668	0.00940	0.00531	0.00301	0.00171	0.00097	0.00056	0.00032
120	0.54963	0.30299	0.16752	0.09289	0.05166	0.02881	0.01611	0.00904	0.00508	0.00287	0.00162	0.00092	0.00052	0.00030

TABLE 3 *(Continued)*

Present Value of $1 at Compound Interest, 7.5–14%

Period	7.5%	8.0%	8.5%	9.0%	9.5%	10.0%	10.5%	11.0%	11.5%	12.0%	12.5%	13.0%	13.5%	14.0%
1	0.93023	0.92593	0.92166	0.91743	0.91324	0.90909	0.90498	0.90090	0.89686	0.89286	0.88889	0.88496	0.88106	0.87719
2	0.86533	0.85734	0.84946	0.84168	0.83401	0.82645	0.81898	0.81162	0.80436	0.79719	0.79012	0.78315	0.77626	0.76947
3	0.80496	0.79383	0.78291	0.77213	0.76165	0.75131	0.74116	0.73119	0.72140	0.71178	0.70233	0.69305	0.68393	0.67497
4	0.74880	0.73503	0.72157	0.70843	0.69557	0.68301	0.67073	0.65873	0.64699	0.63552	0.62430	0.61332	0.60258	0.59208
5	0.69656	0.68058	0.66505	0.64993	0.63523	0.62092	0.60700	0.59345	0.58026	0.56743	0.55493	0.54276	0.53091	0.51937
6	0.64796	0.63017	0.61295	0.59627	0.58012	0.56447	0.54932	0.53464	0.52042	0.50663	0.49327	0.48032	0.46776	0.45559
7	0.60275	0.58349	0.56493	0.54703	0.52979	0.51316	0.49712	0.48166	0.46674	0.45235	0.43846	0.42506	0.41213	0.39964
8	0.56070	0.54027	0.52067	0.50187	0.48382	0.46651	0.44989	0.43393	0.41860	0.40388	0.38974	0.37616	0.36311	0.35056
9	0.52158	0.50025	0.47988	0.46043	0.44185	0.42410	0.40714	0.39092	0.37543	0.36061	0.34644	0.33288	0.31992	0.30751
10	0.48519	0.46319	0.44229	0.42241	0.40351	0.38554	0.36845	0.35218	0.33671	0.32197	0.30795	0.29459	0.28187	0.26974
11	0.45134	0.42888	0.40764	0.38753	0.36851	0.35049	0.33344	0.31728	0.30198	0.28748	0.27373	0.26070	0.24834	0.23662
12	0.41985	0.39711	0.37570	0.35553	0.33654	0.31863	0.30175	0.28584	0.27083	0.25668	0.24332	0.23071	0.21880	0.20756
13	0.39056	0.36770	0.34627	0.32618	0.30734	0.28966	0.27308	0.25751	0.24290	0.22917	0.21628	0.20416	0.19278	0.18207
14	0.36331	0.34046	0.31914	0.29925	0.28067	0.26333	0.24713	0.23199	0.21785	0.20462	0.19225	0.18068	0.16985	0.15971
15	0.33797	0.31524	0.29414	0.27454	0.25632	0.23939	0.22365	0.20900	0.19538	0.18270	0.17089	0.15989	0.14964	0.14010
16	0.31439	0.29189	0.27110	0.25187	0.23409	0.21763	0.20240	0.18829	0.17523	0.16312	0.15190	0.14150	0.13185	0.12289
17	0.29245	0.27027	0.24986	0.23107	0.21378	0.19784	0.18316	0.16963	0.15715	0.14564	0.13502	0.12522	0.11616	0.10780
18	0.27205	0.25025	0.23028	0.21199	0.19523	0.17986	0.16576	0.15282	0.14095	0.13004	0.12002	0.11081	0.10235	0.09456
19	0.25307	0.23171	0.21224	0.19449	0.17829	0.16351	0.15001	0.13768	0.12641	0.11611	0.10668	0.09806	0.09017	0.08295
20	0.23541	0.21455	0.19562	0.17843	0.16282	0.14864	0.13575	0.12403	0.11337	0.10367	0.09483	0.08678	0.07945	0.07276
21	0.21899	0.19866	0.18029	0.16370	0.14870	0.13513	0.12285	0.11174	0.10168	0.09256	0.08429	0.07680	0.07000	0.06383
22	0.20371	0.18394	0.16617	0.15018	0.13580	0.12285	0.11118	0.10067	0.09119	0.08264	0.07493	0.06796	0.06167	0.05599
23	0.18950	0.17032	0.15315	0.13778	0.12402	0.11168	0.10062	0.09069	0.08179	0.07379	0.06660	0.06014	0.05434	0.04911
24	0.17628	0.15770	0.14115	0.12640	0.11326	0.10153	0.09106	0.08170	0.07335	0.06588	0.05920	0.05323	0.04787	0.04308
25	0.16398	0.14602	0.13009	0.11597	0.10343	0.09230	0.08240	0.07361	0.06579	0.05882	0.05262	0.04710	0.04218	0.03779
26	0.15254	0.13520	0.11990	0.10639	0.09446	0.08391	0.07457	0.06631	0.05900	0.05252	0.04678	0.04168	0.03716	0.03315
27	0.14190	0.12519	0.11051	0.09761	0.08626	0.07628	0.06749	0.05974	0.05291	0.04689	0.04158	0.03689	0.03274	0.02908
28	0.13200	0.11591	0.10185	0.08955	0.07878	0.06934	0.06107	0.05382	0.04746	0.04187	0.03696	0.03264	0.02885	0.02551
29	0.12279	0.10733	0.09387	0.08215	0.07194	0.06304	0.05527	0.04849	0.04256	0.03738	0.03285	0.02889	0.02542	0.02237
30	0.11422	0.09938	0.08652	0.07537	0.06570	0.05731	0.05002	0.04368	0.03817	0.03338	0.02920	0.02557	0.02239	0.01963

TABLE 3 *(Continued)*

Present Value of $1 at Compound Interest, 7.5–14%

Period	7.5%	8.0%	8.5%	9.0%	9.5%	10.0%	10.5%	11.0%	11.5%	12.0%	12.5%	13.0%	13.5%	14.0%
31	0.10625	0.09202	0.07974	0.06915	0.06000	0.05210	0.04527	0.03935	0.03424	0.02980	0.02596	0.02262	0.01973	0.01722
32	0.09884	0.08520	0.07349	0.06344	0.05480	0.04736	0.04096	0.03545	0.03070	0.02661	0.02307	0.02002	0.01738	0.01510
33	0.09194	0.07889	0.06774	0.05820	0.05004	0.04306	0.03707	0.03194	0.02754	0.02376	0.02051	0.01772	0.01532	0.01325
34	0.08553	0.07305	0.06243	0.05339	0.04570	0.03914	0.03355	0.02878	0.02470	0.02121	0.01823	0.01568	0.01349	0.01162
35	0.07956	0.06763	0.05754	0.04899	0.04174	0.03558	0.03036	0.02592	0.02215	0.01894	0.01621	0.01388	0.01189	0.01019
36	0.07401	0.06262	0.05303	0.04494	0.03811	0.03235	0.02748	0.02335	0.01987	0.01691	0.01440	0.01228	0.01047	0.00894
37	0.06885	0.05799	0.04888	0.04123	0.03481	0.02941	0.02487	0.02104	0.01782	0.01510	0.01280	0.01087	0.00923	0.00784
38	0.06404	0.05369	0.04505	0.03783	0.03179	0.02673	0.02250	0.01896	0.01598	0.01348	0.01138	0.00962	0.00813	0.00688
39	0.05958	0.04971	0.04152	0.03470	0.02903	0.02430	0.02036	0.01708	0.01433	0.01204	0.01012	0.00851	0.00716	0.00604
40	0.05542	0.04603	0.03827	0.03184	0.02651	0.02209	0.01843	0.01538	0.01285	0.01075	0.00899	0.00753	0.00631	0.00529
41	0.05155	0.04262	0.03527	0.02921	0.02421	0.02009	0.01668	0.01386	0.01153	0.00960	0.00799	0.00666	0.00556	0.00464
42	0.04796	0.03946	0.03251	0.02680	0.02211	0.01826	0.01509	0.01249	0.01034	0.00857	0.00711	0.00590	0.00490	0.00407
43	0.04461	0.03654	0.02996	0.02458	0.02019	0.01660	0.01366	0.01125	0.00927	0.00765	0.00632	0.00522	0.00432	0.00357
44	0.04150	0.03383	0.02761	0.02255	0.01844	0.01509	0.01236	0.01013	0.00832	0.00683	0.00561	0.00462	0.00380	0.00313
45	0.03860	0.03133	0.02545	0.02069	0.01684	0.01372	0.01119	0.00913	0.00746	0.00610	0.00499	0.00409	0.00335	0.00275
46	0.03591	0.02901	0.02345	0.01898	0.01538	0.01247	0.01012	0.00823	0.00669	0.00544	0.00444	0.00362	0.00295	0.00241
47	0.03340	0.02686	0.02162	0.01742	0.01405	0.01134	0.00916	0.00741	0.00600	0.00486	0.00394	0.00320	0.00260	0.00212
48	0.03107	0.02487	0.01992	0.01598	0.01283	0.01031	0.00829	0.00668	0.00538	0.00434	0.00350	0.00283	0.00229	0.00186
49	0.02891	0.02303	0.01836	0.01466	0.01171	0.00937	0.00750	0.00601	0.00483	0.00388	0.00312	0.00251	0.00202	0.00163
50	0.02689	0.02132	0.01692	0.01345	0.01070	0.00852	0.00679	0.00542	0.00433	0.00346	0.00277	0.00222	0.00178	0.00143
51	0.02501	0.01974	0.01560	0.01234	0.00977	0.00774	0.00615	0.00488	0.00388	0.00309	0.00246	0.00196	0.00157	0.00125
52	0.02327	0.01828	0.01438	0.01132	0.00892	0.00704	0.00556	0.00440	0.00348	0.00276	0.00219	0.00174	0.00138	0.00110
53	0.02164	0.01693	0.01325	0.01038	0.00815	0.00640	0.00503	0.00396	0.00312	0.00246	0.00194	0.00154	0.00122	0.00096
54	0.02013	0.01567	0.01221	0.00953	0.00744	0.00582	0.00455	0.00357	0.00280	0.00220	0.00173	0.00136	0.00107	0.00085
55	0.01873	0.01451	0.01126	0.00874	0.00680	0.00529	0.00412	0.00322	0.00251	0.00196	0.00154	0.00120	0.00094	0.00074
56	0.01742	0.01344	0.01037	0.00802	0.00621	0.00481	0.00373	0.00290	0.00225	0.00175	0.00137	0.00107	0.00083	0.00065
57	0.01621	0.01244	0.00956	0.00736	0.00567	0.00437	0.00338	0.00261	0.00202	0.00157	0.00121	0.00094	0.00073	0.00057
58	0.01508	0.01152	0.00881	0.00675	0.00518	0.00397	0.00305	0.00235	0.00181	0.00140	0.00108	0.00083	0.00065	0.00050
59	0.01402	0.01067	0.00812	0.00619	0.00473	0.00361	0.00276	0.00212	0.00162	0.00125	0.00096	0.00074	0.00057	0.00044
60	0.01305	0.00988	0.00749	0.00568	0.00432	0.00328	0.00250	0.00191	0.00146	0.00111	0.00085	0.00065	0.00050	0.00039

TABLE 3 *(Continued)*

Present Value of $1 at Compound Interest, 7.5–14%

Period	7.5%	8.0%	8.5%	9.0%	9.5%	10.0%	10.5%	11.0%	11.5%	12.0%	12.5%	13.0%	13.5%	14.0%
61	0.01214	0.00914	0.00690	0.00521	0.00394	0.00299	0.00226	0.00172	0.00131	0.00099	0.00076	0.00058	0.00044	0.00034
62	0.01129	0.00847	0.00636	0.00478	0.00360	0.00271	0.00205	0.00155	0.00117	0.00089	0.00067	0.00051	0.00039	0.00030
63	0.01050	0.00784	0.00586	0.00439	0.00329	0.00247	0.00185	0.00140	0.00105	0.00079	0.00060	0.00045	0.00034	0.00026
64	0.00977	0.00726	0.00540	0.00402	0.00300	0.00224	0.00168	0.00126	0.00094	0.00071	0.00053	0.00040	0.00030	0.00023
65	0.00909	0.00672	0.00498	0.00369	0.00274	0.00204	0.00152	0.00113	0.00085	0.00063	0.00047	0.00035	0.00027	0.00020
66	0.00845	0.00622	0.00459	0.00339	0.00250	0.00185	0.00137	0.00102	0.00076	0.00056	0.00042	0.00031	0.00023	0.00018
67	0.00786	0.00576	0.00423	0.00311	0.00229	0.00169	0.00124	0.00092	0.00068	0.00050	0.00037	0.00028	0.00021	0.00015
68	0.00732	0.00534	0.00390	0.00285	0.00209	0.00153	0.00113	0.00083	0.00061	0.00045	0.00033	0.00025	0.00018	0.00014
69	0.00680	0.00494	0.00359	0.00262	0.00191	0.00139	0.00102	0.00075	0.00055	0.00040	0.00030	0.00022	0.00016	0.00012
70	0.00633	0.00457	0.00331	0.00240	0.00174	0.00127	0.00092	0.00067	0.00049	0.00036	0.00026	0.00019	0.00014	0.00010
71	0.00589	0.00424	0.00305	0.00220	0.00159	0.00115	0.00083	0.00061	0.00044	0.00032	0.00023	0.00017	0.00012	0.00009
72	0.00548	0.00392	0.00281	0.00202	0.00145	0.00105	0.00075	0.00055	0.00039	0.00029	0.00021	0.00015	0.00011	0.00008
73	0.00510	0.00363	0.00259	0.00185	0.00133	0.00095	0.00068	0.00049	0.00035	0.00026	0.00018	0.00013	0.00010	0.00007
74	0.00474	0.00336	0.00239	0.00170	0.00121	0.00086	0.00062	0.00044	0.00032	0.00023	0.00016	0.00012	0.00009	0.00006
75	0.00441	0.00311	0.00220	0.00156	0.00111	0.00079	0.00056	0.00040	0.00028	0.00020	0.00015	0.00010	0.00008	0.00005
76	0.00410	0.00288	0.00203	0.00143	0.00101	0.00071	0.00051	0.00036	0.00026	0.00018	0.00013	0.00009	0.00007	0.00005
77	0.00382	0.00267	0.00187	0.00131	0.00092	0.00065	0.00046	0.00032	0.00023	0.00016	0.00012	0.00008	0.00006	0.00004
78	0.00355	0.00247	0.00172	0.00120	0.00084	0.00059	0.00041	0.00029	0.00021	0.00014	0.00010	0.00007	0.00005	0.00004
79	0.00330	0.00229	0.00159	0.00110	0.00077	0.00054	0.00038	0.00026	0.00018	0.00013	0.00009	0.00006	0.00005	0.00003
80	0.00307	0.00212	0.00146	0.00101	0.00070	0.00049	0.00034	0.00024	0.00017	0.00012	0.00008	0.00006	0.00004	0.00003
81	0.00286	0.00196	0.00135	0.00093	0.00064	0.00044	0.00031	0.00021	0.00015	0.00010	0.00007	0.00005	0.00004	0.00002
82	0.00266	0.00182	0.00124	0.00085	0.00059	0.00040	0.00028	0.00019	0.00013	0.00009	0.00006	0.00004	0.00003	0.00002
83	0.00247	0.00168	0.00115	0.00078	0.00054	0.00037	0.00025	0.00017	0.00012	0.00008	0.00006	0.00004	0.00003	0.00002
84	0.00230	0.00156	0.00106	0.00072	0.00049	0.00033	0.00023	0.00016	0.00011	0.00007	0.00005	0.00003	0.00002	0.00002
85	0.00214	0.00144	0.00097	0.00066	0.00045	0.00030	0.00021	0.00014	0.00010	0.00007	0.00004	0.00003	0.00002	0.00001
86	0.00199	0.00134	0.00090	0.00060	0.00041	0.00028	0.00019	0.00013	0.00009	0.00006	0.00004	0.00003	0.00002	0.00001
87	0.00185	0.00124	0.00083	0.00055	0.00037	0.00025	0.00017	0.00011	0.00008	0.00005	0.00004	0.00002	0.00002	0.00001
88	0.00172	0.00114	0.00076	0.00051	0.00034	0.00023	0.00015	0.00010	0.00007	0.00005	0.00003	0.00002	0.00001	0.00001
89	0.00160	0.00106	0.00070	0.00047	0.00031	0.00021	0.00014	0.00009	0.00006	0.00004	0.00003	0.00002	0.00001	0.00001
90	0.00149	0.00098	0.00065	0.00043	0.00028	0.00019	0.00013	0.00008	0.00006	0.00004	0.00002	0.00002	0.00001	0.00001

TABLE 3 *(Continued)*

Present Value of $1 at Compound Interest, 7.5–14%

Period	7.5%	8.0%	8.5%	9.0%	9.5%	10.0%	10.5%	11.0%	11.5%	12.0%	12.5%	13.0%	13.5%	14.0%
91	0.00139	0.00091	0.00060	0.00039	0.00026	0.00017	0.00011	0.00008	0.00005	0.00003	0.00002	0.00001	0.00001	0.00001
92	0.00129	0.00084	0.00055	0.00036	0.00024	0.00016	0.00010	0.00007	0.00004	0.00003	0.00002	0.00001	0.00001	0.00001
93	0.00120	0.00078	0.00051	0.00033	0.00022	0.00014	0.00009	0.00006	0.00004	0.00003	0.00002	0.00001	0.00001	0.00001
94	0.00112	0.00072	0.00047	0.00030	0.00020	0.00013	0.00008	0.00005	0.00004	0.00002	0.00002	0.00001	0.00001	0.00000
95	0.00104	0.00067	0.00043	0.00028	0.00018	0.00012	0.00008	0.00005	0.00003	0.00002	0.00001	0.00001	0.00001	0.00000
96	0.00097	0.00062	0.00040	0.00026	0.00016	0.00011	0.00007	0.00004	0.00003	0.00002	0.00001	0.00001	0.00001	0.00000
97	0.00090	0.00057	0.00037	0.00023	0.00015	0.00010	0.00006	0.00004	0.00003	0.00002	0.00001	0.00001	0.00000	0.00000
98	0.00084	0.00053	0.00034	0.00021	0.00014	0.00009	0.00006	0.00004	0.00002	0.00002	0.00001	0.00001	0.00000	0.00000
99	0.00078	0.00049	0.00031	0.00020	0.00013	0.00008	0.00005	0.00003	0.00002	0.00001	0.00001	0.00001	0.00000	0.00000
100	0.00072	0.00045	0.00029	0.00018	0.00011	0.00007	0.00005	0.00003	0.00002	0.00001	0.00001	0.00000	0.00000	0.00000
101	0.00067	0.00042	0.00026	0.00017	0.00010	0.00007	0.00004	0.00003	0.00002	0.00001	0.00001	0.00000	0.00000	0.00000
102	0.00063	0.00039	0.00024	0.00015	0.00010	0.00006	0.00004	0.00002	0.00002	0.00001	0.00001	0.00000	0.00000	0.00000
103	0.00058	0.00036	0.00022	0.00014	0.00009	0.00005	0.00003	0.00002	0.00001	0.00001	0.00001	0.00000	0.00000	0.00000
104	0.00054	0.00033	0.00021	0.00013	0.00008	0.00005	0.00003	0.00002	0.00001	0.00001	0.00000	0.00000	0.00000	0.00000
105	0.00050	0.00031	0.00019	0.00012	0.00007	0.00005	0.00003	0.00002	0.00001	0.00001	0.00000	0.00000	0.00000	0.00000
106	0.00047	0.00029	0.00018	0.00011	0.00007	0.00004	0.00003	0.00002	0.00001	0.00001	0.00000	0.00000	0.00000	0.00000
107	0.00044	0.00027	0.00016	0.00010	0.00006	0.00004	0.00002	0.00001	0.00001	0.00001	0.00000	0.00000	0.00000	0.00000
108	0.00041	0.00025	0.00015	0.00009	0.00006	0.00003	0.00002	0.00001	0.00001	0.00000	0.00000	0.00000	0.00000	0.00000
109	0.00038	0.00023	0.00014	0.00008	0.00005	0.00003	0.00002	0.00001	0.00001	0.00000	0.00000	0.00000	0.00000	0.00000
110	0.00035	0.00021	0.00013	0.00008	0.00005	0.00003	0.00002	0.00001	0.00001	0.00000	0.00000	0.00000	0.00000	0.00000
111	0.00033	0.00019	0.00012	0.00007	0.00004	0.00003	0.00002	0.00001	0.00001	0.00000	0.00000	0.00000	0.00000	0.00000
112	0.00030	0.00018	0.00011	0.00006	0.00004	0.00002	0.00001	0.00001	0.00001	0.00000	0.00000	0.00000	0.00000	0.00000
113	0.00028	0.00017	0.00010	0.00006	0.00004	0.00002	0.00001	0.00001	0.00000	0.00000	0.00000	0.00000	0.00000	0.00000
114	0.00026	0.00015	0.00009	0.00005	0.00003	0.00002	0.00001	0.00001	0.00000	0.00000	0.00000	0.00000	0.00000	0.00000
115	0.00024	0.00014	0.00008	0.00005	0.00003	0.00002	0.00001	0.00001	0.00000	0.00000	0.00000	0.00000	0.00000	0.00000
116	0.00023	0.00013	0.00008	0.00005	0.00003	0.00002	0.00001	0.00001	0.00000	0.00000	0.00000	0.00000	0.00000	0.00000
117	0.00021	0.00012	0.00007	0.00004	0.00002	0.00001	0.00001	0.00000	0.00000	0.00000	0.00000	0.00000	0.00000	0.00000
118	0.00020	0.00011	0.00007	0.00004	0.00002	0.00001	0.00001	0.00000	0.00000	0.00000	0.00000	0.00000	0.00000	0.00000
119	0.00018	0.00011	0.00006	0.00004	0.00002	0.00001	0.00001	0.00000	0.00000	0.00000	0.00000	0.00000	0.00000	0.00000
120	0.00017	0.00010	0.00006	0.00003	0.00002	0.00001	0.00001	0.00000	0.00000	0.00000	0.00000	0.00000	0.00000	0.00000

TABLE 3 *(Continued)*

Present Value of $1 at Compound Interest, 14.5–21%

Period	14.5%	15.0%	15.5%	16.0%	16.5%	17.0%	17.5%	18.0%	18.5%	19.0%	19.5%	20.0%	20.5%	21.0%
1	0.87336	0.86957	0.86580	0.86207	0.85837	0.85470	0.85106	0.84746	0.84388	0.84034	0.83682	0.83333	0.82988	0.82645
2	0.76276	0.75614	0.74961	0.74316	0.73680	0.73051	0.72431	0.71818	0.71214	0.70616	0.70027	0.69444	0.68869	0.68301
3	0.66617	0.65752	0.64901	0.64066	0.63244	0.62437	0.61643	0.60863	0.60096	0.59342	0.58600	0.57870	0.57153	0.56447
4	0.58181	0.57175	0.56192	0.55229	0.54287	0.53365	0.52462	0.51579	0.50714	0.49867	0.49038	0.48225	0.47430	0.46651
5	0.50813	0.49718	0.48651	0.47611	0.46598	0.45611	0.44649	0.43711	0.42796	0.41905	0.41036	0.40188	0.39361	0.38554
6	0.44378	0.43233	0.42122	0.41044	0.39999	0.38984	0.37999	0.37043	0.36115	0.35214	0.34339	0.33490	0.32665	0.31863
7	0.38758	0.37594	0.36469	0.35383	0.34334	0.33320	0.32340	0.31393	0.30477	0.29592	0.28736	0.27908	0.27108	0.26333
8	0.33850	0.32690	0.31575	0.30503	0.29471	0.28478	0.27523	0.26604	0.25719	0.24867	0.24047	0.23257	0.22496	0.21763
9	0.29563	0.28426	0.27338	0.26295	0.25297	0.24340	0.23424	0.22546	0.21704	0.20897	0.20123	0.19381	0.18669	0.17986
10	0.25819	0.24718	0.23669	0.22668	0.21714	0.20804	0.19935	0.19106	0.18315	0.17560	0.16839	0.16151	0.15493	0.14864
11	0.22550	0.21494	0.20493	0.19542	0.18639	0.17781	0.16966	0.16192	0.15456	0.14757	0.14091	0.13459	0.12857	0.12285
12	0.19694	0.18691	0.17743	0.16846	0.15999	0.15197	0.14439	0.13722	0.13043	0.12400	0.11792	0.11216	0.10670	0.10153
13	0.17200	0.16253	0.15362	0.14523	0.13733	0.12989	0.12289	0.11629	0.11007	0.10421	0.09868	0.09346	0.08855	0.08391
14	0.15022	0.14133	0.13300	0.12520	0.11788	0.11102	0.10459	0.09855	0.09288	0.08757	0.08258	0.07789	0.07348	0.06934
15	0.13120	0.12289	0.11515	0.10793	0.10118	0.09489	0.08901	0.08352	0.07838	0.07359	0.06910	0.06491	0.06098	0.05731
16	0.11458	0.10686	0.09970	0.09304	0.08685	0.08110	0.07575	0.07078	0.06615	0.06184	0.05782	0.05409	0.05061	0.04736
17	0.10007	0.09293	0.08632	0.08021	0.07455	0.06932	0.06447	0.05998	0.05582	0.05196	0.04839	0.04507	0.04200	0.03914
18	0.08740	0.08081	0.07474	0.06914	0.06399	0.05925	0.05487	0.05083	0.04711	0.04367	0.04049	0.03756	0.03485	0.03235
19	0.07633	0.07027	0.06471	0.05961	0.05493	0.05064	0.04670	0.04308	0.03975	0.03670	0.03389	0.03130	0.02892	0.02673
20	0.06666	0.06110	0.05602	0.05139	0.04715	0.04328	0.03974	0.03651	0.03355	0.03084	0.02836	0.02608	0.02400	0.02209
21	0.05822	0.05313	0.04850	0.04430	0.04047	0.03699	0.03382	0.03094	0.02831	0.02591	0.02373	0.02174	0.01992	0.01826
22	0.05085	0.04620	0.04199	0.03819	0.03474	0.03162	0.02879	0.02622	0.02389	0.02178	0.01986	0.01811	0.01653	0.01509
23	0.04441	0.04017	0.03636	0.03292	0.02982	0.02702	0.02450	0.02222	0.02016	0.01830	0.01662	0.01509	0.01372	0.01247
24	0.03879	0.03493	0.03148	0.02838	0.02560	0.02310	0.02085	0.01883	0.01701	0.01538	0.01390	0.01258	0.01138	0.01031
25	0.03387	0.03038	0.02726	0.02447	0.02197	0.01974	0.01774	0.01596	0.01436	0.01292	0.01164	0.01048	0.00945	0.00852
26	0.02958	0.02642	0.02360	0.02109	0.01886	0.01687	0.01510	0.01352	0.01211	0.01086	0.00974	0.00874	0.00784	0.00704
27	0.02584	0.02297	0.02043	0.01818	0.01619	0.01442	0.01285	0.01146	0.01022	0.00912	0.00815	0.00728	0.00651	0.00582
28	0.02257	0.01997	0.01769	0.01567	0.01390	0.01233	0.01094	0.00971	0.00863	0.00767	0.00682	0.00607	0.00540	0.00481
29	0.01971	0.01737	0.01532	0.01351	0.01193	0.01053	0.00931	0.00823	0.00728	0.00644	0.00571	0.00506	0.00448	0.00397
30	0.01721	0.01510	0.01326	0.01165	0.01024	0.00900	0.00792	0.00697	0.00614	0.00541	0.00477	0.00421	0.00372	0.00328

TABLE 3 *(Continued)*

Present Value of $1 at Compound Interest, 14.5–21%

Period	14.5%	15.0%	15.5%	16.0%	16.5%	17.0%	17.5%	18.0%	18.5%	19.0%	19.5%	20.0%	20.5%	21.0%
31	0.01503	0.01313	0.01148	0.01004	0.00879	0.00770	0.00674	0.00591	0.00518	0.00455	0.00400	0.00351	0.00309	0.00271
32	0.01313	0.01142	0.00994	0.00866	0.00754	0.00658	0.00574	0.00501	0.00438	0.00382	0.00334	0.00293	0.00256	0.00224
33	0.01147	0.00993	0.00861	0.00746	0.00648	0.00562	0.00488	0.00425	0.00369	0.00321	0.00280	0.00244	0.00213	0.00185
34	0.01001	0.00864	0.00745	0.00643	0.00556	0.00480	0.00416	0.00360	0.00312	0.00270	0.00234	0.00203	0.00176	0.00153
35	0.00875	0.00751	0.00645	0.00555	0.00477	0.00411	0.00354	0.00305	0.00263	0.00227	0.00196	0.00169	0.00146	0.00127
36	0.00764	0.00653	0.00559	0.00478	0.00410	0.00351	0.00301	0.00258	0.00222	0.00191	0.00164	0.00141	0.00121	0.00105
37	0.00667	0.00568	0.00484	0.00412	0.00352	0.00300	0.00256	0.00219	0.00187	0.00160	0.00137	0.00118	0.00101	0.00086
38	0.00583	0.00494	0.00419	0.00355	0.00302	0.00256	0.00218	0.00186	0.00158	0.00135	0.00115	0.00098	0.00084	0.00071
39	0.00509	0.00429	0.00362	0.00306	0.00259	0.00219	0.00186	0.00157	0.00133	0.00113	0.00096	0.00082	0.00069	0.00059
40	0.00444	0.00373	0.00314	0.00264	0.00222	0.00187	0.00158	0.00133	0.00113	0.00095	0.00080	0.00068	0.00058	0.00049
41	0.00388	0.00325	0.00272	0.00228	0.00191	0.00160	0.00134	0.00113	0.00095	0.00080	0.00067	0.00057	0.00048	0.00040
42	0.00339	0.00282	0.00235	0.00196	0.00164	0.00137	0.00114	0.00096	0.00080	0.00067	0.00056	0.00047	0.00040	0.00033
43	0.00296	0.00245	0.00204	0.00169	0.00141	0.00117	0.00097	0.00081	0.00068	0.00056	0.00047	0.00039	0.00033	0.00028
44	0.00259	0.00213	0.00176	0.00146	0.00121	0.00100	0.00083	0.00069	0.00057	0.00047	0.00039	0.00033	0.00027	0.00023
45	0.00226	0.00186	0.00153	0.00126	0.00104	0.00085	0.00071	0.00058	0.00048	0.00040	0.00033	0.00027	0.00023	0.00019
46	0.00197	0.00161	0.00132	0.00108	0.00089	0.00073	0.00060	0.00049	0.00041	0.00033	0.00028	0.00023	0.00019	0.00016
47	0.00172	0.00140	0.00114	0.00093	0.00076	0.00062	0.00051	0.00042	0.00034	0.00028	0.00023	0.00019	0.00016	0.00013
48	0.00150	0.00122	0.00099	0.00081	0.00066	0.00053	0.00043	0.00035	0.00029	0.00024	0.00019	0.00016	0.00013	0.00011
49	0.00131	0.00106	0.00086	0.00069	0.00056	0.00046	0.00037	0.00030	0.00024	0.00020	0.00016	0.00013	0.00011	0.00009
50	0.00115	0.00092	0.00074	0.00060	0.00048	0.00039	0.00031	0.00025	0.00021	0.00017	0.00014	0.00011	0.00009	0.00007
51	0.00100	0.00080	0.00064	0.00052	0.00041	0.00033	0.00027	0.00022	0.00017	0.00014	0.00011	0.00009	0.00007	0.00006
52	0.00088	0.00070	0.00056	0.00044	0.00036	0.00028	0.00023	0.00018	0.00015	0.00012	0.00009	0.00008	0.00006	0.00005
53	0.00076	0.00061	0.00048	0.00038	0.00031	0.00024	0.00019	0.00015	0.00012	0.00010	0.00008	0.00006	0.00005	0.00004
54	0.00067	0.00053	0.00042	0.00033	0.00026	0.00021	0.00017	0.00013	0.00010	0.00008	0.00007	0.00005	0.00004	0.00003
55	0.00058	0.00046	0.00036	0.00028	0.00022	0.00018	0.00014	0.00011	0.00009	0.00007	0.00006	0.00004	0.00004	0.00003
56	0.00051	0.00040	0.00031	0.00025	0.00019	0.00015	0.00012	0.00009	0.00007	0.00006	0.00005	0.00004	0.00003	0.00002
57	0.00044	0.00035	0.00027	0.00021	0.00017	0.00013	0.00010	0.00008	0.00006	0.00005	0.00004	0.00003	0.00002	0.00002
58	0.00039	0.00030	0.00023	0.00018	0.00014	0.00011	0.00009	0.00007	0.00005	0.00004	0.00003	0.00003	0.00002	0.00002
59	0.00034	0.00026	0.00020	0.00016	0.00012	0.00009	0.00007	0.00006	0.00004	0.00003	0.00003	0.00002	0.00002	0.00001
60	0.00030	0.00023	0.00018	0.00014	0.00010	0.00008	0.00006	0.00005	0.00004	0.00003	0.00002	0.00002	0.00001	0.00001

TABLE 3 *(Continued)*

Present Value of $1 at Compound Interest, 14.5–21%

Period	14.5%	15.0%	15.5%	16.0%	16.5%	17.0%	17.5%	18.0%	18.5%	19.0%	19.5%	20.0%	20.5%	21.0%
61	0.00026	0.00020	0.00015	0.00012	0.00009	0.00007	0.00005	0.00004	0.00003	0.00002	0.00002	0.00001	0.00001	0.00001
62	0.00023	0.00017	0.00013	0.00010	0.00008	0.00006	0.00005	0.00003	0.00003	0.00002	0.00002	0.00001	0.00001	0.00001
63	0.00020	0.00015	0.00011	0.00009	0.00007	0.00005	0.00004	0.00003	0.00002	0.00002	0.00001	0.00001	0.00001	0.00001
64	0.00017	0.00013	0.00010	0.00007	0.00006	0.00004	0.00003	0.00003	0.00002	0.00001	0.00001	0.00001	0.00001	0.00001
65	0.00015	0.00011	0.00009	0.00006	0.00005	0.00004	0.00003	0.00002	0.00002	0.00001	0.00001	0.00001	0.00001	0.00000
66	0.00013	0.00010	0.00007	0.00006	0.00004	0.00003	0.00002	0.00002	0.00001	0.00001	0.00001	0.00001	0.00000	0.00000
67	0.00011	0.00009	0.00006	0.00005	0.00004	0.00003	0.00002	0.00002	0.00001	0.00001	0.00001	0.00000	0.00000	0.00000
68	0.00010	0.00007	0.00006	0.00004	0.00003	0.00002	0.00002	0.00001	0.00001	0.00001	0.00001	0.00000	0.00000	0.00000
69	0.00009	0.00006	0.00005	0.00004	0.00003	0.00002	0.00001	0.00001	0.00001	0.00001	0.00000	0.00000	0.00000	0.00000
70	0.00008	0.00006	0.00004	0.00003	0.00002	0.00002	0.00001	0.00001	0.00001	0.00001	0.00000	0.00000	0.00000	0.00000
71	0.00007	0.00005	0.00004	0.00003	0.00002	0.00001	0.00001	0.00001	0.00001	0.00000	0.00000	0.00000	0.00000	0.00000
72	0.00006	0.00004	0.00003	0.00002	0.00002	0.00001	0.00001	0.00001	0.00000	0.00000	0.00000	0.00000	0.00000	0.00000
73	0.00005	0.00004	0.00003	0.00002	0.00001	0.00001	0.00001	0.00001	0.00000	0.00000	0.00000	0.00000	0.00000	0.00000
74	0.00004	0.00003	0.00002	0.00002	0.00001	0.00001	0.00001	0.00000	0.00000	0.00000	0.00000	0.00000	0.00000	0.00000
75	0.00004	0.00003	0.00002	0.00001	0.00001	0.00001	0.00001	0.00000	0.00000	0.00000	0.00000	0.00000	0.00000	0.00000
76	0.00003	0.00002	0.00002	0.00001	0.00001	0.00001	0.00000	0.00000	0.00000	0.00000	0.00000	0.00000	0.00000	0.00000
77	0.00003	0.00002	0.00002	0.00001	0.00001	0.00001	0.00000	0.00000	0.00000	0.00000	0.00000	0.00000	0.00000	0.00000
78	0.00003	0.00002	0.00001	0.00001	0.00001	0.00000	0.00000	0.00000	0.00000	0.00000	0.00000	0.00000	0.00000	0.00000
79	0.00002	0.00002	0.00001	0.00001	0.00001	0.00000	0.00000	0.00000	0.00000	0.00000	0.00000	0.00000	0.00000	0.00000
80	0.00002	0.00001	0.00001	0.00001	0.00000	0.00000	0.00000	0.00000	0.00000	0.00000	0.00000	0.00000	0.00000	0.00000
81	0.00002	0.00001	0.00001	0.00001	0.00000	0.00000	0.00000	0.00000	0.00000	0.00000	0.00000	0.00000	0.00000	0.00000
82	0.00002	0.00001	0.00001	0.00001	0.00000	0.00000	0.00000	0.00000	0.00000	0.00000	0.00000	0.00000	0.00000	0.00000
83	0.00001	0.00001	0.00001	0.00000	0.00000	0.00000	0.00000	0.00000	0.00000	0.00000	0.00000	0.00000	0.00000	0.00000
84	0.00001	0.00001	0.00001	0.00000	0.00000	0.00000	0.00000	0.00000	0.00000	0.00000	0.00000	0.00000	0.00000	0.00000
85	0.00001	0.00001	0.00000	0.00000	0.00000	0.00000	0.00000	0.00000	0.00000	0.00000	0.00000	0.00000	0.00000	0.00000
86	0.00001	0.00001	0.00000	0.00000	0.00000	0.00000	0.00000	0.00000	0.00000	0.00000	0.00000	0.00000	0.00000	0.00000
87	0.00001	0.00001	0.00000	0.00000	0.00000	0.00000	0.00000	0.00000	0.00000	0.00000	0.00000	0.00000	0.00000	0.00000
88	0.00001	0.00000	0.00000	0.00000	0.00000	0.00000	0.00000	0.00000	0.00000	0.00000	0.00000	0.00000	0.00000	0.00000
89	0.00001	0.00000	0.00000	0.00000	0.00000	0.00000	0.00000	0.00000	0.00000	0.00000	0.00000	0.00000	0.00000	0.00000
90	0.00001	0.00000	0.00000	0.00000	0.00000	0.00000	0.00000	0.00000	0.00000	0.00000	0.00000	0.00000	0.00000	0.00000

TABLE 3 *(Continued)*

Present Value of $1 at Compound Interest, 14.5–21%

Period	14.5%	15.0%	15.5%	16.0%	16.5%	17.0%	17.5%	18.0%	18.5%	19.0%	19.5%	20.0%	20.5%	21.0%
91	0.00000	0.00000	0.00000	0.00000	0.00000	0.00000	0.00000	0.00000	0.00000	0.00000	0.00000	0.00000	0.00000	0.00000
92	0.00000	0.00000	0.00000	0.00000	0.00000	0.00000	0.00000	0.00000	0.00000	0.00000	0.00000	0.00000	0.00000	0.00000
93	0.00000	0.00000	0.00000	0.00000	0.00000	0.00000	0.00000	0.00000	0.00000	0.00000	0.00000	0.00000	0.00000	0.00000
94	0.00000	0.00000	0.00000	0.00000	0.00000	0.00000	0.00000	0.00000	0.00000	0.00000	0.00000	0.00000	0.00000	0.00000
95	0.00000	0.00000	0.00000	0.00000	0.00000	0.00000	0.00000	0.00000	0.00000	0.00000	0.00000	0.00000	0.00000	0.00000
96	0.00000	0.00000	0.00000	0.00000	0.00000	0.00000	0.00000	0.00000	0.00000	0.00000	0.00000	0.00000	0.00000	0.00000
97	0.00000	0.00000	0.00000	0.00000	0.00000	0.00000	0.00000	0.00000	0.00000	0.00000	0.00000	0.00000	0.00000	0.00000
98	0.00000	0.00000	0.00000	0.00000	0.00000	0.00000	0.00000	0.00000	0.00000	0.00000	0.00000	0.00000	0.00000	0.00000
99	0.00000	0.00000	0.00000	0.00000	0.00000	0.00000	0.00000	0.00000	0.00000	0.00000	0.00000	0.00000	0.00000	0.00000
100	0.00000	0.00000	0.00000	0.00000	0.00000	0.00000	0.00000	0.00000	0.00000	0.00000	0.00000	0.00000	0.00000	0.00000
101	0.00000	0.00000	0.00000	0.00000	0.00000	0.00000	0.00000	0.00000	0.00000	0.00000	0.00000	0.00000	0.00000	0.00000
102	0.00000	0.00000	0.00000	0.00000	0.00000	0.00000	0.00000	0.00000	0.00000	0.00000	0.00000	0.00000	0.00000	0.00000
103	0.00000	0.00000	0.00000	0.00000	0.00000	0.00000	0.00000	0.00000	0.00000	0.00000	0.00000	0.00000	0.00000	0.00000
104	0.00000	0.00000	0.00000	0.00000	0.00000	0.00000	0.00000	0.00000	0.00000	0.00000	0.00000	0.00000	0.00000	0.00000
105	0.00000	0.00000	0.00000	0.00000	0.00000	0.00000	0.00000	0.00000	0.00000	0.00000	0.00000	0.00000	0.00000	0.00000
106	0.00000	0.00000	0.00000	0.00000	0.00000	0.00000	0.00000	0.00000	0.00000	0.00000	0.00000	0.00000	0.00000	0.00000
107	0.00000	0.00000	0.00000	0.00000	0.00000	0.00000	0.00000	0.00000	0.00000	0.00000	0.00000	0.00000	0.00000	0.00000
108	0.00000	0.00000	0.00000	0.00000	0.00000	0.00000	0.00000	0.00000	0.00000	0.00000	0.00000	0.00000	0.00000	0.00000
109	0.00000	0.00000	0.00000	0.00000	0.00000	0.00000	0.00000	0.00000	0.00000	0.00000	0.00000	0.00000	0.00000	0.00000
110	0.00000	0.00000	0.00000	0.00000	0.00000	0.00000	0.00000	0.00000	0.00000	0.00000	0.00000	0.00000	0.00000	0.00000
111	0.00000	0.00000	0.00000	0.00000	0.00000	0.00000	0.00000	0.00000	0.00000	0.00000	0.00000	0.00000	0.00000	0.00000
112	0.00000	0.00000	0.00000	0.00000	0.00000	0.00000	0.00000	0.00000	0.00000	0.00000	0.00000	0.00000	0.00000	0.00000
113	0.00000	0.00000	0.00000	0.00000	0.00000	0.00000	0.00000	0.00000	0.00000	0.00000	0.00000	0.00000	0.00000	0.00000
114	0.00000	0.00000	0.00000	0.00000	0.00000	0.00000	0.00000	0.00000	0.00000	0.00000	0.00000	0.00000	0.00000	0.00000
115	0.00000	0.00000	0.00000	0.00000	0.00000	0.00000	0.00000	0.00000	0.00000	0.00000	0.00000	0.00000	0.00000	0.00000
116	0.00000	0.00000	0.00000	0.00000	0.00000	0.00000	0.00000	0.00000	0.00000	0.00000	0.00000	0.00000	0.00000	0.00000
117	0.00000	0.00000	0.00000	0.00000	0.00000	0.00000	0.00000	0.00000	0.00000	0.00000	0.00000	0.00000	0.00000	0.00000
118	0.00000	0.00000	0.00000	0.00000	0.00000	0.00000	0.00000	0.00000	0.00000	0.00000	0.00000	0.00000	0.00000	0.00000
119	0.00000	0.00000	0.00000	0.00000	0.00000	0.00000	0.00000	0.00000	0.00000	0.00000	0.00000	0.00000	0.00000	0.00000
120	0.00000	0.00000	0.00000	0.00000	0.00000	0.00000	0.00000	0.00000	0.00000	0.00000	0.00000	0.00000	0.00000	0.00000

TABLE 4

Present Value of an Ordinary Annuity of $1 per Period at Compound Interest, 0.5–7%

Period	0.5%	1.0%	1.5%	2.0%	2.5%	3.0%	3.5%	4.0%	4.5%	5.0%	5.5%	6.0%	6.5%	7.0%
1	0.99502	0.99010	0.98522	0.98039	0.97561	0.97087	0.96618	0.96154	0.95694	0.95238	0.94787	0.94340	0.93897	0.93458
2	1.98510	1.97040	1.95588	1.94156	1.92742	1.91347	1.89969	1.88609	1.87267	1.85941	1.84632	1.83339	1.82063	1.80802
3	2.97025	2.94099	2.91220	2.88388	2.85602	2.82861	2.80164	2.77509	2.74896	2.72325	2.69793	2.67301	2.64848	2.62432
4	3.95050	3.90197	3.85438	3.80773	3.76197	3.71710	3.67308	3.62990	3.58753	3.54595	3.50515	3.46511	3.42580	3.38721
5	4.92587	4.85343	4.78264	4.71346	4.64583	4.57971	4.51505	4.45182	4.38998	4.32948	4.27028	4.21236	4.15568	4.10020
6	5.89638	5.79548	5.69719	5.60143	5.50813	5.41719	5.32855	5.24214	5.15787	5.07569	4.99553	4.91732	4.84101	4.76654
7	6.86207	6.72819	6.59821	6.47199	6.34939	6.23028	6.11454	6.00205	5.89270	5.78637	5.68297	5.58238	5.48452	5.38929
8	7.82296	7.65168	7.48593	7.32548	7.17014	7.01969	6.87396	6.73274	6.59589	6.46321	6.33457	6.20979	6.08875	5.97130
9	8.77906	8.56602	8.36052	8.16224	7.97087	7.78611	7.60769	7.43533	7.26879	7.10782	6.95220	6.80169	6.65610	6.51523
10	9.73041	9.47130	9.22218	8.98259	8.75206	8.53020	8.31661	8.11090	7.91272	7.72173	7.53763	7.36009	7.18883	7.02358
11	10.67703	10.36763	10.07112	9.78685	9.51421	9.25262	9.00155	8.76048	8.52892	8.30641	8.09254	7.88687	7.68904	7.49867
12	11.61893	11.25508	10.90751	10.57534	10.25776	9.95400	9.66333	9.38507	9.11858	8.86325	8.61852	8.38384	8.15873	7.94269
13	12.55615	12.13374	11.73153	11.34837	10.98318	10.63496	10.30274	9.98565	9.68285	9.39357	9.11708	8.85268	8.59974	8.35765
14	13.48871	13.00370	12.54338	12.10625	11.69091	11.29607	10.92052	10.56312	10.22283	9.89864	9.58965	9.29498	9.01384	8.74547
15	14.41662	13.86505	13.34323	12.84926	12.38138	11.93794	11.51741	11.11839	10.73955	10.37966	10.03758	9.71225	9.40267	9.10791
16	15.33993	14.71787	14.13126	13.57771	13.05500	12.56110	12.09412	11.65230	11.23402	10.83777	10.46216	10.10590	9.76776	9.44665
17	16.25863	15.56225	14.90765	14.29187	13.71220	13.16612	12.65132	12.16567	11.70719	11.27407	10.86461	10.47726	10.11058	9.76322
18	17.17277	16.39827	15.67256	14.99203	14.35336	13.75351	13.18968	12.65930	12.15999	11.68959	11.24607	10.82760	10.43247	10.05909
19	18.08236	17.22601	16.42617	15.67846	14.97889	14.32380	13.70984	13.13394	12.59329	12.08532	11.60765	11.15812	10.73471	10.33560
20	18.98742	18.04555	17.16864	16.35143	15.58916	14.87747	14.21240	13.59033	13.00794	12.46221	11.95038	11.46992	11.01851	10.59401
21	19.88798	18.85698	17.90014	17.01121	16.18455	15.41502	14.69797	14.02916	13.40472	12.82115	12.27524	11.76408	11.28498	10.83553
22	20.78406	19.66038	18.62082	17.65805	16.76541	15.93692	15.16712	14.45112	13.78442	13.16300	12.58317	12.04158	11.53520	11.06124
23	21.67568	20.45582	19.33086	18.29220	17.33211	16.44361	15.62041	14.85684	14.14777	13.48857	12.87504	12.30338	11.77014	11.27219
24	22.56287	21.24339	20.03041	18.91393	17.88499	16.93554	16.05837	15.24696	14.49548	13.79864	13.15170	12.55036	11.99074	11.46933
25	23.44564	22.02316	20.71961	19.52346	18.42438	17.41315	16.48151	15.62208	14.82821	14.09394	13.41393	12.78336	12.19788	11.65358
26	24.32402	22.79520	21.39863	20.12104	18.95061	17.87684	16.89035	15.98277	15.14661	14.37519	13.66250	13.00317	12.39237	11.82578
27	25.19803	23.55961	22.06762	20.70690	19.46401	18.32703	17.28536	16.32959	15.45130	14.64303	13.89810	13.21053	12.57500	11.98671
28	26.06769	24.31644	22.72672	21.28127	19.96489	18.76411	17.66702	16.66306	15.74287	14.89813	14.12142	13.40616	12.74648	12.13711
29	26.93302	25.06579	23.37608	21.84438	20.45355	19.18845	18.03577	16.98371	16.02189	15.14107	14.33310	13.59072	12.90749	12.27767
30	27.79405	25.80771	24.01584	22.39646	20.93029	19.60044	18.39205	17.29203	16.28889	15.37245	14.53375	13.76483	13.05868	12.40904

TABLE 4 *(Continued)*

Present Value of an Ordinary Annuity of $1 per Period at Compound Interest, 0.5–7%

Period	0.5%	1.0%	1.5%	2.0%	2.5%	3.0%	3.5%	4.0%	4.5%	5.0%	5.5%	6.0%	6.5%	7.0%
31	28.65080	26.54229	24.64615	22.93770	21.39541	20.00043	18.73628	17.58849	16.54439	15.59281	14.72393	13.92909	13.20063	12.53181
32	29.50328	27.26959	25.26714	23.46833	21.84918	20.38877	19.06887	17.87355	16.78889	15.80268	14.90420	14.08404	13.33393	12.64656
33	30.35153	27.98969	25.87895	23.98856	22.29188	20.76579	19.39021	18.14765	17.02286	16.00255	15.07507	14.23023	13.45909	12.75379
34	31.19555	28.70267	26.48173	24.49859	22.72379	21.13184	19.70068	18.41120	17.24676	16.19290	15.23703	14.36814	13.57661	12.85401
35	32.03537	29.40858	27.07559	24.99862	23.14516	21.48722	20.00066	18.66461	17.46101	16.37419	15.39055	14.49825	13.68696	12.94767
36	32.87102	30.10751	27.66068	25.48884	23.55625	21.83225	20.29049	18.90828	17.66604	16.54685	15.53607	14.62099	13.79057	13.03521
37	33.70250	30.79951	28.23713	25.96945	23.95732	22.16724	20.57053	19.14258	17.86224	16.71129	15.67400	14.73678	13.88786	13.11702
38	34.52985	31.48466	28.80505	26.44064	24.34860	22.49246	20.84109	19.36786	18.04999	16.86789	15.80474	14.84602	13.97921	13.19347
39	35.35309	32.16303	29.36458	26.90259	24.73034	22.80822	21.10250	19.58448	18.22966	17.01704	15.92866	14.94907	14.06499	13.26493
40	36.17223	32.83469	29.91585	27.35548	25.10278	23.11477	21.35507	19.79277	18.40158	17.15909	16.04612	15.04630	14.14553	13.33171
41	36.98729	33.49969	30.45896	27.79949	25.46612	23.41240	21.59910	19.99305	18.56611	17.29437	16.15746	15.13802	14.22115	13.39412
42	37.79830	34.15811	30.99405	28.23479	25.82061	23.70136	21.83488	20.18563	18.72355	17.42321	16.26300	15.22454	14.29216	13.45245
43	38.60527	34.81001	31.52123	28.66156	26.16645	23.98190	22.06269	20.37079	18.87421	17.54591	16.36303	15.30617	14.35884	13.50696
44	39.40823	35.45545	32.04062	29.07996	26.50385	24.25427	22.28279	20.54884	19.01838	17.66277	16.45785	15.38318	14.42144	13.55791
45	40.20720	36.09451	32.55234	29.49016	26.83302	24.51871	22.49545	20.72004	19.15635	17.77407	16.54773	15.45583	14.48023	13.60552
46	41.00219	36.72724	33.05649	29.89231	27.15417	24.77545	22.70092	20.88465	19.28837	17.88007	16.63292	15.52437	14.53543	13.65002
47	41.79322	37.35370	33.55319	30.28658	27.46748	25.02471	22.89944	21.04294	19.41471	17.98102	16.71366	15.58903	14.58725	13.69161
48	42.58032	37.97396	34.04255	30.67312	27.77315	25.26671	23.09124	21.19513	19.53561	18.07716	16.79020	15.65003	14.63592	13.73047
49	43.36350	38.58808	34.52468	31.05208	28.07137	25.50166	23.27656	21.34147	19.65130	18.16872	16.86275	15.70757	14.68161	13.76680
50	44.14279	39.19612	34.99969	31.42361	28.36231	25.72976	23.45562	21.48218	19.76201	18.25593	16.93152	15.76186	14.72452	13.80075
51	44.91820	39.79814	35.46767	31.78785	28.64616	25.95123	23.62862	21.61749	19.86795	18.33898	16.99670	15.81308	14.76481	13.83247
52	45.68975	40.39419	35.92874	32.14495	28.92308	26.16624	23.79576	21.74758	19.96933	18.41807	17.05848	15.86139	14.80264	13.86212
53	46.45746	40.98435	36.38300	32.49505	29.19325	26.37499	23.95726	21.87267	20.06634	18.49340	17.11705	15.90697	14.83816	13.88984
54	47.22135	41.56866	36.83054	32.83828	29.45683	26.57766	24.11330	21.99296	20.15918	18.56515	17.17255	15.94998	14.87151	13.91573
55	47.98145	42.14719	37.27147	33.17479	29.71398	26.77443	24.26405	22.10861	20.24802	18.63347	17.22517	15.99054	14.90282	13.93994
56	48.73776	42.71999	37.70588	33.50469	29.96486	26.96546	24.40971	22.21982	20.33303	18.69854	17.27504	16.02881	14.93223	13.96256
57	49.49031	43.28712	38.13387	33.82813	30.20962	27.15094	24.55045	22.32675	20.41439	18.76052	17.32232	16.06492	14.95984	13.98370
58	50.23911	43.84863	38.55554	34.14523	30.44841	27.33101	24.68642	22.42957	20.49224	18.81954	17.36712	16.09898	14.98577	14.00346
59	50.98419	44.40459	38.97097	34.45610	30.68137	27.50583	24.81780	22.52843	20.56673	18.87575	17.40960	16.13111	15.01011	14.02192
60	51.72556	44.95504	39.38027	34.76089	30.90866	27.67556	24.94473	22.62349	20.63802	18.92929	17.44985	16.16143	15.03297	14.03918

TABLE 4 *(Continued)*

Present Value of an Ordinary Annuity of $1 per Period at Compound Interest, 0.5–7%

Period	0.5%	1.0%	1.5%	2.0%	2.5%	3.0%	3.5%	4.0%	4.5%	5.0%	5.5%	6.0%	6.5%	7.0%
61	52.46324	45.50004	39.78352	35.05969	31.13040	27.84035	25.06738	22.71489	20.70624	18.98028	17.48801	16.19003	15.05443	14.05531
62	53.19726	46.03964	40.18080	35.35264	31.34673	28.00034	25.18587	22.80278	20.77152	19.02883	17.52418	16.21701	15.07458	14.07038
63	53.92762	46.57390	40.57222	35.63984	31.55778	28.15567	25.30036	22.88729	20.83399	19.07508	17.55847	16.24246	15.09350	14.08447
64	54.65435	47.10287	40.95785	35.92141	31.76369	28.30648	25.41097	22.96855	20.89377	19.11912	17.59096	16.26647	15.11127	14.09764
65	55.37746	47.62661	41.33779	36.19747	31.96458	28.45289	25.51785	23.04668	20.95098	19.16107	17.62177	16.28912	15.12795	14.10994
66	56.09698	48.14516	41.71210	36.46810	32.16056	28.59504	25.62111	23.12181	21.00572	19.20102	17.65096	16.31049	15.14362	14.12144
67	56.81291	48.65857	42.08089	36.73343	32.35177	28.73305	25.72088	23.19405	21.05811	19.23907	17.67864	16.33065	15.15833	14.13219
68	57.52529	49.16690	42.44423	36.99356	32.53831	28.86704	25.81727	23.26351	21.10824	19.27530	17.70487	16.34967	15.17214	14.14223
69	58.23411	49.67020	42.80219	37.24859	32.72030	28.99712	25.91041	23.33030	21.15621	19.30981	17.72974	16.36762	15.18511	14.15162
70	58.93942	50.16851	43.15487	37.49862	32.89786	29.12342	26.00040	23.39451	21.20211	19.34268	17.75330	16.38454	15.19728	14.16039
71	59.64121	50.66190	43.50234	37.74374	33.07108	29.24604	26.08734	23.45626	21.24604	19.37398	17.77564	16.40051	15.20872	14.16859
72	60.33951	51.15039	43.84467	37.98406	33.24008	29.36509	26.17134	23.51564	21.28808	19.40379	17.79682	16.41558	15.21945	14.17625
73	61.03434	51.63405	44.18194	38.21967	33.40495	29.48067	26.25251	23.57273	21.32830	19.43218	17.81689	16.42979	15.22953	14.18341
74	61.72571	52.11292	44.51422	38.45066	33.56581	29.59288	26.33092	23.62762	21.36680	19.45922	17.83591	16.44320	15.23900	14.19010
75	62.41365	52.58705	44.84160	38.67711	33.72274	29.70183	26.40669	23.68041	21.40363	19.48497	17.85395	16.45585	15.24788	14.19636
76	63.09815	53.05649	45.16414	38.89913	33.87584	29.80760	26.47989	23.73116	21.43888	19.50950	17.87104	16.46778	15.25623	14.20220
77	63.77926	53.52127	45.48191	39.11680	34.02521	29.91029	26.55062	23.77996	21.47262	19.53285	17.88724	16.47904	15.26407	14.20767
78	64.45697	53.98146	45.79498	39.33019	34.17094	30.00999	26.61896	23.82689	21.50490	19.55510	17.90260	16.48966	15.27142	14.21277
79	65.13132	54.43709	46.10343	39.53940	34.31311	30.10679	26.68498	23.87201	21.53579	19.57628	17.91716	16.49968	15.27833	14.21755
80	65.80231	54.88821	46.40732	39.74451	34.45182	30.20076	26.74878	23.91539	21.56534	19.59646	17.93095	16.50913	15.28482	14.22201
81	66.46996	55.33486	46.70672	39.94560	34.58714	30.29200	26.81041	23.95711	21.59363	19.61568	17.94403	16.51805	15.29091	14.22617
82	67.13428	55.77709	47.00170	40.14275	34.71916	30.38059	26.86996	23.99722	21.62070	19.63398	17.95643	16.52646	15.29663	14.23007
83	67.79531	56.21494	47.29231	40.33603	34.84796	30.46659	26.92750	24.03579	21.64660	19.65141	17.96818	16.53440	15.30200	14.23371
84	68.45304	56.64845	47.57863	40.52552	34.97362	30.55009	26.98309	24.07287	21.67139	19.66801	17.97932	16.54188	15.30704	14.23711
85	69.10750	57.07768	47.86072	40.71129	35.09621	30.63115	27.03680	24.10853	21.69511	19.68382	17.98987	16.54895	15.31178	14.24029
86	69.75871	57.50265	48.13864	40.89342	35.21582	30.70986	27.08870	24.14282	21.71781	19.69887	17.99988	16.55561	15.31622	14.24326
87	70.40668	57.92342	48.41246	41.07198	35.33251	30.78627	27.13884	24.17579	21.73953	19.71321	18.00936	16.56190	15.32040	14.24604
88	71.05142	58.34002	48.68222	41.24704	35.44635	30.86045	27.18728	24.20749	21.76032	19.72687	18.01835	16.56783	15.32431	14.24864
89	71.69296	58.75249	48.94800	41.41867	35.55741	30.93248	27.23409	24.23797	21.78021	19.73987	18.02688	16.57342	15.32800	14.25106
90	72.33130	59.16088	49.20985	41.58693	35.66577	31.00241	27.27932	24.26728	21.79924	19.75226	18.03495	16.57870	15.33145	14.25333

TABLE 4 *(Continued)*

Present Value of an Ordinary Annuity of $1 per Period at Compound Interest, 0.5–7%

Period	0.5%	1.0%	1.5%	2.0%	2.5%	3.0%	3.5%	4.0%	4.5%	5.0%	5.5%	6.0%	6.5%	7.0%
91	72.96647	59.56523	49.46784	41.75189	35.77148	31.07030	27.32301	24.29546	21.81746	19.76406	18.04261	16.58368	15.33470	14.25545
92	73.59847	59.96557	49.72201	41.91362	35.87462	31.13621	27.36523	24.32256	21.83489	19.77529	18.04987	16.58838	15.33774	14.25743
93	74.22734	60.36195	49.97242	42.07218	35.97524	31.20021	27.40602	24.34861	21.85156	19.78599	18.05675	16.59281	15.34060	14.25928
94	74.85307	60.75441	50.21913	42.22762	36.07340	31.26234	27.44543	24.37367	21.86753	19.79619	18.06327	16.59699	15.34329	14.26101
95	75.47569	61.14298	50.46220	42.38002	36.16917	31.32266	27.48350	24.39776	21.88280	19.80589	18.06945	16.60093	15.34581	14.26262
96	76.09522	61.52770	50.70168	42.52943	36.26261	31.38122	27.52029	24.42092	21.89742	19.81513	18.07531	16.60465	15.34818	14.26413
97	76.71166	61.90862	50.93761	42.67592	36.35376	31.43808	27.55584	24.44319	21.91140	19.82394	18.08086	16.60816	15.35040	14.26555
98	77.32503	62.28576	51.17006	42.81953	36.44269	31.49328	27.59018	24.46461	21.92479	19.83232	18.08612	16.61147	15.35249	14.26687
99	77.93536	62.65917	51.39907	42.96032	36.52946	31.54687	27.62337	24.48520	21.93760	19.84031	18.09111	16.61460	15.35445	14.26810
100	78.54264	63.02888	51.62470	43.09835	36.61411	31.59891	27.65543	24.50500	21.94985	19.84791	18.09584	16.61755	15.35629	14.26925
101	79.14691	63.39493	51.84700	43.23368	36.69669	31.64942	27.68640	24.52404	21.96158	19.85515	18.10032	16.62033	15.35802	14.27033
102	79.74817	63.75736	52.06601	43.36635	36.77726	31.69847	27.71633	24.54234	21.97281	19.86205	18.10457	16.62295	15.35964	14.27133
103	80.34644	64.11619	52.28178	43.49642	36.85586	31.74609	27.74525	24.55995	21.98355	19.86862	18.10860	16.62542	15.36117	14.27228
104	80.94173	64.47148	52.49437	43.62394	36.93255	31.79232	27.77318	24.57687	21.99382	19.87488	18.11241	16.62776	15.36260	14.27315
105	81.53406	64.82325	52.70381	43.74896	37.00736	31.83720	27.80018	24.59315	22.00366	19.88083	18.11603	16.62996	15.36394	14.27398
106	82.12344	65.17153	52.91016	43.87153	37.08035	31.88078	27.82626	24.60879	22.01307	19.88651	18.11946	16.63204	15.36521	14.27474
107	82.70989	65.51637	53.11346	43.99170	37.15156	31.92308	27.85146	24.62384	22.02208	19.89191	18.12271	16.63400	15.36639	14.27546
108	83.29342	65.85779	53.31375	44.10951	37.22104	31.96416	27.87581	24.63831	22.03070	19.89706	18.12579	16.63585	15.36750	14.27613
109	83.87405	66.19583	53.51108	44.22501	37.28882	32.00404	27.89933	24.65222	22.03894	19.90196	18.12872	16.63759	15.36855	14.27676
110	84.45180	66.53053	53.70550	44.33824	37.35494	32.04276	27.92206	24.66560	22.04684	19.90663	18.13148	16.63924	15.36953	14.27735
111	85.02666	66.86191	53.89704	44.44926	37.41946	32.08035	27.94402	24.67846	22.05439	19.91108	18.13411	16.64079	15.37045	14.27789
112	85.59867	67.19001	54.08576	44.55810	37.48240	32.11684	27.96523	24.69082	22.06162	19.91531	18.13659	16.64226	15.37131	14.27840
113	86.16783	67.51486	54.27168	44.66480	37.54380	32.15227	27.98573	24.70272	22.06853	19.91934	18.13895	16.64364	15.37212	14.27888
114	86.73416	67.83649	54.45486	44.76941	37.60371	32.18667	28.00554	24.71415	22.07515	19.92318	18.14119	16.64494	15.37289	14.27933
115	87.29767	68.15494	54.63533	44.87197	37.66216	32.22007	28.02467	24.72514	22.08148	19.92684	18.14331	16.64617	15.37360	14.27975
116	87.85838	68.47024	54.81313	44.97252	37.71918	32.25250	28.04316	24.73571	22.08754	19.93033	18.14531	16.64733	15.37428	14.28014
117	88.41630	68.78242	54.98831	45.07110	37.77481	32.28398	28.06103	24.74588	22.09334	19.93364	18.14722	16.64843	15.37491	14.28050
118	88.97144	69.09150	55.16089	45.16775	37.82908	32.31454	28.07829	24.75565	22.09889	19.93680	18.14902	16.64946	15.37550	14.28084
119	89.52382	69.39753	55.33093	45.26250	37.88203	32.34421	28.09496	24.76505	22.10420	19.93981	18.15073	16.65043	15.37606	14.28116
120	90.07345	69.70052	55.49845	45.35539	37.93369	32.37302	28.11108	24.77409	22.10929	19.94268	18.15235	16.65135	15.37658	14.28146

TABLE 4 *(Continued)*

Present Value of an Ordinary Annuity of $1 per Period at Compound Interest, 7.5–14%

Period	7.5%	8.0%	8.5%	9.0%	9.5%	10.0%	10.5%	11.0%	11.5%	12.0%	12.5%	13.0%	13.5%	14.0%
1	0.93023	0.92593	0.92166	0.91743	0.91324	0.90909	0.90498	0.90090	0.89686	0.89286	0.88889	0.88496	0.88106	0.87719
2	1.79557	1.78326	1.77111	1.75911	1.74725	1.73554	1.72396	1.71252	1.70122	1.69005	1.67901	1.66810	1.65732	1.64666
3	2.60053	2.57710	2.55402	2.53129	2.50891	2.48685	2.46512	2.44371	2.42262	2.40183	2.38134	2.36115	2.34125	2.32163
4	3.34933	3.31213	3.27560	3.23972	3.20448	3.16987	3.13586	3.10245	3.06961	3.03735	3.00564	2.97447	2.94383	2.91371
5	4.04588	3.99271	3.94064	3.88965	3.83971	3.79079	3.74286	3.69590	3.64988	3.60478	3.56057	3.51723	3.47474	3.43308
6	4.69385	4.62288	4.55359	4.48592	4.41983	4.35526	4.29218	4.23054	4.17029	4.11141	4.05384	3.99755	3.94250	3.88867
7	5.29660	5.20637	5.11851	5.03295	4.94961	4.86842	4.78930	4.71220	4.63704	4.56376	4.49230	4.42261	4.35463	4.28830
8	5.85730	5.74664	5.63918	5.53482	5.43344	5.33493	5.23919	5.14612	5.05564	4.96764	4.88205	4.79877	4.71774	4.63886
9	6.37889	6.24689	6.11906	5.99525	5.87528	5.75902	5.64632	5.53705	5.43106	5.32825	5.22848	5.13166	5.03765	4.94637
10	6.86408	6.71008	6.56135	6.41766	6.27880	6.14457	6.01477	5.88923	5.76777	5.65022	5.53643	5.42624	5.31952	5.21612
11	7.31542	7.13896	6.96898	6.80519	6.64730	6.49506	6.34821	6.20652	6.06975	5.93770	5.81016	5.68694	5.56786	5.45273
12	7.73528	7.53608	7.34469	7.16073	6.98384	6.81369	6.64996	6.49236	6.34058	6.19437	6.05348	5.91765	5.78666	5.66029
13	8.12584	7.90378	7.69095	7.48690	7.29118	7.10336	6.92304	6.74987	6.58348	6.42355	6.26976	6.12181	5.97943	5.84236
14	8.48915	8.24424	8.01010	7.78615	7.57185	7.36669	7.17018	6.98187	6.80133	6.62817	6.46201	6.30249	6.14928	6.00207
15	8.82712	8.55948	8.30424	8.06069	7.82818	7.60608	7.39382	7.19087	6.99671	6.81086	6.63289	6.46238	6.29893	6.14217
16	9.14151	8.85137	8.57533	8.31256	8.06226	7.82371	7.59622	7.37916	7.17194	6.97399	6.78479	6.60388	6.43077	6.26506
17	9.43396	9.12164	8.82519	8.54363	8.27604	8.02155	7.77939	7.54879	7.32909	7.11963	6.91982	6.72909	6.54694	6.37286
18	9.70601	9.37189	9.05548	8.75563	8.47127	8.20141	7.94515	7.70162	7.47004	7.24967	7.03984	6.83991	6.64928	6.46742
19	9.95908	9.60360	9.26772	8.95011	8.64956	8.36492	8.09515	7.83929	7.59644	7.36578	7.14652	6.93797	6.73946	6.55037
20	10.19449	9.81815	9.46334	9.12855	8.81238	8.51356	8.23091	7.96333	7.70982	7.46944	7.24135	7.02475	6.81890	6.62313
21	10.41348	10.01680	9.64363	9.29224	8.96108	8.64869	8.35376	8.07507	7.81149	7.56200	7.32565	7.10155	6.88890	6.68696
22	10.61719	10.20074	9.80980	9.44243	9.09688	8.77154	8.46494	8.17574	7.90269	7.64465	7.40058	7.16951	6.95057	6.74294
23	10.80669	10.37106	9.96295	9.58021	9.22089	8.88322	8.56556	8.26643	7.98447	7.71843	7.46718	7.22966	7.00491	6.79206
24	10.98297	10.52876	10.10410	9.70661	9.33415	8.98474	8.65662	8.34814	8.05782	7.78432	7.52638	7.28288	7.05279	6.83514
25	11.14695	10.67478	10.23419	9.82258	9.43758	9.07704	8.73902	8.42174	8.12361	7.84314	7.57901	7.32998	7.09497	6.87293
26	11.29948	10.80998	10.35409	9.92897	9.53203	9.16095	8.81359	8.48806	8.18261	7.89566	7.62578	7.37167	7.13213	6.90608
27	11.44138	10.93516	10.46460	10.02658	9.61830	9.23722	8.88108	8.54780	8.23552	7.94255	7.66736	7.40856	7.16487	6.93515
28	11.57338	11.05108	10.56645	10.11613	9.69707	9.30657	8.94215	8.60162	8.28298	7.98442	7.70432	7.44120	7.19372	6.96066
29	11.69617	11.15841	10.66033	10.19828	9.76902	9.36961	8.99742	8.65011	8.32554	8.02181	7.73717	7.47009	7.21914	6.98304
30	11.81039	11.25778	10.74684	10.27365	9.83472	9.42691	9.04744	8.69379	8.36371	8.05518	7.76638	7.49565	7.24153	7.00266

TABLE 4 *(Continued)*

Present Value of an Ordinary Annuity of $1 per Period at Compound Interest, 7.5–14%

Period	7.5%	8.0%	8.5%	9.0%	9.5%	10.0%	10.5%	11.0%	11.5%	12.0%	12.5%	13.0%	13.5%	14.0%
31	11.91664	11.34980	10.82658	10.34280	9.89472	9.47901	9.09271	8.73315	8.39795	8.08499	7.79234	7.51828	7.26126	7.01988
32	12.01548	11.43500	10.90008	10.40624	9.94952	9.52638	9.13367	8.76860	8.42866	8.11159	7.81541	7.53830	7.27864	7.03498
33	12.10742	11.51389	10.96781	10.46444	9.99956	9.56943	9.17074	8.80054	8.45619	8.13535	7.83592	7.55602	7.29396	7.04823
34	12.19295	11.58693	11.03024	10.51784	10.04526	9.60857	9.20429	8.82932	8.48089	8.15656	7.85415	7.57170	7.30745	7.05985
35	12.27251	11.65457	11.08778	10.56682	10.08699	9.64416	9.23465	8.85524	8.50304	8.17550	7.87036	7.58557	7.31934	7.07005
36	12.34652	11.71719	11.14081	10.61176	10.12511	9.67651	9.26213	8.87859	8.52291	8.19241	7.88476	7.59785	7.32982	7.07899
37	12.41537	11.77518	11.18969	10.65299	10.15992	9.70592	9.28700	8.89963	8.54072	8.20751	7.89757	7.60872	7.33904	7.08683
38	12.47941	11.82887	11.23474	10.69082	10.19171	9.73265	9.30950	8.91859	8.55670	8.22099	7.90895	7.61833	7.34718	7.09371
39	12.53899	11.87858	11.27625	10.72552	10.22074	9.75696	9.32986	8.93567	8.57103	8.23303	7.91906	7.62684	7.35434	7.09975
40	12.59441	11.92461	11.31452	10.75736	10.24725	9.77905	9.34829	8.95105	8.58389	8.24378	7.92806	7.63438	7.36065	7.10504
41	12.64596	11.96723	11.34979	10.78657	10.27146	9.79914	9.36497	8.96491	8.59541	8.25337	7.93605	7.64104	7.36621	7.10969
42	12.69392	12.00670	11.38229	10.81337	10.29357	9.81740	9.38006	8.97740	8.60575	8.26194	7.94316	7.64694	7.37111	7.11376
43	12.73853	12.04324	11.41225	10.83795	10.31376	9.83400	9.39372	8.98865	8.61502	8.26959	7.94947	7.65216	7.37543	7.11733
44	12.78003	12.07707	11.43986	10.86051	10.33220	9.84909	9.40608	8.99878	8.62334	8.27642	7.95509	7.65678	7.37923	7.12047
45	12.81863	12.10840	11.46531	10.88120	10.34904	9.86281	9.41727	9.00791	8.63080	8.28252	7.96008	7.66086	7.38258	7.12322
46	12.85454	12.13741	11.48877	10.90018	10.36442	9.87528	9.42739	9.01614	8.63749	8.28796	7.96451	7.66448	7.38554	7.12563
47	12.88794	12.16427	11.51038	10.91760	10.37847	9.88662	9.43656	9.02355	8.64349	8.29282	7.96846	7.66768	7.38814	7.12774
48	12.91902	12.18914	11.53031	10.93358	10.39130	9.89693	9.44485	9.03022	8.64887	8.29716	7.97196	7.67052	7.39043	7.12960
49	12.94792	12.21216	11.54867	10.94823	10.40301	9.90630	9.45235	9.03624	8.65369	8.30104	7.97508	7.67302	7.39245	7.13123
50	12.97481	12.23348	11.56560	10.96168	10.41371	9.91481	9.45914	9.04165	8.65802	8.30450	7.97785	7.67524	7.39423	7.13266
51	12.99982	12.25323	11.58119	10.97402	10.42348	9.92256	9.46529	9.04653	8.66190	8.30759	7.98031	7.67720	7.39580	7.13391
52	13.02309	12.27151	11.59557	10.98534	10.43240	9.92960	9.47085	9.05093	8.66538	8.31035	7.98250	7.67894	7.39718	7.13501
53	13.04474	12.28843	11.60882	10.99573	10.44055	9.93600	9.47588	9.05489	8.66850	8.31281	7.98444	7.68048	7.39839	7.13597
54	13.06487	12.30410	11.62103	11.00525	10.44799	9.94182	9.48043	9.05846	8.67130	8.31501	7.98617	7.68184	7.39947	7.13682
55	13.08360	12.31861	11.63229	11.01399	10.45478	9.94711	9.48456	9.06168	8.67382	8.31697	7.98771	7.68304	7.40041	7.13756
56	13.10103	12.33205	11.64266	11.02201	10.46099	9.95191	9.48829	9.06457	8.67607	8.31872	7.98907	7.68411	7.40124	7.13821
57	13.11723	12.34449	11.65222	11.02937	10.46666	9.95629	9.49166	9.06718	8.67809	8.32029	7.99029	7.68505	7.40198	7.13878
58	13.13231	12.35601	11.66104	11.03612	10.47183	9.96026	9.49472	9.06954	8.67990	8.32169	7.99137	7.68589	7.40262	7.13928
59	13.14633	12.36668	11.66916	11.04231	10.47656	9.96387	9.49748	9.07165	8.68152	8.32294	7.99232	7.68663	7.40319	7.13972
60	13.15938	12.37655	11.67664	11.04799	10.48088	9.96716	9.49998	9.07356	8.68298	8.32405	7.99318	7.68728	7.40369	7.14011

TABLE 4 *(Continued)*

Present Value of an Ordinary Annuity of $1 per Period at Compound Interest, 7.5–14%

Period	7.5%	8.0%	8.5%	9.0%	9.5%	10.0%	10.5%	11.0%	11.5%	12.0%	12.5%	13.0%	13.5%	14.0%
61	13.17152	12.38570	11.68354	11.05320	10.48482	9.97014	9.50225	9.07528	8.68429	8.32504	7.99394	7.68786	7.40413	7.14044
62	13.18281	12.39416	11.68990	11.05798	10.48842	9.97286	9.50430	9.07683	8.68546	8.32593	7.99461	7.68837	7.40452	7.14074
63	13.19331	12.40200	11.69576	11.06237	10.49171	9.97532	9.50615	9.07822	8.68651	8.32673	7.99521	7.68882	7.40487	7.14100
64	13.20308	12.40926	11.70116	11.06640	10.49471	9.97757	9.50783	9.07948	8.68745	8.32743	7.99574	7.68922	7.40517	7.14123
65	13.21217	12.41598	11.70614	11.07009	10.49745	9.97961	9.50935	9.08061	8.68830	8.32807	7.99621	7.68958	7.40544	7.14143
66	13.22062	12.42221	11.71073	11.07347	10.49996	9.98146	9.51072	9.08163	8.68906	8.32863	7.99663	7.68989	7.40567	7.14160
67	13.22848	12.42797	11.71496	11.07658	10.50224	9.98315	9.51196	9.08255	8.68974	8.32913	7.99701	7.69017	7.40588	7.14176
68	13.23580	12.43330	11.71885	11.07943	10.50433	9.98468	9.51309	9.08338	8.69035	8.32958	7.99734	7.69042	7.40606	7.14189
69	13.24260	12.43825	11.72245	11.08205	10.50624	9.98607	9.51411	9.08413	8.69090	8.32999	7.99764	7.69063	7.40622	7.14201
70	13.24893	12.44282	11.72576	11.08445	10.50798	9.98734	9.51503	9.08480	8.69139	8.33034	7.99790	7.69083	7.40636	7.14211
71	13.25482	12.44706	11.72881	11.08665	10.50957	9.98849	9.51586	9.08541	8.69183	8.33066	7.99813	7.69100	7.40648	7.14221
72	13.26030	12.45098	11.73162	11.08867	10.51102	9.98954	9.51662	9.08595	8.69222	8.33095	7.99834	7.69115	7.40659	7.14229
73	13.26539	12.45461	11.73421	11.09052	10.51235	9.99049	9.51730	9.08644	8.69257	8.33121	7.99852	7.69128	7.40669	7.14236
74	13.27013	12.45797	11.73660	11.09222	10.51356	9.99135	9.51792	9.08688	8.69289	8.33143	7.99869	7.69140	7.40678	7.14242
75	13.27454	12.46108	11.73880	11.09378	10.51467	9.99214	9.51848	9.08728	8.69318	8.33164	7.99883	7.69150	7.40685	7.14247
76	13.27864	12.46397	11.74083	11.09521	10.51568	9.99285	9.51899	9.08764	8.69343	8.33182	7.99896	7.69160	7.40692	7.14252
77	13.28246	12.46664	11.74270	11.09653	10.51660	9.99350	9.51945	9.08797	8.69366	8.33198	7.99908	7.69168	7.40698	7.14256
78	13.28601	12.46911	11.74443	11.09773	10.51744	9.99409	9.51986	9.08826	8.69387	8.33213	7.99918	7.69175	7.40703	7.14260
79	13.28931	12.47140	11.74601	11.09883	10.51821	9.99463	9.52024	9.08852	8.69405	8.33226	7.99927	7.69181	7.40707	7.14263
80	13.29238	12.47351	11.74748	11.09985	10.51892	9.99512	9.52057	9.08876	8.69422	8.33237	7.99935	7.69187	7.40711	7.14266
81	13.29524	12.47548	11.74883	11.10078	10.51956	9.99556	9.52088	9.08897	8.69436	8.33247	7.99942	7.69192	7.40715	7.14268
82	13.29790	12.47729	11.75007	11.10163	10.52015	9.99597	9.52116	9.08916	8.69450	8.33257	7.99949	7.69197	7.40718	7.14270
83	13.30037	12.47897	11.75122	11.10241	10.52068	9.99633	9.52141	9.08934	8.69462	8.33265	7.99955	7.69201	7.40721	7.14272
84	13.30267	12.48053	11.75228	11.10313	10.52117	9.99667	9.52164	9.08949	8.69472	8.33272	7.99960	7.69204	7.40723	7.14274
85	13.30481	12.48197	11.75325	11.10379	10.52162	9.99697	9.52185	9.08963	8.69482	8.33279	7.99964	7.69207	7.40725	7.14275
86	13.30680	12.48331	11.75415	11.10440	10.52202	9.99724	9.52203	9.08976	8.69490	8.33285	7.99968	7.69210	7.40727	7.14277
87	13.30865	12.48455	11.75497	11.10495	10.52240	9.99749	9.52220	9.08987	8.69498	8.33290	7.99972	7.69212	7.40729	7.14278
88	13.31037	12.48569	11.75574	11.10546	10.52274	9.99772	9.52235	9.08998	8.69505	8.33294	7.99975	7.69214	7.40730	7.14279
89	13.31197	12.48675	11.75644	11.10593	10.52305	9.99793	9.52249	9.09007	8.69511	8.33299	7.99978	7.69216	7.40731	7.14280
90	13.31346	12.48773	11.75709	11.10635	10.52333	9.99812	9.52262	9.09015	8.69517	8.33302	7.99980	7.69218	7.40732	7.14280

TABLE 4 *(Continued)*

Present Value of an Ordinary Annuity of $1 per Period at Compound Interest, 7.5–14%

Period	7.5%	8.0%	8.5%	9.0%	9.5%	10.0%	10.5%	11.0%	11.5%	12.0%	12.5%	13.0%	13.5%	14.0%
91	13.31485	12.48864	11.75768	11.10675	10.52359	9.99829	9.52273	9.09023	8.69522	8.33306	7.99982	7.69219	7.40733	7.14281
92	13.31614	12.48948	11.75823	11.10711	10.52383	9.99844	9.52283	9.09029	8.69526	8.33309	7.99984	7.69221	7.40734	7.14282
93	13.31734	12.49026	11.75874	11.10744	10.52404	9.99859	9.52293	9.09036	8.69530	8.33311	7.99986	7.69222	7.40735	7.14282
94	13.31846	12.49098	11.75921	11.10774	10.52424	9.99871	9.52301	9.09041	8.69534	8.33314	7.99988	7.69223	7.40736	7.14283
95	13.31949	12.49165	11.75964	11.10802	10.52442	9.99883	9.52309	9.09046	8.69537	8.33316	7.99989	7.69224	7.40736	7.14283
96	13.32046	12.49227	11.76004	11.10827	10.52458	9.99894	9.52315	9.09050	8.69540	8.33318	7.99990	7.69225	7.40737	7.14283
97	13.32136	12.49284	11.76040	11.10851	10.52473	9.99903	9.52322	9.09054	8.69543	8.33319	7.99991	7.69225	7.40737	7.14284
98	13.32219	12.49337	11.76074	11.10872	10.52487	9.99912	9.52327	9.09058	8.69545	8.33321	7.99992	7.69226	7.40738	7.14284
99	13.32297	12.49386	11.76105	11.10892	10.52500	9.99920	9.52332	9.09061	8.69547	8.33322	7.99993	7.69226	7.40738	7.14284
100	13.32369	12.49432	11.76134	11.10910	10.52511	9.99927	9.52337	9.09064	8.69549	8.33323	7.99994	7.69227	7.40738	7.14284
101	13.32437	12.49474	11.76160	11.10927	10.52522	9.99934	9.52341	9.09067	8.69551	8.33324	7.99995	7.69227	7.40739	7.14284
102	13.32499	12.49513	11.76184	11.10942	10.52531	9.99940	9.52345	9.09069	8.69552	8.33325	7.99995	7.69228	7.40739	7.14285
103	13.32557	12.49549	11.76207	11.10956	10.52540	9.99945	9.52348	9.09071	8.69553	8.33326	7.99996	7.69228	7.40739	7.14285
104	13.32611	12.49582	11.76227	11.10969	10.52548	9.99950	9.52351	9.09073	8.69555	8.33327	7.99996	7.69228	7.40739	7.14285
105	13.32662	12.49613	11.76246	11.10981	10.52555	9.99955	9.52354	9.09075	8.69556	8.33328	7.99997	7.69229	7.40739	7.14285
106	13.32709	12.49642	11.76264	11.10991	10.52562	9.99959	9.52357	9.09077	8.69557	8.33328	7.99997	7.69229	7.40740	7.14285
107	13.32752	12.49668	11.76280	11.11001	10.52568	9.99963	9.52359	9.09078	8.69558	8.33329	7.99997	7.69229	7.40740	7.14285
108	13.32793	12.49693	11.76295	11.11010	10.52573	9.99966	9.52361	9.09079	8.69558	8.33329	7.99998	7.69229	7.40740	7.14285
109	13.32831	12.49716	11.76309	11.11019	10.52578	9.99969	9.52363	9.09080	8.69559	8.33330	7.99998	7.69230	7.40740	7.14285
110	13.32866	12.49737	11.76322	11.11026	10.52583	9.99972	9.52365	9.09082	8.69560	8.33330	7.99998	7.69230	7.40740	7.14285
111	13.32898	12.49756	11.76333	11.11033	10.52587	9.99975	9.52366	9.09082	8.69560	8.33330	7.99998	7.69230	7.40740	7.14285
112	13.32929	12.49774	11.76344	11.11040	10.52591	9.99977	9.52368	9.09083	8.69561	8.33331	7.99999	7.69230	7.40740	7.14285
113	13.32957	12.49791	11.76354	11.11046	10.52595	9.99979	9.52369	9.09084	8.69561	8.33331	7.99999	7.69230	7.40740	7.14285
114	13.32983	12.49807	11.76363	11.11051	10.52598	9.99981	9.52370	9.09085	8.69562	8.33331	7.99999	7.69230	7.40740	7.14285
115	13.33008	12.49821	11.76371	11.11056	10.52601	9.99983	9.52371	9.09085	8.69562	8.33332	7.99999	7.69230	7.40740	7.14286
116	13.33030	12.49834	11.76379	11.11060	10.52603	9.99984	9.52372	9.09086	8.69562	8.33332	7.99999	7.69230	7.40740	7.14286
117	13.33051	12.49846	11.76386	11.11065	10.52606	9.99986	9.52373	9.09086	8.69563	8.33332	7.99999	7.69230	7.40740	7.14286
118	13.33071	12.49858	11.76393	11.11069	10.52608	9.99987	9.52374	9.09087	8.69563	8.33332	7.99999	7.69230	7.40741	7.14286
119	13.33089	12.49868	11.76399	11.11072	10.52610	9.99988	9.52374	9.09087	8.69563	8.33332	7.99999	7.69230	7.40741	7.14286
120	13.33106	12.49878	11.76405	11.11075	10.52612	9.99989	9.52375	9.09088	8.69563	8.33332	7.99999	7.69230	7.40741	7.14286

TABLE 4 *(Continued)*

Present Value of an Ordinary Annuity of $1 per Period at Compound Interest, 14.5–21%

Period	14.5%	15.0%	15.5%	16.0%	16.5%	17.0%	17.5%	18.0%	18.5%	19.0%	19.5%	20.0%	20.5%	21.0%
1	0.87336	0.86957	0.86580	0.86207	0.85837	0.85470	0.85106	0.84746	0.84388	0.84034	0.83682	0.83333	0.82988	0.82645
2	1.63612	1.62571	1.61541	1.60523	1.59517	1.58521	1.57537	1.56564	1.55602	1.54650	1.53709	1.52778	1.51857	1.50946
3	2.30229	2.28323	2.26443	2.24589	2.22761	2.20958	2.19181	2.17427	2.15698	2.13992	2.12309	2.10648	2.09010	2.07393
4	2.88410	2.85498	2.82634	2.79818	2.77048	2.74324	2.71643	2.69006	2.66412	2.63859	2.61346	2.58873	2.56440	2.54044
5	3.39223	3.35216	3.31285	3.27429	3.23646	3.19935	3.16292	3.12717	3.09208	3.05763	3.02382	2.99061	2.95801	2.92598
6	3.83600	3.78448	3.73407	3.68474	3.63645	3.58918	3.54291	3.49760	3.45323	3.40978	3.36721	3.32551	3.28465	3.24462
7	4.22358	4.16042	4.09876	4.03857	3.97979	3.92238	3.86631	3.81153	3.75800	3.70570	3.65457	3.60459	3.55573	3.50795
8	4.56208	4.48732	4.41451	4.34359	4.27449	4.20716	4.14154	4.07757	4.01519	3.95437	3.89504	3.83716	3.78069	3.72558
9	4.85771	4.77158	4.68789	4.60654	4.52746	4.45057	4.37578	4.30302	4.23223	4.16333	4.09627	4.03097	3.96738	3.90543
10	5.11591	5.01877	4.92458	4.83323	4.74460	4.65860	4.57513	4.49409	4.41538	4.33893	4.26466	4.19247	4.12230	4.05408
11	5.34140	5.23371	5.12951	5.02864	4.93099	4.83641	4.74479	4.65601	4.56994	4.48650	4.40557	4.32706	4.25087	4.17692
12	5.53834	5.42062	5.30693	5.19711	5.09098	4.98839	4.88918	4.79322	4.70037	4.61050	4.52349	4.43922	4.35757	4.27845
13	5.71034	5.58315	5.46055	5.34233	5.22831	5.11828	5.01207	4.90951	4.81044	4.71471	4.62217	4.53268	4.44612	4.36235
14	5.86056	5.72448	5.59355	5.46753	5.34619	5.22930	5.11666	5.00806	4.90333	4.80228	4.70474	4.61057	4.51960	4.43170
15	5.99176	5.84737	5.70870	5.57546	5.44737	5.32419	5.20567	5.09158	4.98171	4.87586	4.77384	4.67547	4.58058	4.48901
16	6.10634	5.95423	5.80840	5.66850	5.53422	5.40529	5.28142	5.16235	5.04786	4.93770	4.83167	4.72956	4.63119	4.53637
17	6.20641	6.04716	5.89472	5.74870	5.60878	5.47461	5.34589	5.22233	5.10368	4.98966	4.88006	4.77463	4.67318	4.57551
18	6.29381	6.12797	5.96945	5.81785	5.67277	5.53385	5.40075	5.27316	5.15078	5.03333	4.92055	4.81219	4.70804	4.60786
19	6.37014	6.19823	6.03416	5.87746	5.72770	5.58449	5.44745	5.31624	5.19053	5.07003	4.95443	4.84350	4.73696	4.63460
20	6.43680	6.25933	6.09018	5.92884	5.77485	5.62777	5.48719	5.35275	5.22408	5.10086	4.98279	4.86958	4.76096	4.65669
21	6.49502	6.31246	6.13868	5.97314	5.81532	5.66476	5.52101	5.38368	5.25239	5.12677	5.00652	4.89132	4.78088	4.67495
22	6.54587	6.35866	6.18068	6.01133	5.85006	5.69637	5.54980	5.40990	5.27628	5.14855	5.02638	4.90943	4.79741	4.69004
23	6.59028	6.39884	6.21704	6.04425	5.87988	5.72340	5.57430	5.43212	5.29644	5.16685	5.04299	4.92453	4.81113	4.70251
24	6.62907	6.43377	6.24852	6.07263	5.90548	5.74649	5.59515	5.45095	5.31345	5.18223	5.05690	4.93710	4.82252	4.71282
25	6.66294	6.46415	6.27577	6.09709	5.92745	5.76623	5.61289	5.46691	5.32780	5.19515	5.06853	4.94759	4.83196	4.72134
26	6.69252	6.49056	6.29937	6.11818	5.94631	5.78311	5.62799	5.48043	5.33992	5.20601	5.07827	4.95632	4.83980	4.72838
27	6.71836	6.51353	6.31980	6.13636	5.96250	5.79753	5.64084	5.49189	5.35014	5.21513	5.08642	4.96360	4.84631	4.73420
28	6.74093	6.53351	6.33749	6.15204	5.97639	5.80985	5.65178	5.50160	5.35877	5.22280	5.09324	4.96967	4.85171	4.73901
29	6.76064	6.55088	6.35281	6.16555	5.98832	5.82039	5.66109	5.50983	5.36605	5.22924	5.09894	4.97472	4.85619	4.74298
30	6.77785	6.56598	6.36607	6.17720	5.99856	5.82939	5.66901	5.51681	5.37219	5.23466	5.10372	4.97894	4.85991	4.74627

TABLE 4 *(Continued)*

Present Value of an Ordinary Annuity of $1 per Period at Compound Interest, 14.5–21%

Period	14.5%	15.0%	15.5%	16.0%	16.5%	17.0%	17.5%	18.0%	18.5%	19.0%	19.5%	20.0%	20.5%	21.0%
31	6.79288	6.57911	6.37755	6.18724	6.00734	5.83709	5.67576	5.52272	5.37738	5.23921	5.10771	4.98245	4.86299	4.74898
32	6.80601	6.59053	6.38749	6.19590	6.01489	5.84366	5.68150	5.52773	5.38175	5.24303	5.11106	4.98537	4.86556	4.75122
33	6.81747	6.60046	6.39609	6.20336	6.02136	5.84928	5.68638	5.53197	5.38545	5.24625	5.11386	4.98781	4.86768	4.75308
34	6.82749	6.60910	6.40354	6.20979	6.02692	5.85409	5.69054	5.53557	5.38856	5.24895	5.11620	4.98984	4.86945	4.75461
35	6.83623	6.61661	6.40999	6.21534	6.03169	5.85820	5.69407	5.53862	5.39119	5.25122	5.11816	4.99154	4.87091	4.75588
36	6.84387	6.62314	6.41558	6.22012	6.03579	5.86171	5.69708	5.54120	5.39341	5.25312	5.11980	4.99295	4.87212	4.75692
37	6.85054	6.62881	6.42041	6.22424	6.03930	5.86471	5.69965	5.54339	5.39528	5.25472	5.12117	4.99412	4.87313	4.75779
38	6.85637	6.63375	6.42460	6.22779	6.04232	5.86727	5.70183	5.54525	5.39686	5.25607	5.12232	4.99510	4.87397	4.75850
39	6.86146	6.63805	6.42823	6.23086	6.04491	5.86946	5.70368	5.54682	5.39820	5.25720	5.12328	4.99592	4.87466	4.75909
40	6.86590	6.64178	6.43136	6.23350	6.04713	5.87133	5.70526	5.54815	5.39932	5.25815	5.12408	4.99660	4.87524	4.75958
41	6.86978	6.64502	6.43408	6.23577	6.04904	5.87294	5.70660	5.54928	5.40027	5.25895	5.12475	4.99717	4.87572	4.75998
42	6.87317	6.64785	6.43643	6.23774	6.05068	5.87430	5.70775	5.55024	5.40107	5.25962	5.12532	4.99764	4.87611	4.76032
43	6.87613	6.65030	6.43847	6.23943	6.05208	5.87547	5.70872	5.55105	5.40175	5.26019	5.12579	4.99803	4.87644	4.76059
44	6.87872	6.65244	6.44024	6.24089	6.05329	5.87647	5.70955	5.55174	5.40232	5.26066	5.12618	4.99836	4.87672	4.76082
45	6.88098	6.65429	6.44176	6.24214	6.05433	5.87733	5.71026	5.55232	5.40280	5.26106	5.12651	4.99863	4.87694	4.76101
46	6.88295	6.65591	6.44308	6.24323	6.05522	5.87806	5.71086	5.55281	5.40321	5.26140	5.12679	4.99886	4.87713	4.76116
47	6.88467	6.65731	6.44423	6.24416	6.05598	5.87868	5.71137	5.55323	5.40355	5.26168	5.12702	4.99905	4.87729	4.76129
48	6.88618	6.65853	6.44522	6.24497	6.05664	5.87922	5.71180	5.55359	5.40384	5.26191	5.12721	4.99921	4.87742	4.76140
49	6.88749	6.65959	6.44608	6.24566	6.05720	5.87967	5.71217	5.55389	5.40409	5.26211	5.12738	4.99934	4.87752	4.76149
50	6.88864	6.66051	6.44682	6.24626	6.05768	5.88006	5.71249	5.55414	5.40429	5.26228	5.12751	4.99945	4.87761	4.76156
51	6.88964	6.66132	6.44746	6.24678	6.05809	5.88039	5.71275	5.55436	5.40447	5.26242	5.12762	4.99954	4.87769	4.76162
52	6.89052	6.66201	6.44802	6.24722	6.05845	5.88068	5.71298	5.55454	5.40461	5.26254	5.12772	4.99962	4.87775	4.76167
53	6.89128	6.66262	6.44850	6.24760	6.05876	5.88092	5.71318	5.55469	5.40474	5.26264	5.12780	4.99968	4.87780	4.76171
54	6.89195	6.66315	6.44892	6.24793	6.05902	5.88113	5.71334	5.55483	5.40484	5.26272	5.12786	4.99974	4.87784	4.76174
55	6.89253	6.66361	6.44928	6.24822	6.05924	5.88131	5.71348	5.55494	5.40493	5.26279	5.12792	4.99978	4.87788	4.76177
56	6.89304	6.66401	6.44959	6.24846	6.05944	5.88146	5.71360	5.55503	5.40500	5.26285	5.12797	4.99982	4.87791	4.76179
57	6.89348	6.66435	6.44987	6.24868	6.05960	5.88159	5.71370	5.55511	5.40507	5.26290	5.12801	4.99985	4.87793	4.76181
58	6.89387	6.66466	6.45010	6.24886	6.05974	5.88170	5.71379	5.55518	5.40512	5.26294	5.12804	4.99987	4.87795	4.76183
59	6.89421	6.66492	6.45030	6.24902	6.05987	5.88180	5.71386	5.55524	5.40516	5.26297	5.12807	4.99989	4.87797	4.76184
60	6.89451	6.66515	6.45048	6.24915	6.05997	5.88188	5.71393	5.55529	5.40520	5.26300	5.12809	4.99991	4.87798	4.76185

TABLE 4 *(Continued)*

Present Value of an Ordinary Annuity of $1 per Period at Compound Interest, 14.5–21%

Period	14.5%	15.0%	15.5%	16.0%	16.5%	17.0%	17.5%	18.0%	18.5%	19.0%	19.5%	20.0%	20.5%	21.0%
61	6.89477	6.66534	6.45063	6.24927	6.06006	5.88195	5.71398	5.55533	5.40523	5.26303	5.12811	4.99993	4.87799	4.76186
62	6.89499	6.66552	6.45076	6.24937	6.06014	5.88200	5.71403	5.55536	5.40526	5.26305	5.12812	4.99994	4.87800	4.76187
63	6.89519	6.66567	6.45088	6.24946	6.06020	5.88206	5.71406	5.55539	5.40528	5.26307	5.12814	4.99995	4.87801	4.76188
64	6.89536	6.66580	6.45098	6.24953	6.06026	5.88210	5.71410	5.55542	5.40530	5.26308	5.12815	4.99996	4.87802	4.76188
65	6.89551	6.66591	6.45106	6.24960	6.06031	5.88214	5.71413	5.55544	5.40532	5.26309	5.12816	4.99996	4.87802	4.76188
66	6.89565	6.66601	6.45114	6.24965	6.06035	5.88217	5.71415	5.55546	5.40533	5.26310	5.12816	4.99997	4.87803	4.76189
67	6.89576	6.66609	6.45120	6.24970	6.06039	5.88219	5.71417	5.55547	5.40534	5.26311	5.12817	4.99998	4.87803	4.76189
68	6.89586	6.66617	6.45125	6.24974	6.06042	5.88222	5.71419	5.55548	5.40535	5.26312	5.12818	4.99998	4.87803	4.76189
69	6.89595	6.66623	6.45130	6.24978	6.06045	5.88224	5.71420	5.55549	5.40536	5.26313	5.12818	4.99998	4.87804	4.76190
70	6.89602	6.66629	6.45134	6.24981	6.06047	5.88225	5.71421	5.55550	5.40537	5.26313	5.12819	4.99999	4.87804	4.76190
71	6.89609	6.66634	6.45138	6.24983	6.06049	5.88227	5.71422	5.55551	5.40537	5.26314	5.12819	4.99999	4.87804	4.76190
72	6.89615	6.66638	6.45141	6.24986	6.06050	5.88228	5.71423	5.55552	5.40538	5.26314	5.12819	4.99999	4.87804	4.76190
73	6.89620	6.66642	6.45144	6.24988	6.06052	5.88229	5.71424	5.55552	5.40538	5.26314	5.12819	4.99999	4.87804	4.76190
74	6.89624	6.66645	6.45146	6.24989	6.06053	5.88230	5.71425	5.55553	5.40539	5.26314	5.12820	4.99999	4.87804	4.76190
75	6.89628	6.66648	6.45148	6.24991	6.06054	5.88231	5.71425	5.55553	5.40539	5.26315	5.12820	4.99999	4.87804	4.76190
76	6.89632	6.66650	6.45150	6.24992	6.06055	5.88231	5.71426	5.55554	5.40539	5.26315	5.12820	5.00000	4.87805	4.76190
77	6.89635	6.66653	6.45151	6.24993	6.06056	5.88232	5.71426	5.55554	5.40539	5.26315	5.12820	5.00000	4.87805	4.76190
78	6.89637	6.66654	6.45153	6.24994	6.06057	5.88232	5.71427	5.55554	5.40540	5.26315	5.12820	5.00000	4.87805	4.76190
79	6.89640	6.66656	6.45154	6.24995	6.06057	5.88233	5.71427	5.55554	5.40540	5.26315	5.12820	5.00000	4.87805	4.76190
80	6.89642	6.66657	6.45155	6.24996	6.06058	5.88233	5.71427	5.55555	5.40540	5.26315	5.12820	5.00000	4.87805	4.76190
81	6.89643	6.66659	6.45156	6.24996	6.06058	5.88234	5.71427	5.55555	5.40540	5.26315	5.12820	5.00000	4.87805	4.76190
82	6.89645	6.66660	6.45157	6.24997	6.06058	5.88234	5.71428	5.55555	5.40540	5.26315	5.12820	5.00000	4.87805	4.76190
83	6.89646	6.66661	6.45157	6.24997	6.06059	5.88234	5.71428	5.55555	5.40540	5.26316	5.12820	5.00000	4.87805	4.76190
84	6.89647	6.66661	6.45158	6.24998	6.06059	5.88234	5.71428	5.55555	5.40540	5.26316	5.12820	5.00000	4.87805	4.76190
85	6.89648	6.66662	6.45158	6.24998	6.06059	5.88234	5.71428	5.55555	5.40540	5.26316	5.12820	5.00000	4.87805	4.76190
86	6.89649	6.66663	6.45159	6.24998	6.06059	5.88234	5.71428	5.55555	5.40540	5.26316	5.12820	5.00000	4.87805	4.76190
87	6.89650	6.66663	6.45159	6.24998	6.06060	5.88235	5.71428	5.55555	5.40540	5.26316	5.12820	5.00000	4.87805	4.76190
88	6.89651	6.66664	6.45159	6.24999	6.06060	5.88235	5.71428	5.55555	5.40540	5.26316	5.12820	5.00000	4.87805	4.76190
89	6.89651	6.66664	6.45160	6.24999	6.06060	5.88235	5.71428	5.55555	5.40540	5.26316	5.12820	5.00000	4.87805	4.76190
90	6.89652	6.66664	6.45160	6.24999	6.06060	5.88235	5.71428	5.55555	5.40540	5.26316	5.12820	5.00000	4.87805	4.76190

TABLE 4 *(Continued)*

Present Value of an Ordinary Annuity of $1 per Period at Compound Interest, 14.5–21%

Period	14.5%	15.0%	15.5%	16.0%	16.5%	17.0%	17.5%	18.0%	18.5%	19.0%	19.5%	20.0%	20.5%	21.0%
91	6.89652	6.66665	6.45160	6.24999	6.06060	5.88235	5.71428	5.55555	5.40540	5.26316	5.12820	5.00000	4.87805	4.76190
92	6.89652	6.66665	6.45160	6.24999	6.06060	5.88235	5.71428	5.55555	5.40540	5.26316	5.12820	5.00000	4.87805	4.76190
93	6.89653	6.66665	6.45160	6.24999	6.06060	5.88235	5.71428	5.55555	5.40540	5.26316	5.12820	5.00000	4.87805	4.76190
94	6.89653	6.66665	6.45160	6.24999	6.06060	5.88235	5.71428	5.55555	5.40540	5.26316	5.12820	5.00000	4.87805	4.76190
95	6.89653	6.66666	6.45161	6.25000	6.06060	5.88235	5.71428	5.55555	5.40540	5.26316	5.12820	5.00000	4.87805	4.76190
96	6.89654	6.66666	6.45161	6.25000	6.06060	5.88235	5.71428	5.55555	5.40540	5.26316	5.12820	5.00000	4.87805	4.76190
97	6.89654	6.66666	6.45161	6.25000	6.06060	5.88235	5.71428	5.55555	5.40541	5.26316	5.12820	5.00000	4.87805	4.76190
98	6.89654	6.66666	6.45161	6.25000	6.06060	5.88235	5.71428	5.55556	5.40541	5.26316	5.12820	5.00000	4.87805	4.76190
99	6.89654	6.66666	6.45161	6.25000	6.06060	5.88235	5.71429	5.55556	5.40541	5.26316	5.12820	5.00000	4.87805	4.76190
100	6.89654	6.66666	6.45161	6.25000	6.06060	5.88235	5.71429	5.55556	5.40541	5.26316	5.12821	5.00000	4.87805	4.76190
101	6.89654	6.66666	6.45161	6.25000	6.06060	5.88235	5.71429	5.55556	5.40541	5.26316	5.12821	5.00000	4.87805	4.76190
102	6.89654	6.66666	6.45161	6.25000	6.06061	5.88235	5.71429	5.55556	5.40541	5.26316	5.12821	5.00000	4.87805	4.76190
103	6.89655	6.66666	6.45161	6.25000	6.06061	5.88235	5.71429	5.55556	5.40541	5.26316	5.12821	5.00000	4.87805	4.76190
104	6.89655	6.66666	6.45161	6.25000	6.06061	5.88235	5.71429	5.55556	5.40541	5.26316	5.12821	5.00000	4.87805	4.76190
105	6.89655	6.66666	6.45161	6.25000	6.06061	5.88235	5.71429	5.55556	5.40541	5.26316	5.12821	5.00000	4.87805	4.76190
106	6.89655	6.66666	6.45161	6.25000	6.06061	5.88235	5.71429	5.55556	5.40541	5.26316	5.12821	5.00000	4.87805	4.76190
107	6.89655	6.66666	6.45161	6.25000	6.06061	5.88235	5.71429	5.55556	5.40541	5.26316	5.12821	5.00000	4.87805	4.76190
108	6.89655	6.66666	6.45161	6.25000	6.06061	5.88235	5.71429	5.55556	5.40541	5.26316	5.12821	5.00000	4.87805	4.76190
109	6.89655	6.66667	6.45161	6.25000	6.06061	5.88235	5.71429	5.55556	5.40541	5.26316	5.12821	5.00000	4.87805	4.76190
110	6.89655	6.66667	6.45161	6.25000	6.06061	5.88235	5.71429	5.55556	5.40541	5.26316	5.12821	5.00000	4.87805	4.76190
111	6.89655	6.66667	6.45161	6.25000	6.06061	5.88235	5.71429	5.55556	5.40541	5.26316	5.12821	5.00000	4.87805	4.76190
112	6.89655	6.66667	6.45161	6.25000	6.06061	5.88235	5.71429	5.55556	5.40541	5.26316	5.12821	5.00000	4.87805	4.76190
113	6.89655	6.66667	6.45161	6.25000	6.06061	5.88235	5.71429	5.55556	5.40541	5.26316	5.12821	5.00000	4.87805	4.76190
114	6.89655	6.66667	6.45161	6.25000	6.06061	5.88235	5.71429	5.55556	5.40541	5.26316	5.12821	5.00000	4.87805	4.76190
115	6.89655	6.66667	6.45161	6.25000	6.06061	5.88235	5.71429	5.55556	5.40541	5.26316	5.12821	5.00000	4.87805	4.76190
116	6.89655	6.66667	6.45161	6.25000	6.06061	5.88235	5.71429	5.55556	5.40541	5.26316	5.12821	5.00000	4.87805	4.76190
117	6.89655	6.66667	6.45161	6.25000	6.06061	5.88235	5.71429	5.55556	5.40541	5.26316	5.12821	5.00000	4.87805	4.76190
118	6.89655	6.66667	6.45161	6.25000	6.06061	5.88235	5.71429	5.55556	5.40541	5.26316	5.12821	5.00000	4.87805	4.76190
119	6.89655	6.66667	6.45161	6.25000	6.06061	5.88235	5.71429	5.55556	5.40541	5.26316	5.12821	5.00000	4.87805	4.76190
120	6.89655	6.66667	6.45161	6.25000	6.06061	5.88235	5.71429	5.55556	5.40541	5.26316	5.12821	5.00000	4.87805	4.76190

BIBLIOGRAPHY

Brigham, Eugene F., and Louis C. Gapenski. *Intermediate Financial Management.* Fort Worth, Tex.: The Dryden Press, 1990.

CCH Editorial Staff Publication, *1999 U.S. Master Tax Guide.* Chicago: CCH Incorporated, 1998.

Department of the Treasury, *Circular E, Employer's Tax Guide.* Internal Revenue Service, rev. January 2000.

Engel, Louis, and Henry R. Hecht. *How to Buy Stocks.* London, New York, and Boston: Little, Brown and Company, 1994.

Estes, Ralph. *Dictionary of Accounting.* London and Cambridge, Mass.: The Massachusetts Institute of Technology, 1995.

Finkler, Steven A. *Finance and Accounting for Nonfinancial Managers.* Englewood Cliffs, N.J.: Prentice Hall, Inc., 1992.

Hermanson, Roger H., James Don Edwards, and R. F. Salmonson. *Accounting Principles.* Plano, Tex.: Business Publications, Inc., 1987.

Karp, Susan. *Smart Guide to Profiting from Mutual Funds.* New York: JohnWiley & Sons, Inc., 1998.

McMickle, Peter L., and Richard G. Vangermeersch. *The Origins of a Great Profession.* Memphis, Tenn.: The Academy of Accounting Historians, 1987.

McQuown, Judith H. *Inc. Yourself.* New York: Broadway Books, 1999.

Malkiel, Burton G. *A Random Walk Down Wall Street.* New York: W. W. Norton and Company, Inc., 1990.

Mayo, Herbert B. *Basic Finance: An Introduction to Money and Financial Management.* Philadelphia: W. B. Saunders Company, 1978.

Miller, Jan R. *Miller GAAP Guide 1995: A Comprehensive Restatement of Current Promulgated Generally Accepted Accounting Principles.* San Diego, Calif.: Harcourt Brace Professional Publishing, 1995.

Morris, Virginia B., and Kenneth B. Morris. *A Woman's Guide to Investing.* New York: Lightbulb Press and Oppenheimer Funds, Inc., 1998.

Nelson, Carl A. *Import Export: How to Get Started in International Trade.* New York: McGraw-Hill, Inc., 1995.

Nemmers, Erwin Esser. *Dictionary of Economics and Business.* Totowa, N.J.: Littlefield, Adams & Co., 1975.

Pyle, William W., and Kermit D. Larson. *Fundamental Accounting Principles.* Homewood, Ill.: Richard D. Irwin, Inc., 1981.

Quickel, Stephen. *How to Spot Winners in the Stock Market.* New York: Time, Inc., 1995.

Scott, David L. *Wall Street Words.* New York and Boston: Houghton Mifflin, 1997, 1998.

Tracy, John A. *How to Read a Financial Report.* New York: John Wiley & Sons, Inc., 1999.

Welsh, Glenn A., D. Paul Newman, and Charles T. Zlatkovich. *Intermediate Accounting,* 7th Edition. Burr Ridge, Ill.: Irwin, 1986.

Williams, Jan R., Keith G. Stanga, and William W. Holder. *Intermediate Accounting.* Fort Worth, Tex.: Harcourt Brace Jovanovich Publishers, 1989.

Web Site Research

American Institute of Certified Public Accountants
1211 Avenue of the Americas
New York, NY 10036-8775
212-596-6200
www.aicpa.org

American Stock Exchange
www.amex.com

A. M. Best Worldwide Insurance Directory
www.ambest.com

Bureau of the Public Debt
www.publicdebt.treas.gov

Certified Financial Planner Board of Standards
1700 Broadway, Suite 2000
Denver, CO 80290-2101
303-830-7500
www.CFP-Board.org

Commissioner of Patents and Trademarks
Washington, DC 20231
800-786-9199
www.uspto.gov

Dow Jones Publishing
www.dowjones.com

Dun & Bradstreet
www.dnb.com

Federal Reserve System
www.federalreserve.gov/

Financial Accounting Standards Board
401 Merritt 7
P. O. Box 5116
Norwalk, CT 06856-5116
203-847-0700
Fax: 203-847-9714
www.fasb.org

Gomez Advisors
www.gomezadvisors.com

Internal Revenue Service
www.irs.ustreas.gov

International Association for Financial Planning
800-945-4237
www.iafp.org

Investment Company Institute
202-326-5800
www.ici.org

MSN Money Central
www.moneycentral.msn.com/home.asp

NASDAQ
www.nasdaq.com

National Association of Investors Corporation
P. O. Box 220
Royal Oak, MI 48068
877-ASK-NAIC (877-275-6242)
www.better-investing.org

National Association of Personal Financial Advisors
888-FEE-ONLY
www.napfa.org

National Technical Information Service
Technology Administration
U. S. Department of Commerce
Springfield, VA 22161
703-605-6000
www.ntis.gov

New York Stock Exchange
www.nyse.com

Register of Copyrights
The Library of Congress
Washington, DC 20559
www.loc.gov/copyright

Rutgers University
www.rutgers.edu/Accounting/raw/fasb

Charles Schwab
www.schwab.com

Securities and Exchange Commission
www.sec.gov

SmartMoney
www.smartmoney.com

Social Security Administration
www.ssa.gov
(See this web site or your telephone directory for regional office locations.)

Society for Human Resource Management
www.shrm.org

U.S. Department of Labor
www.dol.gov

Value Line
www.valueline.com

Vanguard
www.vanguard.com

World Bank
www.worldbank.org

INDEX

A

accelerated depreciation methods, 88–90
accounting
  career paths in, 9–10
  defined, 2
  finance and, 177
  specialized fields in, 10–13
  types of, 7–8
  value of, 1
accounting clerks, 9
accounting formats, 24–25
accounting periods, 33
Accounting Principles Board (APB), 17
accounting rate of return (ARR), 235–237
accounting staff, 10
accounting supervisors/managers, 10
accounting tools, 23–24. *See also specific tools*
accounting transactions, recording, 33–35
accounts, 30
  accrued federal income tax (FIT), 109
  on balance sheets, 31–33
  general ledger, 31
  past due, 55–56
  reconciling, 48–49
accounts payable (AP), 103, 104
accounts receivable (AR), 46, 54
  bad debts, 58–60
  discounted, 58
  internal controls and, 58
  invoice terms and, 54–55
  managing collections, 55–58
  recording, 57
accounts receivables turnover ratio, 196–197
accredited personal financial specialist (APFS), 179
accrual basis accounting, 34–35
accruals, 35, 272
accrued expenses, 104–105
accumulated depreciation, 30, 91
acid test ratio, 193–194
activity ratios, 194–197
adjustable-rate mortgages (ARMs), 129–130
advances, 105–106
agency problem, 306
aggressive growth funds, 327
aging reports, 56–57
allowance for bad credit, 59–60
American Accounting Association (AAA), 16
American Association of Public Accountants (AAPA). *See* American Institute of Certified Public Accountants (AICPA)
American Institute of Certified Public Accountants (AICPA), 15
  Committee on Accounting Principles, 17
  efforts to create consistency, 16–17
amortization, 99
  loan, 119–123
annual meetings, 172
annual reports, 41–42, 168–169
annuities
  future value of ordinary, 215–216, *408–411*
  present value of ordinary, 222–224, *424–435*
  tax-sheltered, 292–293, 297
annuity due
  future value of, 214–215
  present value of, 220–222
appraised value, 82
articles of incorporation, 304
ask price, 340
asset-backed securities, 322
assets, 26, 31–32, 45. *See also* capital budgeting; intangible assets; long-term assets
  accounts receivable, 54–60
  on balance sheet, 36
  cash/cash equivalents, 46–53
  current, 46
  gifts as, valuing, 81–82

leasing *vs.* purchasing, 252–256
liquid, 45
self-constructed, depreciation and, 81
short-term investments, 53–54
tangible *vs.* intangible, 45
valuing bartered, 81–82
audience, level of knowledge of, 19
auditors, 10–12
bad debts and, 59
tasks of, 12
audits, 12
reasons for, 166
average cost inventory valuation method. *See* weighted average inventory valuation method

B

bad debts, 58–60
balance of payments, 368–369
balance of trade, 369
balance sheet, 36–37
cash flow statement and, 39
changes in stockholder's equity and, 39–40
income statement and, 38–39
recording LCM on, 74
balloon payments, 125
bank drafts, 366
bank reconciliations, 48–49
bankers, 179
banks
cash in, 47
debits and credits and, 27–28
loan-loss reserves, 60
basic accounting model (equation), 26–27
bear market, 345
bearer bonds. *See* unregistered bonds
benefit-cost ratio (BCR), 248–251
beta coefficients, 349–350
bid price, 340
bid requests, for suppliers, 269–270
bills of lading, 366
Board of Governors, 374
bond brokers, 178, 180
bond indentures, 131
bond ratings, 323–324
bonds, 130–131
investing in, 320–321
premiums and discounts, 133–134
types of, 132–133, 322
vs. stocks, 131
yield, 323
bonuses, 282
book value, 145
bookkeepers, 9–10
breakeven point, capital budgeting and, 229–230
broker-dealers, 337
brokers, 178, 180
methods of income, 338
types of, 337–338
using financial reports, 5
budget manager, 178
budgeting, 176, 183–184
long-term forecasting and, 263–264
budgets
items to include, 260–262
preparing, 259–260
buildings, depreciation and, 79–80
bull market, 345
business organization, types of, 299–309
business risk, 209–210
buy-and-hold investment strategy, 316–317
buying futures, 325–326

C

cafeteria plans, 290
call options, 325
callable bonds, 133
capital appreciation, 311–312, 315
investment funds and, 328–329
capital asset pricing model (CAPM), 252
capital budgeting
accounting rate of return (ARR), 235–237
benefit-cost ratio (BCR), 248–251
breakeven point and, 229–230
capital asset pricing model (CAPM), 252
cash flow analysis and, 231–233, *234*
cost of capital and, 228
defined, 227
equivalent annual benefit (EAB), 243–245
infinite net present value (INPV), 245–246
internal rate of return (IRR), 239–241

leasing *vs.* purchasing, 252–256
models, 230–231
net present value (PV), 241–243
opportunity cost and, 228–229
payback period (PP), 237–239
probability index (PI), 247–248
total net present value (TNPV), 251–252
capital expenditures, 83. *See also* capital budgeting
capital leases, 134–135
capital stock. *See* stocks
cash, 46
safeguarding, 50–51
types of accounts, 47
cash basis accounting, 34
cash budgets, forecasting through, 182
cash equivalent basis, 21
cash equivalents, 46
cash flow analysis
capital budgeting and, 231–233, *234*
leasing *vs.* purchasing assets, 252–255
cash flow statement, 39
cash management, 49–53
cash management department, 178
cash shortfalls, 124
cash-to-assets ratio, investment funds and, 327
certificates of deposit (CDs), 322
certificates of manufacture, 364
certificates of origin, 363–364
certifications, for finance experts, 179–180
certified financial planner (CFP), 179
certified management accountants (CMAs), 10
certification requirements, 14
certified public accountants (CPAs), 8
career opportunities, 10
certification requirements, 13
certified public accounting firms, 8
chairman of the Fed, 374–375
change in accounting principle, 21–22
changes in stockholder's equity, 39–40
chartered financial analyst (CFA), 179
chartered financial consultant (CHFC), 180
chartered life underwriter (CLU), 180
chief financial officer (CFO), 10, 178
C.I.F. (cost, marine insurance, freight), 363
citing, 52
clean on board, 366
closed-end mutual funds, 327–328
closing date, 112
Code of Professional Ethics, for CPAs, 18
collateral, 117–118
collections, managing, 55–58
commercial attaché, 364
commercial invoices, 364
commercial paper, 321
commissions, 282
brokers', 338
commodities, 320
common stock, 138–140
paid-in capital and, 143
communication, with general public, 172–173
company loyalty, 287–288
company-specific risk, 348
company stock issuance, 139
shares authorized and, 143
comparability, principle of, 20
compensated absence, 109
compensating balance, lender requiring, 116
compensation and benefits, 289–290. *See also* payroll
changes in, 287–288
health benefits, 290
perquisites, 295
reporting, 295
retirement plans, 290–293
compilation, 12
compound interest, 113–114, 315
present value of money at, *412–415*
compounding, 208–209
comptroller, 10
conservatism principle, 22
consignment goods, inventory and, 62
consistency, 3–4
efforts to create, 16–17
constant dollar plan, 316–317
constraint, 20
consular invoices, 364
contra accounts, 29–30
contra asset accounts, allowance to reduce inventory cost to market, 74
controllable risk, 210
controller, 10

conversion costs, 155
convertible bonds, 133, 324
copyrights, 95
corporate bonds, 322
corporate bylaws, 305
corporate charter, 304
corporate culture, as asset, 101–102
corporations, 303–308
  limited liability, 308–309
  return on investment and, 310
cost of capital, 186
  capital budgeting and, 228
cost of goods manufactured, 150, 151–156
cost of goods sold (COGS), 150–151
  computing/recording, 64–66
  inventory turnover ratio and, 195
cost principle, 21
costs
  capitalizing, 63–64
  fixed *vs.* variable, 230
  managing, 265–270
  organization, 98
coupon bonds, 132
coupon rate, 323
CPA firms. *See* certified public accounting firms
credit lines, 124–125
creditors, using financial reports, 5
credits, overview, 27–29
currency clearing houses, 367
current assets, 46
current liabilities, 32, 103–110
current ratio, 193
current-year earnings, 144
current yield, 323
customers, using financial reports, 5

D

day trading, 339
debits, overview, 27–29
debt
  corporate, fraud and, 310
  secured, 117
  unsecured, 119
  vs. preferred stock, 142
debt covenants, 118–119
debt-to-equity ratio, 198
debt-to-total assets ratio, 198
declaration date, 314
deductions, payroll, 276–280
default, 321
deferred charges, 98
defined-benefit pension plan, *297*
deposits, returnable, 105–106
depreciation, 83. *See also specific methods*
  accumulated, 91
  factors affecting, 83–85
  general depreciation system, *407*
  of long-term assets, 78–81
  manipulating timing of, 86
  methods of, 86–90
  standard timetables, 85
derivatives, 324–326
diluted earnings per share, 163
direct costs, 152
direct labor, 154
  capitalizing costs of, 64
direct materials, 153–154
  capitalizing costs of, 64
disability benefits, Social Security, 280, 289
disclosure, 3
discounting, notes, 126
discretionary accounts, 341
dishonored notes, 126–127
diversifiable risk, 348
dividend reinvestment plans (DRIPs), 319
dividends, 311, 314
  investment funds and, 328
  retained earnings and, 144
dividends payable, 104, 105
document credits, 366–367
dollar cost averaging, 316–317
double-declining-balance (DDB) depreciation, 88, 89–90
double-entry bookkeeping, 30
double taxation, 306
doubtful accounts, 59–60
Dow Jones Industrial Average (DJIA), 346
duties, 368

E

e-trading, 338–339
earnings before interest and tax (EBIT), 158
earnings per share (EPS), 161–163, 347

economic entity, principle of, 20
economies of scale, 153–154
EDGAR (Electronic Data Gathering, Analysis, and Retrieval system), 168
effective annual interest rate (EFAR), 114–116
efficient market theory, 350
embezzlement, 52–53
employee benefits, 281. *See also* compensation and benefits
Employee Retirement Income Security Act (ERISA), 290
employee rewards. *See also* compensation and benefits
  changes in, 287–288
employee stock ownership plans (ESOPs), 293, *297*
employee stock purchase plans (ESPPs), 294
employees
  exempt *vs.* non-exempts, 274
  loyal/committed, 100–101
  using financial reports, 5
employer matching contribution plans, 291
equipment, depreciation and, 80–81
equity, 26
  defined, 137
  market value of, 144
equivalent annual benefit (EAB), 243–245
  leasing *vs.* purchasing assets, 255–256
estimated salvage value, 84
ex-dividend date, 314
EX (EX-warehouse, EX-factory), 363
exchange rate, 358–359
executive stock option plans, 325
exemptions, 278–279
expense accounts, loss on reduction in inventory costs, 74
expenses, 150. *See also* cost of goods sold (COGS)
  accrued, 104–105
  fictitious, 52
  forecasting and, 262–263
  patting travel, 52
  prepaid, 97–98, 272
  special, 99
external auditors, 11
external financial analysts, 5
external reporting. *See* market reporting
extraordinary items, 159–160

F

face value, 112, 321
facts, 4
Fair Labor Standards Act, 273
fair market value, 82
family benefits, Social Security, 281, 289
F.A.S. (free alongside a ship), 363
FASB Concept Statements, 18
federal income taxes, 278
  as liability, 106
  origins of accounting rules and, 16
  paying quarterly, 109
  withholding, 277
Federal Insurance Contributions Act (FICA) deductions, 277, 279
Federal Open Market Committee (FOMC), 377
Federal Reserve banks, 375–376
Federal Reserve System, 373
  organization of, 374–377
  purpose of, 373–374
Federal Unemployment Tax Act (FUTA), 277, 281
Federal Wages and Powers Law, 273
fees
  brokers', 338
  finance, 57
  investment fund, 328
  returned check charges, 58
FICA, 107–108
  as liability, 106
finance
  accounting and, 177
  career paths and, 177–179
  defined, 2–3, 175
  importance of, 175–177
  value of, 1
finance reporting
  market reporting, 165
  SEC requirements, 167–168
financial accounting
Financial Accounting Standards Board (FASB), 15, 18
  key elements of, 19–22
  SEC and, 167
Financial Accounting Standards (FAS), 18

financial analysts, 177
  external *vs.* internal, 5
financial managers, responsibilities of, 175–177
financial models, 185
financial planning, 181–182
financial ratios, 186
  activity, 194–197
  defined, 189–190
  for different industries, 191
  evaluating, 192
  importance of context, 190
  leverage, 198–200
  liquidity, 193–194
  profitability, 197
  "return on . . . ," 191–192
  uses, 190–191
financial reporting, 165. *See also specific reports*
  management reporting, 165–166
  market reporting, 166
financial reports, users of, 4–6
  level of knowledge of, 19
financial risk, 210
financial statement analysis, types of, 169
financial statements, 36–41. *See also specific financial statements*
  analyzing, 169–171
  on annual reports, 41–42
  reporting international operations in U.S., 368
  symbols on, 40–41
financing terms, 110–124. *See also specific terms*
finished goods inventory, 62
first-in, first-out (FIFO), 71, 72
fixed assets. *See* property, plant, and equipment (PPP)
fixed costs, 230
float, 50
F.O.B. (free on board), 363
F.O.B. (free on board) destination, 63
F.O.B. (free on board) shipping point, 63
focus, 154
forecasting, 176, 182–183, 262
  long-term methods, 263–264
  short-term methods, 262–263
  stock-market performance, 347
Foreign Corrupt Practices Act of 1977, 370
foreign currency units, *360–362*
foreign exchange, 358–359
foul bill, 366
403(B) plans, 292–293, *297*
401(k) plans, 292
franchises, 95–96
fraud
  corporate debt and, 310
  types of, 52–53
freight, 151
full-charge bookkeepers, 9–10
full disclosure principle, 22
full-service brokers, 337
full-service discount brokers, 337–338
fund managers, 178, 351
  using financial reports, 5
furnishings/fixtures, depreciation and, 80–81
future value (FV) of money, 213
  of annuity due, 214–215
  of lump sums, 213–214
  of ordinary annuity, 215–216, *408–411*
  using tables to calculate, 216–217
futures contracts, 325–326

G

garnishments, 281–282
general and administrative expenses (G&A), 156–157
general journals, 25
general ledger accounts, 31
general ledgers, 25
general partnership (GP), 301–302
general public, communicating to, 172–173
Generally Accepted Accounting Principles (GAAP), 8, 17–18
gifts, valuation as assets, 81–82
globalization, 353
going concern rule, 20
gold standard, 355
goods, in transit, ownership and, 63
goodwill, 93–94
government accounting, 9
government organizations, using financial reports, 6
gross profit, 156
gross profit margin (GPM), 197
gross revenues, 148. *See also* revenues
growth and income funds, 327
growth funds, 327

H

health benefits, 290
health insurance, Social Security benefits and, 281
hedging foreign exchange rates, 359
historical cost, 21
horizontal analysis, 169

I

income reporting, inconsistent, 16
income statement, 37–38, 147–148
  balance sheet and, 38–39
  basic accounting model and, 26
  cost of goods manufactured, 151–156
  cost of goods sold, 150–151
  earnings per share and, 161–163
  equations for, 163–164
  expenses, 150
  extraordinary items, 159–160
  general and administrative expenses (G&A), 156–157
  gross profit, 156
  income taxes, 158–159
  net income, 160–161
  net income before interest and tax, 158
  net loss, 160–161
  nonfinancial managers reviewing, 257–259
  other income and other expenses, 158
  recording inventory on, 64–66
  revenues, 148–150
  sales discounts, 149
  sales returns, 149
income taxes. *See also* Federal income taxes; state income taxes
  on income statement, 158–159
incorporating, 303
increased specialization, 154
indenture, 321
independent contractors, 283
  reporting income, 283–285
index shares, 329
  major listings, 330
indirect costs, 152
indirect labor, 154
industries. *See also specific industries*
  financial ratios for, 191
industry peculiarities, rules for, 22
infinite net present value (INPV), 245–246
inflation, time value of money and, 204–206
inflation rate, 205–206
initial public offerings (IPOs), 139, 309–310
insider trading, 173
inspection certificates, 365
institutional investors, 339
  using financial reports, 5–6
insurance certificates, 365
intangible assets, 45, 93
  amortization of, 99
  good corporate culture, 101–102
  goodwill, 93–94
  intellectual property, 102
  leaseholds, 97
  legal rights/privileges, 94–97
  loyal/committed employees, 100–101
  management experience and ability, 100
intangible products, 148
intellectual property, 102
interest, 112, 314–315. *See also* compound interest; simple interest
  investment decisions and, 317
  lender requiring up-front payment, 115–116
interest equation, 113
interest rates, 112–113. *See also* effective annual interest rate (EFAR)
  time value of money and, 206–208
  Treasury securities and, 207–208
interest terms
  credit lines, 125
  mortgages, 128–130
  notes payable, 126
internal auditors, 11
internal financial analysts, 5
internal management, 5
internal rate of return (IRR), 239–241
internal reporting, 165–166
Internal Revenue Service (IRS). *See also* Federal income taxes
  payroll taxes and, 108
International Bank for Reconstruction and Development, 357
International Development Association (IDA), 357–358

International Monetary Fund (IMF), 354–356
international trade, 359, 368–371
  documents used in, 363–367
  terms of sale for, 363
inventory, 46, 61
  capitalizing costs and, 63–64
  classifications of, 62
  determining, 67–69
  entering costs on P&L, 64–66
  items included in, 62–63
  lower of cost or market (LCM) rule, 73–75
  net realizable value (NRV), 75
  normal divergence, 69
  valuation of, 69–70
    methods for, 70–73
inventory systems, 68–69
inventory tags, 67
inventory turnover ratio, 194–196
investment. *See also* bonds; commodities; money markets; options; retirement plans; stocks
  factors in selecting, 317–318
  portfolios, 318
  short-term, 53
    recording, 53–54
  strategies for, 316–317
  types of payback on, 313–315
investment clubs, 340
Investment Company Institute (ICI), 329
investment funds, 326–329
investment risk, 292
investor relations, 171
invoice terms, 54–55
IRAs, 297

J

journal entries, 25
  making to accounts, 35

K

Keogh plans, 296, 297

L

land, depreciation and, 78–79
land improvements, depreciation and, 81
last-in, first-out (LIFO), 71, 72
leaseholds, as assets, 97
leases, capital *vs.* operating, 134–135
leasing, *vs.* purchasing, 252–256
legal capital, 139–140
legal rights/privileges, as intangible assets, 94–97
legislation, governing securities, 167
lenders, using financial reports, 5
letters of credit, 366–367
leverage, equity and, 137
leverage ratios, 198–200
liabilities, 26, 32–33, 103. *See also* long-term liabilities
  on balance sheet, 36
  compensated absence, 109
  current, 103–110
liability
  corporations and, 305–306
  partnerships and, 301
lien security bonds, 132
liens, 117, 118
limit orders, 342
limited liability corporation (LLC), 308–309
limited partnership (LP), 301, 302
liquid assets, 45
liquidation value, 145
liquidity ratios, 193–194
loads, 328
loan agreement, 111–112
loan amortization, 119–123
loan amortization schedules, 119–120, *121*, *122–123*
loan closing, 112
loan payoff, 123–124
loans, default on, 117
long-distance fraud, 52
long-range planning, 184–185
long-term assets, 77
  capital expenditures and, 83
  depreciable cost of, 84
  depreciable *vs.* nondepreciable, 78–81
  estimated salvage value, 84
  estimated useful life of, 84–85
  property, plant, and equipment (PPP), 77–78
  repairs and maintenance and, 82–83
long-term debt, current liabilities and, 110

long-term liabilities, 33, 110
  bonds, 130–134
  capital leasing, 134–135
  credit lines, 124–125
  mortgages, 127–130
  notes payable, 125–127
long-term trade receivables, 54
lower of cost or market (LCM) rule, 73–75
lump sums
  future value of, 213–214
  present value of, 218–220

M

machinery, depreciation and, 80–81
major improvements. *See* capital expenditures
management
  experience and ability of, as assets, 100
  internal, 5
management consulting, 13
management reporting, 165–166
managerial accounting, 7
manufacturing costs, types of, 152–155
manufacturing industries
  computing/recording cost of goods sold, 64–66
  cost of goods manufactured, 151–156
manufacturing overhead, 155
margin, buying on, 343
market. *See* stock market
market analysts, 179
market capitalization, 144
market makers, 340–341
market orders, 341–342
market ratios, 347–348
market reporting, 165, 166
market risk, 209, 349
market timing investment strategy, 316
market value, 74
  stock, 138–139
market value of equity, 144
matching principles, 21, 33
  accrual basis accounting and, 34
materiality, principle of, 20
maturity date, 116–117, 318
Medicare, 107–108
  as liability, 106
  Social Security, 289
merchandising industries, cost of goods sold for, 150–151
  computing/recording, 64
minimum investment requirements, 317
modified accelerated cost recovery system (MACRS), 90
money, time value of. *See* time value of money
money markets, 326
money-purchase pension plan, *297*
mortgages, 127–130
multiple regression analysis, 183
municipal bonds, 322
mutual funds. *See* investment funds

N

NASDAQ index, 346
net due upon receipt, 55
net income, 37–38, 147, 160–161
net loss, 37–38, 147, 160–161
net present value (NPV), 241–243
net profit margin (NPM), 197
net realizable value (NRV), 74, 75
net revenues, 148, 150. *See also* gross revenues
net 30, 55
New York Stock Exchange (NYSE) index, 346
nondiversifiable risk, 349
nonmanufacturing costs, 155
normal balances, 28–29
North American Free Trade Agreement (NAFTA), 370
notes payable, 125–127

O

obsolescence, 85
odd lots, 341
office supply fraud, 53
1/10, net 30, 55
open-end mutual funds, 328
operating leases, 134–135
options, 324–326
Options Clearing Corporation (OCC), 326
order bill of lading, 366
organization costs, 98
output method depreciation, 87
overhead costs, capitalizing, 64
overhead expenses, 156–157

P

paid-in capital, 143
par value, 112, 138, 321
partnerships, 300–302
pass-through entities, 309
past due accounts, 55–56
patents, 94–95
payback period (PP), 237–239
paychecks, 278
payment date, 314
payment terms
  credit lines, 125
  mortgages, 128
  notes payable, 126
payout date, 311
payroll. *See also* compensation and benefits
  employer requirements, 274–275
  government regulations, 273
  independent contractors and, 283
  managing, 271
  recordkeeping requirements, 274
  self-employed *vs.* other employed, 280
  supplemental wages, 282–283
  taxes/deductions, 276–280
  1099 forms, 283–285
  union requirements, 276
  wages *vs.* salaries, 274
payroll bank accounts, 275
payroll taxes, as liability, 107–108
periodic inventory system, 69
permanent general ledger accounts, 31
perpetual inventory system, 68
perquisites (perks), 295
personal guarantees, 118
personal item fraud, 52
petty cash, 47
physical assets. *See* property, plant, and equipment (PPP)
physical inventories, 67
  scheduling, 68
P&L. *See* income statement; retained earnings
planning manager, 178
planning staff, 177
plant assets. *See* property, plant, and equipment (PPP)
point-of-sale (POS) inventory system, 68
point system mortgages, 128–129
poison pills, 170–171
portfolios, 318
posting, 25
predictions, 4
preferred stock, 138, 140
  benefits/disadvantages of, 141–142
  reasons for, 142
  types of, 140–141
  vs. debt, 142
prepaid expenses, 272
  as assets, 97–98
present value (PV) of money, 218
  of annuity due, 218–220
  at compound interest, *412–423*
  of lump sums, 218–220
  of ordinary annuity, 222–224, *424–435*
  using tables to calculate, 224–225
press releases, 172–173
price
  bid *vs.* ask, 340
  investing and, 317
  quality and, 269
  securities, fluctuating, 348
  stock, 347
price/earnings (PE) ratio, 347–348
prime rate, 113, 116
principal, 112, 321
  lender limiting access to, 115
principles, of accounting/finance, 3–4
prior-year earnings, 144
private accounting, 8
pro forma forecasting, 182–183
pro rating, 98
products, tangible *vs.* intangible, 148–149
profit and loss statement (P&L). *See* income statement; retained earnings
profit-sharing, 291
profit-sharing plan, *297*
profitability index (PI), 247–248
profitability ratios, 197
project cash flow analysis. *See* cash flow analysis
promissory notes. *See* notes payable
property, plant, and equipment (PPP), 77–78
depreciation and, 79–80
property taxes, 109
protective tariffs, 368

proxy, voting by, 178
proxy statements, 172
public accounting, 8
publicly held corporations, 305–306
purchase discounts, 151
purchasing. *See also* suppliers
  company needs, 265–266
  products/services and, 265
put options, 325

Q

quality, price and, 269
quick ratio. *See* acid test ratio
quota subscriptions, 356

R

ratios. *See* financial ratios
raw materials, 62, 153
real estate taxes, 109
reconciliation, 48–49
record date, 311, 314
redemption value, 145
registered bonds, 132
registered representatives, 178, 180
relevance, principal of, 19
reliability, principle of, 19–20
repackaging costs, 151
repairs and maintenance expenses, 82–83
research and development (R&D), 99
residual value, 84
restricted stock, 283
retained earnings, 26
  defined, 143–144
  prior-year versus current-year, 144
retirement payments, as liability, 107
retirement plans, *297*
  employer-provided, 290–293
  self-employed, 296
  Social Security benefits, 280, 289
return on assets (ROA), 197
return on equity (ROE), 197, 200
return on investment (ROI), 197, 200
  company *vs.* shareholder perspective, 310–311
return on sales (ROS), 197
returnable deposits, 105–106
revenue principles, 21
revenue tariffs, 368
revenues
  on income statement, 148–150
  unearned, 104, 105
reverse stock splits, 319
review, auditing, 12
risk, 209
  controllable *vs.* uncontrollable, 210–211
  diversifiable, 348
  investment, 292
  investment decisions and, 317
  market, 349
  measuring, 349–350
  types of, 209–210
rollovers, 294–295
round lots, 341

S

salary, 274. *See also* payroll
  brokers', 338
sales, 149
sales discounts, 149
sales tax, as liability, 106
savings bonds, 322
scrap value, 84
secured bonds, 132
secured debt, 117
secured note payable. *See* mortgages
securities. *See also* trading; *specific securities*
  marketable, 46
  paying for, 343
  taking delivery of, 343–344
Securities Act of 1933, 167
Securities and Exchange Commission (SEC), 15, 166–168
Securities Exchange Act of 1934, 167
self-employment tax, 108, 280
senior debt, 199
separate entity, principle of, 20
serial bonds, 133
service industries, computing/recording cost of goods sold, 64
servicing debt, 199
shared-appreciation mortgages (SAM), 129
shareholders
  corporation ownership and, 304
  return on investment and, 310–311
  rewarding, 311–312
  trading stock between, 139
  using financial reports, 5

shareholders' equity, 33
  on balance sheet, 37
shareholders meetings, 171–172
shares
  authorized, 143
  defined, 137
shippers export declaration, 365
short-term notes payable, 104
shorthand terms, accounting, 42–43
simple interest, 113, 208–209, 315
simple regression analysis, 183
simplified employee pension (SEP), 296, 297
Social Security, 288–289
  benefits, 280–281, 289
  credits, 279–280
sole proprietorships, 300
special expenses, 99
specialized products and services, locating, 267
specific identification inventory valuation method, 71
spread, 358
Standard & Poor's (S&P) 500 index, 346
state income taxes, 278
  as liability, 106–107
  paying quarterly, 109
  withholding, 277
state unemployment insurance (SUTA), 277
statement of cash receipts and disbursements. *See* cash flow statement
statistical analysis, 186
stock indexes, 345–347
stock market
  bull *vs.* bear, 345
  earnings per share and, 162
  investment theories, 350–351
stock market crash of 1929, 166–167
stock options, 282–283, 294
stock orders, 341–343
stock splits, 319
stock warrants, 133
stockbrokers, 178, 180
stockholders. *See* shareholders
stocks. *See also* capital stock; common stock; investment; preferred stock; trading
  analyzing value, 348–349
  buying and selling, 340–343
  buying back, 142–143
  defined, 137–138
  as employee incentive, 293
  evaluated by price, 347
  investing in, 318–319
  theories for evaluating, 351–352
  vs. bonds, 131
stop orders, 342–343
straight bill of lading, 366
straight-line depreciation, 86–87
subchapter C corporation, 307
subchapter S corporation, 307–308
subordinated debentures, 199
subsidiary ledger, 26–27
sum-of-the-years'-digits (SYD) depreciation, 88–89
supplemental wages, 282–283
suppliers, 266
  bid requests for, 269–270
  evaluating potential, 267–269
  finding, 266–267
  selecting, 270
survivor benefits, Social Security, 281, 289
sweep accounts, 50
symbols, on financial statements, 40–41
synergy, 102
systematic risk, 349

T

T-accounts, 35
tangible assets, 45. *See also* property, plant, and equipment (PPP)
tangible products, 148
tariffs, 368
tax-sheltered annuity, 292–293, 297
tax specialists, 12
taxes. *See also specific taxes*
  corporations and, 306
  on international trade, 367–368
  investment decisions and, 318
  partnerships and, 302
  payroll, 276–280
  retirement investment and, 291
  sole proprietorships and, 300
temporary general ledger accounts, 31
1099 forms, 283–285
10-K report, 167
10-Q report, 168
term bonds, 132
termination date. *See* maturity date

terms of sale, international trade, 363
time assumption, principle of, 21
time fraud, 53
time value of money, 187, 203–204
  compounding and, 208–209
  inflation and, 204–206
  interest rates and, 206–208
  risk and, 211
  tables
    future value of ordinary annuity, *408–411*
    present value of $1 at compound interest, *412–423*
    present value of ordinary annuity, *424–435*
    using to calculate, 216–217, 224–225
time value of money formulas, 212
  future value of a lump sum, 213–214
  future value of an annuity due, 214–215
  future value of an ordinary annuity, 215–216
  present value of a lump sum, 218–220
  present value of an annuity due, 218–220
  present value of an ordinary annuity, 222–224
times interest earned ratio, 198–200
timing, 4
  investment decisions and, 317–318
timing difference, 48
total net present value (TNPV), 251–252
trade deficit, 369–370
trademarks, 96–97
trading. *See also* brokers; securities; stocks
  day, 339
  on-line, 338–339
treasurer, 178
Treasury bills (T-bills), 206–207
Treasury bonds, 207
Treasury notes, 207
Treasury securities, 322
  interest rates and, 207–208
  types of, 206–207
Treasury stock, 142–143
trend percentages analysis, 169
trustees
  for bondholders, 131
  bonds and, 323
2/10, net 30, 55

U

uncontrollable risk, 210–211
underwriters, 130–131
unearned revenues, 104, 105
unemployment rates, competitive compensation and, 287
unemployment taxes, 108
Uniform Commercial Code (UCC), determining ownership and, 62–63
union dues, 277
unit of measure, principle of, 20
units-of-production depreciation, 87
unregistered bonds, 132
unsecured bonds, 132
unsecured debt, 119
useful life, 84–85

V

value-added tax (VAT), 368
variable costs, 230
vertical analysis, 169
vesting, 291–292

W

W-4 form, 278–279
wages, 274. *See also* payroll
wages payable, 104
weighted average inventory valuation method, 71, 73
work-in-progress (WIP), 62
World Bank, 356–358
world trade centers, 370

Y

yield
  bonds, 323
  investment decisions and, 317
yield to maturity (YTM), 323

Z

zero-coupon bonds, 322